Annapurna
South Face

Annapurna
South Face

Sir Chris Bonington

Series Editor, Clint Willis

Thunder's Mouth Press and Balliett & Fitzgerald Inc.

adrenaline classics ®

First Edition

Adrenaline® and Adrenaline Classics® and the Adrenaline® and
Adrenaline Classics® logos are trademarks of Balliett & Fitzgerald Inc.,
New York, NY.

An Adrenaline Classics Book®

Published by
Thunder's Mouth Press
An Imprint of Avalon Publishing Group Incorporated
841 Broadway, 4th Floor
New York, NY 10003

and

Balliett & Fitzgerald Inc.
66 West Broadway, Suite 602
New York, NY 10007

Distributed by Publishers Group West

Book design: Sue Canavan and Mike Walters

Frontispiece photo: Ian Clough crossing snow on fixed ropes on the South Face
of Annapurna © Chris Bonington.

Manufactured in the United States of America

ISBN: 1-56025-315-0

Library of Congress Cataloging-in-Publication Data

Bonington, Chris.
    Annapurna South Face: the classic account of survival/by Sir Chris Bonington.
        p. cm. — (Adrenaline classics)
    Previous ed.: London: Cassell, 1971.
    ISBN 1-56025-315-0
        I.Mountaineering—Nepal—Annapurna. I.Title. II.Series.

GV199.44.N462 A564 2001
796.52"2'092—dc21
    [B]   2001027055

TO IAN CLOUGH
WHO GAVE SO MUCH

CONTENTS

Introduction   xi
by Clint Willis

Chapter 1
Birth of an Expedition   1

Chapter 2
Why Annapurna?   18

Chapter 3
Preparations (October '68–March '70)   30

Chapter 4
Approach March (22–27 March)   50

Chapter 5
The Sanctuary (28–31 March)   70

Chapter 6
First Encounter (1–7 April)   89

Chapter 7
The Col (7–12 April)   106

Chapter 8
Blind Alley (13–18 April)   118

Chapter 9
Back to Base (18-23 April)   136

Chapter 10
Struggle for the Ice Ridge (23-27 April)   152

Chapter 11
Still Struggling (27 April-3 May)   165

Chapter 12
The Ice Cliff (4-9 May)   188

Chapter 13
The Rock Band (10-13 May)   206

Chapter 14
The Flat Iron (13-15 May)   232

Chapter 15
Attrition (16-20 May)   247

Chapter 16
In Support (21-27 May)   261

Chapter 17
The Final Push (17-27 May)   273
    Dougal Haston

Chapter 18
Tragedy (27–30 May)
293

Appendices

Appendix A
Diary and Statistics
305
Nick Estcourt

Appendix B
Equipment
313
Sir Chris Bonington

Appendix C
Oxygen
334
Sir Chris Bonington

Appendix D
Food
336
Mike Thompson

Appendix E
Communications
358
Kelvin Kent

Appendix F
Photographic 364
Mick Burke

Appendix G
Medical 371
Dave Lambert

Appendix H
The People of Nepal 394
Kelvin Kent

Appendix I
Acknowledgements 405
Kelvin Kent

Glossary 411

Index 415

PHOTOGRAPHY
CREDITS

Introduction

nnapurna South Face is a book about a climb—but for more than 25 years I have read it as a book about climbers. I met my first climbers more than 30 years ago, just two years before Chris Bonington and his fellow mountaineers—ranging in age and experience from Nick Estcourt, 26, to Don Whillans, a curmudgeonly 37—left their homes in England and America to climb one of the most formidable mountain walls on the planet.

I was eleven years old in 1968. My parents had scraped together $800 to send me to summer camp in North Carolina because I was desperate to go. When I got there I signed up to go on rock-climbing trips even though I was worried: I expected to be scared.

The young men who led the trips were the first people I knew who seemed to love the world and what they were doing in it. This quality made them interesting—exciting to watch—and cheerful. I watched their behavior and tried to figure out where it came from. The pleasure they took from their work was in their voices and in the way they held their bodies and talked to us—the way they drove a truck full of boys down a narrow dirt road, making fun of each other and finding surprisingly gentle ways to include us.

I stayed in that world as much as I could. In the winter I lived in the lowlands of South Louisiana, surrounded by marsh and cypress trees. The nearest hills I knew about were five hours north, in Shreveport. But I went back to the mountains most summers. When I was 16, I met an older climber—he must have been in his early 30's—who sported the hard-to-forget and not-so-easy-to-spell name of Steve Longenecker.

I'd heard the name from my older brother, who'd done a little climbing himself. I knew that Steve had helped invent the local climbing scene, putting up routes that included a classic called The Nose on Looking Glass Rock in the Pisgah National Forest. He'd fractured his skull and come close to dying not long before. He thought a piece of tape on a sling was meant to mark its midpoint. The tape as it turned out was all that held the sling together, and it stopped doing that when Steve put his weight on it 75 feet off the ground.

But when I met Steve he looked fine—somewhat lean and weather-beaten but healthy. He took me climbing. Eventually, he took me to the bottom of The Nose and told me to lead the first pitch, and held the rope and talked to me while I did it. When I was done, he bought me a pizza to celebrate. I can still taste my fear on the rock and my relief at finishing the climb, and I remember that evening as well. I was happy in a new way, as if I had suddenly somehow become the person I wanted to be.

I climbed with Steve over parts of three summers. He loaned me books about places like Snowdonia and Yosemite and the Alps. One of the books was *Annapurna South Face*. I was 16, and I was trying to learn a way to live in the world—to love it here—and the book told me some of what I needed to know about that. It also confirmed what I was finding out: I wanted to be a climber—not just to climb, but to be with climbers.

Mountaineers ranging from Walter Bonatti to Peter Boardman have written hundreds of expedition books during the past century or so. This one stands out in part because the trip took place during a critical moment in the history of mountaineering. Climbers during the late 60's and early 70's were testing old boundaries and limits, drawing confidence from past achievements. Those achievements had relied upon expedition techniques developed during the early attempts on giant peaks of the Himalaya, including Annapurna as well as its big brothers, K2 and Everest. Large teams of climbers supported by scores of porters systematically laid siege to those peaks, in each case hauling food, fuel, and bottled oxygen to a series of camps—complete with tents, sleeping bags, oxygen, and other supplies—that began low on the mountain and eventually placed a team high enough to make a dash for the summit. Such tactics succeeded in getting climbers to the summits of the biggest peaks. In 1950, the French made the first ascent of one of the world's fourteen 8,000-meter peaks—Annapurna, as it happened—and ascents of mountains such as Everest, Nanga Parbat, and K2 followed.

The period of great expeditions to unclimbed 8,000-meter peaks was a heroic era in mountaineering. Often a team's biggest job was simply to find a route to the mountain; in that sense, the climbers were old-style explorers.

The expedition accounts of the time stress the element of teamwork; each climb or attempt is a shared endeavor. The climbers value two seemingly contradictory elements: self-preservation and self-sacrifice. Thus, Americans on a 1938 expedition to K-2 turned around within striking distance of the summit rather than risk their lives—even though the risk might not seem extreme to today's high-altitude climbers. Their decision was painful but easy: No summit—not even the supremely elusive summit of K-2—was worth a life.

Yet some of the very same climbers made the almost-suicidal choice of trying to rescue their dying teammate Art Gilkey 15 years later on the same mountain. After struggling for three days to lower the incapacitated Gilkey down the peak, the group survived only because Gilkey was swept off the mountain mid-rescue. Even then, the remaining climbers barely made it off the peak.

Again, the contrast with today's climbing ethic is striking: Contemporary climbers on big mountains abandon their partners if they must do so to survive. The change in part reflects modern climbers' ambitions: They often take risks that earlier generations generally shunned, and that leaves them vulnerable to situations where survival requires such choices. But it interests me that earlier generations shunned those risks in the first place.

True, a handful of mountaineers chafed at the limitations imposed on them by more conservative climbers, and at the almost military hierarchy of many old-style expeditions. Englishmen Eric Shipton and Bill Tillman experimented with small parties, travelling light and fast. Hermann Buhl's solo exploits during his 1942 ascent of Nanga Parbat offered a glimpse of what a determined climber could do on a big mountain. Americans Tom Hornbein and Willi Unsoeld again upped the ante in 1963 when the pair completed the first traverse of an 8,000-meter peak: They climbed Everest's West Ridge with minimal support, then descended the mountain via its Southeast Ridge. In 1966, a group of German, American, and British climbers in the Alps put up an extraordinarily difficult route on the Eiger's notorious North Face, bringing modified siege-style techniques to a big mountain wall. Chris Bonington played an important role in that climb as an observer-photographer and support climber, and the lessons he learned there informed his strategy on Annapurna four years later.

Thus encouraged, climbers by 1970 were looking for even greater challenges. During the Eiger climb, Bonington found himself sitting in a tiny snow hole with the American John Harlin. Harlin told Bonington of his plans to tackle a much bigger wall: the Southwest Face of Everest—a snow slope leading up to an enormous gully which in turn leads to a steep rock wall at 26,902 feet.

Harlin was killed on the Eiger, when a fixed rope broke under his weight. But he wasn't the only climber eyeing such challenges. The Japanese made two reconnaissance trips to Everest in 1969, and in 1970 returned with 30 climbers. Their objectives included the Southwest Face that Harlin had coveted. The Japanese climbers turned back at the bottom of the gulley—though they did manage to climb the mountain by the much easier Southeast Ridge and stage a ski descent from the South Col.

INTRODUCTION

• • •

Meanwhile, Bonington and his team had formed their ambition to tackle Annapurna's forbidding South Face. Like Everest's Southwest Face, the climb was a far cry from the technically easy—although grueling—snow slogs that earlier Himalayan expeditions had made to various high summits. The South Face included a 12,000-foot wall of steep rock, ice and snow, leading to a 25,545-foot summit. It would call for the most difficult climbing yet attempted at high altitudes.

The team included eight lead climbers, with three more members in support and six high-altitude porters. Only four members of the climbing team had been to the Himalayas, but the party included several names that were to loom large in the history of modern climbing.

Chris Bonington, Dougal Haston, and Don Whillans were all well-known in British mountaineering circles. Team leader Bonington with another member of the ASF team (Ian Clough) had made the first British ascent of the Eiger's North Face in 1962 and had joined expeditions to Annapurna II (26,040) in 1960 and climbed 25,850-feet Nuptse as a member of a 1961 British military expedition. The Annapurna trip was his first effort to launch and lead a major expedition. Long after, he wrote about the challenge:

> Leading a siege-style expedition in 1970 was a different matter from doing so in the 'fifties and 'sixties. The habit of obeying a leader, inculcated by war service or national service, was no longer there and the climbers themselves were becoming more skilled, competitive, individually ambitious and deserving of their chance to succeed.

Bonington proved a superb leader, tapping the strengths of various team members: Clough's unselfishness, Whillans' tough-mindedness, Haston's drive, American Tom Frost's idealism, Mick Burke's skill on difficult rock. He had chosen those men for his team in part because he knew their strengths. His selections were more than justified by each climber's efforts: Bonington's narrative with characteristic thoroughness and fair-mindedness shows that each man poured enormous energy into the climb. More than that, they often sacrificed their personal agendas in support of the team's effort to get at least some of its members up the route.

The climbers' dedication to their common cause is reflected in the many weary days they spent hauling gear and food to and from various camps low on the mountain. At any given time, only two or three climbers could be out front creating a route; the rest acted as glorified porters, hauling enormous loads up steep terrain, often dangling on ropes that became increasingly worn as the expedition dragged on. Nick Estcourt calculated that the team carried 3,160 pounds to Camp III at 20,100 feet, and that various climbers spent a combined 183 nights there. The group hauled another 2,200 pounds to Camp IV at 21,300 feet, 800 pounds to camp V at 22,750 feet, and 225 pounds to Camp VI at 24,000 feet.

Almost inevitably, some climbers at times disagreed with Bonington's tactics, arguing that his decisions favored the summit ambitions of Haston and Whillans over their teammates' agendas. The mountain in the end decided who would have the best crack at finishing the route, and the climbers seemed to recognize its authority in the matter. Heading for the summit with Whillans, Haston dropped a rucksack and was forced to return for more gear. On his way down, he encountered Bonington and Estcourt at Camp V. Here is Bonington writing about the encounter:

> It never occurred to me, and I don't think that it occurred to Nick, that one of us should take Dougal's place—it certainly never occurred to Dougal. He was going so much more strongly than either of us, and had such a single-minded drive to reach the top of Annapurna.

Haston took Bonington's sleeping-bag and Estcourt's down jacket, and headed back up the mountain.

INTRODUCTION

Some of the climbers who play leading roles in this story went on to even more distinguished careers in the mountains. Several died pursuing their passion for high places. Burke died on Everest in 1975; Haston in the Alps in 1977; Estcourt on K2 in 1978. Bonington went on to become perhaps the central figure of a generation of great British climbers.

Annapurna South Face finds him at an early moment in that distinguished career, coming into his own as an expedition leader. His description of the trip reflects the already thorough and conscientious nature of his leadership. He is attentive to every detail, from shipping arrangements for gear to the intricacies of a difficult section of rock at 24,000 feet. He spent five days above Base Camp, and even his descriptions of other climbers' experiences have the feel of first-person accounts. The nine appendices that accompany the text, meant to help guide future expeditions to the region, are typical of his style: The material is largely dated, but it offers a sense of the kinds of work that Bonington and his mates put into the climb—also how well that work was planned and how willingly it was done.

The years that followed the ASF expedition saw enormous changes at climbing's cutting edge. Peter Habeler and Reinhold Messner in 1978 became the first men to climb Everest without supplementary oxygen. Two months later Messner climbed Nanga Parbat alone—the first solo ascent of an 8,000 meter peak. Climbers today routinely put up spectacular routes on improbable rock spires that combine the hazards and hardships of high altitude, severe weather, and extreme technical difficulty. They do it alone or in small parties, in part to avoid the petty politics and other complications that burden larger expeditions. These climbers often take astonishing risks on incredibly difficult routes, relying upon sheer speed and resourcefulness to survive, often knowing that no one can help them if things go wrong. The modern climbing ethic has evolved to value such independence: Self-sufficiency is the ultimate virtue for many of today's extreme mountaineers.

Bonington's ASF trip was an early step in that evolutionary process. But viewed from our current perspective, the expedition retains much of the flavor of earlier climbs. Unlike today's most extreme mountaineers, Bonington's fellow climbers relied upon each other for encouragement, inspiration, help—and when the time came, comfort. They climbed as friends and teammates, and the work tested and deepened their mutual regard.

Climbers often say they climb to attain some kind of self-knowledge. They rely upon the mountain to teach them what they need to know. Bonington and his friends learned from Annapurna's South Face and from each other—and we in turn can learn from their story. When I read this book more than 25 years ago, I was 16 years old and trying to decide how to be in the world. The lessons I took from it are with me still.

—CLINT WILLIS
SERIES EDITOR, ADRENALINE CLASSICS

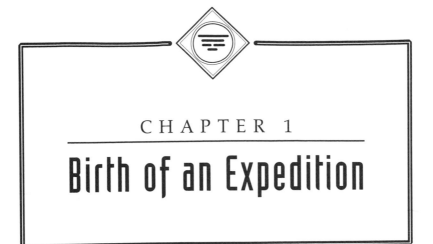

CHAPTER 1

Birth of an Expedition

xpeditions are conceived in many different ways. At one extreme
you have the massive national expedition controlled and directed
by a committee; at the other you have the small group of friends
who get together to climb a mountain. Our expedition to the
South Face of Annapurna in 1970 fell somewhere between these two
extremes.

I had abandoned a conventional career in 1962, after spending eight
years as a Regular Army officer and then nine months as a management
trainee with Unilever, partly through discontent with my work and
partly through a desire to base my life more closely upon climbing. Yet
once having taken this step, I got less climbing than many nine-to-five
workers, for in the three years before October 1968 I had drifted into
the world of journalism, becoming a kind of adventure photographer
and writer. It was a fascinating life, taking me to Ecuador to climb an
active volcano, to Baffin Island in mid-winter to hunt caribou, and in
the summer of 1968 down the Blue Nile with a Service expedition

which made the first ever complete descent—but it was a life that seemed to be taking me further from climbing and one in which all too often I felt I was the onlooker rather than the doer.

In the autumn of 1968 I had just got back from going down the Blue Nile. It had been highly dangerous—I had nearly got myself killed on three different occasions: once when our boat capsized in a cataract and I was caught in the undertow and dragged back under eight times before escaping; and twice when we were attacked by natives. I had certainly been deeply involved, and it had been all too exciting; yet it was unsatisfactory, for I had been outside the environment to which I was accustomed, exposed to too many risks over which I had no control. This expedition heightened my desire to concentrate all my efforts on a mountaineering project, but I was still not at all sure what this should be.

I was pretty mixed up all the way round. My wife, Wendy, and I had been living in the Lake District for the last five years. It was ideal in many ways for climbing, was a glorious setting, and most people thought I was very lucky to be able to base myself there—but I was desperately restless; partly because I wasn't at all sure what I did want to do with my life. Part of me wanted to be a successful photo-journalist, another just wanted to climb. I felt submerged and cut off in the Lake District both from the mainstream of climbing and from what I thought my career should be in journalism and photography. I even thought of going to live in London, and spent several frustrating and very miserable weekends dragging an unhappy wife who loved the Lake District round grotty houses in Muswell Hill and Islington.

Eventually, we reached a compromise and decided to move down to Manchester—betwixt and between, in easy reach of London, Wales, the Lakes and Derbyshire gritstone.

We had bought a house in Bowdon, on the south-west outskirts of Manchester, before I set off for the Blue Nile. Naïvely, I had hoped that Wendy would have moved in and got most of the alterations completed while I was safely out of the way. In the event, the contract had only just been completed when I got back, and the builders took another three months to make various alterations that had seemed necessary to make the house inhabitable.

During this period we stayed with some friends. Nick and Carolyn Estcourt had a two-roomed flat in Alderley Edge. We arrived intending to stay for a few days until we had found a furnished flat, and ended by staying for two months, sleeping on their living-room floor with our eighteen-month-old son. By some miracle we did not get on each others' nerves—certainly a fine test of compatibility for any expedition.

This was when and where the Annapurna South Face Expedition was conceived—or rather, was evolved, for it started out as something very much less ambitious before it took its final shape.

Nick and I, with another friend, Martin Boysen, had been talking about expeditions for the past couple of years without getting very far. That October we decided that come what may we should go on an expedition in 1970, but suitable objectives were limited. At this stage all the mountains of Nepal and most of the better ranges in Pakistan and India were closed to climbers for political reasons, largely the result of tension on the Tibetan border. You could climb in the Hindu Kush in Afghanistan and on the outlying peaks of the Karakorum in Pakistan, but these did not attract me. They seemed overshadowed by the true Himalayan giants. We therefore turned to Alaska, where there are still hundreds of unclimbed walls and the mountains are even more empty and desolate than the Himalayas, though of course very much lower.

I had known Martin Boysen for about eight years, from the days when he was a schoolboy climbing prodigy at Harrison Rocks, a sandstone outcrop just outside Tunbridge Wells. Today, at twenty-eight, he is one of Britain's finest rock climbers, though on first meeting him you would never guess it. At ground level his long limbs seem uncoordinated; his considerable strength is concealed by the way his clothes hang on him. But once he is poised on a stretch of rock he drifts up effortlessly, a smoothly functioning climbing-machine. He is like a huge intelligent sloth, conditioned to a vertical environment.

He and his wife Maggie were frequent visitors at our home in the Lake District, and we had climbed together extensively in this country, but never in the Alps or farther ranges. On leaving school in Tonbridge he had gone on to Manchester University and had then taken up teaching, happy to remain an amateur with the long holidays that teaching gives. For a brilliant climber he was remarkably uncompetitive, secure perhaps in his own natural ability and too lazy to enter into the rat-race that dominates some aspects of British climbing. Even so, some of his new routes in Wales and Scotland are amongst the most difficult and serious ever put up in this country. He also went on to climb at a very high standard in the Alps, making several first ascents and first British ascents.

Nick, on the other hand, was not a natural climber. Wiry yet power-fully built, quite highly strung, very competitive, he had forced himself to a high standard of climbing. In some ways he had the traditional middle-class background of the pre-war climbers, and for that matter of most of the Everest expeditions right up to the successful one of 1953. He went to Eastbourne College, then Cambridge, where he became President of the Cambridge University Mountaineering Club. He was introduced to climbing by his father in the Alps while still at school—something very much in the Edwardian tradition. As a result he gained a very broad mountaineering background in Alpine climbing. While at Cambridge he took part in an expedition to Arctic Greenland, but this was his only experience of climbing outside Europe.

He took a degree in engineering and after spending a year doing vol-untary service overseas in Nigeria went into civil engineering. Although he was following a conventional career he was sufficiently devoted to climbing to try to bend his career to fit in with his sport and, largely as a result of this, abandoned engineering, which tends to be very tying, to go into computers. In 1967 he got a job with Ferranti, based on Manchester, so that he could get plenty of climbing; he and his wife often spent weekends with us in the Lake District.

We now looked around for a fourth member of our team, and chose Dougal Haston. I had been with him on the ascent of the Eiger Direct in the winter of 1966. I went along as photographer and ended up going about three-quarters of the way up the face. I had also climbed with him the previous winter when we set out to make the first winter ascent of the North Face of the Droites, but ended up by climbing the North Face of the Argentière. Martin also knew him well, having been with him to Cerro Torre in Patagonia; though only 10,000 feet above sea level this is probably one of the steepest and most difficult mountains in the world, and has been climbed only once. They attempted a new route up one of its ridges, but were defeated by technical difficulty and appalling weather.

Dougal Haston is certainly one of Britain's most outstanding climbers today: deeply introspective, he has a reserve that is difficult to break through and yet at the same time is a very easy companion, whether drinking at the foot of the mountain or sitting out a storm half-way up. His features have the look of a highly sophisticated primitive man, if ever such a being could exist—definitely a 'pop' figure in the modern idiom—a strange blend of total self-indulgence with a hard ascetism. He went to Edinburgh University, stayed there several years but never completed his degree in philosophy, and finally left to start a climbing school in the Highlands. The group of Edinburgh climbers he went around with were a hard-drinking, antisocial lot who specialized in punch-ups and breaking up huts. He also put in a lot of very hard climbing with Robin Smith, who was probably the most promising of all British climbers before his death in the Pamirs in 1962.

Dougal climbed the North Wall of the Eiger in 1963, then the Eiger Direct, still the hardest route in the Alps, in 1966. He also took over the International School of Modern Mountaineering, which was founded by John Harlin, the man who led the Eiger Direct team but died on the climb. Unlike Martin and Nick, Dougal has committed himself completely to mountaineering, instructing at his climbing school throughout the summer but leaving himself free to join expeditions and climb farther afield in his off-seasons, though he had not as yet climbed in the Himalayas.

And so, in October 1968, there were four of us—though at this stage Dougal didn't know anything of our plans. Then, the news arrived— *Nepal was allowing in climbers* for the first time in four years. We immediately forgot about Alaska and started to think up possible objectives. There were several unclimbed peaks below 24,000 feet, but somehow I wasn't attracted—they would have given me a lesser experience than I had received on the two previous expeditions I had been on, to Annapurna II and Nuptse. The next thought was a major face climb, and this immediately caught our enthusiasm—taut excitement, technical difficulty and little of the slow snow-plodding that can turn Himalayan climbing into a featureless treadmill.

I remembered seeing a photograph of the South Face of Annapurna, sent to a friend by Lt.-Col. J. O. M. Roberts, one-time British Military Attaché at Katmandu and leader of the 1960 Services Himalayan Expedition to Annapurna II, of which I had been a member.

'Let's go for that,' I suggested, with very little idea of what 'that' entailed. The others, all innocent, agreed. Another British expedition had been to Machapuhare, a magnificent snow peak in the shape of a fish's tail, immediately opposite the South Face of Annapurna. Jimmy Roberts had first seen the Face while taking part in this expedition. While waiting for a reply to my query to him, I phoned two of the other members of that expedition who live in this country. 'South Face?' said David Cox, a lecturer in Modern History at University College, Oxford. 'I don't remember much about it; looked huge; yes, there were a lot of avalanches coming down it, but I think they were going down the runnels.' Roger Chorley, a London accountant, was even more discouraging. 'Going for the South Face of Annapurna?'—in a voice of mild disbelief 'It's swept by avalanches the whole time.' By this time I was beginning to think of other objectives, but then Jimmy Roberts's letter arrived:

> The South Face of Annapurna is an exciting prospect—more difficult than Everest, although the approach problems are easier. Certainly it will be very difficult indeed, and although I am not an oxygen fan, it seems to me that the exertion of the severe climbing at over 24,000 feet may demand oxygen.

• • •

I felt encouraged by this letter. Then a few days later I received a colour slide of the Face from David Cox. We projected it onto the wall of my living room, a six-foot picture, and gazed and gazed—excited, then frightened.

'There's a line all right,' Martin said, 'but it's bloody big.'

It was. I don't think I've ever looked at a mountain photograph that has given such an impression of huge size and steepness. It was like four different Alpine faces piled one on top of the other—but what a line! Hard, uncompromising, positive all the way up. A squat snow ridge like the buttress of a Gothic cathedral leaned against the lower part of the wall. That was the start all right; perhaps one could bypass it, by sneaking along the glacier at its foot—but what about avalanche risk? The buttress led to an ice arête; even at the distance from which the photograph had been taken one could see it was a genuine knife-edge. I had climbed something like it on Nuptse—in places we had been able to look straight through holes through the ridge a hundred feet below its crest. That had been frightening; this would be worse. The knife-edge died below a band of ice cliff.

'I wonder how stable they are?' said Nick. I wondered too and traced a line through them with only partial confidence. And that led to a rock wall.

'Must be at least a thousand feet.'

'But when the hell does it start?—could be twenty-three thousand. Do you fancy a bit of hard rock climbing at that altitude?'

'Yes, but look at that groove.' It split the crest of the ridge, a huge gash, but undoubtedly more difficult and sustained than anything that had ever been climbed at that altitude.

The rock band ended with what seemed to be a shoulder of snow that led to the summit.

'But the picture must be foreshortened. That could be a long way below the top.'

I succeeded in unearthing some transparencies I had taken from Annapurna II in 1960. At the time I had been barely aware of the South Face of Annapurna; it had been so far away. At that time, anyway, I would not have thought it possible. Looking at the transparencies we could see that the top of the rock band was at around three-quarter height; another three thousand feet to the top of a steep snow arête, with a rocky crest to finish on.

We were sobered by what we had seen. This was something bigger and more difficult than anything that had ever been tackled before. We flashed a picture of the South Face of Nuptse, which I had climbed in 1961, onto the screen, but it was dwarfed by the huge South Face of Annapurna.

And yet I felt confident that we had a good chance of climbing it with the right team; felt that my own mountaineering background had, partly by chance, built up towards this attempt. We should have to use the techniques developed on the ascent of the Eiger Direct in a Himalayan environment. I had already climbed one Himalayan face— the South Face of Nuptse. Admittedly it had been considerably more straightforward than Annapurna's South Face, but it gave me a yard-stick of comparison. We had climbed Nuptse without oxygen, so I had been to a height of 25,850 feet unaided. On the other hand, we had used oxygen on Annapurna II, so I also had experience in its use, and under-stood the tremendous difference it can make to one's climbing potential.

I had been attracted by the idea of having a small, compact, four-man expedition in the Himalayas—the smaller the party, the closer you can get to the mountains uncluttered by all the paraphernalia and compli-cations of man-management caused by a larger expedition. But the South Face of Annapurna was obviously going to require a larger party than four. We talked of increasing it to six, but this seemed insufficient. We went up to eight.

The next problem was whom to ask. There were plenty of candidates among the leading climbers of Britain. We were going to need a party of men who could climb at a very high standard on rock and ice, had plenty of endurance, would be prepared to subordinate their own per-sonal ambition to the good of the expedition as a whole, and, most important of all, could get on together. Top-class climbers have a touch of the primadonna in their make-up, are often self-centred and are essentially individualists; in some ways the best expedition man is the steady plodder, yet on the South Face of Annapurna it seemed that we were going to require a high proportion of hard lead climbers who would be able to take over the exacting front position as others slowed up and tired. In addition, one can never be sure of anyone's individual performance in the Himalayas, since people acclimatize to altitude at different rates and some never acclimatize at all. The safest bet is to take out climbers who have already proved themselves at altitude, but because of the ban on climbing in Nepal and Pakistan during the late sixties, there was a distinct shortage of top-standard Alpinists with Himalayan experience. The Everest men were getting decidedly long in the tooth, and anyway the problem that the South Face of Annapurna presented was of an altogether different dimension.

I first approached Ian Clough. I had done some of the best climbing of my life with him, on the first assent of the Central Pillar of Frêney in 1961; then in 1962 we had climbed the Walker Spur of the Grandes Jorasses, one of the most beautiful rock climbs in the Alps, finishing it by doing a complete traverse of the Jorasses and Rochefort Ridge, and then two days later climbed the North Wall of the Eiger. Quite apart from being a very capable mountaineer, Ian was also the kindest and least selfish person I had ever climbed with. He was certainly the perfect expedition man, with very little personal ambition yet always ready to do his best for the project as a whole. He had been on three expeditions: one to the Central Tower of Paine in Patagonia with me; one to Gaurishankar, in Nepal; and recently as leader of a successful expedition to the Fortress, also in South Patagonia.

Ian also had made climbing his career, running a small climbing school in Glen Coe. He was a person to whom material gain meant very little, yet he led a very full life with his wife and year-old daughter, based on his small cottage in Glen Coe. He managed to get real enjoyment out of teaching climbing, and at the same time maintained his enthusiasm for pioneering new routes around Scotland, especially in the far North-West in summer and around Glen Coe itself in winter, often with students on his courses.

I then asked twenty-eight-year-old Mick Burke. He comes from

Wigan and has a working-class background. He went to the local grammar school, but left at the age of fifteen to go into an insurance office. He also took up climbing at about this time—largely to get away from home at weekends, he admits. After a couple of years, like many young British climbers, he abandoned his job and settled in the Lake District for most of the year, picking up work where he could and spending the summers in the Alps. He isn't a brilliant natural climber in the way that Martin Boysen is, but by sheer perseverance he has become extremely competent.

I had spent three days with him on top of the Eiger during the final stages of the ascent of the Eiger Direct when he was with me as my assistant. It was a strange, exciting experience wandering around the crest of an Alpine peak in almost unbearable conditions with a temperature of -20° Fahrenheit and a wind of over eighty-five miles per hour. It involved climbing snow-slopes that threatened to avalanche without warning and living in snow-holes for several days with next to no food. I came to like and respect Mick in these conditions.

The third man I approached was in some ways the most obvious choice of all and yet the one I had the most doubts about. I had known Don Whillans for over ten years. He is undoubtedly the finest all-round mountaineer that Britain has produced since the war, but in the last few years he had let himself slip into poor physical condition, developing a huge beer-drinker's pot belly through lack of exercise and a steady intake of beer. He had lost interest in British rock climbing, and even in the Alps, preferring to go on expeditions to the farther ranges of the world. On top of this our relationship had always been strained. But I had done some of my best climbing with Don, and he was certainly the best climbing partner I have ever had. We first met in 1958, when I had set out to make the first British ascent of the South-West Pillar of the Drus with Hamish MacInnes. Don Whillans, with another climber, Paul Ross, arrived at the bivouac that same night. The climb took four days; Hamish was hit on the head by a stone; we ran out of food and were hit near the top by a storm. But for Don's drive and genius as a climber we should have been in real trouble, for I was still very inexperienced.

I climbed with him again in 1961, when we spent most of the summer sitting below the Eiger, made several attempts, but were always turned back by bad weather. We ended up by making the first ascent of the Central Pillar of Frêney, then hailed as the Last Great Problem in the Alps. The following year we climbed together again and were involved in the rescue of Brian Nally from the end of the Second Icefield on the Eiger, but once again weather conditions weren't right.

We then went to Patagonia together on the Towers of Paine expedition, kept apart for almost the entire time, but teamed up at the end to make the final push to the summit.

Although we got on well while on the mountain we were too different, and both probably too strong-minded, to become close friends. I tend to be enthusiastic and fairly emotional, impulsive, change my mind very easily and am constantly cooking up new schemes. Don, on the other hand, is shrewd and cautious, thinks very carefully before he makes any decision, and is rarely, if ever, swayed by emotion. Our backgrounds also were very different.

Don was born and brought up in Salford, a grime-covered town of the industrial North, left school at the age of fourteen and went to work as a plumber. He started climbing when he was sixteen and quickly displayed a genius on rock. He specialized in savage overhangs where a fall would almost inevitably lead to a fatal accident. Even today, twenty years after he made the first ascents, many of his climbs are held in awe and are seldom repeated.

But Don Whillans has an unlucky streak—he had been three times to the Himalayas, performed magnificently, but never reached the top. On his first expedition to the Karakorum, in 1957, he spent eight weeks above 23,000 feet and struggled to within a hundred and fifty feet of the summitt of Masherbrum (25,660 feet) but was forced to retreat when his companion collapsed. On his next expedition, to Trivor, another twenty-five-thousander, he worked himself into the ground getting the party into position for the final assault, and as a result was unable to go to the top.

In 1964 he was climbing leader of the expedition to Gaurishankar of which Ian Clough was a member. Once again he was unlucky. They had a great deal of trouble finding a route to the foot of the mountain and were then forced to make their way round the peak onto the Tibetan flanks, to get a feasible route to the top. Their communications were over-extended, and finally they were forced to turn back.

In build, Don is short and stocky, an Andy Capp figure with a reputation for toughness. There are any number of tales, that have almost reached legendary proportions, of the fights he has been in. These days, he has grown milder, but there is still a brooding belligerence in his make-up: he doesn't argue or discuss; he states a view or decision and does not budge.

Don and I could not have been more dissimilar—each irritating the other and yet at the same time complementing each other's weak points.

Most of the team I had invited so far were comparatively inexperienced, and Don's particular qualities seemed ideally suited to the problem, but I was worried in case he had let himself slide too far into bad condition to function well on the mountain.

I suggested we have a weekend climbing together, without telling him of my plans. We were going to go up to Scotland one Friday night and come back at the end of the weekend. I arrived at his house at about 10.30 that evening to find he was still at the pub, but would be back in half an hour. At 2.30 that morning he got back, having downed eleven pints of beer. We went off straight away—me in a slightly self-righteous bad temper; I kept the wheel most of the way, afraid that Don had had too much to drink, and we reached Glen Coe that morning. The following day we set out to do a new route with Tom Patey, one of Scotland's most brilliant and colourful climbers, tragically killed while we were away on the expedition. It was the first winter ascent of the Great Gully of Ardgour. On the way up to the climb Don lagged far behind, taking his time. On the way up the gully he was happy to stay at the back, accepting a rope on all the difficult pitches which required one—but then on the last pitch, an evil chimney, lined with ice and just too wide for comfortable bridging, he said, 'I think I'll have a try at this. It's about my turn to go out in front.'

There was an icy wind blasting straight up the chimney; it was so wide he was almost doing the splits on the way up, and its top was blocked by ice-sheathed boulders you had to swing out on. Don went up it incredibly quickly and smoothly, without bothering to protect himself with running belays. Both Tom and I had a struggle when it was our turn to follow him. It was then that I made up my mind and that evening invited him to join the expedition. He looked at the photograph I showed him and commented, 'It'll be hard, but it should go all right. I'll come.' He was the obvious person to be Deputy Leader, and I promptly offered him this position.

My selection so far had been a very personal one. I wanted people whom I had climbed with in difficult circumstances, whom I knew deeply, who knew me and knew each other. To me this seemed the soundest basis for a tight-knit group. We all had weaknesses and strengths, knew each other well enough to accept them and had in the past put ourselves and our relationships to the test of physical and mental stress. But now the selection of the eighth member of the team was influenced by finance. Our agent, George Greenfield, said rather wistfully, 'Couldn't you get in an American? It would make my job a lot easier in the States.'

I had some doubts about this, since I did not know personally any American who would be suitable, but we needed the money so I finally agreed. Various names presented themselves, but one climber particularly attracted me purely by hearsay, and this was Tom Frost. Both Don and Dougal knew and spoke well of him.

He is a partner in a mountain hardware factory, and one of America's outstanding rock climbers. The rock walls of Yosemite in California present some of the smoothest and most compact mountain faces in the world. To climb these, Tom Frost and a few others had developed new equipment and techniques. They had since adapted these ideas to tackle even bigger problems throughout the breadth of the American continents, and their approach has influenced climbers throughout the world. His reply to my letter of invitation was characteristic:

I have just returned from Alaska where we succeeded in struggling up

13

the tourist route on Mount McKinley. As a result of this experience I am somewhat confident in being able to ascend to 20,000 feet and on the basis of this credential hereby agree to come to Annapurna with you and will even attempt to climb.

In fact, Tom had already been to the Himalayas on one previous occasion and had climbed Kantega, a peak of 22,340 feet. He had also put up new routes in the Cordillera Blanca and the Alps.

I could not help wondering how he would get on with us, when I discovered he was a practising Mormon, a faith which forbids strong drink, gambling, smoking, bad language, tea and coffee; but Tom turned out to be not only a good Mormon but also a splendidly tolerant one.

The party now numbered eight, and was certainly the strongest that had ever assembled in Britain to tackle a Himalayan peak. We needed this number of hard climbers, but it quickly became evident that we were also going to need some men prepared to concentrate on the more mundane but essential jobs of keeping open the lower part of the mountain and supervising the flow of supplies. I first approached one of my oldest friends—Mike Thompson. Then thirty-two, he was not a brilliant high-standard climber and had done very little in the Alps, but he has an easy, equable temperament coupled with a single-minded individualism. We were at Sandhurst together, but both found soldiering in the Regular Army too limiting; Mike escaped his engagement by standing for Parliament, there being a regulation that no serving soldier could be a Parliamentary candidate. He then went to university to study anthropology, got his degree and spent a period as a builder's labourer while he prepared a thesis that was acclaimed for its original thinking.

We also needed a doctor; someone who was capable of reaching the upper part of the mountain, yet would be content to remain in a support role. It's no good having the doctor out in front. I was just looking round for the right man, when I had a phone call from David Lambert, a thirty-year-old registrar at a hospital in Newcastle. He had heard of the expedition from a friend, and asked if we wanted a doctor. He called at my house the following weekend. Bouncy, talkative, yet full of enthusiasm, he was even prepared to pay his way to come on the expedition. He had climbed in the Alps and was a competent all-rounder without being an ace climber. He seemed ideal for the job and I invited him on the spot.

I was still worried about the start of our supply line—having the right equipment and food flowing up the mountain in the right order would be one of the requisites for success. Some kind of Base Camp manager seemed essential. We could have found an older, experienced mountaineer to take on the job, but he might well have had too many preconceived ideas. I therefore approached Lt.-Col. Charles Wylie, a serving army officer and a member of the 1953 Everest expedition, to ask him if he knew of any soldier suitable for the job. He recommended Kelvin Kent, a Captain in the Gurkha Signals, stationed in Hong Kong. He spoke fluent Nepali, was a wireless expert and had a sound practical knowledge of the logistic planning we required on the mountain. Running an assault on a Himalayan peak is very similar to fighting a war—logistics and planning are the key to success. It doesn't matter how tough or courageous the men out in front are: unless they are supplied with food and equipment they quickly come to a grinding halt.

It has often been said that the ideal age for the Himalayan climber is around the mid thirties. In this case we were slightly below the norm, for the average age of the party was just over thirty, with the youngest at twenty-six and the eldest thirty-five. But I had been twenty-five when I first went to the Himalayas and found that I acclimatized quite satisfactorily; Don Whillans was only twenty-three on Masherbrum and put up an outstanding performance.

A more interesting statistic is that all the party but two—Kelvin Kent and Dave Lambert—were married and four had children.

Our team, therefore, now numbered eleven climbers. We planned to supplement our numbers with six Sherpas—a small figure for an expedition of this size, but the Face seemed so steep that it appeared unlikely that we should be able to use them for more than the lower slopes.

Right at the last minute our strength was still further increased by the addition of a television team. We had succeeded in selling the story to I.T.N. and Thames Television. I had hoped to get away with taking a single cameraman/director with us, but understandably they insisted on our taking a complete film team of cameraman, sound recordist, reporter-director from Thames, and also, since this was a joint venture, a representative from I.T.N. to look after their interests.

I was worried about taking such a large self-contained group along, since an expedition imposes a strain on personal relations at the best of times, and a group reporting on us yet remaining uninvolved could have increased this danger still further. However, we needed the money, and after meeting John Edwards, the Thames Television director, and Alan Hankinson, the I.T.N. representative, I felt reassured. John was a fast-talking extrovert who could obviously fit happily into any group. Alan would be the oldest member of the expedition at the age of forty-four. I

Climbing Team: *(bottom, left to right), Tom Frost, Chris Bonington, Kelvin Kent, Dougal Haston, Mike Thompson, Don Whillans, Nick Estcourt, Mick Burke, Martin Boysen, Dr. David Lambert.* **Sherpas and other porters:** *Tukte, Ang Pema, Gumbahadur Pun, Pasang Kami, Pembatharke, Sonam Tenzing, Nima Tsering, Mingma Tsering, Kancha.* **T.V. Team:** *John Soldini, Jon Lane, John Edwards, Alan Hankinson.* London Sherpas and others: *Frank Jackson, Robin Terray, Cynthia Gilbey, and Barbara Jackson.*

had met him in 1966 when he came out to the Eiger to report for *News at Ten*, and had been very impressed by the way he coaxed a Dutch camera crew across steep, snow-plastered slopes leading to the foot of the Eiger to interview the team. He was a rangy, slightly untidy man with a whimsical yet diffident air, not at all the kind of person you would expect to find in television. He had an unconsummated passion for mountaineering and seemed to be looking forward to our trip with a boyish enthusiasm that was more for the sake of being involved in a mountaineering project than to record it for his employers. I hoped to take full advantage of this, using him as an extra porter on the mountain.

And so the total strength of the party would number twenty-one. Then on top of this we should have mailrunners, cookboys and perhaps some local porters, certainly more people than I had ever been responsible for in the past—twelve men and three tanks had been my biggest command in the army.

CHAPTER 2

Why Annapurna?

When reading expedition books I have always tended to skip the pages dealing with the history of the mountain, previous expeditions, and so on, but I feel it necessary to write about them in this instance to establish the significance of what we were trying to do and its place in the overall history of Himalayan climbing.

At 26,545 feet Annapurna I is the tenth highest mountain in the world. It had already played an important part in the history of Himalayan climbing, for it was the first peak over the magic height of 8,000 metres (26,248 feet) to be climbed, when it was conquered by a French expedition led by Maurice Herzog in 1950. This marked the start of an onslaught on the Himalayan giants, and in the course of the next ten years most of them fell: Everest and Nanga Parbat in 1953, K.2 and Cho Oyu in 1954, Kangchenjunga and Makalu in 1955, Lhotse and Manaslu in 1956. The last of the eight-thousand-metre peaks to be conquered was Gosainthan, in Tibet, by a Chinese expedition in 1964. Today the only unclimbed peak of over 26,000 feet is Gasherbrum III in the Karakorum.

Although there are still many hundreds of unclimbed peaks in the Himalaya, ranging from twenty-one-thousanders to a few twenty-five-thousanders, most of the more attractive ones—those that are steep, with aesthetically pleasing shapes—have now been climbed. The ones that have not, like the Ogre Peak off the Hispar Glacier, Paigu Peak off the Baltoro, and many magnificent peaks in Bhutan, are all unattainable for political reasons.

Before 1968 very few of these major peaks, with the exception of Everest for obvious reasons, had had more than one ascent. Everest was also the only peak of over 25,000 feet with more than one route up it. The Chinese claimed they had climbed the North Ridge, the route attempted by pre-war British expeditions, in 1960, but their evidence was very slight and few Western mountaineers believed them. But in 1963 the Americans made a grand slam, completing the West Ridge of Everest, and then traversing the mountain by descending the South Ridge. Even the West Ridge, though extremely arduous, was not technically difficult in modern Alpine terms.

We had reached much the same stage of development in the Himalayas as had been reached by 1865 in the Alps, with the first ascent of the Matterhorn, which was the last of the major peaks to be climbed. Climbers next turned to successively more difficult routes, at first on the ridges and then on the great walls, developing new techniques and equipment to overcome each successive barrier.

In the Himalayas, however, climbers naturally wanted to jump the slow evolutionary development that took place in the Alps, and, making use of the equipment and skills developed on the lower mountains, tackle the Himalayan equivalents of the North Wall of the Eiger—going straight from the easiest possible routes to the hardest.

Just how big a jump this was can be seen by comparing the time scale in the Alps with that of the Himalayas. The Matterhorn was climbed for the first time in 1865. It was sixty-six years later that its difficult North Face was climbed by the Schmidt brothers.

The equivalent first stage was only reached in the Himalayas in 1964 when the Chinese, spurred on by thoughts of Chairman Mao, conquered Gosainthan. Even by the comparatively easy routes of some of these ascents they were considerable achievements. Everest, for instance, which would be hardly more than an easy scramble at sea level, cost eleven lives in seven expeditions before it was finally climbed by Hillary and Tensing in 1953. Now, only seventeen years later, we were planning to tackle one of the most formidable walls in the Himalayas, as difficult from a technical point of view as the Eiger, but twice its size, with all the problems of altitude thrown in.

We were not alone in our concept. A German expedition was preparing to tackle the huge Rupal Face of Nanga Parbat, and the Japanese were going to attempt the South Face of Everest.

But back in 1950 Maurice Herzog and his team of French climbers were also faced by an unknown set of problems. Nepal was opening its frontiers to climbers for the first time in history. Maps were inaccurate, and therefore climbers first had to find their mountain. The French planned to climb either Dhaulagiri (26,811 feet) or Annapurna I. Dhaulagiri was naturally their first choice, being both the higher and the easier to find. It is a great hump of a mountain towering over entire Nepalese foothills with very few subsidiary ridges or peaks. It is also very steep on all sides, and the French, after skirmishing round its lower slopes, realized it was too hard for them—this was too early a stage in the development of Himalayan climbing.

They therefore turned their attentions to Annapurna. The first problem was to find it, for the mountain hides itself in a complex of subsidiary peaks and ridges. The map marked passes where there were 20,000 foot ice walls, and ridges that did not exist. They spent a month reconnoitering the outer defences before finding the easiest approach into the Miristi Khola, the valley leading to Annapurna's North Face. This was fairly easy-angled up a huge glacier leading into the upper slopes, but the party must have been tired by their exertions and had very little time before the arrival of the monsoon. They only established their Base Camp for the assault on the mountain in mid-May, when most expeditions reckon to have climbed their mountains or least to be very near the top. The monsoon had already broken when Herzog and Lachenal reached the summit. They paid a high price for their victory, losing toes and fingers and narrowly escaping with their lives.

Annapurna I did not have another ascent before 1970, though most of its many subsidiary peaks had now been climbed. Lt.-Col. J. O. M. Roberts, an officer in the Gurkhas and a very experienced mountaineer, was the first European to penetrate the Sanctuary, the huge glacier basin to the south of Annapurna. Its only exit is the Modi Khola, a narrow gorge leading down into the foothills and eventually to the plains of India. This is one of the most incredible glacier basins in the world. Its entrance is guarded on one side by the towering spire of Machapuchare, showing on this flank a sheer rock wall leading up to the summit, and on the other side by Hiunchuli, a 21,000-foot ice peak, still unclimbed. From its Christmas-cake summit a razor-edged ice ridge curls round the summit of Modi Peak (also known as Annapurna South, 22,999 feet); from there the basin is contained by a fluted wall of ice, broken by steep rock buttresses, past the Fang and on to Annapurna, whose three huge buttreses, reminiscent of those of the north side of the Grandes Jorasses in the French Alps, dominate the basin. Beyond Annapurna I the wall becomes more broken, with a whole series of subsidiary ridges and peaks jutting into the Sanctuary. There is Glacier Dome (23,191 feet), the squat triangle of Gangapurna (24,457 feet) and Annapurna III (24,787 feet), whence the eastern retaining wall of the Sanctuary curves down to embrace Machapuchare.

Jimmy Roberts was making a reconnaissance for a British expedition led by Wilfred Noyce that planned to attempt Machapuchare in 1957. They established their Base Camp at the mouth of the Sanctuary, and Noyce and David Cox managed to get within two hundred feet of the summit but were turned back by the steepness and difficulty of the final ice slope.

Machapuchare remains unconquered. Jimmy Roberts, who had a fair amount of influence in Katmandu, suggested that the Nepalese government should keep at least one mountain in Nepal unclimbed, a kind of symbol of the inviolate. They took him at his word, and to this day it is impossible to get permission to climb this most beautiful and accessible of all Nepalese mountains.

Meanwhile, the tail of the Annapurna massif—the mountain formed by Annapurna IV and II, which is divided from the main mass by a 17,000-foot col and really deserves the dignity of a name of its own— had been tweaked.

In 1950 a small expedition led by that great and austere mountain explorer Bill Tillman had attempted Annapurna IV and failed. In 1954 a small German expedition succeeded. Three years later Charles Evans, leader of the successful Kangchenjunga expedition, and Dennis Davies attempted to climb Annapurna II with four Sherpas. This was an extreme version of the lightweight expedition and they did remarkably well, reaching the summit of Annapurna IV but balking at the three-mile-long ridge, all above 23,600 feet, connecting it with Annapurna II.

Annapurna II was climbed in 1960 by a combined Services expedition led by Jimmy Roberts, of which I was a member. I was lucky enough to go to the top with Dick Grant, a Captain in the Royal Marines, and the Sherpa Ang Nyima. We used oxygen, and the final assault was long and exacting, three miles of ridge from the shoulder just below the summit of Annapurna IV, and then a two-thousand-foot climb up the final pyramid, a mixture of snow and rock scrambling. Even so, the climb as a whole was very much in the traditional Himalayan idiom, most of it being simple snow slogging on easy slopes.

The peaks of the main Annapurna mass fell in the next nine years. An Indian expedition climbed Annapurna III from the north in 1961, but it was a Japanese expedition that was first to reach the spine of the Annapurna massif from the south, when they climbed Glacier Dome from the Sanctuary in 1964. The following year a German expedition had permission to attempt Annapurna I from the south, but on reaching the Sanctuary Günther Hauser, the leader, decided to go for the unclimbed Gangapurna.

There was then a gap of four years when Nepal closed its frontiers to climbers. In 1969 another German expedition, this time led by Ludwig

Greissl, attempted Annapurna I from the south, climbing Glacier Dome and then trying to traverse the long summit ridge leading over Annapurna's three tops. It was an ambitious project, involving extended lines of communication at altitude, but it was following the traditional evolutionary pattern of tackling a mountain by successively more difficult ridges. They never even contemplated attempting the huge South Face. They were unlucky with the weather, however, constantly battered by high winds on the crest of the ridge and finally trapped in their camp on top of the Roc Noir (24,556 feet) by a severe storm for eight days. This ended their attempt. Both Günther Hauser and Ludwig Greissl helped me with advice and with photographs of the South Face in the planning stage of our expedition, but neither was over-optimistic about our chances of success.

We were basing our plans on our analysis of a few photographs—an analysis backed by experience on other mountains. But even so I couldn't help being frightened at times by the sheer size and expense of this project, which rested on judgment backed by only limited research. We had talked of making a reconnaissance in the post-monsoon period of 1969, for Don Whillans and myself to go out and have a look at the Face and watch it for a few days to see just how serious a threat there was of avalanche. I was not afraid of technical difficulty, since with modern equipment and techniques almost anything can be climbed, provided one isn't swept away by avalanche on the way up. From photographs the Face seemed fairly safe, though it did flatten out in the middle and the way there was barred by a line of ice cliffs. If these were unstable, the route could be suicidally dangerous, but both Don and I judged them to be solid.

In the event a reconnaissance proved impracticable. We had the money but there was insufficient time to get the expedition properly organized and also fly out to Nepal. In any case, I had already ordered a large quantity of climbing equipment and all the oxygen; we had fixed up a number of contracts, and it would have damaged any chances of getting support in the future if we had turned round and said it was all off. We were, therefore, committed to a project that represented a complete step into the unknown. I had nightmares before setting out for Nepal that we might get to the foot of the Face, look up at it and realize that it was totally impossible. My reasoning said that this was unlikely to happen, but still it was just possible—something that I think all of us secretly feared but did not like talking about.

There are two periods in the year when you can climb in the Himalayas: one sandwiched between the end of the winter and the start of the monsoon, which reaches the Annapurna region around the beginning of June, and the other after the monsoon and before the winter snows set in. Either period has various pros and cons. The weather is more settled in the post monsoon season, but it is also much colder, and expeditions have tended to favour the spring period for assaults on the higher peaks.

We chose the pre-monsoon season of 1970, and I based my programme on leaving Pokhara, a small town with an airstrip about sixty miles from the South Face, on 22 March. We knew that the approach would take us approximately eight days and hoped to start climbing on the Face around the beginning of April; this would give us about nine weeks to reach the top. I had toyed with the idea of going out earlier to give us more time, but then there is always the risk of being held up by winter snows. Ideally, I wanted to get the porters with all the expedition baggage up to the site of the permanent Base Camp, and from all accounts it was difficult to persuade them to carry far above the snow-line.

Our expedition had rapidly developed from a small compact party into something very much larger; our concept had changed from rapid blitzkrieg to a full-scale siege. There is a feeling amongst many mountaineers that the time has come for the Himalayan peaks to be tackled by lightweight parties, treating the climbs as super Alpine problems; this entails tackling the mountain in a single push, without establishing a supply line of fixed ropes with all the paraphernalia of ferrying and support parties. This approach has been used successfully in the American continent on some very big faces—on the West Face of Huntingdon in Alaska by Dave Roberts and his party, and also on the East Face of Yeupaja by the English climber Chris Jones and the American Paul Dix. It is a concept that tries to maintain the elements of chance and commitment, both important ingredients of mountaineering. These days, with modern equipment, particularly the extensive use of expansion bolts to climb where there are no cracks for pitons and fixed ropes to enable a party to retreat, rest, re-supply and return to the assault, no mountain wall below 21,000 feet is unclimbable.

In the Himalayas however it is a different story. Some lightweight pushes have been made, particularly by Austrian climbers. The most successful was in 1957, when an Austrian party of only four led by Hermann Bühl climbed Broad Peak (26,414 feet) then attempted Chogolisa (25,110 feet) but were caught by a storm on their summit bid. They decided to retreat and on the way back Hermann Bühl fell through a cornice and was killed.

The ascent of Broad Peak was a magnificent achievement. More than that, they must have been able to taste the truest joy of mountaineering, being a very small party in the midst of some of the most impressive mountains in the world. There is no doubt that the larger the party, the further you are separated from the feel of big mountains. You lose so much of the silence, the scale, even a full appreciation of their beauty if there are too many people around.

But the route that Bühl and Diemberger made up Broad Peak was comparatively straightforward. It seemed doubtful whether one could employ the same Alpine tactics on a big face climb on one of the major peaks of the Himalaya.

I had considered the possibility of moving up the South Face with a group of six climbers, carrying enough food and gear to last six weeks, and moving as a single body. In theory this is possible, and one day it might well be tried, but the time factor would be against it, for the longer one stays at altitude the more one deteriorates. On this score alone it seems necessary to have a line of fixed rope so that climbers can go back for rest at Base Camp. There is little value in resting at altitude, for above 21,000 feet you are deteriorating the whole time, even when resting. Another factor on a technically difficult climb that is going to take a long time is that people's health at altitude is very unpredictable. One therefore needs a permanent line of retreat so that those who are going badly can get down the mountain reasonably easily.

Even with siege tactics and every possible aid available to us we should still be contending with long odds. We decided that we should have to have oxygen for the upper part, since the Rock Band started at a height of over 23,000 feet and looked as if it could give climbing every bit as difficult as the North Wall of the Eiger, certainly more difficult than anything that had been attempted before at that altitude. We could not possibly predict whether this type of high-standard climbing would be possible at that altitude without the aid of oxygen. For instance, the French had failed on Jannu, a very difficult peak of 25,500 feet, on their first attempt in 1958, largely because they had trouble with their oxygen sets. They succeeded in 1962, using oxygen and backed by a party considerably larger than the one I proposed to take out.

One problem with using oxygen is that it trebles the logistic load on the climb, since it means that a considerable weight of cylinders that have a very limited life have to be carried to the high camps. We also planned to fix-rope almost the entire climb to ensure we had a reliable supply line. For this purpose we took out with us fifteen thousand feet of rope.

When asked why I wanted to climb the South Face of Annapurna, I am tempted to repeat Mallory's famous answer, 'Because it is there.' This is both inadequate yet all-embracing. We climb for so many reasons: the joy of movement and muscular control up a steep face of rock or ice; the satisfaction of exploring new ground, even up a small rock face on the flanks of a hillside; and, perhaps even more important, of exploring one's own reactions to new, at times exacting, experience. There is the sheer beauty and grandeur of the mountains, the soothing balm of solitude. And through it all, is the undercurrent of danger: for this is what climbing is all about—staking one's life on one's judgement, playing the calculated risk. This doesn't mean going blindly into danger, or seeking hazard for its own sake. The climber gains his satisfaction from going into a potentially dangerous situation but then, through his own skill and experience, rendering it safe.

When I started climbing at the age of sixteen I often got myself into positions where I was fighting for life itself, struggling to stay in contact with the rock in a sweat of fear and horror—this was sheer inexperience. I continued climbing because memory is short: I would quickly forget what it had been like to be afraid, and go on to the next climb. The overall feeling was pleasure in the process of climbing, the thrill of discovery and my own development as a climber.

With experience, one gains greater control. This led to a real pleasure in a struggle with the elements at their worst—certainly my most memorable, and in a way most enjoyable, days climbing have been in violent storms in the Alps, when the wind and snow have torn at my anorak-covered body; when my wits and judgement have been extended to the full and yet, in spite of all, I have remained on top of the situation.

At altitude there is little physical pleasure to be gained from climbing—each movement is too exacting and laborious—but the challenge and fascination of discovery are even greater than at lower altitudes.

Climbing a big mountain is essentially a team effort. Only two men out of a dozen might be able to reach the top, through the corporate effort of the entire group. Naturally, one longs to be one of those two men, is tempted at times to nurse one's strength for the summit push, rather than extend oneself to the limit for the good of the team as a whole. At the end of each of my two earlier expeditions there had been an agonizing moment of self-appraisal—the challenge to go back was not only to taste the excitement of discovery, but also to improve my own performance, not just as a climber, but as a member of a team as well.

These were some of the motives that led me to the South Face of Annapurna. It was certainly the supreme challenge of my life, partly because of its magnitude as a climbing problem, but mainly through the responsibility I had accepted as leader of a group of men. Climbing, and I suppose life itself, is a constant process of discovery, of stretching out to find new limits. Each step is all-exciting, yet having made it, there is no going back or even marking time: one must go on to find a new horizon. At the time, one's first tentative step as a toddler must have been all-satisfying, then one's first ascent of a tree at the end of the garden; if you choose climbing as your life's path, the first time you take the lead out in front is as exciting, at that instant of time, as the first time you stand on the summit of a Himalayan peak—and yet each is equally ephemeral.

I often worried about my ability to hold together a group of individualistic and very talented climbers. For the past eight years I had worked as a freelance with very little responsibility to anyone but myself. The last time I had had any kind of command responsibility was back in 1960 when I was in the army, protected by the pips on my shoulder and the might of military discipline. This is very different from conducting a mountaineering expedition, where one's authority rests solely on the loyalty and respect of the team.

Shortly before I set out for Annapurna a reporter asked me how I intended to impose discipline on the team and what I would do if someone turned round and told me to get lost. The answer, of course, was that I could do nothing if this happened, but that I would try to see it did not—in fact, I should already have failed if such a situation ever had arisen.

As leader, it seemed to me I had to be a diplomat and co-ordinator of ideas rather than a disciplinarian. The discipline could only come from the members of the team themselves. If anyone turned round and said he did not want to do something, either because he was too tired or because it was too dangerous, I had to accept it. Yet at the same time I realized I should have to make decisions at times that might be unpopular. Whether I was obeyed or not would depend on the team's respect for my judgement, and their own sense of team spirit.

We were not fighting a war, but rather were playing an elaborate, potentially dangerous game; therefore each individual had the right to decide how far he should drive himself and the level of risk he was prepared to accept.

With the exception of Tom Frost, Dave Lambert and Kelvin Kent, I had known everyone over a period of years. We had climbed together under difficult and dangerous circumstances, had much the same kind of attitude to climbing, and were likely to make similar interpretations of the solution to the various problems we should encounter. I hoped that my own job of leader or co-ordinator would be made easier by the fact that a group of people, however talented and individualistic, have the need for guidance, leadership, call it what you will, in the shape of a plan that can be followed. As we prepared for the expedition my own exploration into the realms of leadership and administration was as much a trip into the unknown as were the problems of climbing the Face.

CHAPTER 3

Preparations
[October '68–March '70]

I built up my team over a period of about seven months, from October '68 through to May '69. At the same time I was trying to get permission to climb the mountain and organize the financial support we should require for the expedition. I was already daunted by what I had taken on. I had been on three previous expeditions and had taken some part in their organization, but I had never taken the lead; had never even considered myself an administrative type.

The actual ascent of a mountain is like the proverbial tip of the iceberg. For the two months of actual climbing there was a year of preparation, of which the last six months were intensive. For me this was one of the most exacting parts of the expedition—a period full of hard grinding work and self-doubt about my ability to carry it through.

I was lucky to come across George Greenfield at an early stage of our organization. He is a literary agent specializing in adventure, having handled Sir Francis Chichester, Robin Knox-Johnston and Wally Herbert. He gave me the first real encouragement I had, was enthusiastic about the scheme and talked confidently of raising at least twenty thousand pounds. My preliminary budgets were in the region of ten thousand, a sum that seemed astronomical, but in fact was well below what the venture eventually cost.

Our expedition seemed to gain in stature almost in spite of ourselves. George Greenfield arranged a meeting with Pat Pirie-Gordon, a director of Glyn, Mills & Co., the bankers, and a power behind the scenes in the world of expedition finance. Largely through his support and enthusiasm we got the full support of the Mount Everest Foundation. Suddenly we seemed to be coming under the wing of the Establishment—something which all of us had regarded with some distrust, having been very much outside these circles. I had certainly come in for a measure of disapproval in the early sixties, when I had started to make my living through lecturing and writing about mountaineering, especially over the publicity associated with the ascent by Ian Clough and myself of the North Wall of the Eiger.

Soon we had a committee to look after us: Sir Douglas Busk, an ex-Ambassador and Vice-President of the Alpine Club, and our Chairman; Pat Pirie-Gordon; Anthony Rawlison, a senior Treasury official; Colonel Charles Wylie; and Tom Blakeney, the Secretary of the Mount Everest Foundation. We used to meet in the boardroom of Glyn, Mills in Whitehall—a solemn room in dark wood, lined with regimental prints, history books and models of soldiers. Lord Hunt, Lord Tangley and Sir Charles Evans kindly agreed to be our patrons.

The Mount Everest Foundation is a trust set up with the profits of the Mount Everest expedition of 1953 to help mountaineering expeditions. It is run by a committee nominated by the Alpine Club and the Royal Geographical Society, the two bodies which sponsored the Everest expedition. It gives grants each year to mountaineering expeditions going abroad, but had only fully sponsored one other expedition, the one to Kangchenjunga in 1955.

It now gave us its full support. This was a tremendous relief, for while George Greenfield was confident he could raise sufficient funds for the expedition, these were all from magazines, television and publishers, and were released according to our level of success, so much when we reached Base Camp, so much on getting quarter-way up. George Greenfield had been sufficiently astute to insist on the total when we reached the Rock Band, but there was always the risk of complete fiasco caused by something completely outside our control which could have stopped us getting started on the mountain. We tried to insure ourselves against this, but the premium asked was astronomical. The Foundation, in taking us under its wing, took away all these worries, but even so I was anxious that the expedition should show a profit at the end. It seemed possible that it would, and the Foundation, with constantly rising costs in Nepal and other mountain areas, needed a shot in the arm.

In addition to this, I had been extremely fortunate in receiving a Winston Churchill Trust fellowship—this too was a great financial help to the whole expedition.

I had never dealt with a committee before, but ours could not have been better, giving me total support and yet leaving me free to get on with the job of organizing the expedition. We did not get permission to climb until July 1969. Before that came there had been a psychological barrier against starting to order equipment and food; I suspect this was more a sop to laziness than anything else. By this time most of the team were in the Alps on their summer holidays and I was still filling in some of my own work on stories I had agreed to do, and needed to anyway to have enough money to keep the family going. As a result I only really got started on the actual business of ordering food and equipment at the beginning of September, though I had already written literally hundreds of letters around the initial planning.

Since most of the team were too far away or had jobs, we decided to concentrate the organization in the hands of a small nucleus. I was to do the bulk of the paperwork from my home, using a secretary, while Don Whillans worked on equipment design and Mike Thompson dealt with the food. Ian Clough came in later that autumn and helped Don and myself. He took a lot of the burden off my shoulders but had to go back to Scotland after Christmas to look after his courses.

The work behind any expedition is much the same: first make out

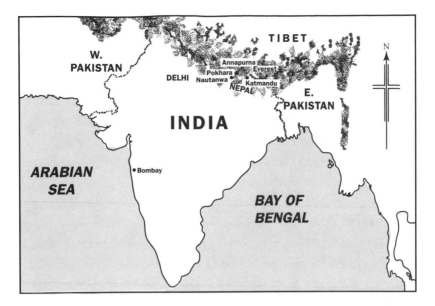

India and Nepal

your shopping-list, then beg or borrow the gear, paying for it only in the last resort. We had considerable success in the begging stakes and ended up paying for comparatively little. We had a quantity of new equipment designed specially for the expedition. Because time was short, inevitably we had many problems sorting out faults in design. I have gone into detail on the design and choice of equipment in Appendix B.

Through most of the autumn I was working a punishing day, getting up at about 6.00 a.m., working through till about 4.30 in the afternoon on the expedition, and then jumping in my car to drive anything up to eighty miles to give a lecture, back the same night and up again at six the next morning. I have certainly never worked so hard in my life as I did that autumn, yet found myself enjoying it. After three years of being involved in other people's expeditions and stories, this was my own venture. I was no longer a spectator but was totally involved. Although I was often frightened by the level of responsibility I had undertaken, at the same time I was elated, glad to be able to make my own decisions, see plans and dreams develop into reality.

At times, though, in these hectic weeks of organization, as I imagine happens with any expedition, it seemed we should never make our deadline for packing all our gear ready to go to India. We used a furniture store near Don's house in Rawtenstall as a packing centre. Fifteen thousand feet of rope, hundreds of pitons, buckets, plates, tents and all the paraphernalia of an expedition slowly piled up amongst the stacked furniture.

Getting the gear to the scene of operations is the most risky and worrying phase of any expedition, and has caused the failure of several before the climbers ever came in sight of their mountain. There are three ways of sending the expedition gear out to Nepal: by air, overland or by sea. The first method was used by the French in 1950, but is exorbitantly expensive; it would have cost us at least five thousand pounds to charter a suitable plane. The overland method has many attractions and is the one I should choose for any future expedition. You at least have all the gear with you, and the roads out to Nepal are reasonably good. We should have had to buy or borrow a couple of large trucks and then part of the expedition would have had to accompany the gear out; this would have meant taking an even longer time away from home, and most of us were married with commitments back in England. There is also the risk of crashing the vehicle, but as it turned out this was nothing to the many pitfalls if you send your gear out by sea.

We chose the sea route so that the entire team could fly out to India. The only ships that have reliable schedules are passenger liners, but the only one going out to India from Britain at round about the right time was the *Chusan*, a P. & O. boat, and she was sailing from Southampton on her last voyage to India at the beginning of January, too early for us to have any chance of getting our gear ready. The only other possibility was a cargo ship, and I booked the gear onto one sailing from Liverpool on 23 January. We were barely ready in time; many of the items we had had specially designed were still not finished. We were only saved in this respect by the fact that an expedition organized by the Army Mountaineering Association, who were flying out to attempt Annapurna by the French route from the north at the same time as ourselves, had very kindly agreed to take fifteen hundred pounds weight of our equipment.

Two days before sailing date I had a phone-call from the shipping agents: 'I'm afraid your boat has gone into dry dock with engine trouble. It won't be ready to sail for another three weeks.' This was disastrous, for we were already tight on our schedule. The boat had been due to reach Bombay on 28 February, which gave Don Whillans and Dave Lambert, who were flying out to meet it, a fortnight to get the gear by lorry across India to Pokhara, where I was planning to meet Don for a reconnaissance of the Face a week in front of the main party. If the boat was delayed for three weeks we should never be able to start on schedule and as a result our chances of success would be jeopardized.

'Isn't there another boat going out?' I asked.

'I'll try,' the shipping agent said, 'but I very much doubt it.'

I was on tenterhooks for the next twenty-four hours. We had quite enough against us on the mountain without this kind of delay. Then next day there was some good news: he had found anther boat, the *State of Kerala*, which was sailing from London on the 23rd, the same date as the original boat.

A frantic dash to the docks to get all the gear loaded in time; more worries that there might be a dock strike or any of the dozen delays that seem to affect cargo ships; but it sailed on time, first stop Bombay.

I felt we had overcome the biggest problem of all. Nothing very much could now go wrong. Don and Dave would meet the ship in Bombay and have an uncomfortable trip across India on the backs of lorries, and we should be ready to tackle our mountain.

Everything was at last falling into place. Captain Kelvin Kent, our intrepid Base Camp manager whom none of us had yet met, was now in Katmandu, paving the way for our arrival. Mike Thompson had already flown out to Katmandu with his wife and two children; he was planning to rent a house there, leave them in Katmandu for the expedition, and then go on to Kulu, an idyllic valley in the Indian part of the Himalayas, to do a year's field work in anthropology. He had it all very well weighed up—no question of leading the primitive life, for he was going to have a five-bedroom chalet with electricity and running water.

Don and Dave flew out to Bombay on 27 February. The boat, which I had checked with the London office of the shipping company, was apparently sailing on time and was due to arrive on the 28th.

That day I was sitting in the office, tying up the few loose strings left undone, when the phone rang—Overseas Cables: BOAT BROKEN DOWN CAPE TOWN. PROBABLE ARRIVAL BOMBAY 13 MARCH, ESTIMATE REACH NAUTANWA 28TH. WHILLANS. My first reaction was one of despair, but then I sat down and started working out how we could minimize the damage. Harking back to army days, I wrote an appreciation of the situation, which summed up the problems involved and my own approach to solving them.

REVISED PLAN—5 MARCH 1970

1. Cause of Change

The boat carrying the expedition's equipment has been delayed by engine troubles at Cape Town. It left Tilbury an 23 January and was due at Bombay on 28 February. Unfortunately, not only did the shipping company agents in London fail to let us know of the breakdown, they even assured us that the boat was sailing on time. This was not entirely their fault since the line's head office is in India.

Don Whillans only discovered the delay on his arrival at Bombay on 27 February. He immediately cabled me the bad news that the boat's new E.T.A. was 13 March in Bombay and that of the gear in Nautanwa 28 March, this period being taken up with off-loading, Customs clearance and the journey across India. Nautanwa is only a day's drive from Pokhara, so the gear would arrive there on the 29th and it would then take a further three days to unpack, sort out loads and be ready to go, taking us up to 2 April before we should be ready to start the approach march.

2. Appreciation of Situation

The departure of the main party was originally planned for 22

March—so this would mean a delay of twelve days, something that we cannot afford on a climb of this magnitude where time will be a critical factor. We must therefore find ways to minimize the loss of time. This will be done in two ways:

(a) By taking every measure possible to hasten gear from the ship to Pokhara, to reduce the time of fourteen days allowed by the agents in Bombay.

(b) By mounting a six-man advance party, with two Sherpas and the T.V. team, to leave on 21 March as originally planned, to establish an advanced Base Camp and to find the route onto the Face. This is logistically possible because we:

(i) have sufficient equipment with the R.A.F. plane;

(ii) shall air-freight approximately 250 lbs. of extra equipment required to fill the gap;

(iii) have been promised 100 man days of compo by the A.M.A. Expedition, which can be supplemented by local rations. We shall return this loan on the arrival of our food.

By taking this course, loss of time will be minimized so that we should only have lost the benefit of the recce by Whillans and myself, and will incur some delay in the build-up of our gear flowing up the Face. Since there might have been a slight bottle-neck before the team became deployed, this latter factor is not too important.

I cabled to Don and Dave to move on to Katmandu; there was no point in their waiting in Bombay for up to a month, letting their hotel bills pile up, and anyway I wanted Don on the mountain. I therefore asked Ian Clough if he would take on the grim job of shepherding the gear through the Customs and across India. He was the ideal man for the job, tremendously conscientious, tactful and very patient. I also decided to fly out to Bombay myself to see if I could smooth Ian's way. Any kind of delay in Bombay would have been disastrous.

When Don heard that I was calling in at Bombay he said wryly, 'Does he think he's going to tow the boat across the Indian Ocean personally?'

There was some justification for his scepticism, but the entire expedition now depended on getting the gear up to Base Camp as soon as possible after the arrival of the main party. I had an unavoidable feeling of guilt that I hadn't managed to get everything onto an earlier boat, even though this would have been impossible in the time available.

I flew from London Airport in a flurry of spring snow and sub-freezing temperature on 10 March. The Air India 707 lifted off effortlessly, but there was no feeling of elation: I was much too worried about the whereabouts of the expedition's gear and was near to exhaustion from weeks of pressured work and worry. The afternoon I flew out another cable arrived stating that the boat had been further delayed and was not expected to reach Bombay till 19 March.

I had amassed a battery of contacts to help clear Customs before leaving England, but in the event found these unnecessary. I spent three days in Bombay meeting representatives of the shipping line and Customs, oozing charm to all and sundry. Our agent, Freddie Buhari-wala, very plump, with a deceptive appearance of softness that hid a keen and determined mind, assured me that they could get the gear through Customs in a couple of days. I felt confident that this was more than just a promise to get rid of a worried customer, and left for Katmandu.

It had been a rather lonely, deflating three days. As I flew up to Delhi, and then changed planes, amid a throng of dough-faced, depressed-looking Russians on some kind of trade delegation, I could not help worrying about our prospects and my ability to see them through.

The plane flew up through the haze of the Indian plains, and then in the distance came the white tops of mountains like the line of breaking surf across the empty sands of a beach. That great hump must be Dhaulagiri; to its right a sprawling mass of mountains could only be Annapurna. I could even see the top of the South Face; from this distance a tiny whaleback of snow leading into a steep head wall, white, mottled with black protruding rocks. And then, as we flew past, the entire line of the Nepalese Himalaya unfolded. On the far horizon was Everest's squat pyramid, hiding behind Nuptse's ramparts. Below us were serried ridges of brown and dusty green, winding paths and villages clinging improbably to crests of ridges. And then we were over the valley of Katmandu, a broad plain amidst the hills, dotted with villages and towns, interconnected with roads and paths. I could pick out Rana palaces with spacious courtyards and rusty, corrugated-iron roofs, pagoda-like temples jutting like rocks out of a sea of close-packed houses. When I had flown in ten years before it had been in a battered Dakota onto a rough grass runway, but now there was smooth tarmac and a solid, if not imposing, terminal building.

Mike Thompson and Kelvin Kent were there to meet me. Kelvin was fairly short, lean and bubbling with a driving nervous energy. He had sharp, rather hard features accentuated by a biggish nose and very firm mouth, yet at the same time there was a warmth about him. He plunged into details about the latest developments almost immediately as he whisked me through the Customs.

'How many cameras have you there?' asks the Customs officer.

'Six,' I reply.

'But you are only allowed to bring in one—I shall have to charge you duty on the rest.'

Kelvin interjects swiftly. 'But these cameras are to be divided amongst the rest of the team,' he says.

The Customs officer accepted the explanation and waved me through. Kelvin was obviously a veteran in this kind of situation, tackling administrative problems with the same enthusiasm and verve that the rest of the team reserved for the mountains. In this respect he climbed a dozen Annapurnas before we left Katmandu.

He had managed to get himself attached to the British Gurkha Headquarters in Nepal after his tour with the 48 Infantry Brigade in Hong Kong had ended at the end of January, to pave the way for both the Army party and ourselves. His time had been well spent. In fact, without someone in Nepal we could have lost several weeks just clearing our equipment with the Customs; several other expeditions had suffered in this way. Being a Royal Signals officer he had proposed having a rear-link wireless back to Katmandu and to Pokhara for the passing of information and particularly for use in emergencies. He got the loan of four Racal Squadcal radios for this purpose, so that we could be in contact with the Army expedition on the other side of Annapurna as well. The Nepalese authorities, like almost all Asian governments, are very security-conscious and did not normally allow expeditions to use long-range radios in Nepal. Even the British Embassy was very discouraging about trying to push the government, mindful of safeguarding their own communication system with the two Gurkha depots in Nepal. Kelvin, however, is not a person who can easily be fobbed off, and he pursued his quest to get permission to use radios with the same tenacity as he employed in every other sphere—a mixture of tact and determination. He eventually got an agreement that the set in Katmandu should be kept in the Nepalese Army headquarters so that they would have control of the wireless net, while we should have another one in Pokhara, operated by Lieutenant Bishnuparsad Thapa, one of Kelvin's subordinates from the Gurkha Signal Regiment in Malaya, and the remaining two sets would be with the two expeditions. Kelvin had secured the release of another Gurkha signals radio-operator, Gambahadur Pun, to operate our set at Base Camp.

In getting this permission Kelvin had secured an important precedent for other expeditions. Wireless communications with Pokhara or Katmandu could mean the saving of a man's life in the event of an emergency. Indeed, they possibly did for the Army expedition: one of their members, Captain Tim Taylor, went down with pneumonia in the latter stages of the approach march. At altitude this illness can be fatal, but they were able to call up a helicopter from Katmandu to take him out.

Kelvin had also found time to visit Nautanwa, the border town where our gear would enter Nepal, to smooth the way with the local Customs man, and had walked to the village of Ghandrung, half-way to Annapurna, accompanied by Mike Thompson, to order all our local purchases of food and fuel. This consisted of paraffin, cooking-oil, rice, potatoes, dhall, fifteen chickens, two goats and even a small buffalo. With the delay to our gear we were going to have to depend entirely on locally bought food, since I did not want to use the compo loaned to us by the Army expedition until we were on the mountain.

He had also organized our low-altitude porters, whose job it was to carry all the gear up to Base Camp. Normally this is left entirely to a government-sponsored organization called the Himalayan Society, which had a representative in Pokhara with the flamboyant title of Coolie Lama. He was responsible for recruiting porters and appointing the Naiks, or foremen of the porters. He would normally make his selection from the riff-raff of Pokhara and the Tibetan refugees from the local camp. The latter were tough and dependable, accustomed to going into the snows, but the townspeople were less reliable. It was particularly difficult on this occasion, and probably will be in future years, because of the huge number of climbing expeditions starting from Pokhara, which is the departure point for all expeditions in central and western Nepal. Kelvin had therefore approached a retired Gurkha officer, Lieutenant Khagbir Pun, who had served in his Gurkha Signal regiment and was now running a little Parbat hotel by the airstrip at Pokhara. Kelvin had asked him to recruit the porters from the hill villages, where the men are more accustomed to hardship and looking after themselves. Khagbir did a wonderful job, walking through thirty-two villages and covering a hundred and fifty miles of switchback footpaths in fifteen days, to collect about eighty porters, while to keep the Coolie Lama happy we allowed him to provide fifty.

Meanwhile, in Katmandu, Kelvin had been unravelling a tangled skein of red tape that would have enmeshed a lesser man. Luckily for us he had managed to enlist the aid of the British Gurkha headquarters and was also working closely with Mike Cheney of Mountain Travel (which organizes tourist treks in Nepal), who spent most of his own time in helping to smooth the way by providing introductions and supplying his own vehicle for helping to collect gear. Jimmy Roberts, proprietor of Mountain Travel, had also generously loaned us vital tentage. From England it was impossible to discover exactly what was required in the way of forms and lists to get import licences for the expedition equipment. Kelvin had sent us details of the requirement: eleven lists of all the equipment, specifying what gear we intended to leave behind in Nepal and what we intended to take out again after the expedition. We then had to value each individual item in both sterling and Nepalese currency.

In the first instance, he took three weeks to set an import permit for our main gear. Subsequently he succeeded in reducing this time through his knowledge of which office to chase into to distribute the various forms and ferret them from the bottom of crowded 'Pending' trays to ram them under the noses of officials.

A day with Kelvin was both instructive and exhausting. I had one, just before we all flew to Pokhara to start the approach march.

6.0 a.m. He is already up, shaved and dressed in sports jacket, tie and flannels. 'If you wear an open shirt you might be mistaken for one of the local hippies. You've got to look the part if you want results.' I am soon to see this in action; you also need the hide of a rhinoceros and the energy of a David Frost, as you constantly barge to the head of queues of patient locals waiting outside interminable offices.

7.30 a.m. He has drafted several letters and now rushes out to the airport to meet the other half of the T.V. team; John Edwards and Alan Hankinson have already arrived, but the camera team are due today with all the gear. But this is a false alarm. The plane is late.

9.30 a.m. I meet Kelvin at the British Embassy and am whisked through several courtesy calls, ranging from the Ambassador down to Cynthia the typist, whom Kelvin has charmed into acting as unofficial expedition secretary in Nepal. I find it both amusing and rather gratifying being the gracious figurehead, murmuring the right words of gratitude as I'm orbited through each office—now I know what Royalty must feel like.

10.30 a.m. Off to the airport again, and this time the camera team do arrive. Jonathan Lane, the cameraman, looks like something straight out of the Underground—flared cord trousers, mauve shirt and drooping moustache—while John Soldini, the sound man, looks improbably plump and comfortable, the kind of man who would be happier watering the garden at home rather than flitting round the world from trouble spot to trouble spot as a member of a news team. They are surrounded by a pile of gear—cine-cameras, tripods and sixty thousand feet of film. For once, Kelvin has met his match in John Edwards, who proves an even faster, smoother talker than our expedition manager. He looks the part: immaculately tailored Vietnam greens, the darkest of dark glasses, kept on in the gloom of the customs shed. He has already persuaded the Customs officer that the camera team are tourists and their forty-two pieces of baggage contain only a couple of ciné-cameras and a few feet of film.

12.00 noon. Off to the Nook, a small café at the back of the American Embassy and expedition meeting-place. On the way we call in at the British Embassy to pick up fifteen copies of the list of items being airfreighted out from England. Dave Lambert is there chatting up his newfound girlfriend and waiting for a briefing from Kelvin. Just time to down a Club Sandwich before we are off again, this time to Rastra Bank, Nepalese equivalent of the Bank of England, to start the process of getting an import licence for some of the extra gear we are having airfreighted out. We fight our way through to a cubby-hole, get a form from the man behind the counter, take it to another cubby-hole to get it stamped, plunge into a maze of corridors to get it signed by yet another official, and then set off for the next set of offices. It's rather like a treasure hunt; small wonder that Kelvin took three weeks to get all the clues when he first went round the course.

2.0 p.m. Now a digression. We go to another bank to get the money we shall use to pay the porters—£2,500's worth of rupees. It takes another hour, and an obstacle course round and over crowded desks, to steer the paying-out slip round the officials who must sign and countersign it. 'It would take all day if I left them to do it,' Kelvin says. We finally collect the money, cramming thick wads of one-rupee notes into our executive briefcases like a pair of bank robbers, rush out and jump onto our bicycles, the most effective means of transport in Katmandu.

• • •

3.0 p.m. 'We've just got time to see if we can find some sunglasses for the porters before my next appointment,' shouts Kelvin. We plunge into the bazaar. This is the old Katmandu: narrow streets, open cavernous shop-fronts with everything being sold from grain and spices to sewing machines or umbrellas; streets packed with honking cars, bicycle rick-shaws, screaming children, drifting hippies, lost-looking tourists. It's a wonderful cacophony of sound, smells and movement. The kind of atmosphere one wants to absorb at leisure, but not a hope with Kelvin. He rides his bicycle as if he was taking part in the Tour de France, bell ringing, dodging cars, buffalo and passersby with equal élan. It's all I can do to keep up with him. In a matter of minutes we have visited four dif-ferent shops in search of glasses, but the price isn't right. He looks at his watch. 'We've got ten minutes to get to the Ministry of Foreign Affairs. Leave your bike here. We'll take a taxi.' We leave the bikes propped against the sidewalk in the main street—equivalent of Oxford Street in London—and jump into a taxi.

3.30 p.m. We reach the Singa Durbar, where almost all the offices of the government of Nepal are concentrated. It was once the private palace—largest in the world—of the Maharaja. Up till 1950 Nepal was ruled by one family, the Ranas. Effective power was controlled by the hereditary prime minister or Maharaja, whilst the King was little more than a puppet, with spiritual rather than temporal power. The Ranas' power was upheld by the British Raj, who wanted a strong, if reactionary, gov-ernment on their northern frontier. Once India gained independence the Nehru government encouraged the exiled opposition to the Ranas and in 1950 they were overthrown. A short period of haphazard demo-cratic government was followed by more positive rule by the King of Nepal. The Ranas have lost their power but many of them still hold high office, particularly in the armed forces. However, most of the old Rana palaces, which anyway were both uncomfortable and expensive to maintain, have now been turned into offices or hotels.

The Singa Durbar is a decaying warren of interlinking courtyards.

We are on our way to see the official in the Foreign Office responsible for expeditions. Once off his bike, Kelvin turns into a road-walker, going at a pace where I find it is almost easier to trot to keep up. We call in at two or three other offices on our way, distributing our copies of the application for an import licence rather like bible tracts.

'Oh, I think you might as well meet the Head of Protocol.' We push open a door and Kelvin jumps in like a jack-in-the-box, myself trailing after him. The Chief of Protocol, a Mr. Remal, seems to be having some kind of meeting but courteously breaks off to talk with us.

Another couple of officials in the Ministry of Foreign Affairs and it is time for a meeting in Army headquarters to discuss the distribution and use of our radios. Kelvin somehow manages to keep to this tight time-schedule without any effort, extracting me and himself from each meeting with a ruthless precision.

We arrive at Army headquarters on time for our appointment, but nobody seems to have heard of us. We are introduced to a few staff officers, chat generally and eventually our meeting materializes. Kelvin plunges into details of frequencies, megacycles and all the other gibberish of technical experts. I'm tired, bored and start thinking of excuses to escape. I look at my watch several times, mutter about an urgent appointment and flee. I return to Mike Thompson's house, a haven of peace in the midst of confusion, fully resolved to write some letters, but end up exhausted on my bed.

7.0 p.m. Kelvin, after one more appointment with the Himalayan Society, gets back just in time for supper and a meeting with Mike Cheney about borrowing more kit, and then retires to his room, to work till three in the morning on our movements schedule to Pokhara. There are very few people I know who could work at such pressure and with such obvious enjoyment. Kelvin somehow manages to be dynamic and forceful and yet at the same time remains an agreeable companion.

I had five days in Katmandu before going on to Pokhara. Kelvin had done his job so efficiently there was very little I needed to do other than make basic policy decisions. Before I had arrived, Don, restless to get onto the mountain, had already decided to press on with the reconnaissance as originally planned, and in fact set off on 15 March with Mike Thompson, who would return to Pokhara once they had reached the Sanctuary, to help Kelvin with the gear coming out by sea. This was essential since Mike had organized the food and was the only person who knew where everything was.

I had not thought of sending Don forward on the reconnaissance, partly because I was not sure how much gear we should be able to borrow in Katmandu, and I knew he had very little with him, but largely, I think, because I had wanted to get that first glance of the Face so very much myself. This was in some way a matter of reassurance that the climb should look feasible when seen in the flesh, but also the sheer intoxication of seeing something for the first time that for the last year of intense work had been my focal point. There was an additional factor—that the prospect of making the approach march as a compact two-man party, instead of with the body of the expedition and all its problems was very attractive. But there was now no question of my going on the reconnaissance since Kelvin would have to stay behind to bring up the rear party and I was the only person sufficiently knowledgeable about problems in Nepal and the expedition in general to look after the main party.

A reconnaissance, however, made very good sense, and I therefore agreed to it, feeling very envious when Don and Mike took the plane the morning after I arrived in Katmandu.

The rest of the team arrived on 18 March.

Tom Frost flew in by himself from Calcutta. He looked very American, with short, almost crew-cut hair and a bulging rucksack, and wearing a tropical suit. His measurements had led me to expect someone of slight build, but he was even thinner than I had anticipated. I could see he had a superb power-weight ratio for high-standard rock climbing, but he seemed too frail for the Himalayas.

The plane carrying Dougal Haston, Nick Estcourt, Martin Boysen and Mick Burke arrived from Delhi about five minutes later. They looked more like a pop group than a climbing expedition, with longish hair and mod-styled clothes. We'd certainly come a long way since the days of Everest when climbers tended to look like clean-living outdoor types.

They had left Ian Clough at Delhi to continue flying down to Bombay to meet the *State of Kerala* which we hoped would be in any day. It had been a close call; back in England I had planned the move out to Nepal as tightly as possible to save time and hotel bills, allowing only a couple of hours in New Delhi and a night in Katmandu. I had not allowed for faulty connections at Delhi, which could easily have caused them to miss the plane to Katmandu. This would have had a chain reaction, for we should then have missed the plane into Pokhara for which we had already booked and it would have been very difficult to get bookings on any subsequent planes, they were in such heavy demand.

The following day Mick Burke, Dougal Haston, Nick Estcourt and I flew into Pokhara. The rest followed during the next few days. Kelvin was already there making last-minute arrangements—as we flew in, he flew out, back to Katmandu to make a few last-minute arrangements before shooting back to Pokhara on the following day. That same day an R.A.F. Bristol freighter had arrived with the Army Mountaineering Association party and fifteen hundred pounds weight of our gear.

Our trip to Pokhara was happily chaotic. We sat for a long time in the International Departures lounge by mistake waiting for our flight to be called and, of course, it never was. We were at last found by Liz Hawley, the indefatigable Reuter correspondent for Nepal, who did a great deal to help us. She shepherded us across to the Internal Departures office, an open shed crammed with Nepalis and hippies. We managed to get ourselves booked onto the plane to Pokhara and our gear weighed in the teeth of a huge scrum of people trying to do the same, and then sat down to wait far another two hours for the plane to take off.

A crowd always meets the plane at Pokhara; today was no exception. Our T.V. team added to the excitement by filming the historic arrival of four tired, slightly bewildered climbers. Gear was piled into a jeep and we were bumped through the dusty streets of Pokhara to the pension paying-post on the other side of the town. This was a huge field with a few corrugated-iron sheds and ridge tents pitched around it. Twice a year retired Gurkhas come in for their pensions; some of them might walk a hundred miles or so in the course of eight or nine days to collect what to us would seem a pittance—a retired rifleman with up to fifteen years' service would receive less than twenty-five pounds a year.

After the push and bustle of the last few weeks, culminating in the worry of getting the team together in Katmandu, the pension paying-post was a peaceful haven. Lieutenant Bishnuparsad, our rear-link wireless operator, was already installed there. Bland, smiling, yet very purposeful, he had already been at work with Kelvin sorting out the gear that had been flown in by the Royal Air Force. He was to stay here at the pension paying-post throughout the expedition, acting as rear link and also handling all our mail and the transit of film being sent to I.T.N. back in England. He also had to cope with a series of commissions that ranged from buying alarm-clocks to finding paraffin for our stoves that was free from contamination; no easy task in Nepal.

He was typical of the new type of Gurkha soldier and, in a way, of the new Nepal. He was no longer a simple hillman. In fact, his father, a retired Gurkha major, had moved down to the plains of the Terrai to be closer to the urban amenities. Bishnu had spent almost a year in Britain taking part in different wireless courses. He had served in the Gurkhas for fourteen and a half years when he was commissioned a Queen's Gurkha officer. This is a rank structure separate from that of the British officers, equivalent in some ways to the Quartermaster ranks in the British Army, but nevertheless of near equivalent status with a Sandhurst-commissioned British officer in that his command of a platoon or troop would involve the same level of responsibility. Bishnu was quite young—around thirty—to get this promotion, though in the next ten weeks he demonstrated to us how much he had deserved it. I couldn't help wondering at times what he made of our casual and very unmilitary ways.

That afternoon we began to sort out the gear, arranging clothing into piles for distribution to the test of the team, testing wireless sets, checking that the tents were complete. It was wonderfully therapeutic work after all the uncertainties of the past few weeks. Admittedly the boat carrying the bulk of our gear was still on the high seas, with Ian sitting out a solitary vigil in Bombay, but it was now easier to put the worry of further delays behind us, with the positive action we were able to take in getting to the foot of the mountain with enough food and gear to last us for the next three weeks.

That night the four of us ate a magnificent curry at the home of a friend of one of our Sherpas. After it we returned to the pension paying-post and sat talking under a clear velvet black sky sprinkled with stars. In the warmth of friendship and the unity of our purpose I found strength and confidence in my own role as leader of this huge under-taking. We were at last getting off the ground.

CHAPTER 4
Approach March
[22–27 March]

We were ready to leave Pokhara only one day late, on 22 March, largely due to the marathon efforts of Kelvin and the generosity of Jimmy Roberts and the A.M.A. party. The boat carrying the bulk of our gear had been due to arrive on the 19th, but we had heard nothing from Ian Clough of its arrival. The hundred and forty porters who were going to carry our loads had arrived the previous day. They ranged in age from about fourteen to fifty-six and many of them had had a three-day walk from their villages into Pokhara. They were tough, wiry little men, dressed in the main with off-casts of service clothing, some of which would be British and others Indian, for this area was one of the main recruiting areas of the Gurkhas. Half a dozen of our porters had served with the British Army, as had all three of the Naiks.

Our Chief Naik, ex-Lieutenant Khagbir Pan, marshalled his men like a company of troops; accustomed as I was to the confusion that I had encountered on previous expeditions, this seemed near to miraculous, as he lined them up in military ranks, called them forward one by one to sit in front of their apportioned loads and then finally gave them a speech which would have rivalled one of Montgomery's harangues to the troops.

On the morning of departure they set off in single file, almost in step, and kept together by the three Naiks. It was a superb morning. We could just see the top of the South Face of Annapurna from the pension paying-post, masked by the curtain wall formed by the great mass of Hiunchuli and Modi Peak on one side and the shapely spire of Macha-puchare on the other. In the thin light of the dawn, through the haze, the mountains seemed to float above the fields and scattered mud-brick houses of the outskirts of Pokhara. The Army Mountaineering Association expedition, who were camped beside us at the pension paying-post, were going to set off on the following day.

The start of our eight-day approach march took us over the gorge of the Seti Khola. Here the river had carved a gorge at least three hundred feet deep though its top was no more than about twelve feet wide. A shaky-looking bridge of cracked concrete spanned it. The porters trooped across it; the expedition was under way.

An approach march falls into a pattern that is very similar on every

The porters lined up behind their loads in preparation for the approach march.

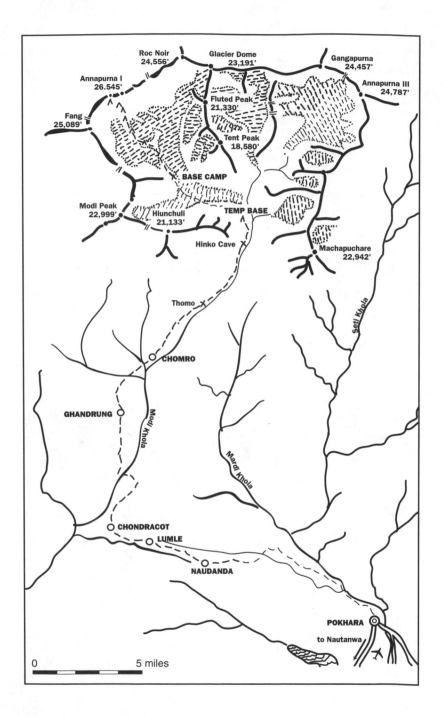

expedition and has therefore been written about a hundred times before. Ours was comparatively short—only eight days. It was the ideal length, just long enough to loosen us up and to start building a measure of fitness, yet not so long as to become repetitive. In addition each day was different, forming a steady crescendo of interest and drama, to the final climax when we rounded the end of the gorge of the Modi Khola and saw before us only seven miles away the upper part of the South Face of Annapurna.

The first day started with a level plod through a broad river valley along a track just wide enough for a jeep; the T.V. team had hired one, ostensibly to get film of the expedition on its first day. They would rattle past us in a cloud of dust, leap out, snipe with their ciné-camera as we plodded past and then leapfrog through again.

As I walked I felt happily relieved of responsibility, even though we had left our super-organizer, Kelvin Kent, behind to wait for Ian and the bulk of our gear. I had delegated responsibility as far as possible. Nick was

The 140 porters of the main party set out on the approach march. In the background are the buildings of the Gurkha pension paying-post where we assembled the loads.

acting as temporary treasurer, Martin was looking after our commissariat, and the Sirdar of the Sherpas, Pasang Kami, with Lieutenant Khagbir Pun, was responsible for the porters. The expedition, almost miraculously, seemed to be running like a well-oiled machine.

We had only two of our high-altitude porters with us, Pasang Kami and Ang Pema; the remaining four were shared equally between Don's recce party and the rear party. I was already very impressed by Pasang. He spoke a fluent, pedantically correct English, addressed me and everyone else on the expedition as an equal, yet got on with the job of organizing the day-to-day management of the party, chasing up the whereabouts of stray loads or any odd items that were wanted by members of the expedition. In appearance he reminded me of a very 'with-it' French guide, for he was always immaculately dressed and wore the white peaked cap much favoured by the Corps of Chamonix guides. He was quite slightly built and had much finer features than the average Sherpa. He was very much more sophisticated than the high-altitude Sherpas I had known on my two previous expeditions, who had spoken very limited English and were essentially simple villagers; shrewd, loyal, tough in any crisis, yet with an almost childlike quality of irresponsibility and petty avarice once the climbing was over. I think Pasang probably represents the start of a new breed of Sherpa, partly spawned by their changing role in Nepal, where the bulk of the work is confined to conducting parties of tourists on treks round the valleys. The ideal qualifications for this job are organizing ability, command of languages and a good manner. Pasang had cultivated all three, although his background was the same as that of the traditional Sherpa. He was born in Namche Bazaar, the administrative capital of Sola Khumbu, home of the Sherpas. His father was a small farmer and Pasang, in common with all Sherpa boys, went to the high pasture in the summer with his father's yaks and sheep. He never went to school, and his command of languages and also his ability to read and write in both English and Nepali were entirely self-taught.

There is a great deal of nepotism associated with getting the coveted job of high-altitude porter, and Pasang had had very few contacts. He started working as a porter, carrying loads for local traders, at the age of eighteen in 1957. He went on his first expedition in 1960 to Langtang, but in 1963 had a setback when he was unable to get a job as high-altitude porter on the American Everest expedition and ended up as a mailrunner. He had better luck on the Indian expeditions and three times went to the South Col, but in no way distinguished himself from the general run of Sherpas. More expeditions followed, but it was in trekking that his abilities as an organizer came out.

Jimmy Roberts, who had already helped us in so many ways with gear, had nominated all our Sherpas from the group that worked for him in his trekking organization. He purposely closes down the trekking in the pre-monsoon period to give his Sherpas a chance to go on expeditions. He had originally selected Ang Temba, a seasoned high-altitude porter of the old school who had been with me on Annapurna II, as our Sirdar. Ang Temba's wife, however, largely as a result of the series of accidents to Sherpas in the last year or so, had forbidden him to go on another climbing expedition. Pasang was his last-minute replacement. I suspect we benefited from the change; although Pasang later had some trouble with his health, his administrative ability amply made up for this.

Ang Pema, the other Sherpa with our party, was an old friend for he had been a cookboy on Annapurna II and a high-altitude Sherpa on Nuptse, when he had accompanied me to the summit, a considerable feat for a twenty-six-year-old on his first major mountain. He was also on the American Everest expedition, and was involved in the accident that killed John Breitenbach in the ice-fall leading into the Western Cwm— his head was smashed in and he was given up for dead, yet he recovered and within a few days was carrying loads. He subsequently made four carries to the South Col and another four to the same height on the West Ridge of Everest. Ang Pema was very different from Pasang Kami, closer in appearance and manner to the traditional Sherpa. He had very broad Mongoloid features, graced normally with a comfortable grin. He was easy-going, not over-bright, yet utterly loyal and superbly strong. Officially he was the Expedition Cook, a job which carries no extra pay but gives him the stature of second-in-command with the Sherpas and a lot of perks around the kitchen. Ang Pema never really filled this job, since

Kent had provided us with the ideal Base Camp cook, in the shape of another Sherpa, Tukte, who had also been a kitchen boy on Annapurna II, but had then abandoned high-altitude portering for the British Army, where he became a mere waiter. He had just finished his service with the Gurkhas, so Kelvin had recruited him as cook. The arrangement worked well, for Ang Pema was invaluable on the mountain as a high-altitude porter while Tukte was a superb chef and major-domo. He was well built, but lacked the inherent toughness of the successful high-altitude porter. He had a very expressive face that easily showed either grief or joy. At first he had no easy task, since we were living off locally purchased food. This consisted of scrawny chickens, frost-blown potatoes and rice, for lunch and supper.

The Sherpas, who hold a monopoly in high-altitude portering, come from Sola Khumbu just opposite Everest, living at a height of around 11,000 feet and taking their yaks to pasture in the summer up to heights of 16,000 feet. They are Buddhists of Tibetan stock, and their entire social structure is more akin to that of Tibet than to that of the rest of Nepal. The Gurkhas, on the other hand, belong to a number of hill tribes who have always lived on the Nepalese side of the watershed and whose religious and cultural ties have been more strongly influenced by India. They are Hindus by religion and observe the caste system, yet they have many Buddhist overtones and even their interpretation of the caste system is very much more liberal than in India. In fact, Nepal must be one of the very few countries in the world where two different racial groups have managed to co-exist in such harmony, in stark contrast to the conflict between Muslims and Hindus in India—or, for that matter, between Catholics and Protestants in Northern Ireland.

Our porters were recruited in the main from two different tribes, the Magars and the Gurungs. Khagbir originally came from a village called Sica and belonged to a *thar* or sub-tribe of the Magars called Pun; as a result, most of his recruits were Puns. He also enlisted the help of another ex-Gurkha called Cheesbahardur, who was from the village of Ghandrung, a stronghold of the Gurungs, on our route to Base Camp. He was to be one of the Naiks and he enlisted sixty of his Gurungs.

Our second day out from Pokhara can act as a model for all successive days.

The cookboys and Tukte woke us up at about 6.00 a.m., going round in a solemn procession, one carrying a huge kettle full of tea, the next a tray full of enamelled drinking-bowls we had bought in Pokhara and the third a plateful of Annapurna biscuits—the local make.

A ritual 'Morning, Sahib', and we could almost feel we were back in the days of the Raj.

We were camped on the crest of a ridge by the village of Naudanda, a straggle of two-storeyed houses and shops on either side of a stone-paved path. No wheeled vehicles, let alone jeeps or cars, could reach the village, yet we were only a few hours' walk from Pokhara. The slopes on either side of the ridge dropped away steeply in serried terraces to the valley a thousand feet below. In the cool stillness of the dawn, the sun was creeping over the hills to the east, glimpsed from behind ragged clouds and painting the country a hazy yellow. Our porters wandered in, still heavy with sleep, picked up their sixty-pound loads and straggled onto the path that serpentined over the ridge we were to follow for the first part of the day.

Most of us had slept under the stars that night; we then packed sleeping-bags and a few personal effects into our rucksacks and wandered off with the porters. You could either be sociable and go in a group, or sink into your own dreams and thoughts and wander off alone, soaking in the atmosphere and beauty of the country. There were no sounds of engines to destroy the peace, just the lowing of cattle, the cry of a baby, the rattle of cooking-pots and the shrill talk of our porters.

We walked for about two hours in the cool of the dawn, along the ridge and then down a rocky, tree-clad valley. The mountains to the north floated in a haze, peering through ragged clouds which gave a tantalizing glimpse of the heights we hoped soon to reach. Our own Face was now hidden by the guardian bastions to the Sanctuary: Machapuchare, a Gothic cathedral; Hiunchuli, only 21,133 feet but still a virgin and very shapely; Modi Peak, squat and massive. Somewhere in front, the gorge of the Modi Khola snaked through these high walls.

We stopped for our morning meal, the inevitable chicken and rice on

The approach march lasted seven days, covering seventy miles of twisting footpaths to the foot of the South Face.

the banks of a small stream that wound its way through terraced fields near the village of Lumle. Some talked, others curled into their cocoons of silence, reading a book or just thinking of the climb ahead.

Twenty yards away villagers paced to and fro; a tinkle of bells heralded the passing of a caravan of gaily caparisoned donkeys probably from Muktinath near the Tibetan border. Travellers rested under the wide-spanned branches of the peepul tree, sitting on the stone benches called *dharmasalas*, often erected by a family in remembrance of the death of one of its members. Tough little Gurkhas plodded past weighed under by huge loads, much heavier than the ones our porters carried. A Gurkha on leave, resplendent in regimental blazer, flannels and jungle boots, strode past, followed by a train of porters carrying his tin trunks.

The Nepalese foothills had lost none of their haunting fascination in the ten years that I had been away, in spite of the fact that one met many more Europeans, wandering along the footpaths between villages. We met drifting hippies, dressed in various interpretations of the local garb, looking far gone on pot, slightly sad, lost yet gentle. A surprising number sported expensive Nikon cameras. Then there were the older trekkers: an earnest Swiss in sandals and flannels, with his eighty-year-old mother; grinning Japanese; groups of hearties who strode along like boy scouts.

Admittedly we no longer had the paths entirely to ourselves; when I had walked both to Annapurna in 1960 and to Everest in 1961 I never even saw a European. But the present invasion in no way intrudes on the character of the Nepalese countryside, and I don't think it will ever do so, unless they start building roads. It is the motor car and jeep, the criss-cross of power lines, that destroy natural beauty. On our approach we seldom saw more than three or four other groups of Europeans in the day. The Nepalese villagers have not yet made any special accommodation for them. The Pathside shops are the same as ever. In these you can buy a little glass full of strong, black, very sweet tea, or the omnipresent packets of Annapurna biscuits.

Nepal is reputed to be amongst the poorer countries in the world, but this is true only in the sense that the bulk of the villagers live on a subsistence economy. In other words, they live on the food and products they farm themselves on their own tiny patches of land. There is not

Terraced fields and a small farm on the route.

much money about, for there are limited means of either earning or spending it. We often had difficulty in buying chickens, eggs or potatoes at any price, since they only had just sufficient for themselves, and paper money is of little use if there is no food available to buy with it. Our own porters were paid fifteen rupees a day, which is just over ten shillings, so that they earned a hundred and ten rupees for the single trip. This is as much as a policeman would earn in a month, but even so some of them were worried about getting back to their fields to tend their annual crop of *makai*, or maize, their main staple, which would be ready for harvesting in May. Once again, money was of little value without the food from their fields on which their families were completely dependent.

But there were no signs of the abject, ugly poverty that constantly hits one in India and throughout Africa. The people are essentially smiling and friendly; there is an atmosphere of relaxed peace about the land.

After lunch we continued our walk, through the village of Lumle, with its solidly built stone houses, window-boxes lining the elaborately carved wooden window-frame, wide verandas opening onto courtyards. Children were playing on a form of hurdy-gurdy wheel by the village pond; women washed clothes and hair under a stone spout at a water point.

And the path winds on, through woods to the sound of chattering monkeys, past terraced fields and onto the crest of a spur that leads down to the village of Chondracot. We are poised over the Modi Khola, which winds its way with ever-steepening flanks into the cloud-clad peaks of the Annapurna massif. From this point on we shall be marching ever closer to our goal, up and down a steadily ascending switchback, as we breast the flanks of the ridges that jab down to the bed of the gorge. We start by losing height, dropping down to the bed of the Modi Khola, where we camp for the second night of the march. Hot and sweaty, we have the agonizing yet delicious pleasure of bathing in the chill waters of the Modi Khola, more reading in the afternoon sun, or a game of 'Piggy', where you throw a small peg into the air, strike it as far as you can with a stick, and nominate the number of strides a member of the opposing team must take to reach the peg; he can challenge you to meet the nominated number of strides. It sounds complicated, but in fact is one of the surest methods I have encountered of ensuring that half your expedition members break their ankles before even getting a sight of the objective. The risks in this case were compounded by the terraced fields we were playing in.

And then supper—chicken and rice washed down by *raksi*, the local spirit made from distilled millet or *codo*, as they call it in these parts. Once again we sleep under the stars to save the trouble of putting up tents, everyone getting into his sack around eight o'clock or so in the evening.

On the third day we reached the village of Ghandrung, its solidly built two-storeyed houses nestling on a terraced spur high above the Khola, with a superb dress-circle view of Machapuchare and Modi Peak. An easy-angled staircase of grey-veined slabs of slate led up to the village which wound round the hillside in clusters of houses amidst the brilliant green of the terraced fields of millet. The houses were uniform in their design, with whitewashed walls of quarried stone and roofs of grey slate. On the ground floor a veranda, roofed in slate and supported by wooden columns, opened out onto a small yard, floored with great slabs of slate similar to those used on the paths. Hens and even goats wandered in and out of the ground-floor rooms; an old woman sat weaving or spinning; a cradle, made from basketwork and slung like a hammock, swayed between the columns. The windows of the upper storey were hidden beneath the broad eaves of the roof—they didn't let in much light, being small and guarded by elaborately carved shutters in wood, darkened by age. There was no glass and inside there was very little furniture, yet this was a prosperous village; in many ways it reminded me of the high villages of the Swiss Alps, yet had and will probably continue to retain an atmosphere of unspoilt peace through the absence of roads and of the roar of motors. It could be argued that these would bring greater prosperity to villages like Ghandrung, but I wonder if this would make all the accompanying pitfalls and problems worth while.

The most serious lack that this and similar villages suffer from is that of medical help. The nearest doctor or hospital is at Pokhara, two hard days' walk away, though their staff do tour the area from time to time. Dave Lambert, our own doctor, was always in great demand with both vil-

The village of Ghandrung, the last major village on the approach march before we entered the gorge of the Modi Khola.

lagers and our own porters; but for him it was discouraging work, for he could do little for serious cases but advise the sufferers to go into Pokhara to get further treatment, something that in many cases was impracticable. By the time we had reached Base Camp he had given out a large proportion of our aspirins, and huge quantities of antibiotics to stop dysentery.

The village did have its own school, which was built and financed by the villagers. We spent the night in it. It was a dusty, uncared-for building on a rocky spur at the end of the village; a bare mud courtyard was surrounded by low open sheds in which were stacked the children's desks and benches. We sat in the shade of its walls and watched our porters in a long ant-like column snake their way up towards the village.

Mike Thompson met us here on the way back to Pokhara to wait for the rest of the gear. He had left Don Whillans two days before camped in the Sanctuary at the old Machapuchare Base Camp with the two Sherpas.

Mike was looking lean and fit.

'What does the Face look like?' was my first question.

'I never saw it,' he admitted. 'It was in cloud the whole time.'

Mike and Don with their two Sherpas had taken only four days to reach the Hinko Cave, the last staging-post before reaching the Sanctuary, on 19 March. They had hit deep snow a short distance above it.

'It's hard going,' Mike told us. 'We were up to our thighs a lot of the time and it was impossible to keep to the path. It's really steep, and you keep slipping on the bamboos that are all covered in the snow.'

They tried to reach the Sanctuary on the 20th, but only got half-way there before they were forced to retreat to the cave, a great overhang beneath a huge boulder that had once tumbled from the retaining wall of the forge. The following day they had reached the site of the old Machapuchare Base Camp.

'I don't think you would be able to see the Face from there,' said Mike. 'The camp is only at the mouth of the Sanctuary and there is a big moraine immediately above it.'

On the 22nd, the day we had left Pokhara, Mike and Don had followed the shallow valley formed by the ridge of the lateral moraine of the Annapurna Glacier and the slopes of Hiunchuli, but the day was cloudy and the Face hidden. That same evening Mike had returned to the Hinko Cave leaving Don established at the Machapuchare Base Camp with the two Sherpas.

'He's quite nervous,' said Mike, 'dead worried about Abominable Snowmen.'

I found it very difficult to believe that the tough, self-sufficient and utterly realistic Whillans could ever be worried by anything so nebulous, but we were to hear a great deal more about Abominable Snowmen when we met him a few days later.

It had been a short day to Ghandrung, for we had camped only just below it the previous night, but that day we had to collect the bulk of our locally purchased food and recruit some fresh porters to carry it. There was pleasantly little that I had to do, for Pasang and Khagbir between them were handling all the purchases, weighing out the rice on a primitive balance and haggling over chickens which we were to carry live to Base Camp.

That night the villagers laid on a dance for our benefit. I had experienced Sherpa dances on my expedition to Nuptse; they tend to be magnificent, boozy affairs, where you all end up dancing a kind of Lambeth Walk, arm in arm in a haze of *chang* and *raski*, but this one was different. It was more a performance, given by two schoolmasters dressed as girls in saris, since it would have been improper by Hindu custom for a girl to dance, though there were plenty watching. It was some time before I realized that, in fact, they were men and not girls, their 'drag' was so good.

The dance itself was essentially Indian in its movements and gestures. It was accompanied by drumbeat and a wailing chant that I found repetitious. We discovered later that this was a manifestation of pop, for there was no tradition of this type of dancing in the hill villages, though there had always been wandering minstrels who had sung ballads. The dancing was then added to the ballad, largely through the influence of Indian films which are shown in small towns like Pokhara.

My enjoyment, however, could have been jaundiced by the fact that I was tired; the dance did not get under way till ten that night and our bedtime was usually eight. The audience of villagers and porters packed solid into the small courtyard of the school enjoyed it immensely, cheering and whooping at every dance.

The following morning the walk from Ghandrung wound its way up the Modi Khola; we were no longer skirting the mountains but plunging into their midst. Machapuchare dominated the skyline, its airy rock and ice ridges making an open invitation to the modern climber. They were easily accessible, obviously technically difficult yet not too high in altitude. Machapuchare is 22,942 feet, an ideal height for a small, compact party. It is sad indeed that the Nepalese Government has placed a firm ban on any expedition's attempting this magnificent mountain.

That day we walked through the rhododendron forests, their trees heavy with dusky red blooms. We reached the small village of Chomro, the last human habitation we should pass, in the gathering dusk of a storm-bound evening. We collected here the remainder of our livestock, a fine-looking goat and a rather pathetic little buffalo. We were told, however, that we should never be able to coax it down the rocks that led into the bed of the gorge a short way beyond the village, so left it there, planning to have it killed once we got ourselves established at Base Camp.

Next day we entered the gorge proper of the Modi Khola. It was an incredibly impressive place, dense forest of gnarled trees and dead bamboos that looked like skeletons in its bed and lower flanks, huge walls towering on either side. Waterfalls cascaded down and the river in the bed of the gorge set up a restless thunder.

The march in had gone well, but I was worried about the fate of the main gear. If it did not catch up with us in a fortnight's time we should start running short of food and climbing equipment on the Face. We had still heard nothing from Ian in Bombay. Every evening Gambahadur Pun, our wireless operator, used to rig the aerial for the wireless and try to get through to Pokhara and Katmandu. In the bed of the gorge this was difficult, especially when the weather was bad, but even so he persevered. That night he got on to Kelvin Kent, who was at the Nepalese Army headquarters in Katmandu. He gave us the good news.

Porters walking below Machapuchare, guardian to the Annapurna Sanctuary.

'Hello, Chris, this is Kelvin. Ian left Bombay by road on 24 March with all the gear, except four boxes.'

My immediate elation was dampened, for the loss of some boxes, particularly the ones containing all the double sleeping-bags or oxygen masks, could have been fatal.

'That's great news,' I said, 'but do you know which boxes were lost?'

Kelvin gave the numbers and I checked them with the master list. We had only lost some oxygen, solid-fuel tablets and gas cylinders for the stoves. There was still ample oxygen for our requirements and we could do without the other items for a time. Kelvin had already succeeded in borrowing some solid fuel and had cabled Sir Douglas Busk to arrange for some more to be sent out.

After this news we all felt in a holiday mood. We were near our objective and would have all the gear we should need; it would be a fair fight—us against the mountain. Admittedly we had barely started, but I was pleased and relieved at the way we all seemed to be getting on together. There was a feeling of accord and unity of purpose in the party.

Members of the team during a lunch break on the way up the Modi Khola.

The T.V. team had already been very much part of the expedition, adapting themselves to conditions considerably rougher, though less dangerous, than they had previously encountered in places like Vietnam or Biafra, where they were rarely away from hotels for more than a few days at a time.

As dusk fell the wood fires of our porters were like so many fireflies in the gloom. They kept them going through the night for we were now about 9,000 feet above sea level and it was decidedly cool after nightfall. The porters had little more than a cotton blanket apiece and makeshift bamboo shelters from the rain. They huddled together for warmth, and you could hear the murmur of their talk throughout the night. In the morning they cooked their *baart* or breakfast over the same wood fires. They messed together in small groups, carrying between them a communal cooking-pot and their ration of rice or maize flour, a little meat and some chillies.

That day we had a short march to the Hinko Cave, for we wanted to get as close as possible to the snow-line, before pushing through to the Sanctuary.

I had decided to push on in front, right through to the Sanctuary if necessary, to meet up with Don and learn about the situation to help decide the best course of action with our porters. We hoped eventually to get a Base Camp close to the foot of the Face, but from what Mike had told me it seemed unlikely that we should be able to get the porters much farther than the mouth of the Sanctuary, the snow was so deep.

As I walked up towards the Hinko Cave I kept getting tantalizing glimpses of the peaks at the head of the Sanctuary. The South Face of Annapurna was still hidden round the corner, but Annapurna's classic triangular summit was framed by the sheer sides of the gorge which, even though it was now nine o'clock in the morning, were still in deep shade. The Hinko Cave was empty but there were signs of recent occupation. Someone had scratched on the rock *Hinko Hilton*. Compared to a bamboo shelter, I suppose it was.

After stopping for a drink of water and some wheat germ offered by Tom Frost, we pressed on towards the end of the gorge. It was here that

Camp site at Thomo in the Modi Khola

we hit the first snow, literally thousands of tons of avalanche debris that must have crunched down from the slopes of Hiunchuli. It filled almost the entire gorge and was like a miniature glacier. Standing on the brink of it, we suddenly noticed a thin plume of smoke about a mile up the gorge. This would almost certainly be Don come down to meet us.

By this time he must have had a view of the Face. His verdict would confirm whether our interpretation of all the photographs we had seen was correct. What on earth should we do if it was continuously swept by avalanche? This had seemed unlikely, though a number of experts, including Joe Brown and another close friend and brilliant mountaineer, Tom Patey, had deemed the route unjustifiable. I remembered a night in the Padarn Lake, the pub used by climbers in North Wales, with Joe shortly before the expedition:

'You'll be swept away by powder snow avalanches in the middle section,' he had commented.

I had a great deal of respect for Don's judgement. As I worked my way over the debris of the spring avalanche, a gruesome omen of what could happen to us, I almost dreaded hearing his verdict.

CHAPTER 5

The Sanctuary
[28–31 March]

Don Whillans, looking like a benevolent gnome, was seated outside a cave under a boulder. In spite of our forebodings and excitement we were all splendidly tight-lipped.

'You're looking a bit slimmer than when I last saw you,' I said. 'How did it go?'

'Not too bad.'

'Did you see the Face?'

'Aye.'

'What does it look like?'

'Steep. But after I had looked at it for a few hours it seemed to lie back a bit. It's going to be difficult but I think it will go all right.'

We dug out a postcard picture of the Face and Don went into greater detail. On the 25th, two days earlier, he had walked up to the top of the lateral moraine to a point where he could see the Face.

'I looked at it for about four hours. A big avalanche came down on the left, but our line looks fairly safe,' he said. 'There didn't seem much point in staying any longer so I returned here to meet you.'

'What's the route going to be like?' I asked.

'Very close to what we had already planned. I think we'll be able to get round the right-hand side of the lower part of the ridge all right. The glacier is broken, but it shouldn't be too bad. There also seems to be a route up to the Col on the Ice Ridge, but the ridge above that looks dicey. It's a real razor-edge with big cornices all the way, but I think there might be a way round it to the left.'

'What about the Rock Band?'

'Steep, but a lot more broken than I thought it would be. I'm pretty sure the big groove up the front of it will be too hard for us, but there seems a line up to the left.'

Don then got onto the subject of Abominable Snowmen. He was convinced he had seen one. He tells the story in his own words.

'It must have been five o'clock in the evening when we reached the site of the Machapuchare Base Camp at the mouth of the Sanctuary. It was just as we put down our loads that I heard a noise on the ridge behind me. Pemba Tharkay looked up and simply said, "Yeti coming."

'I whipped round just in time to see a dark object dropping behind a ridge, and as it vanished two lines of black crows flew up—these are very common in the Himalayas, and the noise we had heard must have been their squawking. But the object was something else; definitely bigger than a bird, though I couldn't be sure what it was since it was now getting dark. I was quite disturbed by the way Pemba mentioned the Yeti. He just made a flat statement, and I felt that if this Yeti did exist this was just the kind of place it would appear. But I didn't continue looking—which was a mistake—because we needed to pitch the tents before dark. I just mentioned to Pemba that I thought that what I had seen was more than a couple of crows and then completely forgot about the incident.

'The following day Mike and I went off to make a reconnaissance for a Permanent Base Camp and left the two Sherpas at the Machapuchare site. At first we climbed up onto the moraine bank intending to traverse the top of it, but there were too many ups and downs—so I dropped back into the valley between the moraine bank and the mountain where there was a smooth, easy slope.

'There had been an avalanche down it several weeks earlier, but it didn't look as if there was going to be any further danger. I had been walking for a few minutes when I was stopped dead by the appearance of a set of deep tracks coming down the mountainside on the left of the valley. I realized immediately that this was the exact point where this whatever-it-was had dropped down behind the ridge the previous evening. The snow had been very soft and whatever it was had made deep tracks in a similar manner to ourselves. Anyhow, I took a picture of the tracks going up the mountainside and called Mike over. There were one or two scratch-marks like claw-marks on the snow, and Mike said, "Oh, it's a bear."

'But there were one or two things that didn't look like a bear to me. I didn't form any opinions at that stage but just looked at all the tracks and the features. It wasn't possible to get a picture of one clear footprint because the snow had tumbled into each hole, which was at least a foot deep. I thought they were about the size of a small man, about my own size foot, which is size 6. We then carried on a little further up the valley but by this time the cloud had come down and we couldn't really see the South Face of Annapurna, so Mike and I went back to the camp and rejoined the Sherpas. I examined the tracks through the binoculars and estimated that they came down to an altitude of around 13,000 feet, and vanished over the crest of the ridge at 15,000 feet. Mike was going back to join the main party at Pokhara and he left me that evening to get back to the Hinko Cave to rejoin the two coolies we had left there. He planned to take them back to the nearest village, load them up with food and send them back up to the Hinko Cave, since by this time I hoped to complete my little reconnaissance and planned to return to the Cave to await the main party.

'That night, after Mike had departed, I began to ponder about the tracks. It did occur to me that it was possible that this creature, whatever it was, might well be around, so I stuck my head outside the tent. It was bright moonlight and the moon was shining straight onto the hillside where the tracks were. It was even possible to read small print, it was so bright. The hillside had gentle undulations, rather like an easy

*Footprints of a creature that Don Whillans saw running away from him in
the light of the moon during his reconnaissance ahead of the main party at
the site of the Temporary Base (12,000 feet). He believes that this could have
been a Yeti.*

ski slope, and I made a mental note of where I could see dark spots which were possibly rocks or trees. If any of these moved they could only be some kind of living creature. It was a fantastically cold night—I was in two sleeping-bags but was still cold. Even so I kept my head sticking outside the tent, and after a time noticed that one of these dark spots appeared to have moved. I couldn't be sure, but I continued watching and then, without a doubt, it started to move quite quickly. There was a monocular in the tent which I focused on the dark, moving shape. It was then that I could definitely distinguish limbs and a kind of bounding movement. It was going directly uphill towards another clump of trees and it was obvious, just by the movements, that it was a reasonably powerful animal and that it was bounding along on all fours. It disappeared into the shadow of a tree, which was leafless, it being winter, and then reappeared wandering from one clump of trees to the next, but it was in a slightly shadowy portion of the hillside at the base of a kind of dune and I couldn't see it clearly. However, when it reached the topmost tree it came into the moonlight. It gave me the impression that it was hunting for food, and then, as if it had decided to abandon its search, it started diagonally downwards across the hillside heading for some cliffs.

'Once it started to move out in the moonlight I could get a better idea of what it was. It was on all fours and it was bounding along very quickly across the snow, heading for the shelter of the cliffs. That was the point at which I thought, That thing is an ape or ape-like creature. Then it just disappeared into the shadow of the rocks and I felt then that that was the last I was ever going to see of this creature, whatever it was. There had been a peculiar atmosphere about the place ever since we had arrived at the Machapuchare Base Camp—and now this seemed to have gone.

'The following morning I went up to make a full reconnaissance to the permanent Base Camp site and I took the two Sherpas along. I thought I'd see their reaction at the point where I'd photographed the tracks the day before. The tracks were so obvious that it was impossible not to make any comment, but they walked straight past and didn't indicate that they had seen them. I had already mentioned that I had seen the Yeti, not knowing exactly what it was, but they pretended they didn't understand and ignored what I said.

'I am convinced that they believe the Yeti does exist, that it is some kind of sacred animal which is best left alone; that if you don't bother it, it won't bother you. I feel very much the same way myself: if it's not a bear and is one of these legendary creatures, and if it's managed to survive so long and under such bitterly cold conditions, it deserves to be left alone.

'When I got back from looking at the Face, I had another indication of the Sherpas' attitude to the Yeti. They had come back in front of me and were playing around, sliding down the snow hummocks on plastic bags; this is a favourite game of theirs.

'I suggested, "Why don't you go over to the other side of the valley, the slope's a lot better there." But before the words were out of my mouth, Kancha chipped in, "It's no good over there, Sahib; been over there, no good."

'But it was obvious they hadn't been anywhere near there, for there were no tracks. I suddenly realized that this was the hillside where we had seen the Yeti, and that the two Sherpas would not go there for this reason.

'Anyway, we packed up our gear and returned to the Hinko Cave to wait for the main party.'

With Don were two more of our Sherpas, Pemba Tharkay and Kancha. Pemba was the biggest and best-looking of all the Sherpas. He was very well dressed, usually in gear from other expeditions, and undoubtedly had a high opinion of himself. He had been on two of the Indian expeditions, and had carried loads up to the top camp at 27,000 feet. He had also been on the German Annapurna expedition the previous year, carrying to their highest camp. In appearance Kancha was less impressive; he had a slightly sullen expression and a manner that seemed surly, yet when we got to know him he opened out and worked well on the expedition.

The Face looked feasible, but the next problem was to reach it, for this spring the late winter snows had been especially heavy and very slow in clearing. The snow-line started only just round the corner from where we were camped in the gorge, a good four hours' march from its end and at an altitude of only 10,000 feet. Don had his camp at the site of the Machapuchare expedition's Base Camp at a height of around 12,000 feet, a good seven miles from the foot of the South Face and four thousand feet below the top of the Rognon, where we hoped to make our first camp.

He had spotted a good site for Base Camp on the side of the glacier about four miles up from his temporary camp, but it seemed unlikely at this stage that we should be able to get our porters that far. We certainly could not manage it in the day from where we were camped that night by the Hinko Cave, and we did not have sufficient tentage for them to spend a night out in the snows at the mouth of the Sanctuary.

None of them had any socks, half were without shoes and their clothing was inadequate. We had brought with us a supply of cheap snow goggles and gym shoes, but it is no joke wading through snow with this type of footwear. We reckoned we could coax them up to the mouth of the Sanctuary, but no farther. In this respect the delay to the rest of our gear was to prove a blessing, for we could hope that some of the snow would have melted by the time our rear party caught up with us and by that time we should have consolidated a track to the site of our eventual Base Camp. Even if we were unable to keep all the porters, I hoped we should be able to retain sufficient to ferry the gear fairly quickly from the site of our Temporary Base to permanent Base Camp.

That night it rained and the porters must have had a miserable time, for their bamboo shelters were barely waterproof. Dave Lambert had had a particularly large sick parade, attended by a good third of our porters, most of them complaining of bronchial troubles. It was a tribute to Khagbir's leadership and magnificent rhetoric that they were all prepared to press on above the snow-line. Fortunately the next day dawned fine; if the weather had been bad, we might have had trouble in getting the porters any farther up the gorge and this would have been disastrous, for it would have taken many days to ferry all the gear from there up to Base Camp.

Porters, few of whom owned any footwear, were issued with gym shoes for the last leg of the approach march to the mouth of the Sanctuary.

In the morning we issued the porters with their gym shoes and goggles. We tried to get away with only giving out footwear to those that did not have any, but in a trice our entire band of porters were barefoot and so we had no choice but to make an issue to all of them. Many did not risk dirtying their new shoes, but wore them round their necks, wading barefoot through the knee-deep snow.

A short way beyond the camp-site we passed another huge pile of avalanche debris. Don told us that much of this was fresh since he and Mike had walked up only four days before. On their way back the previous day, Don and his two Sherpas had found the carcass of a deer that had been swept down in it. It was difficult to say how long it had been dead, but since it had been in cold storage we added it to our larder; it had a rich, gamy flavour.

In the cool of the dawn the debris was frozen solid and we had to hack out a path for the porters. Beyond this the gorge began to open out and the snowy thickets became more sparse; the sun peered round the shoulder of Machapuchare, now grossly foreshortened, and bars of dazzling light, etched out by jagged shadows, spread over the bed of the gorge. We stepped from shivering cold into the heat of the sun, and then back again into chill shadows. It was an exciting walk, with the vista of snow peaks ever opening out as we came out of the dark throat of the gorge into the Sanctuary. A group of porters were resting on a hummock.

'Come up here,' shouted Mick Burke. 'You can see the Face.'

I scrambled up a bank of deep, soft snow and there, up the valley, peering over the top of the high bank of the lateral moraine of the glacier, was the top of our objective. It looked surprisingly close, though it was a frightening thought that the summit was still fourteen thousand feet above our heads. We could just see the top of the Rock Band, but it looked reassuring, as Don had observed; much more broken than it had seemed in the photographs.

A straggle of porters had already started back, running, whooping through the snows. The site of our Temporary Base was only a few hundred yards ahead in a small flat area squeezed between huge boulders,

The winter snows were unusually late in clearing, making it difficult for the porters. Pasang, the Sirdar, helps one of the porters over an awkward snow step.

just below the lateral moraine of the glacier. The top of the bamboo skeleton of a summer hut was just protruding above the snows. At the height of summer the villagers of Ghandrung send their goats up to the high pastures in the Sanctuary, but that day it was difficult to believe that the snows would ever clear, they were so very deep.

There was no question of retaining any of the porters to help us carry loads up to Base Camp, for we had insufficient tentage. They were all anxious to get below the snow-line. Even so, their morale was high. The previous evening I had heard the wonderful news that Ian had succeeded in reaching Nautanwa. This was much sooner than I had dared expect and was a considerable achievement on his part. He had rushed the gear through Customs, using his combined powers of persuasion and firmness. He had then travelled day and night across India, spending most of the time on top of the lorry, choked with dust and grilled under the blazing sun. Towards the end of the journey he had had his money stolen by the crew of the lorry. He had undoubtedly carried out one of the most important, yet most unpleasant and least spectacular, tasks of the entire expedition. In doing so, he made a tremendous contribution to our eventual success.

I asked Khagbir whether he could take the porters back to Pokhara as quickly as possible to help bring up the gear, since I knew Kelvin Kent might have trouble in recruiting sufficient numbers, there had been so many expeditions starting out from this centre. Khagbir promised to do this, and a high proportion of the porters returned for a second trip.

It was very satisfying to be able to start planning the actual onslaught against the mountain. I had already given a great deal of thought to the basic principles of our plan of attack, while back in England. I had decided to use a basis of four men out in front actually forcing the route, leaving fixed ropes in position on difficult ground, while the rest of the climbers and Sherpas would be divided between the camps already set up, to ferry loads up the mountain. As the lead party slowed up or became tired they would retire for a rest and then start ferrying at the back of the queue while the group that had been immediately behind the front party would move up to take their place. In this way all the climbers would have a turn out in front.

I wanted to get things moving on the mountain as quickly as possible. Don was the obvious choice to go out in front for the first stint since he was the only person who had examined the route. I now had to decide who to team up with him; this question of pairing could be critical, for one could get so much better or worse results from the way individuals managed to get on together and complimented each other's strengths and weaknesses. I was still not entirely certain how well Don would go; he was obviously not yet a hundred per cent fit, and his pot belly, though on the wane, was still there. It was seven years since we had climbed together in South Patagonia and I did not know whether he still had that tremendous fire that I had once known.

I therefore selected Dougal as Don's partner, for of all the team he seemed to have the greatest drive. On the approach march he was like a compressed spring, held under tension, just waiting to get at the mountain. On the way to Base Camp he was either striding, long-legged, out in front or resting sprawled on the grass. He read a great deal, talked little and rarely took part in horseplay or general discussion. He was a living example of the military dictum 'economy of effort'. Yet somehow he avoided being a tight-lipped, hard man, was too thoughtful and introspective. It was as if he was preserving every little bit of strength and energy for the conflict ahead.

I have a deep respect for Don's mountain judgement; in fact, I have never climbed with anyone else who has had such a 'feel' for the mountains. This is a combination of intuition, profound common sense and the ability to interpret both the features of a mountain and the many factors associated with any mountaineering problem. I hoped that Dougal's superb fitness and climbing ability coupled with Don's experience would carve out rapid results on the lower slopes of the mountain, where the route-finding seemed the most tricky. Any basic route-finding mistake could not only waste a lot of time but also increase the level of danger.

The rest of the day was spent putting up tents, sorting out loads and making our Temporary Base a comfortable place to live in. The following day, 29 March, Don and Dougal, with Mick Burke and the Sherpa Kancha, moved up to the eventual site of Base Camp. At this stage I was still planning to have four men out in front: this had the advantage that if one person was feeling off-colour, progress could still be made by the other three. It also meant that Don, Dougal and Mick could have the luxury, for a few days longer, of a Sherpa to look after them. Traditionally, the Sherpas do the cooking and most of the chores around the camp.

The rest of the team were to carry loads up to Base Camp and return that evening. I should have liked to go out myself but had a mass of administrative duties to plough through, writing letters to our sponsors and making a logistic plan for the next few days. A lot of these were duties that Kelvin Kent would eventually take over once he caught up with us. Even so, I could not resist walking in the early dawn to a point where I could see the entire Face, and the glacier we should have to cross to reach it.

Before the sun rose above the basin formed by the spire of Machapuchare the snow was frozen hard and it was pleasant, easy walking up the shallow valley alongside the lateral moraine of the glacier. Even so I could already feel the altitude and found myself panting as I plodded slowly upwards. It was three-quarters of an hour before I was far enough up the valley to clear the rocky spur on the other side of the glacier, which was obscuring the lower part of the Face. I scrambled up the moraine ridge and gazed for the first time at the entire South Face of Annapurna.

My own reaction was the same as Don's: the first impression was one of size—it was a really huge face; the next, one of steepness and then, as I examined each feature through the binoculars, I realized that the Face could be broken down into arêtes, ridges, gullies, separate snowfields and rock walls. This was something that we could climb, and from that moment I felt confident that we had a good chance.

I then started examining the approach to the foot of the Face. Günther Hauser and Ludwig Greissl, the leaders of the two German expeditions to the south side of Annapurna, had assured us that the glacier looked straightforward, and from the photographs I had thought that this would probably be the case, though Nick Estcourt had muttered words of warning and had been convinced we might have trouble in getting to the start of the climbing. Now, looking through the binoculars, I felt that Nick might well be right. The glacier was very broken and obviously contained a maze of crevasses and ice walls.

It took Don and Dougal a complete day to follow the slopes above the glacier to a point where they thought they would be able to cross to get to the foot of the Rognon, or rock island, on whose crest we hoped to establish the first camp. The slope was covered in deep snow which softened as soon as the sun hit it in the early morning. It took them another day to thread their way across the glacier. It was even more intricate than it had seemed from a distance—once they were on it the immediate horizon was reduced to the next ice tower or ridge a few yards in front. There was a constant grumble and grind from under the quilt of snow that still covered the crevasses. It was like crossing a nerve-racking obstacle course, as they cut steps in the ice around tottering towers, felt every step of the way in the soft snow for hidden crevasses and leapt the ones that were open.

They managed to get across, but were forced to find another way back since they had made several irreversible leaps. The last part of the crossing was beneath a huge mass of decaying sérac towers.

'You're only in the danger area for a few minutes,' Don told me that night, 'and I think you'd have a good chance of dodging any ice avalanche because you're some way below it, but even so I'd like to find a safer route.'

That same day Nick Estcourt had made a survey of the Face, using a theodolite. This was something that Charles Evans, who had led the Kangchenjunga expedition and was one of our patrons, had suggested. It is always difficult to estimate heights on a mountain from immediately below because of foreshortening, and measurements actually on the climb taken with an altimeter can be inaccurate. We needed to know the relative heights of the various features before starting up the Face, to help planning.

We appointed Nick Expedition Surveyor, since he had done some survey work on his expedition in Arctic Greenland. He set up his theodolite on the crest of the moraine ridge and, muttering about baselines and log tables, took his readings.

He gave us the results quite diffidently. Nick tends to be over-modest; and this was compounded by the memory of the time when, as a civil engineer, he had built his half of the concrete base of a large power-station eighteen inches too low, with the result that it failed to meet up with the other half. In this instance, however, his results seemed credible and they were subsequently borne out by readings with the altimeter. He computed that the small peak just above the Col was 20,250 feet above sea level, the bergschrund below the Rock Band was 22,750 feet, and the top of the Rock Band was 24,750 feet. This meant that the Rock Band would be two thousand feet high at its lowest point, but, if we were forced off to the left, as seemed possible, it could give us anything up to four thousand feet of climbing. Nick had also tried to measure the top of the Ice Ridge where it joined the snowfield in the centre of the Face, getting a reading of 21,650 feet, but he was not certain of the accuracy of this one, since it was difficult to find a posi-tive feature to sight on.

Don had made an estimate in planning tentage that we should need six camps: Camp I on the top of the Rognon, II at the side of the ice Ridge, III on the Col half-way up, IV below the Rock Band, V immedi-ately above it and VI, the top camp, just below the summit. I had some reservations on this, thinking that we should probably need interme-diate camps on top of the Ice Ridge and the Rock Band, but in the main the route that we had picked out was the one eventually followed.

Meanwhile back at Temporary Base every available person, including some of our cookboys, was ferrying loads up to the eventual site of Base Camp. Tukte had dug out the summer shelter for his kitchen and our hens had been released to run free around it, never straying far from the warmth of the fire. The Expedition goat was tethered on top of a boulder where there was some exposed grass for it to eat; it looked mournfully aware of its inevitable fate.

On 30 March another expedition arrived at our camp. This was the Japanese women's expedition to Annapurna III, consisting of nine petite ladies and nine Sherpas to look after them. We entertained some of them with tea, amidst giggles and clicking of camera shutters. We had

crossed each other's paths on several occasions on the way from Katmandu to Pokhara, and we had been impressed by their fanatical keep-
fit routine. At Pokhara they had carried out early-morning P.T. and
gone for long runs. They put up their camp a few yards from ours,
intending to ferry all their gear themselves on the long haul up a subsidiary glacier to the foot of the gully that leads up to the col between
Annapurna III and Gangapurna.

That night Alan Hankinson and Mick Burke made a social call on the
girls but were firmly shepherded away by the leader to talk to the
Liaison officer, a Nepalese police inspector. After this occasion both
teams were too busy to have very much to do with each other.

I intended to treat our Temporary Base as a base camp until the
arrival of the rear party, merely filtering food, tentage and equipment
through to the site of Base Camp and then up the mountain, as
required, making as much progress as possible before 8 April, when our
reinforcements were due to arrive.

On 31 March I decided to move up to Base Camp to join Don,
Dougal, Mike and Kancha, since Temporary Base felt too far away from
operations. You could not see the Face or the approach of it, and finding
a safe straightfoward route to it quickly was of vital importance.

At this stage, Base Camp was no more than a staging camp, with a
two-man tent and two Whillans Boxes. These boxes were one of the
most revolutionary innovations we used on the climb. We had been
worried that ordinary tents might prove inadequate on the very steep
ground we should almost certainly encounter. Back in 1963, on the
Towers of Paine, we had a different problem, in that none of our tents
could stand up to the high winds that batter South Patagonia. Don had
come up with the solution, designing a prefabricated, box-like structure,
with a framework of timber and an outer covering of proofed nylon. It
weighed about a hundred pounds and we carried it in sections up to the
foot of the Central Tower, where it withstood every storm and enabled
us to wait, poised for a summit assault the moment the weather cleared.

Two years later Don took a more sophisticated model with him to
Gaurishanker. It had a framework of Dexion and an outer covering of

canvas, both fairly heavy, but even so it proved invaluable and they used it for their top camp, where they were able to slot it into a hole they had dug out of a steep snow slope.

For our expedition Don had managed to get the weight down even further, by using aluminium tubing for the frame and a combination of proofed nylon and cotton terylene for roof and walls. In shape it was rectangular: six foot long, four foot high and four foot wide. It weighed about thirty pounds, heavier than the average high-altitude tent, but it had the great charm that once it was up you could be confident that it would never blow down and that it was unlikely to be crushed by powder snow, as can happen to an ordinary tent. A side benefit was that snow melted on the roof, providing a ready supply of water. This was to prove of immense value for it saved a great deal of time and fuel which otherwise would have been expended in melting snow.

Inside the box one had a comfortable feeling of security. As we cooked the evening meal we kept open the entrance and gazed up at the Face; this gave an orchestra-stalls view of the mountain, for the camp was situated in the shallow valley between the lateral moraine, which formed a ridge of about sixty feet between us and the glacier, on one side and a spur running down from the vast bulk of Modi Peak on the other. This protected it from the threat of avalanche—a very real one, for the walls around us calved a series of huge avalanches in the next few weeks. Our little valley pointed straight up to the Face which towered above us about three miles away. It formed a magnificent centrepiece to what must be one of the most impressive mountain cirques in the world; the ridge linking Modi Peak with our mountain was like a turreted wall linking two fortresses and never dropped below 21,000 feet.

Modi Peak from the Sanctuary looked impregnable. Steep, furrowed ice flutings led up to summit cliffs capped by bulging ice walls that threatened to engulf any midget men struggling on the lower slopes. The wall between the two mountains was ploughed with ice flutings that swept down gracefully between angular rock buttresses; its turreted crest was dominated by the Fang, well-named, for it was shaped like the tooth of a wolf and framed from forbidding black rock. There seemed no

Permanent Base Camp was established in early April, after the arrival of the rear party, on the side of the Annapurna South Glacier at a height of 14,000 feet.

lines of weakness in the wall and certainly no line free from threat of avalanche.

To the right, or east, of the Face, the retaining walls of the Sanctuary were less uncompromising. A tumbling glacier swept down from the rounded hummock of Glacier Dome, which in its turn thrust out a subsidiary ridge that jutted out into the centre of the Sanctuary, with its minor summits of Fluted Peak, a classic wedge of 21,330 feet, and Tint Peak, an undistinguished jumble of ice and rock at 18,580 feet.

But the entire cirque was dominated by the bulk of the South Face. From this aspect—and, for that matter, from any other aspect—Annapurna could never be described as a beautiful mountain in the sense that Machapuchare undoubtedly can. Annapurna has no real shape or form. It is like the body of a great octopus, its tentacles of subsidiary peaks thrown higgledy-piggledy from the central mass—yet its South Face is immensely impressive live. It reminded me of the North Face of the Grandes Jorasses with its three huge buttresses, but it was three times the size and very much more complex. And here there was a beauty in the way the line up the left-hand buttress was so positive, and

The top 8,000 feet of the South Face viewed from Base Camp

yet in places tenuous. That night as we stood outside the tents and looked up at the dark mass of the Face dimly lit by the stars, I think we were all asking ourselves the many imponderable questions that the Face presented. Was there a line round to the left of the Ice Ridge? How stable were those ice cliffs half-way up? Would the Rock Band really go?

CHAPTER 6

First Encounter
(1–7 April)

The summit ice cliff of Modi Peak seemed to hang over us.

'If that lot came away,' Mick said, 'it'd sweep the whole glacier.'

We were very conscious of the danger of avalanche. Two expeditions in Nepal had been wiped out by big avalanches in the past year; the scale of everything is so much greater in the Himalayas than in any other mountain region in the world that it is all too easy to underestimate the extent of the danger zone of potential avalanche threat.

Mick Burke and I were reconnoitring an alternative route across the glacier to the foot of the Rognon, whilst Don and Dougal were crossing it by the line of their return the previous day. It was essential to find a safe and straightforward approach to the foot of the Face, since we hoped to use local porters to supplement our numbers.

Going out in front on this kind of ground is rather like going into a minefield, for there are concealed dangers on every side: a hidden crevasse, unstable ice towers, or the more distant threat from the huge mountain walls. We had not yet got the feel of the mountain as we ploughed through the soft snow at the side of the glacier, tensed and rather nervous. There was a big ice cliff just ahead, with avalanche debris scattered round its foot. We looked across the glacier, hoping to find a corridor higher than the line that Don and Dougal had taken, for this would have made it possible for us to avoid the area of dangerous séracs at the other side of the glacier. But however hard we looked, there seemed no possible line. The glacier was a chaos of huge ice blocks covered in a mantle of snow. We tried to start one line but almost immediately were halted by yawning black gulfs dropping away into the innards of the glacier.

We returned to the bank and climbed higher to try to get a bird's eye view of the barrier. Looking through the binoculars we could pick out Don and Dougal, two tiny, black dots, starting up the long slopes of the Rognon. It was now midday—time for the radio call we had agreed on. We each had a Pye Bantam walkie-talkie set which we had taken with us for the day so that we could co-ordinate our search for the best route across the glacier. The walkie-talkie sets had already proved invaluable for keeping contact with Temporary Base. In spite of the fact that the two camps were over three miles apart and not in line of sight, we had reasonable communications with them.

'Hello, Dougal, this is Chris. Come in, please. Over.'

'Hello, Chris, you're loud and clear.'

'How are things going with you?'

'The route across the glacier isn't too bad, though I think you could straighten it out a bit. There is certainly no way across at this end higher up.'

'O.K., Dougal. It looks bad from here as well; we'll work on the route across the glacier. What's it like on the Rognon?'

'Straight snow plodding. We'll try to get to the top of it today.'

Mick and I spent the rest of the day straightening out the route which Dougal and Don had taken across the glacier, finding a better, more direct line than the one they had used. It was enjoyable yet tense work as we ferreted our way round ice towers and through narrow corridors, leaving fixed rope on awkward sections and marking the route with bamboo wands.

We returned to camp having had quite a short day, to find Dave Lambert lying flat out in our tent. He had felt the altitude badly on the way up, but had forced himself on, collapsing once he had reached our camp. He was one of the least experienced members of the party and being tremendously willing had driven himself beyond the limits of his own endurance, something that one tries to avoid at all costs in the Himalayas, since one can end up by putting more people than just oneself in jeopardy. We had no spare sleeping-bags or room in the tents for an extra person, and so I persuaded, or rather bullied, him into going back down. As soon as he had set off to cross the glacier back towards Temporary Base I began to worry about his being alone, and whether he might collapse on the way back. I thought of accompanying him part of the way myself, but feeling tired at the end of our day had convinced myself he would be all right—but would he? This was an unaccustomed feeling of responsibility that I now had to bear as leader of the expedition.

Ang Pema had come up to the camp that same day to bring up our strength to six. Don and Dougal got back late that evening, having reached the top of the Rognon, returning in the afternoon snowstorm that was to form a regular weather pattern throughout most of the expedition.

'It's heavy going in the snow,' reported Don, 'but perfectly straightforward and there's a good camp-site once you've got to the top of the Rognon.'

We had been worried whether the top of the Rognon would be far enough out from the foot of the Face to be free from avalanche danger, but Don reported that it was. They were tired after two long days' work and so we agreed that they should have a rest the following day, while Mick Burke and I moved up to the site of Camp I, supported by Kancha, with Nick Estcourt and Pemba Tharkay who had come up to Base Camp that same day.

As usual, the morning was fine and we made steady progress to the glacier and across it to the point where it was threatened by séracs. I was

Sherpas starting to cross the glacier barring the way to the Rognon, or Island, in the middle right of picture. Camp I was on top of the Rognon.

feeling the altitude, not yet being acclimatized. I tried to hurry below the threatening séracs but found the effort too great, preferring to take the thousand-to-one chance of being hit by an icefall to blowing up with the effort of running. I slumped onto the snow at the other side of the glacier. It was like coming to shore after fording a treacherous, fast-flowing river; I started up the Rognon. Don and Dougal's tracks were covered by the previous evening's snowfall so it was up to us to make the route. The two Sherpas quickly pulled ahead, breaking trail in the knee-deep snow; Nick was also going well, whilst Mick and I were considerably slower. Getting acclimatized and load-carrying in the Himalayas is a desperately slow, tedious business. For every day you spend out in front, there are at least a dozen of monotonous carrying. The final slope of the Rognon was a straight pull of about a thousand feet. The Sherpas were now well ahead, but had left marker flags every hundred yards or so. I picked on each flag and then tried to will myself to reach it. This was to be the pattern for the rest of the expedition. Endless effort, forcing ourselves beyond what we thought our bodies could take. The plod up the Rognon at sea level would be an easy walk, the equivalent of climbing Scafell, but at this stage of the expedition it was an exhausting grind. Once we were acclimatized, it was very much easier; but the process of acclimatization is painful—no sooner have you accustomed yourself to one altitude than you have to press ever higher, going through the same painful process all over again.

Mick was just behind me, and we were going at about the same slow rate, at least a good augury for our working together in the next few days. There is nothing more discouraging than having one member of a pair going very much better than the other.

By the time we reached the top of the Rognon, the Sherpas were

Seracs on the glacier between Base Camp and Camp 1. Machapuchare is in the background.

Camp I with the 6,000-foot wall of the connecting ridge between Modi Peak and the Fang in the background.

already putting up the tent. The crest of the Rognon curved round in a crescent enclosing a flat dip. The Face now looked very much closer, towering over us, very foreshortened at a distance of about a mile. The glacier between us and the Face abutted onto the upper edge of the Rognon like a huge wave threatening to engulf it. There were no ice cliffs, however, and the risks of avalanche seemed slight. Even so, I insisted on the tent's being moved from the place where the Sherpas had pitched it, in front of a large boulder, to a place behind it, which would give it at least psychological if not real shelter. I was still afraid of the risk of big avalanches reaching us from the Face itself.

Nick and the two Sherpas started back down as the afternoon cloud swirled in over the camp-site, leaving Mick and myself in solitary possession. It was a good feeling to be alone; suddenly we had ceased to be part of a big expedition and were just two climbers on a mountain. We also had the luxury of the compo rations which the A.M.A. expedition had loaned us. We had lived on rice and stringy chicken for the last fortnight, and a meal of stewed steak followed by apple pudding was sheer

Camp I at 16,000 feet

95

luxury. But the paraffin stove was a sore trial. The bulk of our stoves had come out on the boat, and the one we had at Camp I was bought at the last minute in London and was a little half-pint picnicker's stove. The jet was not the correct type for altitude, and, even worse, the paraffin we had bought in Pokhara was full of impurities and burned with a dirty, yellow flame. The stove required constant pricking and it took over an hour to melt down and boil a single pan of water.

With the aid of a sleeping-pill, I slept quite well that night, and woke at about six in the morning, to wait for the sun to strike the tent. It was bitterly cold at night and it took a severe effort of willpower to get out of a sleeping-bag before the sun began to warm the tent. That morning, and on most subsequent ones, we discovered that it took over three hours from the point of waking up to the moment we were ready to set out for a day's climbing. It was always best to melt some water the previous night so that we had a panful of ice in the morning, to avoid the unpleasant necessity of getting out of one's sleeping bag to fetch snow and then wait for it to melt. In addition, it took several panfuls of snow to make a single one of water. An hour for the first brew, then a can of beans and an oatmeal biscuit. We stayed in our sleeping-bags to the last possible minute; yet another brew at the end of breakfast and over two hours have slipped by. The sun is beginning to warm the tent, painting its interior a rich orange. We lie back and put off the moment of getting up and then, willing ourselves to the effort, crawl out of our sleeping-bags.

Dressing is another ritual: You don't take any clothes off at night. If anything, you put more on, so it is simply a matter of putting on windproofs if it's cold outside; but at this altitude, around 16,000 feet, the sun is already hot and there isn't a breath of wind. The snow is still frozen solid from the night's frost, crunching under foot. There isn't a cloud in the sky and across the valley Machupuchare is no longer foreshortened, but towers gracefully above the site of Temporary Base which is tucked away into a shaded fold out of sight. Base Camp is fully three miles away and two thousand feet below us, lying by the side of the Annapurna Glacier, which winds down the valley like a huge white motorway. The winter's mantle of snow still covers the Sanctuary.

Time to set off—we were at last breaking new ground. A corridor ran between the two branches of the glacier, divided by the ridge running down from the centre of the Face. The bottom of the ridge and most of its flanks had been carved away into a sheer cliff by the action of the glacier. This would have made it difficult to get onto the ridge in its lower part—this, anyway, would have taken too long since the crest of the ridge a nearly always difficult to follow.

The corridor to its foot seemed straightforward with rolling mounds of snow between the walls formed by the upper glacier and the chaotic jumble of ice on the lower. We soon roped up, fearful of hidden crevasses, and slowly plodded up the corridor, weaving our way timorously from one snow wrinkle to another, marking the route with bamboo wands. We were both being cautious, awed by the sheer size of our surroundings and a feel of lurking threat emitted by the glacier.

Two hours later we were at the end of the corridor.

'The glacier looks very broken.'

'We could try the ridge,' Mick suggested. 'There is a route straight up the front, and then left along the corridor.'

I think we were both frightened by the glacier, but the cliff barring the foot of the ridge looked too difficult, certainly at this early stage on the climb.

'Come on,' I decided. 'We'll have a look at the glacier and see if we can work out a safe route up the side of the ridge.'

A steep but fairly smooth-looking ramp ran up the side of the glacier between broken ice walls. I kicked up this, sweating under the blaze of the sun. It was easy enough and led onto a small ledge. It was obvious that we were going to need a fixed rope on this, and I buried our first 'dead man'. I had never used one before and was slightly skeptical of their value. They are shaped like the blade of a shovel, with a wire cable threaded through a couple of holes. You bury the shovel part at an angle which will cause it to be pulled deeper into the snow when weight is applied to the cable. They were first developed in the Antarctic as

On reaching the foot of the Ridge running down from the centre of the Face it was necessary to climb a complex ice-fall. It was here that the accident occurred at the end of the expedition.

anchors to hold dog teams, but may work equally well as belays or for holding fixed ropes. That first dead man I buried lasted the entire expedition and what must, by the end, have been several hundred ascents and descents.

Another steep snow slope over concealed ice bulges led us onto a short level section. It was difficult to tell where there were safe corridors or what was hidden by the blanket of unspoilt snow. We moved slowly and cautiously towards the ridge, weaving our way past hidden crevasses. By midday we had reached a point about a thousand feet above Camp I. Ahead was an obviously dangerous sérac region; we were tired, barely acclimatized and not feeling at all bold.

'We might as well go back,' I suggested.

Mick did not demur, and we wandered back to Camp I, where we found Don and Dougal, who had come up that morning after their day's rest. Don, with his proprietary interest in boxes, insisted on putting one up, and then they crowded into our two-man tent and spent the rest of the afternoon brewing tea and talking. Throughout the expedition there never seemed any tension between groups living and working together. We always seemed to enjoy each other's company and get on well together. The tension came between groups working at different camps and it was usually a matter of lack of communication, the conviction that Group A was having an easier time than oneself. In almost every instance, however, when individuals from two dissident groups met, the tension vanished, the grievances either forgotten or discussed and solved.

On his return to the camp, Mick had a bad headache; he was obviously suffering from altitude. Dave had given each of us a small plastic container holding a range of drugs to meet almost any eventuality. They ranged from headache pills through anti-diarrhoea tablets to an ampoule of morphia for use in the event of really severe pain. There were also some altitude sickness pills. These apparently were the very latest thing in treating pulmonary oedema, which is one of the most deadly of the many illnesses that can hit the climber at altitude. It is a form of pneumonia which, in a very short period, can flood the lungs and cause the patient to die, in effect by drowning. Don Whillans had had direct experience of this on the Masherbrum expedition in 1957, when Bob Downes contracted the illness and died in a matter of hours, having pushed up to one of the high camps after a spell of convalescence.

The pills in Dave's box had the effect of dehydrating the patient by making him want to urinate, and hence reducing the likelihood of fluid's forming in the lung. Mick decided to try out the treatment and took the prescribed dose. As a result, he had to get out of bed every half-hour or so through the night, a grim and exhausting experience in sub-zero temperature. His plight was all the harder to bear because I snored peacefully through everything, both keeping him awake and rubbing in my own good fortune. The following morning he was barely conscious, and so we decided to leave him to sort out the camp, while we pushed on up the glacier in search of a site for Camp II.

One of the features of Himalayan climbing is that the ground you crossed very cautiously and rather fearfully on the first occasion becomes commonplace on greater acquaintance. We quickly reached our high point of the previous day, Dougal moving very quickly and easily, Don bringing up the rear, plodding slowly but very surely in our tracks.

From our high point, the route lay up a snow corridor close in to the cliff of the ridge. In the heat of the sun a steady bombardment of icicles and rocks rattled down its flanks onto the snow below. It was a question of keeping as far out as possible, plodding hard and hoping for the best. Above this, an ice cliff curled across the glacier, merging into a shattered maze of crevasses and towers. There was a chimney where it leant against the rock wall, but it was full of debris, a black, noisome place, threatening to disgorge rocks and boulders embedded in the ice. We worked our way round the cliff, keeping a healthy distance from its base, for it was obviously unstable. There was a narrow shelf that stretched diagonally across it and seemed to offer a way. Dougal and I roped up and cut up a little shoot of ice to the start of the shelf. It was overhung by the wall above, huge icicles drooping down. We paused to anchor a rope in place to safeguard the way up to it, and while we fiddled with an ice-screw Don caught up and pushed through following the shelf, unroped. It was very much in keeping with Don's temperament on a mountain. I did not feel safe on the glacier without the security of a rope just in case I fell into a crevasse, but Don seems to have absolute faith in his own judgement. He is one of the safest climbers I have ever known, and yet will often go solo in places where most people would be happier with a rope, simply because of self-confidence.

He shouted back a warning: 'Don't waste any time under this, there's a crack running down the back and it's going to break away sooner or later.'

We followed him as quickly as we could, to find when we looked back at the overhanging wall that it was slowly peeling away from the glacier and must inevitably collapse. From this point the route lay under a couple more icy overhangs before it led to an easy slope above the cliff. A few hundred feet further up we could see a place where the rock wall of the ridge overhung the glacier. It seemed a likely spot for Camp II.

The way up to it lay over a big snow cone, a relic of powder snow avalanched down the flanks of the ridge. Another fifty yards and we were at the overhang; it was squeezed between two avalanche cones, but seemed protected by the amount of snow jutting out above it. Dougal, ever thrustful, ploughed through the snow above to see round the corner, but came back a few minutes later to report.

'There doesn't seem to be any better camp-site higher up. It seems to curve round into a big gully which with a bit of luck might lead up to the Col.'

Water was running down the cliff to the side of the camp-site and Don, reverting to his early profession, said, 'We'll see if we can do a bit of plumbing here. We might as well have running water in the camp.'

He promptly took off his crampons and started climbing the rock face to the left of the overhang. It looked difficult climbing on very soft, rounded rock. He was even able to find a use for the whammer, a space-age style piton-hammer of his own design, when he tried to chip a hold out of the rock. After climbing about thirty feet he managed to hammer a piton into a crack in the line of the waterfall, and cautiously abseiled down. A certain amount of water trickled down the rope, providing a somewhat haphazard water supply.

We reckoned we were at a height of about 17,500 feet, not as high as we had hoped for Camp II, but still, it was a step on the way to the Col, two and a half thousand feet above.

I was beginning to feel acclimatized and was able actively to enjoy pottering around the glacier at this comparatively low altitude in the full heat of the sun. On the way back we looked for an alternative route to avoid the dangerous gangway, but the glacier was so heavily crevassed there seemed no alternative. This was yet another objective

Camp II (17,500 feet) was tucked under an overhanging roof beneath the retaining cliff of the Ridge. This was the only safe camp site available.

danger we had no choice but to accept. We called the ice overhang the 'Sword of Damocles', because of the way it loomed over our path with its battery of sword-like icicles. It was obviously going to collapse very soon, but one was only beneath it for a few seconds so that the chances of being in the danger area at the moment of collapse seemed remote.

These are the type of risks one must accept if one wants to climb anywhere in the Himalayas and, for that matter, very often in the Alps. Our Sherpas commented that neither this nor the lower glacier was as dangerous as the icefall from the Western Cwm of Everest.

Back at Camp I Nick Estcourt, Martin Boysen, Alan Hankinson and two of the Sherpas had made a carry from Base Camp. As a result we now had all the gear we should need to establish our next camp. Mick Burke was still feeling very weak, and we decided he should go down the following morning if he was still unwell. As usual, before the evening radio call I had to work out the movements of everyone for the following day. The rear party, with the bulk of the food and gear, was now due to reach Temporary Base on 8 April. This was just about the right time, for we were getting low on both food and tentage. Although I should have liked to stay out in the front it was obviously essential for me to go back to meet our reinforcements and co-ordinate the move up to Base Camp. Once Kelvin Kent was fully briefed and installed as Base Camp manager, I should then be able to turn my attention once more to the Face. That night I therefore asked Martin and Nick to move up to Camp I, while I planned to carry a load up to the site of Camp II with Don, Dougal and Mick, if he was fit, and then return to Base Camp that same evening.

But the next morning, Mick was still feeling ill and had a splitting headache, so the three of us set out for Camp II. Having pioneered the route, we found the way easy—a short burst of speed below the Sword of Damocles and in little more than an hour and a half we were there. I left Don and Dougal digging out a tent platform and returned to Camp I. Mick Burke, still feeling very ill and complaining of very bad piles, had already gone down to Base Camp. Nick and Martin were waiting for me. I was brimming over with good spirits but they were very cool, almost surly.

'What on earth's got into you?' I asked.

'The camp's a bloody tip,' Nick said. 'You might at least have washed up before you got away in the morning. Look at all that rubbish. Couldn't you have dug a trash hole? The place'll be alive with flies if we're not careful.'

It was a cold douche to my own exuberance. My first reaction was to be defensive, the next to argue, but I managed to suppress both: this was a good example of the kind of friction that can develop between groups on a mountain. They were almost looking for something to be self-righteous about, still had very little idea of just how hard it was to get away in the morning and leave everything tidy. Most grievances on a mountain, taken out of their context, seem incredibly petty, yet all too easily they can get out of hand and undermine the morale of an expedition. On the other hand, I am sure that a certain amount of grumbling and character-stripping helps to relieve tension. It is just a matter of keeping it all in proportion.

On the way down I used the method of descent perfected by the Sherpas, sliding down the snow on my backside on a plastic bag. What had taken hours to slog up took a matter of seconds to descend. I spent the night at Base Camp, which was still little more than a transit camp with its huddle of two-man tents, and the following morning walked down to Temporary Base. Even after only a few days on the mountain it was a luxury to strip off and wash in the sun. At the same time, I was disturbed by the amount of snow that was still on the ground. We were obviously going to have a difficult time getting the porters up to the site of our permanent Base Camp.

On the way back across the glacier a snow ledge had collapsed and I had nearly fallen into a cleft in the ice. I had just saved myself; but in doing so had grazed my hand. At the time I had thought nothing of it, but on the morning of 7 April, down at Temporary Base, I woke up to find that my thumb had swollen into a huge, septic lump, and that the glands in my armpits were also swollen, a sure sign of blood-poisoning.

Fortunately, Dave Lambert was still at Temporary Base and was able to give me a mammoth injection of penicillin.

I had arranged to go down to the Hinko Cave that afternoon to meet Kelvin Kent and the rear party, but was feeling much too ill, and therefore asked Dave Lambert to go in my place. There seemed nothing I could do but concentrate on getting rid of my blood-poisoning.

CHAPTER 7

The Col

[7–12 April]

My ailment very nearly had disastrous repercussions for the entire expedition, through an unfortunate chain of circumstances. That night the porters should have stopped at the Hinko Cave, to give them an easy walk the following morning to Temporary Base. In the letter I had hurriedly written and dispatched by mail runner to Kelvin the day before I had been ambiguous, and he had understood it to mean them to reach Temporary Base on the 7th— not the Hinko Cave, which I had meant. They had spent the night of the 6th at Thomo, an easy day's march from Hinko but a very long one from our camp. They had already had some trouble with the porters, who had found the previous day's march from Chomro to Thomo very tiring. Thirty of the porters recruited by the Coolie Lama had refused to go any farther and Kelvin had had to pay them off. This meant that several of our porters were having to take double loads for double pay.

Ian Clough told the story of what happened in a letter he wrote to his wife, Nikki, the following day:

Yesterday, the 7th, was a great cock-up really. We walked to a good resting-place just beyond the place called Hinko [the place I expected them to spend the night-C.B.]; Chris was supposed to meet us there but never turned up. Mike Thompson and I were both feeling a bit seedy and thought that the coolies had probably had enough, about five hours' walking, especially as there weren't many good stopping-places ahead. Anyway, Kelvin was keen to keep some of them going on.

That morning, due to paying off thirty coolies, we had to reshuffle loads and the Sherpas and Sahibs were asked by Kent to carry more. The Sherpas and he took sixty pounds or more, but Mike and I told him we weren't taking more than we had—I had got fifty pounds, anyway—since we were both ill and needed to pamper ourselves for the Face.

Anyway, Kelvin and Khagbir came to a funny kind of compromise arrangement where Mike and I would go up with some of the porters and stop at Machapuchare Flats which are about two hours short of Temporary Base. The weather was obviously breaking and we two set off expecting to go only a very short distance. As it turned out we should have put our foot down and said we were stopping by Hinko, but one didn't like to, since there is no official ranking on the expedition except for Don and Chris, while Kelvin was more or less the official transport officer.

To cut a long story short, we walked and walked, and climbed and climbed; it thundered and hailed and then became a full-blown snow-storm. Some of the coolies didn't have shoes although we had issued most of them with gym shoes the previous day. They only had rags of clothes and were carrying very heavy loads.

We met Dave Lambert at the Machapuchare Flats but you couldn't stop there. They were covered in snow and there was no kind of shelter, so we continued to stagger on.

At Temporary Base it was about two o'clock in the afternoon when I heard a commotion outside the tent. It had now begun to snow quite hard and icy gusts were playing around the guy-lines of the tent. I poked my head out and saw blurred figures materializing out of the blizzard; some of our porters must have pressed on ahead. A few minutes later Mike Thompson and Ian Clough arrived, covered in snow, looking tired and haggard. I was feeling too ill to give Ian much welcome and anyway the commotion outside was rising to a crescendo. The porters were near exhaustion, bitterly cold and many of them were already quite serious exposure cases. There was still no sign of Kelvin, for he was bringing up the rear. For as long as possible I tried to ignore the commotion outside—I felt much too ill even to think of rushing out to try and bring some semblance of organization to the chaos.

An hour or so went by, and finally Ian came into the tent.

'I think you should get up and try to sort things out,' he told me. 'If we don't do something fast we'll have some dead porters on our hands.'

I felt near death myself, but was spurred to activity and staggered out of my sleeping-bag. Outside it was a nightmare scene: porters, some of them barefoot, kept arriving out of the snow to dump their loads in a pile; they then just stood around in listless, wailing groups. Ian was trying to persuade them to go back down to the Hinko Cave below the snowline; but they wouldn't budge; they were much too tired, and anyway hadn't been paid.

'We must get some carbohydrates into them,' shouted Ian.

Mike was rushing around with a boxful of sugar cubes handing them out. I found myself clutching a box, and handed a few cubes out as well. Our T.V. team, with camera and microphone, were having a field day filming the shambles. At this point Kelvin Kent arrived. He was half-frozen, shivering and exhausted. On the way up he had given all his outer clothing to a man who had collapsed at the side of the track. This was the last he ever saw of his gear, for as soon as Kelvin had gone out of sight, the man must have high-tailed it for the valley, rejoicing in his booty. In spite of his fatigue Kelvin immediately plunged into the fray, trying to organize tentage for our 240 porters. He had with him three large base tents and these were all erected. Soon there were about fifty porters crammed into each. Meanwhile, Pasang had taken the unwise step of making a *raki* issue to some of them. In their exhausted state this was disastrous, and we soon had helplessly giggling coolies slumped into the snow, in a state of near-insensibility. We bundled these into Tukte's kitchen shelter to try to thaw them out, an action which outraged Tukte'a sense of propriety. He and all the Sherpas were indifferent to the fate of the despised porters, and it was very difficult to make them do anything to help them. I think they felt it was beneath them to care for or serve people whom they considered were socially inferior.

Slowly the crisis sorted itself out. We unpacked the primus stoves and used them to heat the tents, somehow got all the porters into some kind of shelter, under tarpaulins draped over boulders, into caves and in the tents we specially erected. Dave Lambert was treating the worst of the exposure cases; Mike and Ian were still taking around food; Tukte had been bullied into preparing a great bowl of soup.

It was 5.0 p.m. and I took the walkie-talkie set to a good vantage point to make the evening radio call. It brought an encouraging piece of news: Don Whillans and Dougal Haston, who had moved up to Camp II the previous day, had pushed through to the Col on the Ice Ridge at a height of 20,100 feet. This was an important achievement for it meant that we had climbed half the height of the Face in only ten days from reaching the Sanctuary, though admittedly we had only just reached the start of the difficult climbing.

Don and Dougal had pressed on in savage conditions. The previous night their tent, snagged under the rock overhang of the retaining wall of the Ice Ridge, had been very nearly engulfed in powder snow avalanches.

'It was the only time on the expedition that I was ever frightened,' Don told me later. 'You could hear the snow thunder down outside but you couldn't see a thing, and didn't dare open the door of the tent, for spindrift just poured into it even if you only opened up a chink. I told Dougal to get into the back of the box so that if the avalanche did hit us we'd at least have a chance of it just crushing the outer part of the frame. We couldn't tell whether the snow was coming round the side or straight over the top of the cliff above us, but in the morning we could see that the snow had come from the side and had missed us by about three feet. I never really worried after that.'

The site we had picked for Camp II was probably the only safe position on that part of the mountain because the rock overhang protected it from stonefall, and a small spur to its side deflected the powder snow avalanches round the flanks of the ridge. Even so, the odd deflected stone or lump of ice from above sometimes fell on top of the tent and later a small boulder came crashing down from a position slightly higher than the camp-site and went straight through the RAFMA tent. Luckily, no one was inside at the time.

On the 7th, while we struggled to cope with the unexpected influx of porters, Dan and Dougal left Camp II and struck up for the ridge. At first the going was straightforward, ploughing through deep, fresh snow on the glacier to the side of the ridge. This led into a basin at the foot of the Face proper. It was a dangerous place, threatened by hanging glaciers on the lower part of the Face. The best route seemed up a big, powder snow avalanche cone at the foot of a subsidiary gully to the left of the main gully, whose lower part was badly threatened. They were then able to gain the main gully that seemed to lead straight up to the Col, by crossing a broken rock buttress about three hundred feet up.

By the time they had reached this point the weather had set in. It was snowing hard and bitterly cold, yet they pressed on, determined to keep going as long as they did not meet any difficult sections. Don had only a pair of lightweight gloves which barely kept his hands warm, while Dougal had Dachstein Mitts, made of very thick matted wool, which have proved to be the warmest gloves available today. To avoid frostbite they had to swap gloves from time to time.

It was like climbing upwards in a white vacuum, slowly plodding up steep, knee-deep snow that merged into the falling snow around them. The occasional rock was just a misty dark shape which gave them only a faint feeling of orientation. Powder snow avalanches swirled down past them, but they were careful to keep into the side of the gully where they were only struck by side eddies.

They reached the head wall of the gully in the early afternoon. There was just a short rock wall between them and the Col. Well satisfied with their day's climbing, they hammered in a piton and abseiled down. (Plate 53 demonstrates the method of abseil.)

Out of all the confusion of the last few hours we seemed to be emerging triumphant. Our main gear had arrived at just the right time, we had reached a height of 21,000 feet, and the porters were finally settled for the night. With the arrival of the main gear we at last had a stock of whisky, and down at Base Camp that night we happily swilled Scotch and talked of knocking off the Face in the next fortnight.

The following morning dawned fine. Don and Dougal at Camp II went back up their route of the previous day, fixing ropes in position on the traverse across the buttress leading into the main gully. Having done this they returned to Base Camp for a well-earned rest. Meanwhile, Martin Boysen and Nick Estcourt moved up to Camp II, with the task of consolidating the route up to the Col and establishing Camp III.

Back at Temporary Base, confusion reigned under a hot sun. The porters had spent a chilly night in spite of being packed together in their shelters with primus stoves burning the whole time. (They had supple-

Looking down on Camp III (20,100 feet). The route up to it follows the gully that is out of sight on the other side of the Col.

111

mented the heat of the stoves by piling brushwood on top.) They were now working themselves into a pitch of indignation, accusing Kelvin of trying to kill them all, and more, to the point, of cheating them of a day's pay, for they had just made a two-day carry in one. Kelvin was surrounded by a crowd of angry, shouting porters. Fortunately, our Naiks, Khagbir Pun and Cheesbahadur, who had been ineffective the previous night because they themselves had been so cold and exhausted, were now back to their normal form and did everything they could to pacify the porters.

Khagbir had done a magnificent job of coaxing 139 out of the 140 Gurkha hill porters he had recruited up to Temporary Base. One man had fallen out through illness. This can be compared with the fact that 38 of the 80 men appointed by the Coolie Lama in Pokhara abandoned their loads at Thomo, well below the snow-line, and refused to go on.

Meanwhile, Kelvin was dealing with another crisis. The previous evening at the height of the storm, the aerial of our Racal h/f wireless, which was our rear link with Pokhara and Katmandu, was struck by lightning and badly damaged. Kelvin tried to effect some repairs on the spot but was unable to do so. We had become very dependent on our rear link, not just in the event of an emergency, but as a means of calling up supplies at short notice from Pokhara. The T.V. team made even greater use of it, getting rapid reports back on the quality of the film they were sending out by mailrunner. Kelvin wrote an urgent letter to Racal in England for a replacement and, in the meantime, asked the Military Attaché in Katmandu to try and arrange for the set left with the Nepalese Army to be sent to Pokhara. This was achieved, but nevertheless we were to be without communication with the outside world.

I was anxious to keep as many porters as possible for another few nights at Temporary Base so that we should be able to ferry all the gear up to Base Camp over the space of the next few days.

It was one o'clock in the afternoon before we had paid off the bulk of the porters, who fled from the inhospitable moors of Temporary Base whooping with joy and relief. We retained forty of the porters under one of the ex-soldier Naiks, Corporal Ganga Bahadur Pun, planning to ferry up as many loads as possible and then retain twenty of the strongest for a further week or so to clear Temporary Base. It was already becoming evident that our manpower was going to become very extended once we had established another two camps. We had planned to use local porters for the carry to Camp I, but the glacier was much more complex than I had anticipated. Even so, I decided we should have to see if the best of our Gurkhas could cope with this type of ground, even though they had never before been above the snow-line.

It was so late when the forty porters whom we had retained were ready to do a carry to Temporary Base that they had only walked half-way across the glacier when the usual afternoon snow-fall started. I didn't dare have a repetition of the previous night's fiasco and therefore told them to dump their loads and return to the shelter of Temporary Base. I was now feeling much better and, recruiting the few porters who possessed anoraks, pressed on to the site of Base Camp.

The following morning we were able to make an early start, cleared the dump on the glacier and ferried more loads up to Base Camp, which at last was getting a more permanent appearance with one of the big cottage tents pitched and a growing pile of stores. The next few days were spent consolidating our position on the mountain. Martin and Nick spent 10 April digging out the fixed ropes left by Don and Dougal, all of which had been swept away by powder snow avalanches. On the 11th, they pushed up to the Col, carrying a Whillans Box, and dug it into position. That night on the evening radio call Nick reported, 'There's a flat space the size of a football pitch up there; it's perfect as a camp-site, completely free from objective danger.'

This was excellent news. Meanwhile, Tom Frost and Ang Pema had moved up to Camp II to join Nick and Martin, while I walked up to Camp I with Mingma, one of the Sherpas who had come with the rear party. He was the quietest and I think the most pleasant of all our Sherpas. He was also the oldest at thirty-seven, and had carried to the top camp on Everest with the Indians in 1965. On our expedition he was

The four tiny figures at bottom centre are carrying loads from Camp II (beneath the cliffs, lower left) up to Camp III by the gully slanting up to the left. This area was threatened by both powder snow and ice avalanches.

always willing and cheerful, getting on with the work in hand unobtrusively but very effectively. Our sixth Sherpa was Nima Tsering, at twenty the baby of the party. He was very much the representative of a new generation of Sherpas, for he had been to one of the schools set up by Sir Edmund Hillary in Khumjung, spoke fluent English and could read and write. He was well built, very self-confident yet not loudmouthed. This was his first expedition.

I was planning to move up to Camp III to start forcing the route up the Ice Ridge in the next two days. Martin and Nick wanted to come down for a rest and anyway needed to go through their kitbags of personal equipment, which had been brought up with the rear party. Planning the movement of our team up the mountain was like sorting out a complicated game of snakes and ladders. In my original planning I had banked on an average of fourteen out of the seventeen climbers and Sherpas fit and working at one time, but in the event this proved optimistic. In spite of the arrival of our reinforcements we were not much better off than we had been before. Mike Thompson and Ian Clough were weakened from an attack of flu; Mick Burke was still laid low with an appalling set of piles and Dave Lambert seemed to be a slow acclimatizer. On top of this Don and Dougal were having a necessary rest, and as soon as they returned to the fray Martin and Nick would have to come back down. Another factor one had to reckon with was that people moving back up the mountain, as opposed to ferrying, could carry only a very limited payload of supplies, if any, since they would be carrying their own personal equipment. Ideally, one would keep everyone at his allotted camp on the mountain with the minimum change of position, so that one could get the maximum ferrying potential from the entire team. This approach, however, would take no account of the human factor, in terms both of a growing fatigue in the face of altitude and, perhaps more important, of the psychological factor of boring repetition of work. Ferrying loads up the same length of mountain day after day is a monotonous, soul-destroying business. All eight of the mountaineers in the party were eager to get out in front to carry out the exciting work of pioneering the route. It seemed essential to change the front people fairly frequently, both for their own sakes, to give them a rest before they had taken too much out of themselves, and for the sake of the others ferrying loads down below.

Another problem was that the Sherpas had just heard over the radio of an appalling accident on Everest, in which their friends and relatives had been involved. Six Sherpas had been killed by an ice avalanche in an Khumbu Icefall, while working for the Japanese ski expedition which was attempting to ski down the upper slopes of Everest. This naturally shook the Sherpas badly, and the way they continued to work for us is a tribute to their loyalty.

I spent a large part of each evening trying to work out the best permutation of movement on the mountain for the next few days. On 12 April I moved up to Camp II to join Tom Frost. I had hoped I should find it easy, being acclimatized to this altitude, but it was still a hard grind. On the way up I met Nick Estcourt returning to Base Camp. That morning he had set out with Martin Boysen, Tom Frost and Ang Pema to do a carry to the Col, but he had burnt himself out the previous day, when he had pressed on in front, ever competitive and over-willing, to carry a heavy load up to the Col. He had felt completely shattered the night before and had decided to go straight down in the morning, but now, feeling better because he was going down rather than up, he was racked by qualms of conscience. I shared a drink with him, and slowly plodded on towards Camp II. I could not even raise an increase of pace under the Sword of Damocles. At Camp II the others had already returned. Martin was obviously going very well indeed and regretted having to go down for a rest.

That night Tom Frost and I shared Camp II with Pemba Tharkay and Ang Pema. I was immediately impressed by the way Tom shouldered a rucksack and went off to collect ice. Most of us—including, I must confess, myself—would have left this task to the Sherpas. We were undoubtedly spoilt when we had the Sherpas with us. They automatically did all the chores around the camp, cooked the meals and delivered mugs of tea through the tent door. This was a relic of the old days when

Sahibs were waited on hand and foot—a relic I quite enjoyed taking advantage of.

Throughout the expedition we had wonderful service from our Sherpas, both in load-carrying and in helping around the camp. I think this was largely because we never expected them, or for that matter even asked them, to wait on us, but left it entirely to them. They responded to this approach accordingly. We certainly always treated them as fellow climbers and never allowed a Sherpa-Sahib relationship to creep in. They were undoubtedly fitter than we were, and on the carries were nearly always out in front. We openly respected them for this; they, on the other hand, respected our greater climbing experience on difficult ground.

Tom and I were both excited that night as we lay in the Whillans Box. Tomorrow we should be going up to Camp III; the day after we should be getting to grips with one of the key sections of our route—the Ice Ridge.

CHAPTER 8

Blind Alley
[13—18 April]

The ice arête above Camp III was like a fragile buttress, its crest crenellated with a thousand spires, leaning against the massive wall of a Gothic cathedral. On its left a broad shelf of snow ran up to the foot of the wall; there was a gully in the corner where the arête joined the Face proper, but this was a natural avalanche channel, dominated by the ice cliffs far above and the pendulous cornices on the ice arête. The entire left flank of the arête was furrowed with ice flutings over which curled still more cornices.

It was 14 April. A week had elapsed since Don and Dougal had reached a point just before the Col, but it had taken us all this time to redeploy after the arrival of the rear party. Tom and I now had a difficult decision to make. We could either follow the crest of the ridge, which would avoid the threat of avalanche and collapsing cornices, or try to bypass it by going up the easy shelf to tackle the gully or either of its walls at the end of the arête. Don had recommended the shelf to the side and I had agreed with him, but now we were immediately below it, it looked less desirable. The ridge, grossly foreshortened, looked more straightforward; the side route seemed menaced by hidden threats.

That morning I had said to Tom, as we finished the slow process of cooking, getting out of bed and dressing, 'Let's go and have a look at the best route.'

'You go and have a look if you like, I'll just get started up the ridge.'

Tom had obviously made up his mind that the crest of the ridge gave the best route. He had some experience of this kind of climbing for he had been on an expedition to Peru, where they had climbed the North Ridge of Chacaraju, a particularly difficult peak in the Cordillera Blanca. Tom observed that our ice arête looked no harder than this one; he obviously did not like the look of the bypass route. I still had an open mind, but was slightly shaken by Tom's confidence.

'I'll go and have a look at the side of the arête,' I said, and started to plod through the snow up the shelf. It was about a hundred yards broad, shelving gently to what seemed a steep drop to the broken glacier hundreds of feet below. My progress was painfully slow; out of the corner of my eye, I could see Tom pulling up onto the first step of the ice arête, almost at the front door of our camp. A few more steps; I focused onto an ice block that had fallen from the crest of the ridge, and headed for this. Although it was only a hundred yards away it took me twenty minutes to reach it.

I paused and looked up at the arête; the serried cornices had a silent threat about them, even on this dazzling, cloudless morning. I noted the huge avalanche cone at the foot of the gully, the way the snow was scarred from previous falls. I was full of doubt and, in the face of Tom's quiet confidence about the crest of the ridge, I adopted his course and ploughed back to join him at the foot of the ridge.

Even the first step was harder than it looked, an augury for the future. Tom had just nearly fallen down a concealed crevasse, so we promptly roped up, and I started up the first main step. From the bottom it had looked easy, but almost immediately it steepened. The snow was aerated, had hardly any substance to it, baked even at this altitude by the fierce

119

heat of the sun. Even the ice was rotten and flaked away under foot. I ran out about eighty feet of rope and came to a point where it steepened to the vertical for the last few feet to the top of the step. It was no good putting in an ice-piton for it just pulled out again. I was suddenly aware of how far I should fall if I slipped; I looked down and saw four tiny dots at the foot of the gully leading up to Camp III. They must be our two Sherpas with Don Whillans and Dougal Haston, who were making a carry up to our camp.

I tentatively carved out another hold with my axe but did not reach any stable snow; I should have had to pull on this unstable mass to get over it and did not fancy the idea. I looked over to the right and it seemed at an easier angle. Cautiously I worked my way down and across; it was all hideously loose, but at least it was not pushing me out of balance. A last pull and I was at the top of the first step on the ridge, a mere hundred feet above Tom.

Two hours had gone by, and we barely seemed to have scratched the problem. We had now reached a point where we should have to leave fixed ropes all the way to safeguard the route and enable us to ferry loads up it in the wake of the lead climbers. It is like making a road up a mountain and requires even more thought than the initial climbing to ensure that the ropes are easy to climb, that they are correctly anchored and on traverses give adequate support. Once the ropes are in place, the climbers no longer move roped together, but simply dip onto the rope, using on the upward sections a device called a jumar clamp. This is a metal handle, with a knurled lever which is fitted over the rope. It works on a ratchet principle, sliding easily up the rope, but biting into it when put under tension. (See Appendix B.)

But Tom and I in our haste had not worked out how we should actually fix the ropes in position. There are various alternatives: I had thought of using the rope I had climbed on as a fixed rope, anchoring it into position with a dead man buried in the snow, and then letting Tom climb up the rope. Tom had other ideas. We were barely in shouting distance, and it was soon obvious that we were getting nowhere. I decided to come back down to get things properly sorted out before we started, and abseiled back down the step, leaving the rope in place. By this time Don and Dougal, obviously going very strongly, had reached our box on the Col. Feeling sheepish, we went down to meet them.

'We didn't like the look of the shelf,' I said. 'At least the arête will be free of objective danger. I'm afraid we've been pretty disorganized this morning.'

'One usually is the first day out,' Don said. I felt grateful to him for his tact; Tom and I had made a poor start. We had a brew of tea, ate some biscuits and returned to the fray.

'How about the second man carrying the fixed rope in his rucksack, with one end attached to the last piton?' Tom suggested. 'The leader can then climb on an ordinary climbing rope, take the second man up on it in the usual way, and he will then be automatically paying out the rope.'

It seemed a good idea and was typical of Tom's methodical approach to all problems. We quickly reached the top of the first step and Tom went out ahead, following the curving crest of the arête to the next steep section. It looked easy, but the snow was so soft that he sank up to his thighs in it. He ended up using a snow shovel to dig out a path up the ridge. He was advancing at a snail's pace, and I felt sleepy under the hot rays of the sun. After about fifty feet the arête was barred by a mushroom of snow which he tried to traverse under, but the snow and unconsolidated ice was near vertical and honeycombed with holes. He pushed in a long Dexion strip for protection, but it slid in as if it was going into melted butter and gave no sense of security. After working away for a little longer, he came back and took a belay just short of the steep section.

By this time I was seething with impatience, but once I had swum up the soft snow to him and then ventured onto the slope beyond I saw why he had gone so slowly: I had never been on such appalling snow. I managed to work my way precariously round a corner and up a shallow gully leading back to the crest of the arête. I had the feeling that the entire ridge was honeycombed and could just come tumbling down about me. There were snow mushrooms and little cornices on every side, any of which could have swept me away if they collapsed. I reached a point just short of the arête and called Tom up. He came quite quickly, carrying the rucksack full of fixed rope, with a tail of rope trailing behind him. At least this part of our system seemed to work. It was now Tom's turn out in front. The snow in the gully was more consolidated and he kicked his way quickly to the top.

A near-vertical step now barred our way. It was getting late and we decided to leave this till the following morning. On our way back we tried to straighten out and improve the route, cutting away great bollards of snow but never seeming to get down to anything stable.

We returned to the box in the late afternoon. This had been the first day of the entire trip that it had not clouded over, but I couldn't help feeling worried that we might have made the wrong choice. Progress along the ridge was obviously going to be slow. Should I have made a more thorough reconnaissance of the way round the side?

We were both tired and had headaches either from lack of acclimatization or from the intensity of the sun, which seemed to burn straight through the tinted lens of our sunglasses. Even so it was a good feeling to be there in the top camp on the Face. We might be part of a big and complex expedition, but we were alone for just a few hours and might almost have had the entire mountain to ourselves. From the open door of the box we were looking straight across the gulf of the Sanctuary to the forked peaks of Machapuchare, well named the Fish's Tail. We could now see over Tent Peak and gaze at the full sprawl of the Annapurna range laid out before us: Gangapurna with its wedge-like summit, the solid mass of Annapurna III, and beyond it the black, triangular summit of Annapurna II, guarded by the squat barrier of Annapurna IV and its long-lying summit ridge. It was difficult to believe that I had stood there fully ten years before.

We now had our proper high-altitude rations, designed by Mike Thompson. They had tasted delicious when we had tried them out in North Wales, but already I was beginning to have my doubts about their palatability at altitude. He had chosen interesting, tasty morsels. As a result every pack had pumpernickel, a packet of rather pungent, black, wafer-like slices of rye bread, that we quickly became tired of.

Another innovation was fruit drink as a substitute for tea or coffee; very quickly I found myself longing for a mugful of good, strong, sweet tea, but this arrangement suited Tom, as his faith did not allow him to drink tea or coffee. That night I prepared a supper of soup, followed by stew, made from a can of sweet-corn, a tin of pork and one of new potatoes. Having prepared it I found I had to force it down against a feeling of rising nausea, while Tom gulped his down with little or no trouble.

As the sun dropped down over the western retaining wall of the Sanctuary, the tip of Machapuchare was lit a dusky red, that faded imperceptibly into dark grey then black. It was a scene of ineffable peace. Tom and I stayed outside in the gathering dark taking photographs of the incredible change of tone and colour in the rock, snow and sky around us. A plume of snow blown from the summit of Annapurna was lit a fiery gold, the last splash of light in a darkening world. Tom and I returned to the box, crept into sleeping bags and lit a candle, me to read *Decline of the West*, a novel of sex, lust and violence, he to read his Mormon testament, the only reading matter I saw him look at during the entire trip.

I couldn't help respecting Tom for his religious faith and the way he refrained from ramming it down any of our throats. It was only when I raised the subject that night that he showed how happy he was to talk about it. He also let me read his diary at the end of the expedition, which revealed his evangelistic aspirations. Just before leaving for Nepal he had written:

> But it was not until one week before leaving Ventura [Tom's home town is California—C.B.], in a ten-minute meeting with Pres. Joseph Chapman, that the tone of the expedition was set and the reason and meaning of going was partially understood. As he explained it, the entire expense and effort of building up the Church was worthwhile if only one individual was converted, so great is a soul's worth in the sight of God. He explained that the individuals I will come into contact with on this trip probably do not even realize that the Lord has re-established his true

Church among men in these present times. I may have the opportunity to explain this and be a proper example of the word of wisdom.

Tom certainly was this; in one of my letters to Wendy I wrote:

He is tall, slightly built; reminds me of one of Steinbeck's farmers from the Dust Bowl in The Grapes of Wrath. *He is a convinced and fervent Mormon, never rams it down your throat, yet his faith has given him a code of conduct that puts him way out in front of most of us.*

That night we got onto the subject of religion and had a long discussion, but I'm afraid Tom failed to make any inroads on my own scepticism. In desperate situations, in the mountains or in my own family life, for instance when our first child was born, when I was not allowed into the room with my wife yet could hear her cries of pain, I have prayed. But this was the cry of one who was desperate and could see no one to help him—more an instinctive desire for help than any kind of faith. When we had stood outside the box that evening and gazed in wonder around us, Tom felt he was looking at God's creation, and wrote in his diary: 'We are treated to a once or twice in a lifetime's view of Heavenly Father's mountains.'

The beauty of the mountains certainly had a mystic quality of infinite peace, size and power that stirred my emotions to a great depth and made me feel at that moment that there must be some greater spiritual power, but once again the feeling was passing, one of extreme emotion rather than faith or reason.

We slept badly that night, both suffering from headaches and feeling claustrophobic inside the box. I woke at five in the morning, couldn't get to sleep and so started to cook, to ensure that we could make use of all the hours of daylight to make some progress on the ridge. We were away by 7.15, quickly climbed the fixed rope that we had spent the whole of the previous day fixing, and were standing at the foot of the next step.

'Do you want to have a go?' I asked Tom.

'Yeah, sure thing. It looks great climbing.'

He moved off from the stance, festooned in ice-pitons, snow-stakes and dead men. Even early in the morning the snow was insubstantial and even the ice seemed fragile. Tom moved up slowly and methodically, treating the snow and ice as a rock problem, cutting very few steps, but getting protection from above by pushing in the long Dexion stake and passing his rope through a karabiner attached to it. Towards the top the angle reared up to the vertical. He straddled out widely, moving with an engineer's precision, and pulled over the crest. When it was my turn to follow I had a struggle. I was carrying Tom's Kelty pack frame full of rope. It was superbly comfortable to carry, but had a high frame that made it difficult to bend my neck backwards to look upwards. Even with the security of his rope above, I found the climbing hard and marvelled at the neat, controlled way he had vanquished the problem.

By the time we had both reached the top of the step it was ten in the morning. We could already see the tiny dots formed by the four climbers coming up from Camp II. That day Don and Dougal were moving up to our camp in support of us. To us, it acted as a spur; we wanted to show a good bit of progress to justify our choice of route.

The ridge now opened out a little, sweeping in an easy curve to a set of snow mushrooms about a hundred feet beyond. It looked easy and I pushed ahead, wading through the snow. At first it *was* easy, but as I reached the point where it started to steepen once again, I was slowed down by the appalling state of the snow. It was like candyfloss, and however much I shovelled away I never came to a solid base.

'Looks better round to the left,' shouted Tom. 'How about trying that?'

I agreed, and worked my way back to his belay. Time fled by unnoticed; I had spent over an hour out in front and the others had very nearly reached Camp III. Tom was feeling tired that morning, and therefore let me go on in front once again. I swung round the ridge into one of the ice runnels, looked down it and realized with a sick feeling that we could have come straight up it to our present point, and thereby have saved a great deal of time. I traversed several more hoping to reach a point where we could climb straight up and rejoin the ridge at an

ow was better consolidated on this side since it did
1.

1 had joined me, Don and Dougal had reached our
ting their way round the bottom of the ridge on the
⸻gui pushed a little beyond the place that I had reached
the previous morning. Meanwhile I pushed straight up the gully
towards the crest; it was easy enough going, for the angle was only about
forty degrees and the snow was firm, so that I could kick good steps, but
our efforts to avoid objective danger already seemed wasted, for there
was a huge cornice overlooking the gully which, if it collapsed, would
sweep anyone in it.

I had run out two hundred feet of rope and was near the top. The
angle had steepened perceptibly and at the same time had deteriorated.
I felt cautious and a little demoralized but was determined to see over
the top. I pushed in a snow-stake, but it went in too easily and would
almost certainly be pulled out if I fell on it. I bridged up with little of
Tom's grace and peered over the top, to see that the ridge was now
razor-thin and looked even more difficult beyond the point I had
reached.

A shout came from below. 'I think there's a good route round here,
Chris, which will bypass the whole of the ridge.'

There was nothing for it. We had made a mistake and would have to
return. I felt bitterly disappointed and was furious with myself for
being caught out; I couldn't resist hitting out at Tom, saying, "I wish I
hadn't listened to you about the ridge.'

Almost as soon as I had let rip, however, I realized the injustice of my
complaint, for the decision, good or bad, was ultimately mine. In the circumstances our course had seemed sensible, since the ridge, if it had
been possible, would have given us a route almost entirely free from
objective danger. But I could not help feeling depressed and uncertain of
myself as I returned to the camp to meet the others. I think my distress
was caused more by uncertainty in myself than anything else. I could
not help worrying how the rest of the team would accept my decisions
and leadership after making such a basic route-finding mistake.

Back at Camp III, Don and Dougal could not have been more forbearing. They gave us a warm welcome and we made our plans for the following day, agreeing that we should all go to the end of the shelf and try to find a route bypassing the ridge. But we had lost two perfect days, and the fact was rubbed in still harder the next morning, when it dawned overcast with a web of gossamer-like cloud drawn across the day. We made a latish start, getting away at 8.30, Dougal out in front forcing the trail. He slowly but steadily ploughed through the knee-deep snow, never thinking to pause to allow someone else to take on this tiring drudgery. I think he regarded it as a challenge to himself; he probably found it no easier than any of us but was determined not to let up.

As we neared the end of the shelf, a huge powder snow avalanche swept the wall at the Fang just opposite. It started with a wisp of snow near the top, then grew into a huge boiling cloud as it dropped down the near, sheer face of ice and rock, dividing round a prominent buttress near the bottom into two great floods of snow that hit the glacier far below us and engulfed entire networks of crevasses, until the whole basin was filled with swirling cloud. And then it dissipated to nothing in a matter of minutes—this was the most frightening thing of all, for we could see no trace of this avalanche that had just fallen five thousand feet and had contained literally thousands of tons of snow. Snow had merged into snow; perhaps a few crevasses had been covered; perhaps the glacier was more heavily scored with avalanche trails, but you could barely tell if this was so. Yet any of the team or a camp that had been in the path of that avalanche would have been as totally obliterated.

Suddenly the entire mountain assumed an atmosphere of quiet menace. We became painfully aware of the size of the avalanche cone at the foot of the gully leading into the upper part of the Face, noticed the depth of scoring in the snow—it was very similar to what we could see on the glacier far below.

We had been following a course well out from the side of the ridge, to avoid any avalanches caused by collapsing cornices, but we were now getting into the danger area threatened by the gully.

'We want to get into the side here,' observed Don.

Two climbers follow the shelf that bypasses the lower part of the Ice Ridge on their way up to Camp IV.

I agreed, and we now clung to the edge of the ridge, where the threat of a falling cornice seemed much less than that posed by the yawning gully above.

'If anything big comes down we can at least jump into the bergschrund,' I suggested. The bergschrund was partly covered in and not too deep, forming a perfect bolt-hole from any big avalanches.

The closer we got to the gully, the less I liked it: Don obviously shared my doubts. Looking up it one could see that anything falling down the ice cliffs that barred the snowfield above the end of the Ice Ridge would be channelled into it.

'We can cross the gully,' said Dougal, 'and then follow up those flutings on the other side. That should give you a fair amount of cover and we can then get out onto the snowfield.'

'I'm not so sure. Even the flutings look as if they're dominated by those ice cliffs above.'

'Well, how else can we get up it?'

'How about that arête leading up onto the ridge? It looks easier from where it joins the crest and should be a lot safer.'

A huge powder-snow avalanche pours down the 8,000-foot wall of the Fang, just opposite the South Face.

An arête ran up from the foot of the main gully, back onto the ridge that Tom and I had spent the two previous days trying to climb. It ran up towards a huge ice wall that seemed fairly stable, though over it curled a pair of cornices which at some stage would inevitably collapse. There seemed a way round the ice wall to its right which would take us onto the ridge at a much higher point than Tom and I had reached the previous day.

'It's difficult to say which is best,' Don said. 'I suggest we start up the ridge arête, gain a bit of height and then we can at least look at the gully.'

Whilst we were talking, Dougal had already uncoiled a rope and was starting to climb the arête. He reminded me of an impatient racehorse, raring to go. He was only able to kick steps for a few feet before he had to start cutting with his short axe. It took him an hour to run out the full two hundred feet of rope.

At the end of the rope, Dougal secured it to a snow-stake and Don followed up using his jumar clamp for security, carrying up another rope for the next pitch. As soon as he reached the top and had belayed I followed up myself. The higher I got, the more unpleasant the gully looked and the more inviting the arête leading up onto the ridge.

'I might as well have a go at the arête while you look at the gully,' I shouted.

Tom came up behind me and I started up the arête. It was a wonderful feeling getting out in front once more, hacking away steps in the compact snow. Dougal had now started working his way across the side of the arête into the gully. It was even wider than it had looked from below, and very much more threatening. One felt very exposed in the gully and was all too conscious of the ice cliffs poised above and the huge curling cornices of the upper part of the ridge. I don't think I have ever been anywhere in the mountains that was so still and yet had such a strong feeling of potential danger. This had even affected Dougal, whose forward progress had slowed down.

Meanwhile the weather had begun to deteriorate; a sea of cloud had crept into the glacier basin below us, ragged wisps curled round the ridge and suddenly the thin air was full of snow. Don and Dougal turned back suddenly. Don was suffering from a recurrence of an old ailment; he had an attack of vertigo. He felt as if the mountains were spinning around him and it was all he could do to stay upright clinging onto the rope. He had had several of these attacks in the past, one on the lower slopes of the Eiger while carrying a load up the Face during the ascent of the Eiger Direct, but he had had no recurrences for some time and had hoped that he had got over the trouble. All he could do now was to hurry back to the camp while he could still walk.

I carried on for a little longer, but the wind was beginning to rise and it was getting bitterly cold. I reached a point about half-way up the arête, anchored the rope to a dead man and slid back down it towards Tom, who was already on his way back before I reached his belay. Little powder snow avalanches had already started to pour down the gully and the flutings in the ridge beside us. It was very nearly a white-out, but we could just pick out the marker flags we had left on the way up.

By the time we got down Don had recovered from his attack of vertigo but was obviously worried about a recurrence. That night we had further problems: Don and Dougal were very nearly asphyxiated by paraffin fumes, while Tom and I in our box were suffering from severe headaches. The cause was almost certainly the inferior paraffin we had bought in Pokhara. The following morning at the seven o'clock call, I asked Kelvin down at Base Camp to see if he could order some better fuel from Pokhara. He promptly called up Bishnuparsad, who in turn made contact with a fellow officer, Major Peter Ridlington at the British Gurkha base at Paklihawa. They chased up some good-quality paraffin for us and sent it up to Pokhara, from where our mailrunners could pick it up and bring it to us.

That day Don decided to take it easy to try to shake off any likelihood of getting another bout of vertigo. We agreed therefore that Tom and I should press on toward the crest of the ridge, while Dougal rescued the ropes he had left in place the previous day. On the way up the fixed rope I dug in some intermediate anchor points to shorten the distance between anchors. This lessens the stretch in the rope and means there is less delay for people coming up the fixed ropes, since you can have only one person between anchor points at a time.

From my high point of the previous night I continued hacking steps up the crest of the arête. I was now becoming more aware of the ice cliff that towered above me. If it had collapsed we should have had no chance of survival, but it seemed unlikely that it would—it was just another risk that we had to calculate and then accept. A snow gully led up to the side of it, to what seemed the crest of the ridge. I brought Tom up to the edge of the gully, and asked, 'Do you want to have a go out in front?'

'You're going great, Chris. You push on ahead.'

I couldn't help being glad. I at last felt acclimatized and hardly noticed the altitude at all while concentrating on forcing the route. I now lowered myself into the gully and started kicking my way up it. The snow was quite soft but at first it was easy going. After a hundred feet or so it began to steepen, and the snow, resting on a bed of ice and rock, felt unpleasantly insecure. I pushed in a dead man but had little confidence that it would hold me in the event of a fall.

In my concentration I had not noticed a change in the weather. It had been bright sunlight when I had started and I was only wearing my Borg fur jacket without any windproof over it. Suddenly I noticed that it was snowing, though I was still barely conscious of the growing cold; my position felt much too precarious. I dug away the snow and tried to put in an ice-screw, but found that there was rock only an inch or so beneath the ice; I worked my way up a little farther, trying to limit the weight I placed on each crumbling snow hold, dug again and found some ice; I got out an ice-screw and started screwing it in, but could not get any purchase.

Tap it, you fool, I told myself, and I did; edged it in a little farther; *Thank God, it's biting;* and, using the pick of my ice-hammer as a lever, I wound the screw round and in.

Suddenly I felt safer and was able to notice my surroundings once again. The crest of the ridge was only fifty feet above.

A muffled shout from below.

'What are you planning to do, Chris? I'm freezing down here.'

'I'll try to reach the ridge,' I shouted back, and fixed a sling on my ice-screw. But once I started to move again, I realized how cold I was. My rucksack with my anorak was down below, and the rising wind was whipping through my jacket. After a few tentative moves, my resolve weakened and I returned to my peg, fastened the rope to it and slid back to Tom. It was midday and we had only gained two hundred feet.

We got back to camp in the early afternoon. At least this gave me plenty of time to plan movements for the next few days. I used a note-book and a kind of snakes-and-ladder system, to calculate movement of personnel and loads. My other task was to sort out priority of loads. At the moment we needed the tentage for Camp IV and ever more rope. Rations were easy to calculate, for they were in two-man-day packs, weighing about eight pounds each. At this stage I was concerned with all movement above Base Camp, while Kelvin was still supervising the ferrying of equipment from Temporary Base, with the twenty porters he had held back. We had equipped them with anoraks, trousers, boots and blankets, specially brought out for this purpose. In addition, Kelvin scrounged as much spare gear as he could from the rest of the team, and with characteristic generosity gave up almost all his gear and quite a few items belonging to other people as well.

The 5.0 p.m. call was the main one of the day, and could take anything up to three-quarters of an hour by the time I had given out my orders, discussed modifications to them, and dealt with all the individual requirements of the different camps. And then there was always a good session with John Edwards, our T.V. producer, on distribution magazines for the little autoload cameras we were using, the instructions for their use, discussion on exposures and so on.

It was very noticeable how quickly everyone's use of the wireless improved, and by the end of the expedition it was a really swinging wireless net. Even the taciturn Dougal lent a certain dry humour to the evening's wireless conversation.

That evening I had to make some major adjustments. It was time for Tom and myself to go back to Base Camp for a rest; this also would give me a chance to see the state of all the camps and co-ordinate with

Kelvin, who had now very nearly cleared Temporary Base, how we could boost the flow of supplies up the mountain.

We were short of manpower. Pemba Tharkay and Ang Pema, who had been carrying loads from Camp II to Camp III for the last fortnight, were also in need of a rest, and I decided to send them back to Base Camp the following day. Dave Lambert, who had moved up to Camp II three days before, had failed to acclimatize and after one carry to III had returned to Base to organize medical supplies for the Face and recuperate. This meant that five of the team would be at Base Camp, while Nick Estcourt and Martin Boysen, who had just finished their rest, were now on their way back up the mountain. But as far as load-carrying went they were unproductive, for they could only carry their personal belongings yet needed three days to get back up to Camp III, and were using up tent space on the way.

Mick Burke, only just recovered from his attack of piles, and Mike Thompson and Ian Clough, who were still only partially acclimatized, were at Camp I with four Sherpas. I decided to move Mike, Ian, Mingma and Nima up to Camp II the following day, which would leave Pasang, Kancha and Mick Burke to do a carry. I also asked Kelvin, now established at Base Camp, if he could start using our local porters on the carry up to Camp I. He agreed to send three the following day, though we were all worried about the technical difficulty and danger of the glacier they would have to cross.

Don now felt rested, so we agreed that Don and Dougal should try to reach the ridge next morning, supported by Tom and myself, who would then go straight back down to Base. It was a bitterly cold morning and Don was obviously having trouble on the feed ropes. It was so cold that it made him feel sick and giddy. I couldn't help fearing that this might be a recurrence of his attack of vertigo. At one point he paused to take his boots off and rub his feet to get warmth back into them. But he was determined to go on, and slowly worked his way up the rope. Tom and I had brought up loads of rope, and while we waited for Don, Tom said, 'May I make a suggestion?' (He always prefaced his good and well-thought-out ideas with this modest opening. 'I think there's going to be quite a delay here, so I might just as well go back to the camp and pick up another load of rope, while Dougal leads the next pitch.'

It was not far back to camp, but it meant using five hundred hard-earned feet in deep powder snow. Admittedly the track had now been made, but it took a lot to go all the way back and ferry up another load.

And time fled by; clouds were already creeping up the valley, drawing a curtain across the sheer walls of Modi Peak and the Fang. I couldn't help envying Dougal as he pushed up to my high point of the previous day, and then slowly worked his way above it. It was even steeper than it had looked. Don straddled across the groove, trying to get extra purchase from his crampons. The snow was soft and insubstantial, and underneath it the ice was full of holes. At the top it reared into a real wall. He tried to hammer in a snow-stake, but it only went in a few inches. Holding it gingerly, he bridged his legs across the ice runnel, cut holds for his hands and pulled up onto the crest in the gathering storm. We could only just hear his voice.

'What's it like?'

'Ne'er so good . . .' and the rest was blown away with the racing snowflakes.

'Well, there's no point in going up in that,' Don observed matter-of-factly, and he shouted up into the mist, 'Come on down, Dougal.'

When he joined us Dougal told us that the gully didn't extend to the top of the ridge, as we had hoped, but merely onto a subsidiary spur. There was still difficult ground beyond.

It was 18 April. Eleven days had ticked by since Don and Dougal had reached the Col, and we were now only a thousand feet above it. I couldn't help worrying about the slowness of our progress as Tom and I started back down.

Nick and Martin had already reached Camp III when we passed through it. They had had a hard time ploughing up the gully in all the soft snow and were feeling the altitude. Martin just plunged into the box and lay back exhausted. Nick fussed around and exasperated me by saying, 'I can't think why you tried to go up the ridge; I should have thought it was obvious to anyone that you had to go round the side.'

CHAPTER 9

Back to Base
[18–23 April]

om and I finished packing our rucksacks, leaving a proportion of
our gear in polybags outside the boxes to reduce the weight of our
loads when we returned up the mountain, and plunged down the
couloir.

Tom went first, glissading down, and I followed. It was an exhila-
rating yet slightly scary plunge down the gully into a white mist of
nothingness, and I kept braking myself with the ice-axe to avoid going
out of control. At the bottom Tom took a different route from the one
we had followed on the way up, farther across to the left. It took us close
to the ice cliffs that threatened the basin at the foot of the gully, and for
a few minutes we were scrambling over ice blocks that had fallen from
the séracs. We wound our way down the glacier, stopping for a cup of
tea at Camp II, and meeting Mike Thompson and Ian Clough on their
way up to the camp. They seemed to have recovered from their bouts of
flu, though both were still coughing.

We continued past Camp I, down the long slopes of the Rognon and across the bottom glacier. It was now almost free of snow, a mysterious place in cloud reminiscent of those Victorian Alpine prints with improbable ice towers, huge over-dramatic crevasses and spidery arêtes—it was a place of many different tones of grey, from the rocks scattered over its surface and the grit that discoloured its ice. The route had also changed and at one stage we were lost on the way across.

We reached Base Camp just in time for the five o'clock call. It was a different place from what it had been ten days before. The snow had melted, revealing grassy meadows scattered with alpine flowers. There were four big two-man tents, all dominated by the radio aerials of our rear link to Pokhara. Kelvin had demonstrated his military background by erecting notices all over the place— one outside his own tent stating: *Headquarters, Annapurna South Face Expedition.*

Tukte greeted us with a broad grin and mugs full of tea. We had arrived just in time for supper—soup followed by steak from the Expedition buffalo—now slaughtered—and chips; Tom and I managed two large helpings each. It was like being in a different world from that of the mountain, though in a matter of time it had only taken us four hours to get all the way from the high point, just below the crest of the Ice Ridge at an altitude of around 21,000 feet, back to Base Camp.

The following morning we were able to lie watching Don and Dougal through the binoculars: two tiny black dots seeming almost motionless, like tiny insects on the ruffled cockscomb of the Ice Ridge. Here at 14,000 feet we could strip off without being flayed by the savage rays of the sun, but on the ridge it was more like being on the moon; it was a place of extremes in heat and cold. One moment, in the morning sun, it was stupefyingly hot, yet you could not strip right off for fear of having the skin burnt off you, and even with a protective covering of glacier cream faces were burnt raw; then in a matter of minutes, when the afternoon cold rolled up the mountain, you were freezing cold, toes nipped by frostbite; clothes dampened with sweat from the heat of the sun became chilled and clammy. There was no in-between—just blazing heat or icy cold emphasized by the ever-present glare of snow, even in heavy cloud. This might sound over-dramatic, good tabloid stuff, but this is what Himalayan climbing is like. It is difficult to comprehend the harshness of the extremes unless you have actually been at altitude. It is the nearest thing we have on earth to the moon. And yet man is adaptable, and we quickly came to accept this way of life as the norm, not even mildly amazed as we lay in the sun at Base Camp, watching the little black ants slowly plod up the mountainside. Don and Dougal on the ice ridge, Ian, Mingma and Nima toiling up the long gully leading to Camp III.

Altitude was taking its toll: at Camp II Mike Thompson had decided to take the day off, he was feeling so ill, largely from the after-effects of flu; at Camp III Nick and Martin were also laid out, partly the result of altitude sickness and partly from the effects of the paraffin fumes given off by the stoves. The Camp III headache became familiar to all members of the expedition whenever they arrived at this camp for the first time, or even when they returned after a rest back at Base Camp; 20,000 feet seemed to be a critical height for all of us. At the time Nick and Martin felt they had got little benefit from their rest and, in fact, felt less acclimatized than when they had been up before.

Don and Dougal had therefore gone out on their own, trying to push the route up onto the crest of the ridge. Once again Dougal took the lead. At this stage of the expedition Don was happy to stay in the support position, nursing his strength and slowly building up fitness. It was a combination that worked well, for Dougal loved to be out in front, using his skill and drive to the full, yet relying a great deal on Don's considerable mountain wisdom. In this respect they formed a balanced team, Don being the brain and Dougal the muscle. Around camp, they divided tasks equally happily; Dougal did all the cooking while Don did the practical jobs of securing the box or tent, or repairing a primus stove.

Don's approach to climbing and, for that matter, to most problems in life is that of a craftsman, eminently practical, down to earth and set within definite limits.

They both climbed the fixed rope left by Dougal on his high point the previous day. This was a small, knife-edged saddle on a subsidiary arête about fifty feet below what seemed to be the main ridge. It was an awe-inspiring spot. Above them the arête soared in a fragile wafer of snow into a curling wavelike cornice; no hope there. To the right lay a near-vertical gully that also vanished into the cornice, while on the other side was a preposterous mushroom of decaying snow. Dougal chose this as the only course remotely possible.

He teetered across the head of the gully, taking some tension on the rope from Don. The snow was similar to what Tom and I had encountered near the foot of the ridge. There was no substance to it, however much you cut away, and here it was so steep that Dougal was afraid he might be undermining the entire ridge.

He reached the corner and found that the mushroom was even more unstable than it had seemed from a distance. It must have weighed hundreds of tons, yet seemed fastened to the ridge only by a honeycomb of rotten ice, which Dougal had to climb over. He bridged out between the wall and the mushroom of snow, trying not to put more pressure than necessary on the unstable mass of snow. It was no use putting in ice-screws or snow-stakes for they would inevitably have been pulled out if he had fallen, and anyway there was the fear that they could have pinned him like a helpless butterfly if the mushroom collapsed.

At midday the afternoon clouds rolled in, blotting the pair from our view down at Base Camp. With the cloud came the snow and soon Dougal was forced back. He had reached the crest of the ridge, but that day he had only advanced fifty feet and what he had seen in front was not encouraging. They abseiled back down the fixed ropes to spend the rest of the afternoon cramped in their box, brewing unpalatable fruit drinks and meditating on the future.

Back at Base Camp it was time for lunch—salmon, oysters, tuna fish, anchovies and Russian salad, accompanied by smoked cheese and pâté, washed down with pint mugs of coffee. Such was the comparative luxury of Base Camp living.

Life at Base Camp fell into a placid routine. Early-morning tea was brought round at about 6.00 a.m., just before the morning sun had crept above the ridge linking Machapuchare with Annapurna III. At about 6.30 the warm rays of the sun touched the big mess tent, which the climbers made their transient home during their short stays below. Another half-hour and the seven o'clock radio call would drag us out of bed.

From that moment on, Kelvin Kent had a full day. Immediately after the radio call he sorted out the loads for the local porters carrying up to Camp I. The twenty men we had retained to ferry all the loads from Temporary Base to Base Camp had now completed their task, and he had retained six of the strongest men for the carry forward of Base. None of these men had ever been on glaciers before, but they took to it like naturals. Their loyalty and enthusiasm were undoubtedly largely due to Kelvin: he could speak to them in their own language, and made sure they were adequately equipped and well looked after. We had brought a certain amount of gear for our auxiliaries and he supplemented this by giving up almost all his own clothing and scrounging from the rest of the team, often being as generous with other people's gear as he was with his own.

Kelvin ran Base Camp rather like an Army barracks. As a result meals were on time, the porters got away from camp fairly early in the morning, stores were kept tidily so that one could find any items one wanted. Some members of the team were undoubtedly irritated by Kelvin's hyperefficiency, so different to the easy-going ways of climbers. He laid himself open to criticism at times through a combination of over-enthusiasm and lack of mountain experience. But even so everyone came to respect him for the amount of work he managed to get through, and there is no doubt at all that his efforts on the lower parts of the mountain made as important a contribution to our eventual success as those of any other member of the team. Before we met, I had once written to him: 'I am sure you are going to be a very efficient staff officer to a pretty scatterbrained general.' In the event this proved very true.

While Kelvin chased around on his administrative chores the three members of the T.V. team, the other permanent inhabitants of Base Camp, adopted a more pedestrian routine, spending the mornings doing a little filming around the camp or endlessly washing their clothes or themselves. This perhaps delineated one of the big differences between climbers and ordinary mortals, for the climbers rarely washed either themselves or their clothes. On the mountain we didn't wash at all, since it would have used up too much fuel to melt the necessary snow. I usually had one all-over wash when I got back down to Base Camp after a spell on the mountain of ten days or more and that sufficed for the time down at Base Camp, so I'd have my next wash two or three weeks later when I next came down. Other members of the team were on the Face for even longer periods; for instance, Mick Burke had one spell of twenty-eight days on the Face. Climbers are undoubtedly an untidy bunch, and the state of the communal mess tent rapidly deteriorated whenever climbers were resting at Base Camp.

As Nima Tsering, our youngest Sherpa, summed it up very aptly when he looked in one morning after a hard night's drinking: 'You Sahibs are like buffalo; filthy lying, filthy eating.'

But the T.V. team were very much more civilized. Their presence at Base Camp undoubtedly helped to keep standards up and at the same time provide a broadening influence, for although they became deeply involved in the climb, their interests were wider than ours. Even T.V. shop provided a welcome break from climbing shop.

Everyone met for lunch, the key meal of the day, and we sat outside talking or gossiping until we were driven back into the tents by the afternoon cloud. Everyone then took a siesta, meeting again at the evening radio call, which the T.V. team usually put on tape. This was followed by pre-supper drinks and then supper. After the meal we played liar dice or Scrabble, with our tape-recorder blasting out music in the background.

The expedition provided a change from the normal existence of the T.V. team. Alan Hankinson immersed himself completely in the life of the expedition, carrying loads first up to Camp I, and eventually to Camps II and III. The remaining three took a less active part but were nevertheless very much part of the team—John Edwards acted as Base Camp manager in the latter stages of the climb when Kelvin was ferrying loads on the mountain.

They only once ventured onto the mountain, when they crossed the bottom glacier to film the séracs that threatened our route. They ensconced themselves on the slope overlooking the glacier in what they thought was a safe place, set up the camera and sat down to wait for a good sérac avalanche. Suddenly they heard a rattle of falling stones behind them. Some icicles on the rock wall above had been melted in the sun, had collected some rocks on the way down and were rattling down the hillside towards our intrepid T.V. team. John Edwards dived for cover, but Jonathan Lane, the cameraman, played it cool, pausing to switch on the camera before getting out of the way. The camera was hit by one of the stones and its zoom lens irreparably smashed, but it made a dramatic finish to one of John Edwards's news reports. This was the last time they ventured out of Base Camp, however, before the end of the expedition, when they went to the glacier edge to welcome Don and Dougal.

Tom and I had chosen a good time to come down for a rest, for on our second day down it snowed all day, the first and only time this happened until the later stages of the expedition. There was no movement on the mountain and from Camp II Ian Clough reported that avalanches were pouring down both round and over the tents, which were only saved by the way they were tucked under the rock overhang.

The following morning, 21 April, dawned fine. I was planning to return to the Face that day but decided to wait till after lunch, to get in one more good meal before returning to austere living.

Meanwhile the parties on the Face were having a hard time. Two feet of new snow had fallen the previous day. Mike and Ian, with Mingma and Nima, tried to force their way up to Camp III. They were up to their knees in fresh snow, but more serious than that, powder snow avalanches were pouring down the sides of the ridge and the gully itself. They got about half-way up but were then forced to retreat. On the way up, however, Ian fixed some more rope in position. It was obvious that we should have to fix-rope the entire gully if we were to keep the route open after snowfall.

At Camp III all four climbers got out onto the ridge. Dougal once again took the lead and tackled a knife-edged arête leading onto the top of the big ice cliff. It was still hard, nerve-racking climbing on insubstantial snow. It took Dougal all day to make fifty feet of progress onto the crest of the ridge. Watching him through binoculars and seeing just how far he had to go before getting to the end of the ridge, I could not help worrying about whether we should be able to climb the ridge at all, for though we had bypassed the lower section we were still only just over half-way along it. The previous day Dougal had mentioned that he had not seen any avalanches coming down the gully to its side, even after heavy snowfall, and had suggested that we might think of following it if the ridge took too long. I suggested this to Tom, but he was so convinced of its potential danger that he said, 'If you go into that gully I guess I won't be going above Camp III.'

At the evening radio call I was still worried about our progress and opened to Dougal, 'Looking through the binoculars it looked very hard. I imagine you've got bad news for us.'

'On the contrary. It looks good. I reached a perfect camp-site today. The ridge opens out into a crescent of fairly easy-angled snow above the ice cliff. We'll be able to fit a box onto it without any trouble and are going to take one up tomorrow.'

The route eventually taken went up the gully to its immediate right.

143

Haston, on the first ascent of the spur leading to the rest of Ice Ridge, investigates the possibility of turning to the left of the huge ice above him.

'What's it like beyond?'

'Not too bad; it should be a lot easier than what I've just done.'

I had a tremendous feeling of relief and jubilation at this encouraging news.

We had had another bonanza back at Base Camp in the shape of unexpected reinforcements. Just as we were sitting down to lunch two men and a couple of girls walked into the camp. We invited them to join us, and over lunch learnt that they all came from Essex, were climbers and had driven out by Land-Rover hoping to climb in the Hindu Kush. A collision in Austria had delayed them and they had reached Afghanistan too late to do any climbing but had spent the winter there, planning to visit Nepal in the spring. They had driven the Land-Rover to Katmandu and had then flown to Pokhara, from where they had trekked across to the foot of the Dhaulagiri Massif and then back over the Deroli Pass to Chomro, to have a look at the Sanctuary.

Almost jokingly, I suggested, 'You can pay for your lunch by doing a carry up to Camp I.'

Their leader and spokesman was Frank Jackson, a big, well built man with a huge beak of a nose, jet black hair and a black beard. We gave him the nickname of Black Jack.

'That'd be great. We'd like to get above the snow-line anyway.'

'Well, in that case,' chipped in Kelvin, 'you could always stay at Camp I and do a few carries up to Camp II.'

'Suits us, but we'll have to go and get our gear.'

And in this way we recruited the 'London Sherpas', as our own Sherpas labelled them. The two girls stayed at Base Camp while Black Jack and Rob the Gob, so named because he ate so much, carried loads as high as Camp III and even made one trip up to Camp IV. We were so short on manpower that the help they gave us was a very real contribution to our eventual success. The presence of Babs and Cynth at Base Camp was also welcome, giving it a more relaxed and civilized atmosphere.

After their arrival we had a fairly steady stream of visitors, many of whom were recruited into making at least one carry up to Camp I and some higher. This influx was very different from what I had experienced on either of my two other Himalayan expeditions, and enhanced the almost Alpine character of the climb. The fact that from Base Camp one could watch the action on the Face with an orchestra-stalls view of the stage; the fact that Base Camp was in a meadow of brown sun-dried grass; that people could call in to see us; that we had with us a television team—all this turned the expedition into a kind of Eiger Direct ascent on a vastly greater scale, rather than an old-style Himalayan expedition.

For instance, when Maurice Herzog and his team arrived at the foot of Annapurna in 1950, their biggest problem was finding a route onto the mountain. We didn't even need a map to find ours. There was nothing unknown about the terrain; the mystery was entirely that of the climbing, whether we could contend with the complex difficulties of the Face at altitude. Once on the Face one felt as isolated and at as great a risk as one would have done on any mountain in the world; but this feeling is absolute for any big face. For instance, you can feel it on the North Wall of the Eiger in winter, with the skiers flashing down the Lauberhorn just opposite.

The difference on the South Face was that it all lasted so much longer, that altitude took such a heavy toll of one's endurance and, perhaps above all, the feeling of lurking threat on a great face. The scale of everything was so huge—the glacier, the ice cliffs, the avalanches that came creaming down from the walls around us. It was now three weeks since Don and Dougal had reached the Col, at the start of the real difficulties, and we had only advanced a further twelve hundred feet.

I was anxious to get back onto the mountain and found the walk up to Camp I, which had been so laborious only ten days before, comparatively easy; I was at last becoming acclimatized. I now had to work out our movements for the next two days. Don and Dougal were due for a rest, so the obvious step was for Nick and Martin to move up to Camp IV as soon as it could be established, to try and force the route to the end of the Ice Ridge. This meant that another pair needed to move up to Camp III, in support. Mick Burke was now on his way back up the mountain and was at Camp II with Mike Thompson and Ian Clough. In some ways the logical step would have been to move two of them up to Camp III, and for Tom Frost and me to have worked our way up the mountain behind them. If I had carried out this course I should have been following our original plan of pairs slowly working their way up the mountain, ferrying loads and then having a spell out in front before going down for a rest. I was anxious, however, to get up to Camp III as quickly as possible, to be immediately behind the front pair. This seemed the best position to control events and to keep an eye on the route being made up the Ice Ridge, and also on the stocking of Camp II, which was obviously going to become a vital camp, a kind of advanced base. Back at Camp I, or even tucked away under the Ice Ridge at Camp II, it was very difficult to conceive what was going on out in front.

I therefore decided to break up the pairing and move up to Camp III with Ian, since he now seemed to be getting acclimatized while Mick Burke, still recovering from his attack of piles, was an unknown quantity. Meanwhile, the same day that I slogged up to Camp II, Don, Dougal, Nick and Martin carried the gear for Camp IV up onto the Ice Ridge. I don't think any of the people who went there later realized how much hard work went into digging out the platform for Camp IV, for the slope was around thirty degrees, and they had to dig out a considerable depth of snow to get the box horizontal. Martin told me afterwards, 'Don quickly assumed the role of site foreman, keeping us digging in ten-minute shifts until the job was done.'

The supply problem, however, was now becoming critical, for while the front four were establishing Camp IV, Ian Clough and his party at Camp II had failed for the second day running to reach Camp III. They had got half-way up the couloir, when Mick Burke had been nearly swept away by a powder snow avalanche. It had seemed much too dangerous and so they had retreated. I reached Camp II, coming up on my own, in the late afternoon. Tom Frost was to follow the next day. On the way up I had noticed with relief that the Sword of Damocles had collapsed, probably that morning. The collapse had been much more extensive than I had anticipated, and a section of cliff about a hundred feet long had obviously come away, littering a wide area with a frightening debris of ice blocks. If anyone had been in the area at that time he would almost certainly have been killed.

I couldn't help feeling nervous as I picked my way through this graveyard of destruction; one could move so very slowly oneself, whilst the collapse must have been so devastatingly sudden. I glanced up at the cliffs brooding silent above me and hurried fearful along the gangway over the piled ice blocks. The effort had been too much, and the last few hundred feet up to Camp II seemed never ending. Mingma must have noticed me slowly toiling up the slope and came down to carry my rucksack the last few yards. It was a very kind gesture and typical of the consideration of our Sherpas.

At the camp I found that they were all seething with plans.

'We must get some food up to the lads,' said Ian. 'They're very nearly out. We've decided to have another try to reach Camp III tonight when it's dark. I think this is the only time when the gully will be safe, because there's still a hell of a lot of fresh snow to come off the ridges on either side of it.'

I wasn't over-enthusiastic, largely, I suspect, because I was tired from

Erecting the Whillans Box, a revolutionary development in high-altitude tentage. It is roomy inside and will withstand the weight of considerable quantities of powder snow piling around and on top of it. In this respect it was superior to a conventional tent.

my afternoon slog up to the camp and anyway never function very well at night. If I have a lot of work to do I prefer getting up in the early hours of the morning.

'How about trying to get away before dawn?' I suggested.

'You'd have to get away bloody early. The sun hits the gully at about 6.0 a.m., and the avalanches start soon after that. I'd rather get going in the evening before settling down than have the business of getting out of sleeping-bags and trying to cook in the early hours of the morning.'

Since they had made their plans and were obviously keen to go through with them I had no choice but to concur. I also felt obliged to volunteer to help in the carry.

We had a leisurely supper prepared by our two Sherpas, and then sat packed into the Whillans Box drinking coffee laced with whisky and waiting for the cold of the night to freeze the snow. It was a superb night and a three-quarter moon brightly lit the peaks about us. We started to get ready at about nine o'clock. It was then that we discovered that Nima had never worn crampons before; this didn't seem to disturb him, however, and we showed him how to fit them to his boots and were soon ready to set off. We all had head torches, but barely needed to use them, it was so light.

Once we started moving my lack of enthusiasm for the project vanished. The mountains had a mysterious beauty they never had during the day. As we plodded up by the side of the glacier we could look down and over it to the dark gulf in which was hidden our Base Camp. There was none of the glare or blazing heat of daytime; just a clear-cut gleam that left opaque shadows in the storm-racked waves of the glacier, and a cold, as hard and clear-cut as the light itself, that froze the snow into a crisp, firm surface. Crampons bit with an incisive crunch into snow, and for the first time on the expedition I felt I could plod on for ever without pausing every few steps for a rest.

We followed the fixed ropes left by Ian earlier that day. When we reached the high point he towed another five-hundred-foot spindle of rope behind him to get more fixed ropes in place. Ian, ever conscientious, always did that little bit of extra work, in fixing rope, improving a route or carrying an extra heavy load. We could see his head-lamp bobbing up and down far below us as we plodded steadily up the gully.

We reached the top at midnight, letting out a war whoop to let the occupants of Camp III know we had arrived. They did not appreciate being woken up but were certainly glad to get some food.

Going back down is always more difficult than going up, and we had fixed rope in place only part of the way up the gully. It was a hard test for Nima Tsering cramponing down fairly steep, iron-hard snow, but he moved as if he had been using crampons for years. We got back to Camp II at about two o'clock in the morning and tumbled into our sleeping-bags.

We had planned to sleep in the following morning, but it is not easy to alter sleeping habits and we were all awake by seven. There was no question of going up to Camp III that morning, but Mick and Ian were quite keen to try going up again the following night. I was not so happy: it was all right in bright moonlight, but in cloud or once the moon began to wane it would have been less pleasant and, anyway, we didn't have enough torch batteries to keep the head-lights going. In addition the Sherpas were not keen to go out again at night. We hummed and hawed and eventually reached a compromise solution that we should set off in the early evening once the couloir was in shadow. Mick Burke set off first, but was soon back.

'It's no good,' he told us. 'The snow is still much too soft; we were going up to our thighs in it.'

'In that case,' I said, 'I think we should wait till tomorrow morning. It'll mean we shall have lost today, but at least we can get things back onto a regular routine.'

That same day Don and Dougal returned to Base Camp for their allotted rest. Mike Thompson decided to join them. He was still suffering from the after-effects of flu. Meanwhile Nick and Martin had moved up to Camp IV to settle themselves in. Although it had been heavy going to the foot of the fixed ropes up the arête leading to the crest of the ridge, it was both shorter and a great deal safer than the route between Camps II and III. As the climb progressed we were to find that the higher we got the easier it was to keep going in the face of heavy snowfall.

Don and Dougal had also carried loads up to Camp IV prior to descending to Base Camp. Before leaving Camp IV Don had turned to Martin and said:

'Don't mess around, lad, and don't let those ice towers stop you.'

CHAPTER 10

Struggle for the Ice Ridge
[23-27 April]

amp IV was like the eyrie of a lammergeier, dug into the crest of the ridge, its front zip entrance looking out onto the yawning gulf of the Annapurna South Glacier below and framing the cleft peak of Machapuchare, some eight miles away. Above, the crest of the ridge was barred by a series of towers that looked like a jumble of ice-cream cornets that had overflowed their cones. Beyond these, the ridge became wafer-thin with cornices overhanging the left-hand slope, but resting on a solid rock base that was visible on the right. If Martin and Nick could reach this we hoped that they would have cracked the main difficulties.

Next morning (24 April) they were both excited at the prospect of getting out in front. They had now been on the mountain for three weeks, but this was their first opportunity to get out in front and pioneer part of the route, something that made all the days of arduous load-carrying seem worth while.

'I felt like Jack the Giant Killer,' said Martin afterwards, 'as we stepped into the shadow of the first Ice Giant.'

They didn't have to go far to start climbing. The slope above the box steepened quickly to a corridor nestling between a small ice gendarme and the overhanging base of the first ice tower. They first looked at a gully that went round the left-hand side of it. From a distance they had been able to see that this turned the first two towers, but once Martin climbed into it he found it was full of steep, rotten snow that slid away as soon as he put any pressure on it. It was much too nerve-racking at such an early stage of the climb.

He then tried to get round to the right of the tower where the way was barred by an overhanging ice wall. The only way to surmount this was to put in ice-screws, and pull on these, but the ice was honeycombed and insubstantial, fracturing as the screw went in. There seemed little hope in this direction either. It was at this point that Martin noticed a hole that looked as if it might lead through the ridge. He took off his rucksack and plunged into it. The tunnel was about twenty feet long and only two feet high, running horizontally through the ridge. In places the way was partly blocked by icicles which Martin had to clear out of the way. It was like potholing in a deep freeze, with a dim, greenish light filtering through the icy walls. He was hoping that the tunnel would lead right through onto easier ground, but it didn't. He could see its end, a glaring porthole of dazzling light, and eventually poked his head out to find himself looking onto a sheer ice wall that seemed to drop away to the glacier two thousand feet below. The only hope seemed to be a traverse across the wall to where it went round the corner and the angle seemed to ease off. At least the ice here seemed fairly solid, and Martin was able to place a screw just beyond the exit of the tunnel and, swinging on this, hauled himself out onto the wall.

It was even steeper than it had appeared from the tunnel. He had to cut handholds in the ice to hold himself in balance, leant out on the screw and started hacking a line of foot- and handholds across the wall. He moved very slowly, yet very relaxed; this is Martin's style of climbing. You work out the sequence of steps and then cut them; you can't afford to waste energy on steep ice even near sea level, let alone at 21,000 feet. A few careful steps edging crabwise across the wall, the wall getting steeper, bulging above him so that he hangs on, arms, muscles aching; a step crumbles beneath his feet, but he adjusts his balance, fumbles with an ice-screw with one hand for he needs the other to cling onto the ice. It's difficult to get an ice-screw started, rather like an ordinary screw in hard wood—you first have to tap out a little hole to allow the thread to get a purchase.

He gets it in, it bites, but then it's hard to turn just one-handed. He slots the pick of his axe through the eye of the screw, turns it this way, but can only manage a short fraction of a turn each time for the axe keeps jamming against the ice, and his other hand is tiring. Eventually, the screw is right in and he is able to swing onto it, taking the weight off his arms. Time slips by imperceptibly, one hour then two. He reaches the corner, pulls himself round. The angle eases off very slightly, but he is now in a repulsively steep gully encrusted with shreds of half-melted snow.

He lunged round and slightly down into the gully, but his footholds collapsed beneath him. He began a desperate swimming motion, digging elbows, knees, feet, ice-axe into the bodiless wet sugar that just seemed to slip away from under him, until he managed to get himself precariously lodged on a slightly firmer layer below.

'I had been so frightened I had held my breath and now my lungs and heart were ready to burst,' Martin admitted. 'Only Nick will know how long I rested, but eventually I continued, feeling my way upwards, expecting to be disgorged at any minute.'

The rope behind Martin was dragging badly because of the friction caused by its passage through the tunnel and various piton runners. Towards the top the snow steepened, yet was as insubstantial as ever, and so he traversed out onto a vertical ice arête on the edge.

He was now fifty feet above his last running belay but had at last reached some ice that was sufficiently solid to take an ice-piton. He hammered one in, clipped in the karabiner, but was so exhausted that he forgot to clip in the rope. He then continued up the ice arête, his renewed confidence based on the false premise that a fall would be quickly arrested by the running belay he thought he had placed. If he had fallen he would have gone a long way, for in actual fact he was still fifty feet above that last running belay.

His arms were tiring from the incessant cutting and holding himself in to the sheer ice. By the time he reached the crest of the ridge he had used up the full hundred and fifty feet of rope, though he was only fifty feet or so immediately above Nick Estcourt, so wide had been his diversion.

This was the hardest piece of ice climbing that Martin, who is amongst the best climbers in the country, had ever tackled, more difficult even than many Scottish winter climbs that have the reputation for being the toughest in the world.

The next problem was to get Nick up.

'I'll drop the rope straight down to you,' Martin shouted. 'You can jumar up it.'

He threw the rope down, but it dangled about fifteen feet out from the base of the ice tower, because of the huge cornice that capped it. Nick eventually managed to rescue its end by climbing some distance down the slope below, but as soon as he pulled it tight the rope cut into snow of the cornice. To climb it Nick would have to tunnel up through the cornice with the ever-present risk that the whole mass would collapse on top of him.

He therefore decided to follow in Martin's footsteps, safeguarded by the climbing rope. Even this though was a difficult undertaking, in some ways harder than Martin's original ascent. Beyond the tunnel the rope gave him no support for it was running through a series of pitons on a slightly descending traverse leading round the corner. The steps had just taken Martin's weight but were now flaking away.

As Nick said afterwards, 'It was frightening enough on a rope; it must have been terrifying to lead.'

It took him nearly two hours to repeat the pitch, it was so difficult, and in fact on the traverse he probably got even less help than Martin had done from the rope, which was running away from him slightly downwards through the pitons. If he had slipped he would have spun into space on the end of the rope, the ice wall he was crossing overhung so much.

When he reached Martin on the ledge he was too tired to go through to lead the next pitch and so Martin, who was now well rested, continued in the lead.

Camp IV (21,300 feet) was a Whillians Box dug into the slope. Above, on the crest of the Ice Ridge, Boysen is tackling some of the most difficult ice climbing of the entire ascent, working his way round and up the ice towers towards the rocks just below the right-hand crest of the ridge.

He first tried to climb into the couloir on the left which they had first looked at, but it was appallingly loose and he very nearly fell off. Rebuffed, he returned to the arête and tackled a short ice wall that led onto another platform. From this he could see that the steep ice climbing probably finished about forty feet above; there was an obvious break in the ridge slightly to the right, but to reach it would have meant climbing a steadily overhanging ice wall. The arête to the left looked slightly easier, though it was still very steep, so he followed this, cutting a furrow in the honeycombed ice and then wriggling up to it. At least it enabled him to gain some height, though he was not at all sure where it would lead him.

It was just beginning to get uncomfortably steep when he pulled up onto a narrow shelf that had been completely invisible from below; overhung by the ice wall, it stretched horizontally across the Face towards the break in the arête they had seen from below. He started along this, wriggling along on his stomach. Slowly the shelf grew narrower and the roof above lower, thrusting his body from out of its slippery grip. About twenty feet short of the corner it dwindled away completely. He now had to use ice-pitons, but he had already used most of his stock on the lower part of the pitch. The rope had also got into a bad tangle and he was near exhaustion. He put in a couple of ice-screws, then, having run out of these, hammered in ordinary rock-pegs, which are much shorter than ice-screws and not nearly as secure. He was still a few feet from the arête when the rope behind him jammed solid. By the time they had cleared it, it was nearly five o'clock and they retreated for the day. 'He had got the ropes in an incredible tangle,' Nick said later, 'and in the end he stopped thinking and let me do the thinking for him. I lowered him back down to the ledge.'

And then a quick abseil back to the box. It was amazing, having spent all day in climbing less than three hundred feet up the ridge, to get back down again in a matter of minutes. The Ice Ridge obviously wasn't going to be easily cracked in spite of what Dougal and Don had said when they first arrived at the site of Camp IV.

They returned to the fray the next morning, with Nick having his turn out in front. Even getting to the previous day's high point was difficult, for their rope was draped over a huge cornice and they had to burrow their way through it to get back up. From the end of the traverse that Martin had almost completed, Nick worked his way across the last five feet of wall, swinging in étriers suspended from ice-pitons till he could pull up onto the corner.

He was back on frighteningly loose insubstantial ice; levering himself as high as he could from his last good ice-screw he managed to tap a long icepeg into a nose of rotting ice that jutted out from the profile of the arête. He then demolished all but the hard core of the nose to give him something to stand on and very, very gently transferred his weight onto it. As he pulled up onto the peg it came out in his hand. He very nearly teetered backwards, but somehow readjusted his balance and hugged back onto the ice. He clawed for handholds but the ice crystals just broke away under his grip. Somehow keeping himself in balance he pushed the ice-piton back into place and edged round the corner into a gully very similar to the one that Martin had climbed the previous day. He climbed this to the crest of the ridge and then, finding no ice solid enough for ice-pitons, dug a hole, buried a dead man in it and sat on top of it to hold it down in the event of any strain coming onto it. The crest of the ridge was a frightening place, for the ice that comprised it was so insubstantial that he felt the entire mass could collapse without warning.

There was no question of following the crest of the ridge, for it soared in a genuine knife-edge up to a fragile cornice. About a hundred feet to the right, however, rocks projected from the snow, a solid, safe-looking haven after all the insecurity of the Ice Ridge. It was now Martin's turn; he followed the crest of the ice arête for a short distance to where it steepened and then, digging a dead man into the insubstantial ice crystals, let Nick lower him into the gully which barred the way to the rocks on the right.

There was a terrifying moment when he first put his weight on the rope. He shot down for about three feet.

God, I've had it, he thought. Nick wasn't safely belayed, and it looked as if the dead man had pulled out.

But then he was abruptly brought to a halt. The dead man had been dragged deep into the crest of the arête until it bedded itself down. Martin was then lowered a further sixty feet or so into the bed of the gully, which was near vertical and composed of hideously unstable snow, until it was possible to edge over to the relative safety of the rocks, using tension from the rope to do this.

At least he was now on stable ground, but his problems were far from over. The rock was near vertical and sheathed in ice. There were plenty of piton cracks, but he couldn't use them for this would have caused too many complications with his rope as it would then have gone up through the dead man, down to a peg in the rock then up to Martin like a letter Z tipped on its side. This inevitably would have caused the rope to jam.

He therefore had to climb without any protection from pitons, though if he had fallen off he would have had a punishing pendulum back into the gully, something that could have imposed an excessive strain on the dead man through which the rope was running. The higher he got up the rock rib the fiercer would have been his fall, and the greater the likelihood of pulling Nick off his precarious belay.

The rock was plastered in ice, and though there were good holds underneath, it was very steep, tiring work, clearing away the ice and pulling up on the sheer rock blocks that seemed embedded in the ice. To make matters more difficult Martin was wearing rubber vapour-barrier boots, which were very warm, but which were more like ordinary Wellington boots than climbing boots. The soles were flexible and even with crampons on were unpleasantly bendy for hard climbing. It was a superb but very nerveracking lead.

Eventually Martin climbed the rib to a point slightly higher than the level of the dead man, put a peg in and slid back along the rope to the col just above Nick.

It had been another punishing day, as much from nervous tension as from the effort of doing complex, high-standard climbing at altitude. They were still only three hundred and fifty feet or so above Camp IV, but in those two days they had undertaken the most difficult ice climbing we encountered on the South Face, and I shouldn't be surprised if this was the toughest climbing ever tackled at this altitude.

They were so tired that the following morning Ian Clough and I, who had now reached Camp III and were ferrying loads up to Camp IV, caught them in bed. They made their way up to their high point, improving the fixed ropes on the way, and Martin once again went into the lead, climbing up the broken rocks that led up alongside the ridge above them. From a distance this had seemed straightforward, but as with so much of the Ice Ridge, closer acquaintance showed it to be both steep and difficult—great shattering blocks of smooth, hard rock piled one on top of the other, morticed together by flaky, crystalline ice. That day Martin reached a point only thirty feet or so above Nick, though to do this he had climbed very nearly a hundred, in an arching course, trying to probe the defences of the ridge.

That night, over the radio, Nick confessed, 'We're dead tired, Chris: we'll have to come down tomorrow.'

'Can't you go up and try to make a bit more progress before

Nick Estcourt on the 'Traverse of the Devil', pulling along the fixed ropes that lead to the end of the Ice Ridge.

returning?' I said. 'Otherwise we'll lose a complete day while we move up to take your place.'

'I'm sorry, but I don't think you can have any idea how tiring it is on this kind of ground. Martin's hands are torn to shreds and anyway we're both feeling pretty shattered. Even if we did manage to get up to our high point, we wouldn't be in any state to push on any farther.'

I had no choice but to accept their decision. They had done a really magnificent job, and we were soon to find that more than three days in succession of hard climbing was more than anyone could take. I don't think that any of us really appreciated just how hard was the climbing that Nick and Martin undertook, for the route we subsequently followed on the fixed ropes took a direct line where they had to weave their way from side to side to make the first ascent, and so none of us really experienced it.

While Martin and Nick had been battling with the ridge, Ian and I had been ferrying gear up to them, watching and filming them each day, before returning to Camp III. On our way up to Camp III on 24 May, Ian had completed the line of fixed ropes to the top of the gully and had tried to install a pulley system for hauling loads up through the snow from the top of the gully. We had brought out with us a windlass winch, designed for yachting but fitted on an alloy frame, so that it could be fastened in place on a ledge on the mountain. The windlass worked well, but we had to use three five-hundred-foot ropes tied together, and there was too much stretch. In addition the loads, packed in special hauling sacks, tended to dig themselves in the snow. As a result, the loads were pulled up the gully at a snail's pace, advancing a few feet only for half an hour's hard winding on the winch.

Tom Frost and Mick Burke took turns at winching, but even so it took several days of spasmodic effort to haul one, admittedly heavy, load all the way up the gully. After this experience we abandoned the winch and resorted to normal load-carrying. The fixed rope fitted by Ian made this both easier and safer, for with it there was less risk of anyone being swept away in the small powder snow avalanches that swept the gully after every snowfall.

On the lower slopes our two London Sherpas were supplementing the efforts of our Gurkha porters on the carry up to Camp I. They also did some valuable work straightening out the route across the glacier, which altered from day to day as the protecting mantle of winter snow thawed away. More and more crevasses were uncovered, and though the glacier became safer as a result, it also began to resemble an obstacle course. They even had to utilize some of the sections of ladder we had brought out to build makeshift bridges across the crevasses.

Meanwhile, down at Base Camp, Don and Dougal were relaxing in their own special way.

Each pair that went down to Base Camp for rests behaved differently. I tended to spend a lot of time catching up on administration when I was down, and in the evenings enjoyed playing Scrabble or liar dice. Nick and Martin tended to lie around reading and talking in the evenings, favouring Scrabble as a pastime—they were perhaps the most intellectual pair. Tom, of course, just sat quietly reading his Bible, while Ian was the most active, for ever teaching people to jumar on the crag immediately above the camp or helping Kelvin, who never seemed to stop working. Unlike the majority of climbers, Kelvin seemed to love work for its own sake, was for ever writing reports, planning logistic movement or organizing the kitchen. Even in play he put everything into it, whether it was liar dice or volleyball on a makeshift court. He didn't read much, simply because he rarely had the time. Mick Burke read widely and loved a discussion; he had a tendency to lay down the law and took himself rather seriously, and yet he also has a natural clowning ability and can be amazingly funny. He and I often argued, perhaps because I am equally fond of laying down the law.

Don and Dougal simply relaxed at Base Camp playing non-stop beat music over the tape-recorder; Dougal reading and Don, who very rarely reads, just sitting in the sun or lying in his sleeping-bag thinking his own thoughts.

On their first night down at Base Camp they had one of those wild, impromptu parties that always seem more memorable than anything one carefully plans in advance.

I think the booze-up was a form of total relaxation, a release from the tension of the Face. It started after supper with the group down at Base Camp passing the bottle of whisky round the circle. The T.V. team had gone off to bed, so there were just the London Sherpas, Kelvin, Mike, Don and Dougal.

They talked and drank—Don at his wittiest, for he is a superb raconteur—and they passed the bottle round, and talked some more and drank some more and drank.

Don suddenly realized it was time to go to the dance at Chomro, and dashed out of the tent to find his van. The others followed, to find him sitting on a packing-case, lit by the bright moon.

'The bastard won't start,' he told them. 'You'll have to give me a push.'

They duly pushed him off the packing-case, but the van still wouldn't start, so they decided to hold the dance at Base Camp. By this time the girls and Kelvin had made their escape, but Don and Dougal gyrated slowly round the tent to the beat of the music before returning inside to get back to some serious drinking. Half an hour went by.

'I'm going to the bloody dance,' said Don as he staggered up and tried to walk through the wall of the tent.

Kelvin, who looked out of his own tent at this stage, reported that the entire tent seemed to be moving. Eventually Don was slotted into his sleeping-bag and Mike, who is a very careful, calculating soul, had tucked himself safely out of harm's way in a corner, realizing the danger of people being sick. It must have been a weird, Rabelaisian affair, strangely enjoyable to take part in. It took a further two days for Don and Dougal to recover from their hangovers, during which time they succeeded in reducing John Edwards to the same dire straits that they had been in the previous night.

This was the only hard drinking session on the entire expedition. We had plenty of whisky—over four hundred miniatures and seventy-two full bottles—but people tended just to have a tot or so during the course of the evening.

Two days later, still recovering from hangovers, Don and Dougal were on their way back up the mountain. Next day, on 27 April, Ian Clough and I moved up to Camp IV, hoping to push on to the end of the ridge. Time now seemed to be running against us, for it was fully three weeks since Don and Dougal had reached the crest of the ridge at the site of Camp III, and since then we had only made about fifteen hundred feet of vertical progress.

CHAPTER 11

Still Struggling

[27 April–3 May]

L ife at Camp IV was that much sterner than in the lower camps. The box was exposed to the wind which bit, hard and cold, past the entrance, blowing flurries of powder snow in through the smallest chinks. The floor of the box had been moulded by the warmth given off from the bodies of Nick and Martin into a rounded depression, so that inevitably Ian and I ended up by sleeping on top of each other. It was difficult keeping the primus stove upright, and if one was untidy, which I am, the interior of the box soon became hideously squalid, with spilt food, clothing, film, cameras and sleeping-bag mixed together in a chaotic heap. We tried to hang up as much as possible from the frame, but this diminished the mess only very slightly. During the night the hoarfrost from condensation precipitated by our breathing formed on the roof, and each day, as soon as the sun came up, it melted, dripping onto our clothes and sleeping bag. If it was sunny all day there was a chance of drying out, but the weather now seemed to have settled into a pattern of afternoon snow, which seemed to arrive a little earlier every day. As a result everything, imperceptibly, became steadily damper.

We achieved comparatively little on our first day out in front. Martin and Nick had had enough on their hands just getting up this section for the first time. It was up to us to improve it before pressing on to new ground. Our first job was to cut away the huge cornice over which the rope ran. It was an impressive situation, for the rope was hanging free about two feet out from the sheer ice wall. To start climbing one had to swing out into space, over a drop of around three thousand feet down to the glacier below. I am sure this was the first time that this type of free jumaring had ever been necessary at this altitude in the Himalayas. Nick had already carried out the difficult task of making the initial passage through the cornice, but it still needed a lot of shovelling to make it practical for regular use by ferrying parties. We were then faced with the diagonal pitch across the wide ice gully leading to the rocks. We came to call this the 'Terrible Traverse'. I went across first. It was a frightening and exhausting experience, for I did not entirely trust the dead man anchoring the lower end of the rope, and a diagonal traverse on jumars is always arduous, particularly at 21,500 feet. The jumars tend to pull off the rope, and there is a great deal of friction. I tried to improve this section by lengthening the rope so that one started by abseiling into the gully and then swung across onto the rocks, following these on very much the same course that Martin had adopted. However, this merely prolonged the agony and sent one swinging over the sheer rocks on the side of the ridge. By the time I had reached the ledge on which they had left all their ropes the weather had broken. The ropes were in a tangle of knitting, half submerged in fresh snow. I struggled with frozen fingers for half an hour and then retreated back down the ropes to Camp IV, very impressed with what Nick and Martin had achieved in the past three days.

Usually the wind dropped at nightfall and the cloud cleared, but this time it kept up throughout the night, hammering at the box with an incessant roar. We settled down for the night at around 7.0 p.m. when it got dark. We had books, but reading became too great an effort by the

Reaching the top of the jumar pitch before the terrible traverse.

light of a candle. I drugged myself with a couple of sleeping-tablets, each of which was meant to guarantee eight hours' sleep, but in spite of these I woke up around midnight and dozed off and on for the rest of the night, my mind over-active with expedition problems. At dawn the wind was still hammering at the tent and it was bitterly cold outside. We even wondered if we should be able to get out at all, but by 7.0 a.m. the wind had dropped a little and we resolved to start.

Once we were both at the ledge just below Martin's high point, I jumared up the rope to the lip of an overhang where he had anchored. It was a stirring yet slightly frightening moment when I handed myself round the corner and was once again on virgin ground. I had pulled up over the overhang onto a sloping ledge. There seemed a way round to the right over a complex series of ice gullies and broken rock, but the line seemed too devious, as if it would be very difficult to make an easy ferrying route across it and it would also be a fair way from the crest of the ridge, and therefore more prone to avalanche and stonefall.

I then looked up to the left; a slightly overhanging corner led back

Looking down at Camp IV from the top of jumar pitch

towards the crest of the ridge. Getting a piton into its base I worked my way up, straddled out across the rock, jamming hands into the ice-filled cracks. I could not help being aware that even a slight fall could be fatal; it would have been desperately difficult getting back even with only minor injuries. The rope, running through several karabiners and round the lip of the overhang below, was beginning to drag badly. I had just reached the crest of a projecting nose, jutting out from the ridge, There was no ledge, just a couple of footholds and a crack for a piton, but above the rock reared in a steep groove to another overhang. I therefore decided to bring Ian up to me.

There was a long delay. You have to be very patient in this kind of climbing, for you function slowly anyway as a result of the altitude, and on top of this you have to sort out all the ropes. We did not want to make the route I had followed the permanent line of fixed ropes—it was much too awkward for that. By working my way back to the crest of the ridge I hoped we might be able to cut out the Terrible Traverse altogether. Ian was therefore carrying up the entire load of fixed rope left by Nick and Martin, a rucksackful weighing around forty pounds.

It was now his turn to lead; he worked his way slowly and methodically up the groove, placing pitons for his protection. An hour slipped by. I could watch the sea of clouds below slowly flow in through the gorge of the Modi Khola, then fill the basin of the Sanctuary, creep up the sides of the peaks, first engulfing Tent Peak, now far below us, then creeping up to the crest of Fluted Peak. It wouldn't be long before we also were engulfed. But for the moment we were in the sun. I felt tired and drowsy in its glaring heat. My clothes were damp with sweat from my exertion on the pitch I had just completed. I let my eyes wander across the Face, with its serried icefields and sheer rock walls—you could have fitted the North Wall of the Eiger into this huge area of snow, rock and ice six times over. Yet there were many reminders of the Eiger. A powder snow avalanche careered down the slope to the immediate right in a great, white cloud. Stones falling from the Rock Band whistled and warbled, landing in the snow just below me with a dull, sickening crunch. I couldn't help wondering if the upper snowfields above the ridge were going to be like this if and when we reached them.

And Ian continued climbing, absorbed in the task of making just those few feet of upward progress. He was now on the brink of the over-hang, cramponed boots scraping on iced rock, thrust out of balance by the overhang above.

'I'll have to use a sling here,' he called down.

Standing in a rope sling, suspended from a peg, he was able to reach up to another crack above the overhang and hammer in a further peg, clipped in another sling and pulled himself up. He was standing on a narrow ledge about forty feet above me.

'What's it like?' I shouted.

'Not too bad,' he replied. 'But I don't think it gets much easier ahead.'

I had to wait another hour while he safeguarded his stance with care-fully placed pitons. During this period the cloud crept up and engulfed us. Within a matter of minutes it had started snowing, and where I had been sweating only a short time before, I was now shivering with cold, my clothes chill and dank from sweat. By the time I had reached Ian there was no question of making any further progress, for it was obvi-ously going to take us some time to re-rig the fixed rope on the easiest possible line back down to the Terrible Traverse. I swung across onto an ice arête barring the view back down the ridge and looked over the top. We were looking straight down a rock ramp to the end of the traverse. There seemed no way of bypassing it, for the other end was still a long way across to the right.

We tried to improve the line of the fixed rope and returned to the box. I found there a little note from Dougal. He had pushed up to Camp III the previous day all the way from Camp I, a sign of how strongly he was going—while Don had taken a more leisurely two days for the trip. In his note he wrote: *Everyone seems very lethargic at Camp III; we must get things moving soon. Don has some ideas that he'll talk over with you on the radio.*

While out in front it was very difficult to keep a perspective of the entire expedition and to do all the necessary planning for the movement up and down the mountain. At the end of a hard day, like the one we had just had, when our horizon had been limited to the few feet of rock immediately in front, and nerves had been stretched by the stresses of leading, I just felt like collapsing into my sleeping-bag to drink endless brews and sink into a comfortable coma in preparation for the effort of next day. In this respect I always found it easier to plan and control the expedition from farther back, ideally at the camp immediately below the top one, where it was possible to keep in direct contact with the front party and at the same time get a broader view of the climb as a whole.

That night on the wireless Don came up with his ideas.

'I've been thinking on the way up from Base,' he said, 'and it seems obvious to me that we must stop people going all the way back to Base Camp for rests. In this way we are losing too many people and if we're not careful we'll lose all our momentum. I suggest, therefore, that we keep all the climbers at Camp III and above and let the Sherpas look after the carry from I to III. This means that people will rest at Camp III instead of Base; we'll save three days doing this.'

It sounded a good, obvious idea; one that I hadn't thought of at this stage largely because I had my nose too close to the immediate problem of pushing the next few feet of the climb farther forward. The only snag was that it was questionable whether one could gain sufficient effective rest as high as Camp III. Even so, I said, 'Sounds good, Don, let's stick to that.'

Don had already put his idea into practice. On arriving at Camp III Mick Burke had told him that he was still feeling shattered and that he intended to return to Base Camp for a rest. That day it had been all he could do to carry fifteen pounds of food up to Camp IV; a normal load would have been in the region of thirty pounds. He had been badly weakened by his piles and had had difficulties in acclimatizing. Don and Mick have a kind of love-hate relationship; from very similar back-grounds, in character they are similar yet very different. Mick pushes himself to the very limit; Don, on the other hand, tends to stand back and wait for people to come to him. He resented Mick's thrustfulness, and yet they had climbed and worked together over a period of years, quarrelling frequently, criticizing each other to their friends yet retaining a grudging respect and friendship.

Don went straight into the attack.

'You're always grumbling about not being out in front, but I don't see how you can expect to go into the lead if you can't even carry a few loads up the mountain. You've had more rest days than anyone else on the expedition.'

'What about you? You've only just got back from a rest down at Base and you've done precious little load-carrying.'

'That's as may be, but we've established every single camp so far. Anyway, if you want to go out in front on this trip, you'd better prove you can keep going.'

This kind of needling was the ideal treatment for Mick. I would probably have let him go down, for I believed that each person should make up his own mind about what he could or could not do, but Don was perfect in this situation, even if what he said was unjust.

Mick responds to challenges, to the degree that next day he broke trail almost all the way up to Camp IV, just to show Don that he could burn him off. It suited Don admirably and he coasted quietly along behind, taking advantage of the staircase of footsteps.

That day we had only made about a hundred feet of vertical progress and I was determined to do better than this. I woke up as usual about midnight and then didn't sleep at all, tossing plans and counter-plans around in my overactive brain. I stuck it out till three o'clock in the morning and then decided: to hell with it, let's start cooking. We can at least guarantee a start at the crack of dawn.

I squirmed round to the front of the tent in my sleeping-bag and lit the primus—always a long process, and particularly unpleasant by the light of a glimmering candle in sub-zero temperature. It took over an hour to melt a panful of snow, collected the night before. I woke Ian up with a mugful of hot 'Cola', the least unpleasant of the fruit drinks. We lay back in our sleeping-bags savouring the hot liquid, delaying the next step. I then prepared some kipper fillets, frying them in their can; another long delay. It was now 5.30—two and a half hours had slipped by. A glimmer of light began to filter into the box and I looked out. The stars had been washed out by the pallid light of dawn and glare behind Gangapurna showed where the sun would soon creep up over the far mountains. It was a fine day, but a tidal wave of cloud in the bed of the Modi Khola was a sure sign that the tide of cloud would roll in before the afternoon was out.

'It's bloody cold out here. Let's have another brew,' I suggested, and reached over the roof to scoop off some frozen snow. This would at least delay things till the sun hit the box.

The glare over Gangapurna increased, a segment of burning white light crept over the side of the wedge-shaped peak, and then within a matter of seconds the sun climbed up over the mountains, bathing us in a soft glow that had very little warmth in it. We lay in our sleeping-bags and waited for the box to warm up; another few minutes and we had no more excuses for staying put. Even so it needed a distinct effort of will to crawl out of the warm comfort of the bag, to force on frozen boots. I kept the felt inners inside the sleeping-bag, but the outers were too bulky and I used these as a pillow; even so, each morning they were frozen solid. We put on windproofs while still in the box and then crawled out to don our crampons and elaborate sit harnesses that Don had designed specially for climbing the fixed ropes. It was 6.30 before we were ready to set out, three and a half hours after I had woken up; this was slow, but of course the earlier one started the longer everything tended to take because of the dark and cold.

It took us over three hours to reach the high point of the previous day, for there was still quite a lot of work to be done in improving the route. In addition, we were short of rock-pitons and therefore had to remove any that were not essential. By the time we had both reached the high point and sorted out ropes, and Ian had belayed ready for me to try the next pitch, it was ten o'clock. The rock above was sheer, and though there were handholds they seemed few and far between. To the side of the rock was steep snow, and I opted for this. But it was similar to the snow lower down, rotten and honeycombed; however much I cleared away I never seemed to reach anything solid. Eventually I dug a

he side of the rock pinnacle and burrowed up alongside
p, exhausting work, shovelling away with the ice-axe
y head. It took me nearly an hour to reach the top of the
here I found a kind of ice cave. It was obviously out of
the question to follow the crest of the ridge. Our only chance of success
seemed to be a traverse round the broken rocks on the flank. I was only
thirty feet above Ian, and now started to work my way round a rock
corner clearing the piled encrustations of snow with my axe, placing
pitons for protection where I could and ever edging round the ridge. I
was soon out of sight of Ian; it was even difficult to hear him with so
many rock corners and projections to muffle our shouts. The rope
behind began to drag more and more, and the climbing seemed to be
getting more difficult. A frightening slab of soft snow led to a jutting
overhang formed by a great boulder that seemed embedded in the ice.
Swinging under this on a precariously placed peg, I was spreadeagled
across a sheer wall of ice, the rope behind now tugging me back at every
step I tried to edge forward. This was no good, and I resolved to return
to the last ledge to bring Ian up to a position where he could give me
more support. I edged my way back along my airy highway, and
brought Ian up to the cave at the start of the traverse. Three hours had
slipped by; I had gained thirty feet and traversed another sixty.

I always feel happier when I can see my second man. It gives one a
feeling of real support. But the weather was now turning against us; the
tide of cloud had risen around us, drowning us in its cloying embrace. A
few snowflakes were blowing around the ridge and suddenly in the flat,
white light the ridge looked even more menacing than it had before.

It was nearly two o'clock but I wanted to try to make at least a little
more progress that day, and so returned along the traverse. At least
there was now no rope drag, and I was reassured by the sight of Ian
peering round the corner of the ridge. I swung up onto a rock nose and
beyond this saw that I had a choice, either up a steep ramp onto the top
of a rock tower near the crest of the ridge, or round a steep-looking traverse line over near-vertical snow at its base.

I chose the high road and began edging up the ramp. The handholds were so small that I had to take off my gloves. I managed to hammer in a peg, but it had a dull, flat sound as I hammered, never a good sign, for this usually indicates that the peg is insecure. My hands were rapidly getting numb with the cold. I could no longer feel the slightly iced rock I was gripping, my crampons were scraping on rock, and suddenly I was very frightened. You couldn't afford to fall off in this kind of situation.

I slipped back down to my piton and looked round the lower traverse. At least this looked a little safer, but it was now snowing hard; I was shivering with cold and therefore returned to Ian, who was in an even worse state than I.

That afternoon as I returned to the box I was profoundly depressed and desperately tired. We had expended so much effort for so very little progress.

Ian said, 'At this rate I don't think we've got much hope of success; at least we've put up a good show.'

I think I agreed with him, but obstinately was not prepared to admit it. 'We must get to the end of the ridge soon,' I said. 'Things will speed up then.'

'Well, I'm going to have to go down tomorrow for a rest. I'm shattered.'

'That's O.K. We can get one of the others up. I'd like to stay up here until we get to the end of the ridge. Can you do one more day out in front though, so we don't waste tomorrow?'

'I'll do that all right if only I can make it back up the fixed ropes.'

When we got back to the box we made ourselves a brew and slumped into sleeping-bags in near coma condition, we were both so tired. It was an effort to get out the walkie-talkie set at 5.0 p.m. and to start thinking once again about what the rest of the team were doing on the mountain.

I got through to Camp III and asked to talk to Don. He very rarely came on the air, preferring to leave it to Dougal.

'Hello, Don, Ian wants to come down for a rest tomorrow. I want to stay on up as I seem to be going well, but could you send someone up to help? I leave the selection to you.'

'In that case I'll send Dougal up. When are you thinking of coming down?'

'Probably the day after tomorrow. Someone else can then take my place.'

I broke off from Camp III and contacted Kelvin at Camp I. He had the lower part of the mountain well in hand. He and the two London Sherpas had now moved up to Camp I, while the local porters were managing the carry from Base to Camp I on their own.

All the excitement seemed to be on the lower part of the mountain. Kelvin seemed to attract trouble with the power of an electromagnet. He had had one slip on the lower glacier and had been involved in two minor avalanches. Our two London Sherpas had both had narrow escapes. Black Jack had dropped through a hidden crevasse on his way up to Camp II. As Kelvin, who was carrying a load just behind him, described it, 'One moment he was plodding in front of me and I looked up a second later and he had vanished.' Kelvin crawled forward cautiously to look down a gaping hole in the surface of the snow, fully expecting to find that Jack had fallen into a deep crevasse. Fortunately it was shallow, but it was filled with water and he was soaked to the skin. That same day Rob the Gob slipped on the icy traverse below the Sword of Damocles and fell about fifty feet, scraping himself on the way down. Fortunately neither of them was too badly shaken by his misfortune, and they continued humping loads.

More serious was Pasang's state, and that of most of the occupants at Camp II. Pasang never really became fit, suffering recurrent attacks of dysentery throughout the expedition. At this stage he was at Camp II and the other Sherpas and Dave Lambert were also troubled. Dave even wondered if Pasang was perhaps a carrier.

On the wireless that night Dave warned that they were all going badly as a result of severe diarrhoea. The carry from Camp II to III was punishing anyway, because of its length and the afternoon fall of fresh snow that had become a daily occurrence. Each day they had to break a fresh trail. Without the fixed ropes put in place by Ian this part of the route would have been impassable.

Down at Base Camp John Edwards, who had taken over from Kelvin as temporary manager, had a slightly more light-hearted message, a bizarre reminder that the rest of the world was still grinding on in the same way that it always has done.

'Hello, Kelvin, at I. Do you read me?'

'Yes, John, loud and clear.'

'I've got a cable for you from your unit in Hong Kong. They want to know where the signature for authority is for a typewriter you had purchased before you left.'

Kelvin dictated a detailed explanatory cable that seemed strangely unreal in this little world of ours. To me nothing really seemed to exist beside the mountain. Our world was limited by the retaining walls of the Sanctuary. We had heard about the crisis of the Apollo XIII moonshot, but its return to earth, which had gripped the rest of the world, passed almost unnoticed. Our own struggle for survival and even more, our eventual goal, were too engrossing.

That night I took three sleeping-tablets, in the misguided expectation that I should be knocked out for at least twelve hours. In practice they gave me ten hours' deep sleep and I woke at 5.20 that morning.

Ian was still desperately tired, even talking of going straight down without having a session on the ridge, but I managed to persuade him to come up with me.

We set out at about eight, and I could see immediately that Ian was near the end of his tether. He had been on the Face for a week longer than myself, a fortnight altogether, and I don't think he had ever had the chance of recovering from his gruelling trip across India.

He succeeded in getting across the Terrible Traverse, but on the vertical ropes leading up to the crest of the ridge he just hung there like a lifeless sack.

'It's no good, Chris. I'm pilloxed. I'll have to go down,' he shouted.

'You've only got another hundred feet to climb and you'll be at our high point,' I shouted back. 'All you'll have to do then is hold the rope, so that I can at least get another pitch done.'

'I don't think I could even do that.'

I was desperate to make some progress that day, especially as I felt I was going quite well.

'In that case, I'll just have to press on and climb solo. I'll be able to get a bit of protection from the rope.' I'm not sure if I would have done but it had the desired effect.

'I can't let you do that, I'll get up somehow.'

Ian now moved slightly more quickly, but was obviously very tired. It was eleven o'clock before I reached my high point of the previous day. This time, instead of trying to climb the ramp up the side of the tower, I swung under it, making a slightly descending traverse across a near-vertical depression banked with snow. I was able to get some tension from the rope to the side, and, shovelling away the snow, eventually reached the rock core underneath, where I was able to find further cracks for my pitons.

Even so, it was slow, exhausting work. I pulled up onto a nose round another corner, and reached a huge mushroom of ice that seemed to be defying all the laws of gravity in the way it clung to the sheer rock above. The only possible route was down and under it, onto a fragile, wafer-like snow arête. I was able to hammer a piton into a crack just short of the ice mushroom, but I was still frightened that it might come away the moment I touched it, crushing me and perhaps cutting the rope.

I moved slowly and fearfully, edged my weight onto the wafer of snow, which collapsed beneath me, kicked frantically and found a solid purchase. At least I was now out of the fall line of the snow mushroom. A pull across onto a slab, and I was standing on a sloping ledge. The afternoon cloud had crept up unnoticed, and once again it was snowing. I could see that a deep-cut chimney led up round the corner, and at its top it even looked as if the difficulties might ease off.

I searched for ice-gummed cracks, eventually placed a piton, tied the rope to it and returned, tying off the fixed rope into each piton on the way back to turn my climbing-rope into a handrail for subsequent parties.

We returned in the usual afternoon snowstorm to find Dougal waiting in the box at Camp IV. Ian plunged on down towards Camp III, while I lay back in my sleeping-bag, happy to let Dougal brew a mug of tea. That night he made supper, a magnificent concoction of fried Spam and fried new potatoes.

'Don'll have a good try at stopping Ian going down farther than III,' predicted Dougal. He was right. Don tried to persuade Ian to rest at

Bonington jumars up a rock wall while taking part in the initial ascent of the Ice Ridge.

Camp III, but Ian was persistent. He was feeling badly run down and realized that he had little chance of recuperating at 20,000 feet. It was all very well for Don, who had only just come up from a rest at Base Camp, to decide that everyone should stay on the mountain to rest. And so Ian insisted on going down, reaching Base just before dusk that evening.

On the radio call Mick Burke came on the air.

'Look, Chris, when are Tom and I going to have a go out in front? It's beginning to look as if Don and Dougal are going to leapfrog through once again. We've been up here for nearly a fortnight and at this rate we'll be shattered, humping loads, before we ever have a chance at getting out in front.'

'Mick, I can appreciate how you feel,' I replied, 'but the trouble is, on evidence you don't seem to be going well enough at the moment to go out in front. You've had almost every other day off for a rest, up to now. As soon as you seem to be going well we can put you in front, but not before.'

This closed the argument, but that night Dougal and I talked over the ethics of who should go out in front. I had hoped that we should be able to do it on a rota system, with each pair taking it in turns to lead and then to carry loads, but it hadn't worked out like this, mainly as a result of differing rates of acclimatization and a certain amount of minor sickness.

'One of the first things I realized on this climb,' Dougal observed, 'was that it wasn't a matter of people taking turns; it's a matter of priorities.'

So far we had managed to effect an uneasy compromise between the two systems, though Dougal and Don as a pair, and myself, had undoubtedly tended to push through to the front. Replacing Ian with Dougal, rather than with Tom Frost or Mick Burke, had brought the problem to a head.

Tom summed it up in his diary.

Thus far the expedition has run smoothly as a team without obvious

personality conflicts. Now our time is fifty per cent used up. We have
already spent eighteen days on the Ice Ridge and are not yet up. The per-
sonal desires of many of the members to: (1) Get things moving; (2) be
out in front; (3) be on top; are beginning to become apparent in ner-
vousness and directiveness. All these intense, driving, talented personal-
ities have distinguished themselves by a tendency to direct others and
not always without self-interest first.

Today's case in point, my companion Mick Burke (14 days out of
Base) and I (10 days out of Base) were passed over for the move to IV by
Dougal (4 days out of Base)—Don's decision.

On the other hand, Mick doesn't hesitate to use the oxygen reserved
for the summit assault for his endless headache, and Chris seems to be
almost always out in front, but seems to have the strength and ability to
be there and still, mostly, directs the operation.

In fact, Don had recommended Mick Burke to use the oxygen to help him
to stay up at III rather than return to Base for a rest. All of these arguments really came back to the question of fairness or expediency. Don and
Dougal had a single-minded drive to get to the summit. They had done
comparatively little load-carrying, but at the same time they seemed to
have a greater corporate drive than any other pair.

Dougal was undoubtedly the right person to come up to join me at
that moment, for I was now getting tired and needed his forceful energy
to keep up the momentum of the next day's advance. It could have been
argued that I should have gone down for a rest or a spell back at Camp
III with Ian, but getting to the top of the Ice Ridge had become a very
personal challenge as well as being vital to the success of the expedition
as a whole.

On the climb at this stage I undoubtedly tended to thrust up to the
front, though not, I hope, from purely egotistical motives but mainly
because this seemed the best way of controlling the situation and getting things moving. That night, in the box, I also discussed with Dougal
the possibility of splitting him and Don, both to widen our own base of
experience and push and to ensure that some pictorial record was kept

of their activities; neither Don nor Dougal could be persuaded to use his camera to any extent.

Dougal was very much against this. He felt, and I think he was right, that Don and he made a very well-balanced team, that could not be replaced by any other kind of pairing. Although very different in character, interests and outlook on life, in their single-minded determination to climb the mountain and their mutual respect for each other's ability they had an extraordinary unity—almost like a long-married couple— as long as they were on the mountain, yet once they were off it they immediately went their own ways.

'I've learnt a great deal from Don,' Dougal said. 'Simple things that I had never really thought of, but which are of vital importance in this kind of climbing. He sites a camp like a real craftsman: thinks very carefully of just where to put the box, taking every possible factor, of avalanche potential, drifting snow, exposure to wind, into consideration. When he digs the platform or erects the box, the same thoroughness goes into it.'

Dougal also felt that my own worry about getting a photographic record was out of proportion. 'Let's get our priorities right. If we don't climb the mountain, your record won't be much good anyway.'

'In that case,' I pleaded, 'for heaven's sake start taking a few pictures of each other.'

Next day (2 May) I was glad of Dougal's freshness, for I was feeling heavy and tired as I struggled up the fixed ropes to the high point, very happy to let Dougal take the lead. I had tried to make an early start, cooking breakfast at 5.20 a.m., but although it was a clear day an icy wind was whipping across the Face, blowing spindrift in great clouds and making the prospect of hard climbing exceedingly unpleasant. We lay in our sleeping-bags listening to the wind and only set out at 8.0 a.m., when it began to drop in intensity.

Dougal disappeared round the corner into the narrow gully I had spied the previous day. The rope ran out slowly and then he came into sight again, about half-way up. The bed of the gully was filled with blocks of rock gummed into the ice; none of them felt over-secure and he had to balance delicately over them, getting the minimum of security from an occasionally placed piton. The top of the gully was barred by a huge block that formed a jutting roof. It wasn't the kind of place you liked hammering pitons for fear of bringing the whole mass toppling down on top of you. Dougal managed to get one piton into the side of it and swung across to the right, wide bridging across the gully; clearing holds in the ice, he pulled up onto the top of a small spur, letting out a shout of victory.

'It doesn't look too bad from here. I think we might be able to see the end of the ridge from round the next corner.'

He fixed the rope to a complex of angle-pitons hammered into cracks behind the block, and I jumared up to him carrying a rucksack, heavy with ropes for the next section.

It was my turn to lead, but I had been dropping off to sleep on the stance below; I felt incapable of any kind of action. I had a cough that had steadily been worsening over the past few days. I had not worried too much about it, though, for it did not seem to be on my chest—it was just an irritating tickle at the back of my throat that sent me into paroxysms of coughing that lasted for minutes at a time. All I could do was to sag on the rope and cough my guts out until the attack died away.

And so I asked Dougal to stay in the lead. Always eager, he started on the next pitch. A slab-covered scoop barred our way to the crest of a subsidiary snow aréte, from where we hoped we should be able to see the top of the ridge. But first, to get there. The rock slab was steep and holdless; the snow overlapping its top just slid away as Dougal tried to dig out hand- and footholds. Into a crack revealed by his digging he tapped one of our few remaining rock pitons—we had now used up almost the entire stock we had at Camp IV and were waiting for another consignment from Base Camp. Taking tension on the piton he gingerly worked his way across the slab, crampons scraping on sloping footholds, fingers digging into the yielding snow above. A final pull and he was around the corner.

'Can you see the end of the ridge?' I shouted.

'No, but it looks straightforward.'

He fixed the rope once more and I swung across on the horizontally stretched rope. We were now standing on the top of a rock prow, about two hundred feet below the snow crest of the ridge. Almost unnoticed, the afternoon snow had crept in, spreading its chill over us.

Even so, Dougal set out on another pitch, kicking into deep, soft snow that was still frighteningly steep. There was a firm ice base about two feet below, and using this he was able to get the occasional ice-piton runner. Perched on my rock, I was shivering with cold and praying that he would decide to return, yet did not like to suggest it. At last, as the storm built up to a crescendo, Dougal lost his enthusiasm for masochistic pursuits, fastened the end of the rope to a piton hammered into a crack in a small rock island protruding from the snow, and retreated. We fled back, swinging Tarzan-like across the handrail of rope, a karabiner attached to a sling from our harness clipped into it for safety, then an easy abseil down to the Terrible Traverse, the inevitable struggle on that, and back to the box.

We got back at about 4.0 p.m. I felt totally shattered and doubted if I should have the strength to go back onto the ridge to finish off the Ice Ridge the next day. I had already decided to call one of the others up to replace me when, at the 5.0 p.m. radio call, Don beat me to it.

'We've decided that Tom, Mick and myself should come up to join Dougal tomorrow,' he said. 'Since the afternoon snow seems to be arriving at around eleven o'clock in the morning it would be best if you could stay at camp tomorrow and dig a platform for the second box before we arrive.'

I was so tired that this sounded an easy let-out, and I agreed.

'Well, that lets us off the hook,' was Dougal's only comment.

I woke up at six o'clock the following morning (3 May). It was a clear, windless day and, refreshed by a good night's sleep, I felt a lot better.

'We might as well go up the hill,' I suggested to Dougal. 'It won't do the others any harm to dig a platform.'

We informed them of the change of plan at the seven o'clock radio call and set off up the fixed ropes. I seemed to have received a new lease of life, and climbed the ropes more quickly and easily than I had ever done before. Dougal started out on the first pitch and, fresh in the bright morning's sun, worked his way quite quickly across the snow slope from one rock outcrop to the next. He had brought with him one of the ex-army entrenching-tools we used for digging out platforms. This proved an ideal tool for shovelling away a route in soft snow. I followed, and, feeling strong and confident once more, volunteered to do my share of leading. Dougal had a belay in a small hollow and the best route seemed to be out to the right across a broken rock wall up onto a snow spur which we hoped would lead straight up to the top of the ridge.

I worked my way out across the rocks, feeling good to be out in front once more, confident in the strength of my arms and the points of my crampons. The rock was steep, but there were good peg cracks. I took off my gloves, stuffed them into the open pouch pocket on my chest to handle a piton more easily. Arching across a blank wall to wedge the peg into a crack, I brushed my chest against the rock, and one of the gloves, insecurely lodged, was knocked out. I lunged to save it; the foothold I was standing on broke away from under me, and I was swinging on one handhold. If I had fallen I should have dropped about twenty feet before the rope held me. But I managed to hang on, readjusted my balance and, cursing my carelessness, got back into a safe position.

Once I had hammered in the piton I took stock. Dropping things on a big climb is a cardinal sin; what was worse, I had not brought with me a spare pair of gloves. My gloveless hand was already becoming numb with cold and it was out of the question to continue gloveless, yet we were so tantalizingly close to success. Even getting back could be dodgy, for hands can freeze fast in the Himalayas and the chill clouds were already licking at our feet.

Dougal saved the day.

'I've got some spare gloves in my sack, Chris. You'd better come back and get them.'

I returned to the fray; a few holds cut in the snow, a sling threaded underneath a boulder embedded in ice, an awkward pull up on side holds onto a sloping ledge, as slippery as the slide of death, and I was on the snow slope. Boots dug into the firm snow reassuringly; the shaft of

my axe plunged in up to the pick; but most important of all I could see
the col where the Ice Ridge abutted onto the main Face.

I kicked up the slope, hardly noticing the altitude, to the full length
of the rope, slotted in a dead man and fastened the rope to it, and Dougal
came up to join me.

We now had another problem, for we were rapidly running out of
rope. We had about two hundred feet left and it looked farther than this
to the col. The slope was no longer so easy, for the snow was now getting shallow, lying on a bed of hard ice. Dougal, now leading through,
shouted down, 'Watch the rope. It's getting dodgy. It'll take all day if I
cut steps, but this snow might slip any minute.'

He was relying on a couple of inches of sugary snow to hold his
weight and stepped up delicately to avoid collapsing his precarious
holds. All too soon he ran out the rope. We now had only one length left
to reach the crest of the ridge, and it still looked a long way away.

Once again I led through, pressing up towards the col, but the angle
was now steepening and the layer of snow getting progressively steeper.
We were too far to the left and I had no choice but to make a traverse
to reach our objective.

'How much rope?' I shouted down to Dougal.

'About twenty feet.'

'It won't be enough. I'll just have to get as far as I can.'

I was now cutting steps in the hard ice. It was so steep I had to cut
handholds to keep me in balance as I hacked away at the glassy surface.
Another five feet to go and at least I should be on easier ground just
below the col.

'You've only another three feet or so,' called Dougal.

But I was nearly there. The rope came tight as I kicked into some
deep snow once more, just twenty feet below the crest. I fastened the
rope to a combination of snow-stakes and dead men, and while Dougal
climbed up to join me, I started out solo to cut steps up those last few
feet leading to the col. It was now snowing hard, but that didn't seem to
matter; a final step and I was able to pull up onto the crest. I could gaze
down into the swirling clouds on the other side of the ridge, where the

retaining gully of the Ice Ridge yawned down, menaced by a huge, wave-like cornice, breaking upon the ridge that we had just bypassed. Looking up, I could just see our next serious problem, the band of ice cliffs stretching across this part of the Face. They were about a thousand feet above us and the route to them looked straightforward, up a long, easy snow slope, but it was impossible to tell through the scudding clouds whether there were any weaknesses in the next line of defences. We had now spent five weeks in just cracking the Ice Ridge. If the Rock Band was to prove as difficult we should have little chance of eventual success.

Even so, Dougal and I had a feeling of euphoria as we returned down the fixed ropes in the storm. Suddenly our horizons had opened out. We felt we had made a breakthrough.

CHAPTER 12

The Ice Cliff
[4–9 May]

We had at last climbed the Ice Ridge. On 4 May, Don and Dougal, with Mick Burke and Tom Frost, carried a load of ropes up to the col at the head of the ridge. Dougal then struck out towards the ice cliffs, running out a complete five-hundred-foot reel of rope. After all the time-consuming difficulties of the lower stretch this was straightforward, if monotonous, climbing; just a question of slow plodding in knee-deep snow. Ice-axe in, kick, step up, pant and axe in again, step after step, always fighting against the enervating effects of altitude.

They came back the next day and reached the foot of the ice cliff in heavy cloud. Each day the cloud flooded in a little earlier, though fortunately it was not accompanied by wind. Dougal described it.

'Visibility was about ten feet. It seemed as if I was alone on the mountain, with only the drag of the ice-encrusted rope to remind me that I was linked to anyone else. The first thing I knew about the ice cliffs was when the angle of the slope suddenly changed from forty-five degrees to vertical.'

The foot of the ice cliff was to be the site of Camp V. That afternoon they started digging out a platform, but were driven back by the rising wind and rushing snow slides that came pouring over the ice cliff.

The following day Don and Dougal moved up to Camp V supported by Tom Frost and Mick Burke. They spent the entire afternoon digging out a platform, but as fast as they dug waves of spindrift, pouring from the ice cliff above, filled the space they had cleared. It was dusk before they were ready to start erecting the tent. Instead of a Whillans Box they were using a RAFMA tent. These were lighter and more commodious than the boxes, though, as we were soon to discover, not nearly as robust. The poles fit through sleeves and are gently curved to give the tent a hooped shape similar to that of wartime Nissen huts. In these conditions, struggling with frozen fingers against stiff canvas, erecting the tent was a sore trial. By the time they had pitched it, the interior was full of powder snow and it was well into the night before they could settle down to cook and rest.

Meanwhile, I had been resting down at Camp III, trying out Don's idea of resting there rather than returning to the foot of the Face. Camp III had turned into an advanced base, with three boxes and a RAFMA tent pitched and a plastic tarpaulin covering a fast-growing dump of supplies. Martin Boysen and Nick Estcourt, on their way back up the mountain, were in one tent, Mike Thompson in the other. I moved in with Mike. One could not have a better tent companion: he is highly domesticated, very methodical and tidy, and an excellent cook.

He was finding life on the mountain hard, however. He had never really thrown off the flu he had caught on the approach march. In addition, this was the first time he had done any serious mountaineering. He had never worn crampons before, never used jumars. He had fulfilled his role admirably, in spite of acclimatizing slowly. It was a particularly difficult role, for without the stimulus of the expectation of leading or going to the top, the climb inevitably must become a long, grinding drudgery. This had affected Mike in the shape of minor complaints that were beginning to oppress him. He had severe sores on his tongue through breathing in the cold, dry air through his mouth. These

Mick Burke jumars his way up the fixed rope over an ice cornice. the jumars clip on to the rope on a ratchet principle, sliding up the rope, but biting into it when under tension.

were extremely painful and unpleasant and had begun to affect his performance. Even so, day after day he dragged himself out to ferry loads
between Camps III and IV. Even when forced to take rest days, he fulfilled a vital role just by staying up at Camp III, and later at IV, acting,
in effect, as a kind of advanced base manager, keeping a careful tally of
the supplies filtering up the mountain. It was always important to avoid
running out of any commodity completely at the front, say at Camp V,
for it took fully five days to ferry anything up to the front line all the
way from Base Camp.

That night, after my seven days out in front, I was happy to slump
into the box and let Mike cook me a magnificent meal of soup, chicken
supreme and sweet corn, followed by fried Christmas pudding. The next
morning I felt totally indolent and weak and happy to spend the entire
day in my sleeping-bag, as I did my second rest day as well.

Meanwhile, Martin, Nick and Mike ferried loads each day up to
Camp IV. On 6 May, the day after Don and Dougal moved up to Camp
V, I planned to go up to Camp IV with Nick Estcourt. This was once
again a question of jumping out of turn, but I realized that the carry
between Camps IV and V was going to be specially tough and crucial to
our success. I wanted, therefore, to get up into a position immediately
behind the front pair, so that I could assess the situation easily, both
from the carrying point of view and also the problems that Don and
Dougal might encounter.

I had also decided to start using the Sherpas on the carry from Camp
III to IV, since it was becoming very obvious that the ten climbers would
be unable to keep supplies flowing through the upper camps without
reinforcements. In a matter of days, I hoped, Camp VI would be established, probably somewhere on the Rock Band. This meant we should
then need two men there, at least two at Camp V and four at Camp IV,
leaving only two for Camp III; this did not take into consideration the
likelihood of anyone becoming sick and being forced down for a rest.

Our position on the lower part of the mountain was now quite
healthy, since we had the London Sherpas and Dave Lambert working
on the carry from Camp I to II; Kelvin was also now proposing to use

Looking out from a Whillans Box. We always cooked in the entrance because of fumes. Note the inner tent made of fire-proof material.

some of the Gurkha porters, who had distinguished themselves on the carry across the glacier, for the carry to Camp II. In addition, the dump of supplies was now growing to a respectable size, as a result of consistent carries by the Sherpas up the gully.

Camp IV, on the other hand, was still only lightly stocked and we were barely keeping up with day-to-day needs, let alone building up a stockpile for the upper slopes. Particularly worrying was the oxygen situation. We now had about fifteen cylinders at Camp III, but only four had reached Camp IV. If we were to be faced with a siege on the Rock Band and were to find it necessary to use large quantities of oxygen, our supply problems would become all the more critical.

Ian Clough had now finished his rest and was on his way back up the mountain. Ang Pema and Pemba Tharkay, the most experienced of our Sherpas, had been doing a stint of carrying between Camps I and II, easiest of all the runs. I therefore asked them whether they would be prepared to try the run from Camp III to IV, knowing that this would be on considerably steeper ground than they had ever been before.

Although they were used to fixed ropes they had never been on a climb that necessitated the use of jumars—in fact, I don't think jumars had ever before been used in the Himalayas, certainly never as extensively as we had already used them.

They agreed to give it a try, and Kelvin arranged for them to have a rest on the 6th, the day that Ian was due to move up to Camp II, and then to move straight through to Camp III on the 7th with Ian. They preferred to do it this way, confident that they could move straight through the two camps without undue fatigue. In this way I hoped to build up the stocks in Camp IV fairly rapidly, with Don and Dougal working up towards Camp VI, Tom Frost, Mick Burke, Nick Estcourt and myself ferrying gear up to Camp V, and Mike Thompson, Ian Clough and the two Sherpas ferrying to Camp IV. The trip from Camp III to IV had been getting progressively harder as a result of increasingly heavy afternoon snowfall. On the morning of the 6th, when I was due to go back up the Face, we all prevaricated as long as possible, sitting around talking and filming in the morning sun until about nine

Inside the Box, this time without an inner tent. Spare clothes, etc., are hung up from the frame but even so the Box is a tight fit for two climbers.

193

o'clock. The first three hundred yards from the camp were set at an easy angle, and with the trail broken by the three in front it should have been no more than a plod, but almost immediately the others pulled away from me. It was a strange feeling, not so much of breathlessness as of complete listlessness, where each step required a supreme effort. I had been confident that I was probably better acclimatized than anyone except Dougal before I went down for my rest; I had hoped that after two days in my sleeping-bag I should feel completely recovered and be going better than ever before.

As I plodded slowly behind the others, the gap between us ever increasing, I tried to dismiss it as a temporary lapse caused by my rest.

I'll be all right once I've got into the swing of it, I told myself, and stopped for yet another rest. Four steps, rest, not panting, just standing slumped over my axe, trying to will myself to start again. I felt perfectly normal when I was stationary, but the moment I started to move lethargy took over. It was as if my body did not want to function and was going on strike the moment I put it to work once more.

It took me an hour to cover four hundred yards with a vertical rise of only three or four hundred feet. But I was catching up on the others. They had reached the section where it steepened for the last three hundred feet to the foot of the spur and start of the fixed ropes. They were floundering in thigh-deep snow, getting nowhere, it was so soft and deep. Mike was out in front for a time, but burnt himself out in his efforts to struggle upwards. Martin then took over, finally making progress by lunging his body forward onto the snow and almost swimming up it—a painfully slow, exhausting progress. By the time we reached the foot of the fixed ropes, two hours had gone by.

Mike was shattered.

'I'll never make it up the fixed rope,' he said. 'I'll dump my load here and come back tomorrow.'

Martin agreed to add part of Mike's load to his own. Nick set off first, then Martin and finally myself. I had a long wait at the foot of the rope to allow the others in turn to get past the first anchor, which was about two hundred feet up.

By the time my turn had come the cloud had crept up on us; flurries of snow were whispering down the slopes and the basin had turned from a blazing furnace of reflected light to an icy deep freeze, all in a matter of seconds. I started up the fixed ropes, trying to do ten successive pushes of my jumar clamps at a time before pausing for a rest.

It's all in the mind, I told myself. Will yourself to keep going. But my willpower wasn't enough. Martin and Nick were drawing ahead, though even they were going very slowly. Soon I was on my own in a world of swirling snowflakes on the crest of a snow arête leading up to a notch in the ridge that never seemed to get any closer. My progress had dropped to a single push of my jumar clamps at a time; my feet slipped on the snow steps, and I pendulumed clumsily across the arête into the gully.

I lay sobbing on the slope from a mixture of frustration and exhaustion. I looked up at the top of the ridge. *I'll never make it. Must go down for a rest. What good would I be anyway, even if I do get up to Camp IV? If I'm like this tomorrow I certainly won't manage the carry along the ridge.*

I decided to go down, turned round and slid a few feet down the rope, but the thought revolted me. How could I expect others to grind their guts out if I wasn't prepared to do it myself? A spasm of coughing hit me, and I hung on the rope, amidst tears and coughs, trying to bolster my resolve.

I turned back up the rope and made a few steps. It had taken a matter of seconds to drop back thirty feet on the rope. It took me a quarter of an hour to regain those few feet. The contrast was too much. My body was screaming to go down, my logic told me that I could do no good by going up, yet a sense of duty, mixed with pride, was trying to force me on. I felt torn apart by the two conflicting impulses, weakened and degraded by my own indecision.

But it was no good. I looked up once more. The others had gone out of sight; I couldn't even warn them I was going down, but felt that I should never have the strength to reach the crest of the ridge, let alone follow that last awkward stretch to the camp. I turned round and plunged back towards Camp III. It was so hideously easy to go down—the broad, easy path down to a personal hell—so hard to go up.

It was good to find Mike at Camp III, but there seemed no point in staying there. I had learnt the hard way that if you get over-fatigued, rest at 20,100 feet does very little to help you recover. At this stage I did not think there was anything wrong with me, other than over-fatigue; although I had noticed for the first time, while struggling on the fixed ropes on the way up to Camp IV, a stabbing pain in my chest whenever I coughed, I dismissed this as a muscular pain caused by the constant coughing.

I had a brew of tea with Mike and then set off down the couloir back towards Base Camp, planning to spend a couple of days there before returning to the fray. I had a bitter feeling of failure, of having let down the rest of the team through my own personal weakness, at a time when we were desperately short of manpower.

I met Ian Clough at Camp II, on his way back up the mountain. We discussed the situation and I continued down. At Camp I Pasang pressed a cup of coffee on me. I mentioned the pain in my chest to Dave Lambert, but he thought it was probably no more than a muscular ache. It was now six o'clock in the evening but I wanted to get back down to Base that night and left the relative comfort of Camp I to stagger down the long slopes of the Rognon to the glacier below. The snow that had covered it a month before had now completely vanished, exposing a long, easy-angled scree slope that led down to grassy hummocks. The glacier had also lost its mantle of snow. It was now a mournful place of grit-covered ice, decaying towers and dark, yawning holes. In bright sunlight it would have been a drab, almost ugly place like an abandoned scrap yard, but in the mist it had a strange beauty that even I, in my exhaustion, could wonder at. The mist softened the outline of towers and gaping holes, magnified and distorted them in a fairy-tale landscape. The route across had altered again since I had last been there and I kept getting lost in the gathering dusk, going into blind alleys or finding myself on feathery peninsulas of ice jutting into an opaque sea of shadow-filled chasms. Coming to the other side of the glacier was like dragging myself out of a nightmare; all that was left was the long plod across grass-covered slopes down to Base Camp.

Tukte had come out to meet me, carrying a torch, just in case I was caught out by the dark. I was both glad and sorry to be down in the lush comfort of Base. Glad to rest yet longing to be back on the mountain. That night I slept in the Base tent, warmed by a good meal and whisky fumes; dry sleeping-bag, no hoar frost forming on the roof of the tent, to be woken in the morning by Tukte with a mug of tea—but I envied Don and Dougal up at Camp V, snagged beneath the ice cliff, 8,500 feet above me.

And at Camp V, the spindrift avalanches swished down all night, filling the platform, burying the tent. Sleeping-bags were encased in an icy armor that seriously reduced their insulating qualities. That morning (7 May) it had dawned cloudy with flurries of powder snow gusting down the ice cliff, but Dougal was determined to see what was round the corner. Anyway, life at Camp V was so exceedingly uncomfortable that a struggle with the elements outside seemed preferable. Don belayed Dougal from the door of the tent and he started working his way across the top of the snowfield below the ice wall. Cataracts of spindrift kept pouring over the cliffs above and his feet and hands were numb with cold. He could hardly see where he was going but just kept edging across on the points of his crampons.

He had run out about three hundred feet of rope when there was a slight break in the clouds. He saw that he was in a little bay in the centre of the ice barrier; there was a gangway of ice swinging up to the right that seemed to lead to the top.

And then the cloud swirled in once more and the avalanches of snow came flooding down. Dougal had no means of communicating with Don, so he fixed the end of the rope to his ice-axe thrust into the snow and returned to the bleak discomfort of the tent and a second breakfast.

Around midday, the roof of the clouds seemed to drop and they found themselves above a cloud sea, which still engulfed the rest of the camps. They immediately got out of their sleeping-bags and set out along the fixed rope left in place earlier that morning by Dougal. Once again he took the lead and started up the steep ice gangway, chipping away holds in the hard, sticky ice, using the occasional ice-screw for protection. It was steep but straightforward climbing, as he hung dizzily over the sheer walls of the ice cliff, and worked his way up to the right. This was one place where Dougal found a use for the Whillans Whammer, Don's space-age climbing tool, for its squat, triangular-shaped pick proved ideal for this type of ice, slicing in and out of the hard yet glutinous surface without sticking as the pick of Dougal's ice-axe did.

He was now climbing in dazzling sunlight. The Rock Band, like the tower of a huge cathedral, soared above, its base a mere three hundred feet above, up an easy snow slope. He shouted the good news down to Don and then brought him up to the top of the ice cliff. They had now run out of rope, but Don was determined to reach the Rock Band and hammer in a ceremonial piton. They soloed up the last few feet to the lip of the bergschrund, which seemed a perfect camp-site, and hammered a piton into a crack in some rock protruding out of the ice, actually within the bergschrund.

Meanwhile, Nick Estcourt had been making a solitary carry up to Camp V. Mick Burke and Tom Frost, who had carried gear up to the foot of the ice cliff on the two previous days, were in urgent need of a rest and spent the day in their sleeping-bags. We were already beginning to find that two consecutive carries up to Camp V were as much as anyone could be expected to undertake without a rest day, the going was so very arduous.

For Nick it was a lonely and exhausting carry, loneliness emphasized by the swirling cloud that enclosed him, cutting him off from the rest of the team and from everything but the ice and rocks immediately around him. His security was the lifeline of fixed rope snaking away into the driving snow, but there was no one else to talk to, to bolster resolve in the face of exhaustion. Yet he knew that the five-hundred-foot reel of rope he was carrying was vital, since Don and Dougal were sure to run out of rope that day—and so he kept plodding on. It took him ten hours of harsh, grinding effort to reach Camp V and return to Camp IV—twice as long as a normal day in the Himalayas.

That same day Mike had tried to reach Camp IV on his own but turned back exhausted, while Ian and the two Sherpas plodded up the long snow gully to Camp III.

Back at Base Camp it had been difficult to believe that any progress had been made at all, the weather had been so bad, with the Face covered in cloud throughout the day. We learnt of Don and Dougal's success at the five o'clock call that night.

KELVIN: Hello, Camp V. This is Base. Are you on the air? Over.

DOUGAL: Hello, Base. Reading you loud and clear. How do you read me? Over.

KELVIN: We read you O.K. A little bit distorted. Any progress today?

DOUGAL: News is: Today Don and I planted the top piton in the Rock Band.

KELVIN: Congratulations to all concerned. Understand you put the first piton in the Rock Band. Is that right?

DOUGAL: Roger. Is Chris there, please, and if so could we speak to him?

CHRIS: Hello, Dougal. Chris on the air.

DOUGAL: Did you get that message that we reached the Rock Band?

CHRIS: Yes, that really is tremendous, Dougal. What does it look like?

DOUGAL: It looks very impressive but should be feasible. The thing is, Don and I now would like to come right down because we are feeling . . . er . . . *comme-ci, comme-ça.* How does that sound?

CHRIS: Roger. If you could do, say, one more day tomorrow and ideally get a camp established at the foot of the Rock Band we could push Mick and Tom through to the new camp and then you could come down for a rest. I think this would be ideal. It would then mean that you would be really fit for the final assault. How does that sound to you?

DOUGAL: Wait out. *[A long pause—he was obviously talking it over with Don.]* The thing is, this present Camp V is one hell of a place and Don has this idea that we could transfer Camp V to the bergschrund at the foot of the Rock Band, which is about half an hour away, and use this as a dump. This would save a camp, save establishing V and VI very close together, and I think it would also relieve the carrying situation. It would mean that people could come down from Camp V and then carry back up.

CHRIS: Roger. Do I understand you to mean that you shift the present Camp V complete to the bergschrund and actually establish tents there?

DOUGAL: Roger; yes.

CHRIS: Would it make sense in that case if you and Don at least helped Tom Frost and Mick, who I think are going well, into place on the bergschrund and then came down for a rest?

DOUGAL: Wait out. *[Another long pause for consultation.]* Tomorrow we could go up, dig out a site and carry some gear. We can't do any climbing because we haven't any more rope. How does that sound?

CHRIS: O.K. That sounds good. Now, is it practical for the three at Camp IV to move straight up through your present site to the dump and establish gear there?

DOUGAL: Yes, this is practical unless the weather is bad, because it is only a very short distance from our present camp to the future one.

CHRIS: Roger. In that case I think the best thing is that tomorrow we should concentrate on moving the camp to the dump and the day after, Mick and Tom actually move up to the bergschrund camp. Out to you. Hello, Mick, at Camp IV. Did you hear that?

MICK: The only problem is, Camp IV at the moment is almost empty completely of food, completely empty of rope, though we do have pitons. What's the situation as far as once we've moved up there? We haven't any food to take with us. Don and Dougal might have a pack left. Is there any rope left for us to climb with the next day?

CHRIS: No. You are not moving up to Camp V tomorrow; you're moving up to Camp V the day after. Martin Boysen is going to move up to Camp IV tomorrow. The actual plan is this. Roger so far?

MICK: Roger.

CHRIS: Dougal and Don will take up tomorrow just about everything except for the tent and the foams. You and Tom should travel up to Camp V lightly laden tomorrow, taking with you what you have of pitons and so on, pick up the camp at Camp V with the foams and take that on to the new site at the big bergschrund below the Rock Band. Roger so far?

MICK: Roger.

CHRIS: Meanwhile—are you listening in Camp III?

MIKE: Yes.

CHRIS: Meanwhile, tomorrow Martin will move up to Camp IV and the two Sherpas plus Mike will bring maximum quantity of food and rope up to Camp IV. Roger so far?

MICK: Roger from Camp IV.

MIKE: Roger from Camp III.

CHRIS: Roger. And then the day after tomorrow Tom and yourself will move up with your personal kit and Nick and Martin will be able to take rope up to the new site of Camp IV— correction, Camp V.

MICK: O.K. from here.

CHRIS: Hello, Dougal. Does that sound all right to you?

DOUGAL: Sounds fine to me, yeah.

CHRIS: O.K. Well, that can remain as the plan, and if anything goes wrong or alters the situation we will have to think again.

• • •

I have written out the entire radio conversation from tapes taken at the time to give some idea of how I reached decisions and to show what a vital role the radio played in our ascent. We were still badly stretched, for with Tom and Mick up at V we should need at least three, ideally four, carrying up from IV and the same number at III.

Next day, the 8th, Don and Dougal shifted all the gear less the tent up to the bergschrund as planned, while Tom and Mick Burke, leaving Nick Estcourt resting at IV, carried light loads up to Camp V, picking up the tent on the way. The carry was already excessively long, just as far as the foot of the ice cliff—it was now a further four hundred feet. This turned it into a marathon obstacle course, acrobatics on the traverse followed by the soul-destroying plod up the thousand-foot snowfield, and then the strenuous pull through the ice cliffs. Tom described 8 May in his diary.

> I had a terribly groggy time waking up on 8 May and it was only with luck that I made it by 5.00. The pumpernickel and cheese spread were frozen solid this morning and went down only with difficulty. Mick finally arose at 6.30 and Nick was impossible to arouse; apparently sleeping-pills and feeling rough from the previous day's carry. I was feeling rough too actually, but didn't fully realize it.
>
> Nick was off first and I followed at 8.30 moving very slowly and sickly up the ropes in Mick's steps. I felt almost unable to proceed. It was a very humbling experience.

That same day, Pemba Tharkay and Ang Pema made their first carry to Camp IV, shepherded and instructed by Ian Clough. The two Sherpas took to the steep section and the use of jumars amazingly well, making up for a lack of technique with sheer fitness and physical strength. Their deep affection for Ian was strengthened by this experience: a superb instructor, he devoted a lot of time on the way up, in spite of his own fatigue, to showing them the best method of using jumars, and on the way down how to abseil. The success of the experiment was a great relief to me down at Base Camp, for this meant that we could now start building up Camp IV and break the bottleneck at this point on our supply line, though I could fore-see that ferrying supplies up to V was going to provide even greater problems. That night on the radio I asked Ian to move up to Camp IV to reinforce Nick and Martin, while Mike, who was now feeling badly run down, stuck it out at Camp III. I also told Nima and Mingma Tsering to move up to III to bring our Sherpa strength up there to four.

I had now had two days back at Base Camp, was still feeling tired and lethargic, and was worried by the pain in my chest which seemed to be getting worse rather than better, but the manpower position on the mountain was so bad that I decided to start back up the mountain, hopeful that my two days at 14,000 feet had rested me sufficiently.

Leaving Don and Dougal at Base Camp, I set out for Camp I on the 9th, reaching it in just over two hours—a fairly fast time and one that convinced me that I was now fully recovered, in spite of the stabbing pain in my chest whenever I coughed.

Camp I had developed into a kind of advanced base, with two large tents and an impressive stockpile of gear and food which was now sufficient to last out the rest of our stay on the mountain. As a result Kelvin had been able to move the most agile of our local porters up to Camp I for the carry to II, at the moment under the command of Gambahadur, our Gurkha radio operator, who had asked Kelvin if he could take a turn at load-carrying. He was tall and well built for a Gurkha, back at Base Camp the champion volleyball player of the expedition.

Alan Hankinson, looking rather tired and haggard, was also there. At forty-seven he was the oldest member of the expedition, yet had thrown himself into it with an almost boyish enthusiasm. He had been sent out by Independent Television News with the slightly ambiguous position of watchdog to guard their interests. He took advantage of this by leaving the filming strictly to John Edwards and his camera team, while he took a very active part in the expedition, carrying loads on the lower slopes of the mountain. His help and that of the London Sherpas had enabled us to use the Sherpas higher up the mountain where they were urgently needed.

On the upper part of the mountain Tom Frost and Mick Burke were moving up to Camp V for their assault on the Rock Band, while Nick Est-court and Martin Boysen accompanied them to make a carry. It took them seven hours to reach the bergschrund at the foot of the Rock Band. Nick only managed to get as far as the foot of the ice cliff, and then felt so ill and weak he had to share his load out between Tom and Mick. Meanwhile Martin, going very strongly, had pushed on up to the bergschrund and was on his way down, doing a dramatic sitting glissade down the long snow slope, with a karabiner clipped into the fixed rope for safety.

When Tom and Mick finally reached the bergschrund they were faced with the task of stamping out a platform and pitching the

Martin Boysen climbs the fixed rope through the ice cliffs that bar the snow field just below the Rock Band.

RAFMA tent, which was now frozen into an almost solid lump. They were panting with exhaustion and lack of oxygen as they struggled with the frozen canvas, amazed at how much even the slightest effort took out of them.

They were both worried by the huge overhang of snow that reared over the schrund like a breaking wave. It protected them from the worst of the spindrift avalanches from the Face above, but if it had collapsed they would have no chance of survival, for it jutted out a good twenty feet and must have weighed several hundred tons.

It was nearly dark before they had pitched the tent and unpacked their rucksacks inside it. Befuddled as they were with exhaustion, even filling the primus became an exacting task; and then, once they had got it burning, with a pan of boiling water bubbling on top of it, Tom knocked it over, sending the liquid slooshing over the tent floor—an hour's effort wasted, clothes and sleeping-bag soaked.

That night, when eventually they had finished cooking supper, they were close to exhaustion, yet the fact that they were going out in front the next day to tussle with the final barrier, and perhaps the most difficult of all, gave them a feeling of excited anticipation that already seemed capable of overcoming their fatigue.

CHAPTER 13

The Rock Band
[10–13 May]

The climb was developing into a slow war of attrition, which we seemed to be losing; just keeping the upper camps supplied, let alone building up a stockpile of oxygen and gear for the final assault, was proving as great a struggle, and certainly every bit as dramatic, as the job of forcing the route up the Face.

This was especially the case at this stage of the climb, when we were faced by two inter-related problems: climbing the Rock Band and ferrying supplies between Camps IV and V. Don had suggested that we should try to establish a further pair at Camp V, so that we could have one pair going down to the Col at the end of the Ice Ridge and another going up to the Col from Camp IV, using the Col as a dump for supplies. This seemed a sound idea, since it was becoming increasingly obvious that the carry right through to Camp V would inevitably exhaust anyone undertaking it for more than a few days at a time. But it was to prove impractical, for we were too short of manpower ever to put it into practice. Each time we seemed on the point of building up enough people at the front, someone inevitably was struck down by exhaustion.

On 10 May, when Tom Frost and Mick Burke did their first day's work on the Rock Band, Ian, Martin and Nick all managed to make a carry through to Camp V, but they could only take an average load of twenty-five pounds each, and this was the biggest load to go up for nearly a week.

That same day, hoping to reach IV three days later, I set out for Camp II, but was aware almost immediately that I was moving less well than on the previous day; more frightening, the slightest jerk caused a painful spasm in the bottom of my chest. Whenever I coughed I bent over double, hugging my chest in my arms, trying to hold the muscles tight to reduce the agonizing stabs of pain that I was experiencing with each cough. The only thing that kept me going was the knowledge that Dave Lambert was at Camp II; at least he might be able to tell me what was wrong and do something to cure it.

When I reached II, I found Dave Lambert in residence with Pasang Kami and our two London Sherpas. They were all suffering from dysentery and were taking a day off. I told him of my symptoms and he listened to my chest.

'It's probably pleurisy,' he said.

'What the hell's that?'

'Inflammation of the walls of the chest. You can't be too bad or you would never have got up here, but I'd advise you to go back down for a rest; it could easily develop into pneumonia up here. I can put you on a course of penicillin; that should clear up the infection.'

'But how long will it be before I can get back up?'

'Four or five days at least—you definitely mustn't try coming up in less than four.'

It sounded like a life sentence, but I had no choice but to return to Base Camp. That night on the radio it became obvious that everyone was getting badly run down. Pasang returned to Base Camp with me. Ang Pema was already there resting with an eye infection and very bad piles. The climbers on the mountain did not seem to be in a much better state, as I gathered that night on the 5.0 p.m. call.

Camp V was established at 22,750 feet in a Bergschrund immediately below the Rock Band.

CHRIS (*at Base*): Hello, Mike. This is Chris. Come in please. Over.

MIKE: (*at III*): You're loud and clear, Chris. Over.

CHRIS: I'm afraid I've gone and got pleurisy and have had to come down to Base and will be out of action for about four days. Now, can you—are you fit enough to go up to IV tomorrow?

MIKE: Well, I was wondering about this, and, the last two days, I've been bad with this [*ulcered*] mouth and haven't made it up to IV at all. Today I got up to IV all right with a load but I felt very weak—much weaker than the last few times I've been up there. I have a feeling that, you know, to be honest, being realistic, I suspect that even if I got to IV I wouldn't be able to manage a carry to V because I'm badly run down now.

CHRIS: I see. Roger. That's fair enough; out to you. Hello, Camp IV. Come in, please.

IAN: Hello, Chris. Sorry to hear you're not going to make it for a few days. We're getting a bit sort of drawn out ourselves.

CHRIS: I know. It's a bastard. Just what kind of state are you, Nick and Martin in?

IAN: Well, Nick isn't back yet. We set off late this morning. Nick's not so good. We left about nine o'clock and we've only been in an hour or so and Nick's not back yet.

CHRIS: I see. Roger. How soon can you, in fact, establish the second tent and camp unit at Camp V?

IAN: We can't do it in the next two days without a fourth person—that's for sure. It's really knackering and we've got rope priority to try and get up there.

CHRIS: Roger. I see. That really means that until Don and Dougal get up, as Mike doesn't seem to be able to do it, we'll have to keep the Camp IV to V run as it is and I presume that is going to really knacker you after about three days of doing it.

IAN: Yeah—correct.

CHRIS: Roger. I don't really at the moment see that there is very much we can do though besides just keeping at it, but what I do suggest you do is just try to do two carries per day with one man resting.

IAN: Yes, that's a good idea, actually, 'cause after two days it gets a bit desperate and we're just about tired out.

CHRIS: Roger. The other thing is—are you trying to take some oxygen in the evenings? This could make a difference.

IAN: We haven't tried yet but we will do. We took some up today for Tom and Mick and told them to start taking it as well.

CHRIS: Roger. Well, you probably need it more than they do. Don and Dougal are starting up tomorrow and I hope I'll be able to follow in a couple of days.

IAN: O.K. We'll stagger on.

CHRIS: Good on you, mates. That's all from me. Out.

• • •

The following day we were weakened still further. Nick still felt exhausted in spite of a night's sleep and complained of stabbing pains in his chest; he therefore rested at Camp IV. Martin and Ian set off for Camp V but at the Col Ian turned back. He described his feelings in one of his letters to Nikki:

13 May. I am at Base Camp; yes, Base Camp again. In my last letter written at Camp IV I was going well, I think. The day before yesterday, I was carrying a load on the IV to V run with Martin again; Nick had a day off. Anyway, I got a pain, or rather pains down my left side and was very worried about it, dumped my load at the top of the ice ridge and rushed back down to Base for a rest. I saw Dave briefly at Camp III and he said he thought it was just muscular pains, probably from carrying loads in Don's special frame sack. I'm glad I came back though, as I definitely felt a bit chesty and had strained a muscle in my groin. It's daft staying up high as you never recover any fitness or strength at that altitude and if you do have something wrong with your chest it can all too rapidly develop into pneumonia.

Chris is down at Base with pleurisy; he's not allowed up for a few days yet and it is unlikely that he will be fit enough to go very high. It sounds as if Nick is also developing pleurisy. He's at Camp IV resting again today, trying to hold out but it is silly really because he won't improve until he drops down here for a stay, but we are terribly short of manpower. Everyone is getting a bit run down, I think. We've had dysentery at several camps and I seem to have caught a cold at Base. However, I am off up again this afternoon. It's a slow process going up through the camps. I won't be at IV again until the 16th. We are very short-handed at the front and should be making the summit push in the next couple of weeks. Don and Dougal are two days ahead of me going from II to III today and Chris hopes to follow in a couple of days. However, I guess everyone up at front must be really tired even though they are taking the odd day off for a rest, but as I say, resting up there doesn't do anyone any good.

The plan now is to reduce the amount of tentage, etc., needed at the

Mick Burke filming, ubiquitous cigarette in hand.

front and to squeeze four men into one two-man tent at Camp VI. The proposed Camp VI is to be half-way up the rock band. If it proves in the next day or so that we are going to need to siege the top of the Face, Chris may bring everyone back to Base Camp for a good rest before the big push to the top. Perhaps it will be better to get it over with though; most of us, probably all of us, have had enough of this place and are looking forward to going home.

On re-reading this it all sounds very depressing; things aren't as bad as I make it sound, but I am not feeling good myself and I can't see myself doing more than helping the summit bid in a supporting role; indeed, I might not even do that. However, I shouldn't be feeling as sorry for myself as Chris and two of the Sherpas, who are all worse off than I am and are unlikely to be able to go very high. I think I am just generally run down and maybe when I get back up the hill I will feel a lot better.

Ian's retreat caused yet another crisis in our supply line, for Tom Frost and Mick Burke needed at least one five-hundred-foot reel of rope each day as well as their food and fuel. We also needed to build up a stockpile of oxygen at Camp V, in addition to the tentage, which we had already reduced to a minimum, for Camps VI and VII.

I had been considering the possibility of pulling everyone down for a rest, or alternatively pulling back a potential assault group while the Sherpas and two or three of the climbers tried to build up a stockpile at Camp IV and perhaps Camp V. This move, however, did not seem popular with anyone—it would have been bad for the morale of the people left on the mountain, and could even have been detrimental to those pulled back, for throughout the team there was the feeling of 'Let's get up the bastard and go home'. There was also the risk that the weather might change for the better over the rest period and then worsen once we returned to the fray.

I therefore maintained a policy of plugging the gaps as they occurred and trying to maintain at least a trickle of supplies flowing up the mountain.

It is difficult to conceive just what that carry between Camp IV and

V was really like, without having made it several days running. Martin Boysen made five complete carries and one to the dump in a period of seven days, giving himself only one rest day. His description of one of these carries could apply to any of them.

The bright sun of morning brings little cheer; today as yesterday and the day before I'm carrying loads up from Camp IV to V.

The brilliant morning sun begins to beat on the box and I slowly rouse myself out of a deep, drugged sleep. I feel depressed and tired, today, another carry to Camp V. The drudgery of cooking, dressing, packing, to be followed by five or six hours of back-breaking monotony. Nick, the bastard, is resting today. God, I hate the mornings.

Automatically I start counting steps, forty-five, fifty, stop, lean back on the rope, take twenty breaths and off again. An overhanging prussic at 23,000 feet—I ask you. Ah well, get it over, chop off first and second prussic and on to next rope. Launch out and swing to and fro for a few moments, crampons scratching the ice, then push one jumar up, push second up and flop back. The aerial traverse follows, the first rocks, a ledge.

Sweating freely now I begin to feel better. The surroundings are magnificent; the traverse is fun and it gives a rest from everlasting step counting. Lean round the corner, your hand in familiar crack. Curious how satisfying it is to know every hold and have every move thought out.

The traverse ends, the ropes lead upwards, the wearisome snow slopes have begun. No more swinging about in exciting positions, just kick one foot in after the other.

At last the col, somewhere to sit down and have a fag. Light up, inhale and relax. How many more times will I sit here? I can't face doing it again tomorrow. I need a rest, mentally as much as physically. The constant effort, the incessant counting to fifty. God, it gets you down. Still, it won't go on for ever; in a few days we should take over from Mick and Tom. But will we? I can feel myself getting run down and what about Nick? Will he feel any better? Why the hell did Ian shoot down? Mike shattered, so for the time being that leaves us.

Swing the rucksack onto back, switch onto automatic control and

*start counting. One more rope to go, the ice cliffs loom up green and for-
bidding. Clouds start closing in as I reach the next resting spot, and as
usual I sit in the last sun and have a smoke until it begins to snow. Soon
spindrift starts snaking down the cliffs and a grey coldness settles in. The
awful traverse, left through deep powder snow, the steep gangway
cutting through the sérac barrier and then the endless slog to Camp V,
sitting cheerlessly deep in the bergschrund.*

*One, two, three, a footstep collapses, my rhythm is lost, my body
revolts, it won't go on. I gasp for breath every few paces. A stone clatters
down hidden in the mist, and thuds into the snow near by. I am too tired to
care much. Can I hear voices up on rock band? The blank gape of the
bergschrund appears and with utter relief I collapse into the tent. It's done.*

Meanwhile, out in front, Mick Burke and Tom Frost were contending
with the Rock Band. The weather had at last improved and we had three
cloudless days in succession. It meant that down in the hot sun of Base
Camp we could watch them through the binoculars, two tiny dots, moving
imperceptibly on the huge Face. From below, the best route up the Rock
Band seemed to be across to the left up a series of icefields, broken by rock
walls leading to a prominent rock spur, reminiscent of the Flat Iron of the
Eiger. By this time we had abandoned all thought of attempting the huge
groove that cleaved the front of the buttress formed by the Rock Band. In
Tom's parlance it was the 'true aesthetic line on the Face', and would
obviously give magnificent and probably feasible climbing, but at this
stage we were looking for the easiest possible way up.

Tom and Mick started their first day of climbing on the morning of
10 May. Don and Dougal had already suggested that the best route
would be a traverse below the bergschrund to the left of the camp-site,
until it was possible to climb up over some iced-up slabs to a big snowfield that led straight up to the Flat Iron. Tom and Mick started out on
this route that morning, climbing unroped, because the angle was fairly
easy. Mick went first and Tom followed. They had only gone a few
yards, however, when the snow caved away beneath Tom and he found
himself wedged in the bottleneck of a huge crevasse, his feet kicking in

the dark void. He hastily scrambled back, badly shaken. Looking down into the gaping hole, he could see that it was at least sixty feet deep and widened out to six feet. They discussed what to do, divided by the crevasse line, which one or the other would have to cross. From this point they could look up at the Rock Band, and saw an inviting-looking groove leading up onto what seemed to be a line of ledges of snow slopes leading across to the snowfield they were trying to reach. After Tom's narrow escape the firm rock seemed all the more inviting.

And so they resolved to turn tail, return to the camp and strike up to the lowest point of the rocks, which they could skirt in relative safety. But Mick, without a rope, first had to get back to Tom. He edged his way, crablike, across the snow still covering the crevasse, adrenalin, from nervous tension, pumping hard. Once reunited they quickly got back to the camp and Mick thrust into the front once again; there is something irrepressible about Mick.

A short struggle with the bergschrund and Mick was able to pull up onto the snow above it and front-point on his crampons up to the foot of the Rock Band some fifteen feet above. He hammered in a rock-piton, clipped his rope into a karabiner on it and continued up the side of the buttress on ice that was now around fifty degrees in angle. This is steep by Alpine standards, similar to the Second Icefield on the North Wall of the Eiger. He was using a combination of ice-axe and ice-hammer; the latter was specially designed by Yvon Chouinard, Tom Frost's partner in their climbing hardware factory. It had a gently curved pick, with a number of serrations on its end, so that swung hard into the ice it bit in deep, like a fish hook, and could hold a man's weight. The pick on Mick's axe was less well designed and was blunt anyway, as were the points of his crampons—the results of weeks of climbing over ice-encrusted rocks and ice.

He whammed in the ice-hammer, pulled up on it, kicking with the two front points of his crampons into the ice, which had a thin covering of snow, giving a little extra support to his feet, and then jabbed ineffectually with the blunt pick of his axe, and held himself on it while he got a more secure point of contact with the ice-hammer, which bit into the hard ice about a quarter of an inch. And so he went on. It's strenuous, precarious climbing even at sea level, and he was at 23,000 feet.

He ran out a hundred and fifty feet before reaching a point where he could get back into the rock to get a secure rock-piton belay to bring up Tom. He had nearly reached the top of a bay in the icefield and his route now lay across the ice towards a rocky depression on the left-hand side of the bay. The ice was now both steeper and harder, without a protective covering of snow—it was like the smooth steel breastplate of a sleeping giant. His crampons kicked and skated ineffectively on the hard gleaming surface. Only the sharp pick of the Chouinard hammer enabled him to stay on his front points without resorting to the time-consuming measure of cutting steps.

Mick was climbing close to his limit and perhaps befuddled by lack of oxygen; it never occurred to him to hammer in an ice-piton to protect himself. He was now fifty feet above and to one side of Tom Frost, and if he had slipped he would have fallen nearly a hundred feet before being held on the rope. He had not cut any steps, and as a result was in a state of uncomfortable insecurity, hanging on the pick of his ice-hammer, his front points barely taking his weight. He could not even try to cut a step for fear of disturbing his precarious balance by the action of swinging his axe. He just froze, in a rising panic.

'Watch the rope, Tom,' he called. 'I could come off here.'

'How about putting in an ice-peg, Mick?' came the cool reply.

'Christ, I'd forgotten about them!' Mick fumbled at the karabiner on which he had slung half a dozen pegs. A one-handed struggle to free one from the gate of the karabiner, stab it into the ice to make it stand on its own—he can only use one hand for the other is clutching his axe; tap the pick of the axe into the ice to get a better hold, and then gently tap in the ice-piton.

'I got myself into a real panic there,' he admitted.

But now, reassured by the security of the piton, he once again picked his way across the steep ice, mainly on the front points of his crampons but cutting the occasional step. He was heading for a rock bay at the foot of a groove which he hoped would lead onto the next snow-band. And then he was in trouble again.

'My crampon's come off,' he shouted down to Tom. 'Watch the rope.'

The nylon straps had worn loose and his right crampon was dangling ineffectively from the ankle-strap. If he dropped it he would have a difficult time in getting it back, and it would be at least a day, perhaps longer, before he could get a replacement—and this would mean one day or more wasted. But at that instant Mick was much more concerned with the immediate problem of staying in contact with the ice. He was about five feet above his last ice-piton—somehow he had to get back to it without falling off and without losing his crampon.

Stabbing the pick of his hammer into the ice at about waist level, he cautiously let himself down till he could reach down for the piton, grasped it and let himself slide, at the same time grabbing for the crampon that was falling off his foot. It took him another ten minutes to get the crampon back on and fasten the straps. He still had to reach the security of the rocks—he was heading for a big flake that seemed to offer good handholds and an easy swing into the groove. Three staccato kicks with his crampons and he teetered within reach of the flake, seized it, but it moved. If it had come away it would inevitably have crushed him. There was a crack for a piton just in front of his nose, but he could only free one hand to get at his pitons. There were too many of them clipped onto the karabiner, and as a result the one he was trying to free jammed in the gate. His other arm was tiring from the strain of holding most of his weight, as he struggled to free the recalcitrant piton. At last he was able to pull it free and slotted it into the crack; a few blows of the hammer and it was home. He lowered himself carefully to a small ledge about eight feet below, just round the corner, pulled in what was left of the five hundred feet of rope on the reel, attached it to a couple of pitons, and slumped back for a rest and a cigarette while Tom jumared up the rope to join him. On his way up Tom tied off the rope at each intermediate piton to make it easier for the parties following up.

And then Mick set out up the next pitch. The bed of the groove was lined with smooth ice, from which protruded loose-looking flakes of rock. To the right, on the other hand, the rock was steeper, but looked more secure with plenty of small, incut holds for fingers and boot edges. As Tom jumared up the rope to join him, Mick got ready for the next pitch, removing crampons and overboots in readiness for what was obviously going to be a hard piece of free rock climbing, racking his pitons on karabiners slung to one side so that he could free them easily, and hanging the empty karabiners on the other, for clipping into the pitons.

'I'm not going to be caught out again,' Mick said, as Tom arrived at his stance.

Mick set off in the lead once more and Tom settled down for another long, patient wait, paying out the rope to the leader. In his diary that night he wrote:

> It is frigidly cold up here at 23,000 feet. Although the sun beats straight down, the wind and below-freezing temperature overpower it. We are quite comfortable climbing in all our clothing including down jackets. I am in ecstasy to be on rock again and busy myself collecting numerous small samples—the most beautiful ones to show my Love. The rock band is composed of various types of metamorphic rock, all of which seems to be good quality; what a beautiful creation this, and what a joy to climb on.
>
> I spend part of my time at one of my favourite pastimes, sitting on small ledges admiring the beauty below. Here the scale and magnitude are overwhelming and from our high vantage point we can see the minute workers setting out from each camp with their burdens, inching their way up the endless ropes.
>
> In the early daylight hours clouds begin forming in the floor of this huge Annapurna South Basin and as the morning hours pass they steadily grow and rise, blotting out each group of carriers and each camp in turn. We watch the clouds march like an invincible army until in the earliest hours of the afternoon at nearly the top of their surge, they swallow us up too, almost like an old friend who returns regularly and whom you are sure you will see again tomorrow.

Mick Burke led all the way across the lower part of the Rock Band to just below Camp VI, including very difficult rock sections of up to Grade V plus standard.

Out in front, Mick Burke was grappling with sheer rock and holds covered with a thin veneer of ice. His big double boots felt clumsy on the tiny incut edges and without crampons his feet slipped on any ice that he had failed to clear.

Mick thinks his way up the pitch.

. . . Tom is now about seventy feet below me; I look down and he gives me a grin. Just to the right is a crack, so I take a peg from my sling and knock it in. I'm beginning to tire and the next thirty feet also look hard. After resting for a few minutes and smoking a Gauloise, I launch myself from the safety of the piton. There's only a scrape on the surface of the rock for my feet and hardly anything to hang on to; reach up for a spike of rock, but it moves as I pull it. The only hope is to use the edge of a crack and lay back, leaning back on my arms, feet thrust in opposition against the blank wall opposite.

My hands are tiring; shove a foot out onto a flake, and it crumbles; only six feet above my peg; should be all right if it holds me, but will it? There's no choice, I must get the weight off my arms; cock my feet up to the flake, press gently against it, straighten up and reach for a ledge. I feel like a ballet dancer wearing diving-boots as I try to edge daintily up the flake and onto secure holds.

Time for another piton, but can I afford it? If I put one in here it'll make the rope drag badly behind me as it pulls over those flakes of rock. A gangway leads off to the left and I follow it, working my feet along it, finding a reassuringly sharp hold for my hand. Another pull and I'm back in the bed of the groove, the angle eases and I quickly climb to a ledge. . . .

Mick brought Tom up once again and, with what was left of their five-hundred-foot reel of rope, ran out another pitch to the top of the rock groove and the start of a snow-covered ledge leading back to the big snowfield. As they climbed, stones and larger rocks, loosened from their beds of ice in the heat of the afternoon sun, came whistling down, shattering on the rocks around them or thudding into the icefield below. In his diary Tom managed to be very resigned about the threat:

• • •

The high whistlers were coming down, occasionally landing close by (one on top of my Kelty Pack) and I gave thanks many times for the protection I am being given. Sooner or later someone will probably be hit by this falling rock or ice.

Another danger was that the fixed rope might easily have been hit and damaged, with the risk of its parting under the weight of anyone climbing it. This would almost certainly have led to a fatal accident. There was nothing they could do about it but hope for the best. On reaching the ledge leading into the main icefields, Mick hunted around for piton belays, eventually found a couple of suitable cracks and abseiled back.

Tom takes up the story in his diary:

The 11th was one of those mornings when you just wake up tired. As a result I kept on sleeping until Mick got up at 6.30. Breakfast was its normal unpalatable frozen self, except for some kippers which we fried in their tin.

The difficult climbing below Camp VI linked rock with long traverses across steep ice fields.

• • •

After breakfast Mick and Tom had the closest to an argument they had during their partnership on the Face. The smoking and drinking of most of the team had proved a sore trial to Tom, and he had teamed up with the heaviest smoker of the lot. Mick had a passion for Gauloises and had brought out 7,000 with him, most of which he managed to smoke himself. That morning Tom was feeling particularly queasy, the tent was zipped up and Tom was struggling to force on frozen boots. He suffered Mick's first cigarette of the morning in tight-lipped silence—and then Mick lit up a second and the explosion occurred. Suddenly Tom slammed his sleeping-bag down onto the floor. Hello, wonder what's wrong with him, thought Mick—then realized—the tent was like a London smog.

'Sorry, Tom, I just didn't think.' And he threw the offending cigarette out of the entrance.

'It's O.K., Mick,' Tom said, and the outburst was over. After this Mick was always careful to smoke by the entrance of the tent.

It was 9.30 before they were ready to leave. They carried another five hundred feet of rope and jumared up their fixed ropes to the previous day's high point. It was a superb day—completely windless, and the sun even had some heat behind it—but with the heat came heavier stonefall. Once again Mick Burke took the lead, climbing up to the rock wall above and then following its foot across the top of the snowfield that led straight up from near the bottom of the Rock Band. It was enjoyable, exciting climbing with sound running belays from pitons hammered into cracks in the rock, steep ice dropping away below their feet. A stretch on ice was followed by a few moves on rock, with good ledges for foot- and handholds, then some more moves on ice. The angle was as steep as that of the Third Icefield on the North Wall of the Eiger; the situation infinitely more impressive. Looking down, Mick could see every single camp on the Face—the boxes or tents, black blobs; the people, minute dots. The Annapurna South Glacier was eight thousand feet below. Above him the brown rock of the band reared endlessly, but to the left the Flat Iron, which he was trying to reach, jutted like the prow of a monster battleship out of the wall. He could only see its top, which looked sheer and unclimbable; another spur immediately in front of him blocked his view of the rest of the feature. Until he managed to round it he would be unable to tell whether it was climbable. He judged that the edge of the spur, which seemed to have a gully running up to the foot of the Flat Iron behind it, was fifty feet away, but as Mick edged his way across Tom called up, 'Only twenty more feet of rope.'

They had very nearly run out their ration of five hundred feet; Mick had no choice but to search for a piton belay and return, with the tantalizing question of what the route up the Flat Iron was going to be like still unanswered.

Back at Base Camp we had watched their progress through the binoculars. They were like tiny, black dots, even through high-powered binoculars. They seemed to move so slowly and it was impossible to tell just how difficult the going was. Even the distance they had covered did not seem very great, and we were worried, indeed aggrieved, because they had not taken the line straight up the snowfield, which seemed to give the most straightforward route and which would certainly be easier to follow on fixed ropes than the line they had selected. But it was all too easy for us to be critical, lying out in the hot sun at Base Camp on the flower-strewn grass. It was impossible to conceive just what it was like on the Rock Band, or just how exhausting was the carry from Camp IV to V. It was obvious, however, that Nick and Martin could not keep it up for very much longer. On top of this we were running out of time. It was now 11 May, less than three weeks before the possible arrival of the monsoon. From Base Camp we were painfully aware of just how much of the Rock Band was still towering above Mick and Tom. In trying to turn the steep front of the Band, we were increasing the amount of difficult climbing we should eventually have to face, for round to the left the Band increased in height, stretching up the side of the summit ridge; we could only hope that it would prove easier than it looked.

It was in this atmosphere that I came to a difficult but logical decision—to let Don and Dougal push straight through to the lead, rather than allow Martin and Nick their turn out in front. The latter

Martin Boysen (right) and Nick Estcourt showing signs of fatigue that was hitting the entire team.

pair were obviously very tired from their exhausting yet absolutely vital struggle to keep the line between Camps IV and V open. On top of this Don and Dougal undoubtedly had a drive and feel for the mountain that I felt no other pair had. We could not afford a route-finding mistake in the upper part of the Rock Band, and the Band looked as if it could be complex in the extreme. Don and Dougal also had the advantage of having spent a couple of days examining the route from the bottom through the binoculars. When on the Band it was impossible to see more than a few feet ahead and everything was very much foreshortened when one looked up.

Don and Dougal decided they had had enough rest after only two days and started back up the mountain on the 11th, the day that Ian Clough came back down for a rest.

It snowed that night, filling in everyone's hard-won steps up the fixed ropes, and at Camp V very nearly engulfed the camp. Mick and Tom were beginning to feel the effects of their two days of hard effort out in front. They felt tired and lethargic that morning, especially after a bad night, most of which they had spent trying to shake the fast-gathering snow from the roof of their tent, pushing it away from the entrance. In spite of this, Tom managed to wake at 4.30 and start breakfast. By this time everyone was getting tired of the high-altitude packs and had discovered two of their main inadequacies—lack of easily edible cereal for the mornings and of conventional hot drinks such as tea. This morning, Tom and Mick were able to enjoy some special luxuries brought up the previous day by Martin Boysen on his solitary carry to Camp V. They had instant porridge and some condensed milk. This was the ultimate in luxury, for you just had to warm some water and pour it over the porridge and you had a hot, palatable food that simply slooshed down the throat. Instant porridge, perhaps partly through its rarity value, was the favourite food of the entire expedition while on the mountain.

When eventually they were ready to start, they had to dig out their dump of supplies, which was covered by several feet of fresh snow. When eventually they had dug it out, they found that the five-hundred-foot reel of rope they needed for their day's climbing had disintegrated in the snow and had become inextricably tangled. It took them two hours to untangle it; they had also been delayed by some filming that John Edwards had asked them to do, with Mick filming Tom talking into the radio to link up with some film and sound that the T.V. team was taking of me down at Base Camp. They had warned me that if it took them too long to untangle the rope they might have to take a rest day. Fortunately, however, Tom succeeded in unravelling the rope by nine o'clock that morning and so they decided to try to push the route a little farther, at least to see round the corner of the spur to their immediate front.

Just climbing the fixed ropes was a nerve-racking, exhausting business and they now had very nearly a thousand feet in place; steep vertical pulls alternating with awkward traverses, where all they could do was hang on the ropes, cramponed boots slipping on the ice as they swung hand over hand from one piton anchor to the next. They reached the previous day's high point at about 12.30, and Mick once again went into the lead.

He found that morning that it was a great deal farther to the corner of the spur than the forty feet he had estimated the previous day. It was also harder, a mixture of steep, hard ice and smooth, ice-worn rock; nowhere to rest, nowhere to put in a protective piton. Suddenly he became painfully aware of what could happen if he did fall off and injure himself—it would have taken at least two days for any help to arrive, and that would only be Nick and Martin from Camp IV. Getting back across the traverse would be almost impossible with an injured arm or leg, and a night out almost certainly fatal. He just couldn't afford to fall.

He was nearing the foot of the gully—rock jutted out of the ice like splintered bones out of the skin in a compound fracture. Boots or crampons? He'd be better off with the cleated rubber sole of his boots on the rock, but near helpless on ice. With crampons, on the other hand, he would be unable to use small rock holds, but would be better off on the ice. He opted for boots, removed his crampons and overboots, and started up the rocks. Every hold had to be wiped clear of snow, some chipped clear of ice.

A hundred feet of rope ran out and he at last reached a small ledge with a good piton crack behind it—the first real resting-place he had passed. He wondered whether to make this a stance, but there seemed to be a better ledge about thirty feet higher, so he hammered in a piton, left a runner there and continued climbing. He now had nearly two hundred feet of rope running round corners and through several pitons trailing behind him; it felt as if Tom was hanging on the end of it pulling him back each time he tried to thrust himself forward.

Mick reached the ledge and curled his fingers over its edge, but the rope held him back.

'Let the rope loose, Tom,' he shouted, but knew already that it was no good, for Tom was paying the rope out as best he could. It was sticking somewhere in between.

He pulled a short length of slack, heaved up onto one elbow then the next, tried to straighten out, but the rope was pulling him back—it was a sixty-foot, bone-breaking fall if he came off. Feet scrabbled on the rock, he got one knee over onto the ledge, then the other, and slowly straightened out, panting his lungs out.

He was still just short of the couloir, but while Tom jumared up the rope he had fixed, Mick tried to work out the route into it, and also looked down the Face to see what else was happening on the mountain. Suddenly he did not feel quite so alone as he watched a tiny, solitary figure plod up the long snow slopes towards Camp V; others starting down the ridge back towards Camp III.

'Lucky beggars, they've got some good food down there; I wonder why the hell it never seems to reach us.'

And then Tom, tired and panting, arrived at the ledge.

'Which way do you think, Tom? I don't fancy the gully; it looks desperate to me. This last pitch was hard enough. I reckon we want to get on the rock.'

'I'm not so sure, Mick, at least the gully's a definite line. You might get yourself into trouble out on the rock; looks steep to me.'

'O.K. I'll have a look at the couloir anyway.'

Mick put his crampons back on and started across towards the gully—it felt good to be able to slam the points into ice again after the previous pitch of dainty, nerve-racking edging from one slippery hold to the next. Eighty feet of rope ran out and he had reached the gully.

'It doesn't look too bad,' he shouted back. 'It only goes up for about a hundred feet and seems to fizzle out into the Face, but it looks as if there's a way across from the top to the Flat Iron.'

'Sounds good to me.'

'Anyway, I'll pull the rope in and fix it here. I've done enough for one day.'

'It's quite early yet. Don't you think we should try to get up to the top of the gully and see what it's like?'

'I'm bloody tired. I don't fancy any more today.'

'O.K. Come on back.'

They turned tail and started swinging back down the ropes. Before they had completed a rope-length the afternoon storm hit them. It was as if someone had thrown a switch. One minute it was sunny and sufficiently warm to climb without gloves; the next, the temperature had dropped about thirty degrees, powder snow avalanches were pouring down the Band in huge cascades and the wind was tearing at their clothes. By the time they got back to the camp-site, the tent was already very nearly buried under the spindrift.

That day Nick had managed to reach Camp V carrying another coil of rope and a little food, while Martin had rested at IV, his first rest day after three successive carries. That same day Mike Thompson had moved up to IV to try to reinforce this exhausting carry.

That night in the storm-battered tent both Mick and Tom were beginning to feel the strain. Tom wrote in his diary:

> 14 May. Tonight I am exhausted, or at least overtired. I have trouble eating—a rarity—and we both suffer mild headaches. I don't know how many more days we can last up here. It is not a matter of my wanting to stay out in front like Mick, but a question of who can replace me at the moment. Don and Dougal only arrived at Camp II tonight (carrying the sealed autoload camera reserved for the summit bid). Nick and Martin (and now Mike) are unable to keep the desired amount of supplies moving from IV to V, the present bottleneck now that so many of the team are fizzling; the altitude is taking its toll.

Mick, on the other hand, who felt he was climbing well, still saw himself at the front, writing:

> Heavy snow falling and lots of powder snow avalanches. Well, we might get a chance to consolidate our position even if we can't climb. We are very short of things at Camp V, in fact, we are still living from day to day. Nick is pretty tired, Martin is having trouble with his hands and Ian has gone down. Don and Dougal are on their way up so they should be able to inject some new life into the bad carry from IV to V. Soon though we shall have to put up another camp. That means we need at least two more people to carry from V to VI.
>
> The snow is building up outside. Every so often we have to flap the

sides of the tent to stop the build-up and push it away from the doors. While we cook we have to have the doors open otherwise we suffer from the paraffin fumes. I take this opportunity to have a cigarette, but I have an idea we won't be keeping this door open for much longer. Every few minutes we hear the sound of another avalanche flowing over the overhang. We rush to get the door closed before it flows inside, and then as soon as it's stopped we open up again. It's proving quite hard to live up here.

That night their tent was very nearly buried by the almost non-stop torrent of powder snow avalanches. Inside it was now desperately uncomfortable as a result of the hollows melted by their bodies. This meant that everything rolled into the middle of the tent, and it was becoming increasingly difficult to cook without upsetting the stove. On top of this, Tom and Mick were tired from three days of difficult climbing—probably the hardest that has ever been attempted at altitude. When they described their condition on the seven o'clock call I suggested they take a day off to dig out a platform for another tent or box at Camp V and for one of them to go down to the Col to pick up a load from there. I hoped that Tom and Mick would reach the top of the Flat Iron in the next day or so, and that we should be able to establish Camp VI there. Don and Dougal were due to reach Camp IV the following day, and at this stage I was planning for Martin to move up to Camp V the next day, either to take over from Mick or Tom, or to pick up loads from the Col, and then for Don and Dougal to move through to Camp VI once it was established.

Tom, who was the more tired of the pair, spent the day clearing the camp—no easy task, for even shovelling snow at altitude was exhausting. He described it in his diary:

It had turned out a beautiful, near cloudless day and I spent much of the time admiring the view from our near 23,000-foot platform, in between huffing and puffing over the simplest and most minor chores.

Meanwhile, Mick dropped down to the Col, wading out a trail through the deep snow. Even in descent it took him an hour, and without his trailbreaking from above Martin and Mike Thompson would have had an exhausting time forcing the route from below. He met Martin at the Col and was immediately impressed with the speed at which Martin was climbing; he slogged up to the ice cliff with hardly a pause. Mike Thompson, on the other hand, was not going nearly as well. This was the highest he had yet been and he had certainly never used jumars on a section as steep and difficult as the Terrible Traverse. On top of this he was badly run down as a result of spending eighteen days consecutively on the Face.

Mick Burke waited for Mike to arrive at the Col and the two started together back up the fixed ropes leading to the ice cliff, but Mick soon found that he was pulling ahead. At the foot of the ice cliff he waited once again, thinking that he might have to relieve Mike of some of his load, for he was carrying some of the luxury foods—coffee, tinned milk and porridge, which Mick was determined to have at Camp V that night.

Mike had reached the stage where he had to halt for a rest at each step, where each step required a superhuman effort, repeated step after step after step, like an endless, punishing treadmill. The ice cliff became the focal point of his entire being—at all costs he had to reach it— another step, another rest, sagging on the fixed rope, and it never seemed to get closer. An hour slipped by unnoticed—an hour, and a hundred feet gained—a distance you could cover at sea level in five minutes. And he willed himself on, until at long, weary last he reached the ice cliff.

He slumped into the slope, panting hard.

'You O.K., Mike?' Mick Burke asked.

'No, I feel desperate.'

'Have a rest here and you'll feel better in a few minutes.'

Mike Thompson got out some nuts and offered them to Mick Burke, but Mike's condition worsened. His breathing seemed to have got out of control, rising to a crescendo of raucous pants. He was convinced he was dying; it was as if his heart and lungs were exploding. Mick Burke was equally convinced and began to wonder how to give the kiss of life if he stopped breathing. It just didn't seem possible that anyone could keep up these lung-tearing, hacking gasps for breath for long.

'I tried to remember what the symptoms of pulmonary oedema were,' Mick Burke admitted later. 'I just stood there, waiting for him to die, and then, I suppose to relieve my own tension as much as anything else, asked him what he had done with the nuts. This seemed to bring him round a bit. His breathing slowly returned to normal, so I relieved him of his goodies and carried up to Camp V. Mike said he would wait where he was until Martin got back, and then return with him to Camp IV.'

Martin and Mike got back to Camp IV in time for the five o'clock radio call. This was when I gave out my orders to cover the next few days and, in doing so, introduced the only serious argument we had on the entire expedition.

CHAPTER 14

The Flat Iron
[13-15 May]

It was five minutes to five on 13 May. Everyone down at Base Camp gathered round the walkie-talkie set for the evening radio call. This was the focal point of the day, when for a few minutes the entire party, scattered up ten thousand feet of the mountain in six different camps, were united and could tell of their progress and supply requirements. This was also my only means of controlling the logistic build-up of the expedition and the movement of the climbers.

This evening Tom Frost and Mick Burke were up at Camp V, Martin Boysen, Nick Estcourt and Mike Thompson at Camp IV, Dave Lambert with four of the Sherpas in residence at Camp III, while Don and Dougal were staying the night there on their way back up to the front. Alan Hankinson, with the two London Sherpas, was at Camp II, and Ian Clough, on his way back up the mountain, was stopping at Camp I, which was occupied by four of our local porters.

At Base Camp, Kelvin Kent was holding the Bantam radio and I took the microphone. The T.V. team and a few cookboys were standing round. Three minutes to five; the walkie-talkie sputtered with atmospherics and then Nick Estcourt from Camp IV came on the air.

NICK: Hello, Base, do you read me? Over.

CHRIS: Hello, Camp IV, you're loud and clear. Over.

NICK: So are you.

CHRIS: Roger. How did the carry go today?

NICK: I didn't go, but Mike and Martin went—they got the rest of the gear and food up. I think Mike is very tired and won't be going tomorrow anyway.

CHRIS: Well done. We were actually able to watch them. Did Mick or Tom come all the way down? We thought we saw a third man.

NICK: Mick came all the way down, yes.

CHRIS: I see. So am I right in thinking that we have now got the complete box plus a camp kit at Camp V?

NICK: Yes.

CHRIS: In that case how does it seem to you up there if Martin actually moved up to Camp V tomorrow so he can do the carry down and Mike and yourself do the carry up to the col?

NICK: Yes, that's what we had already decided. Martin's going to move up tomorrow. I'll do a carry up tomorrow and then, from then onwards we'll just have to see what happens.

CHRIS: Well, you'll have Don and Dougal arrive at your camp tomorrow night.

NICK: Yes, we are aware of that.

CHRIS: So that means if Martin goes up I think it will pay for Don and Dougal to do one carry right up to Camp V to get some stuff up there, and then the following day for them to move up to Camp V. This will mean pulling back one of the three to Camp IV.

NICK: What about me?

CHRIS: We are going to use their freshness to push them out in front and make a bit of progress. I think that is the only thing practical.

NICK: No, I was only half joking. All right, anyway, so far as tomorrow is concerned I'll be doing a carry the whole way. Martin will be moving up and Don and Dougal will be moving up to this camp-site.

CHRIS: That's right, out to you. Hello, Camp III. Are you on the air?

DOUGAL: Roger, Chris. Hearing you clear.

CHRIS: Hello, Dougal. Did you hear what I was saying to Nick?

DOUGAL: Yes, I heard it. It sounds O.K.

CHRIS: Once you're up at Camp IV it will be easier for you to work out just who comes back, but I think it would pay to use your and Don's fitness and freshness just for one carry to get as much as possible—particularly the complete Camp VI kit—up to Camp V; and then the following day— it will be the day after the day after tomorrow—for you actually to move up to Camp V.

DOUGAL: That's probably O.K. We were thinking it might save time to put a very heavy load on ourselves plus our personal gear, and move right through because there definitely needs to be a little bit of . . . well, a need of freshness at the front.

CHRIS: That would mean what? You would go up there the day after tomorrow, then?

DOUGAL: Ah . . . yes, that is what we are thinking of.

CHRIS: That actually is a better idea than for you to hold back even another day. I agree with that—out to you. Hello, Camp IV, come in please.

NICK: Nick here, Chris. There is a fantastic pile up of oxygen, food, rope and everything else building up out here, you know.

CHRIS: I know that, but I think the thing is that we want to start pushing out the route as fast as possible because the faster we can push the route out the less oxygen we need to use. I think anyway, in principle, we are going to have to use the minimum of oxygen and if climbers find that they can climb without oxygen fair enough. We'll just use the oxygen for the summit bid.

NICK: Yes, all right, and the ones that climb without food?

CHRIS: I think we can cope with the food fairly easily. I think in that case, if Dougal and Don move straight through—and I think there are some strong arguments in favour of this—it would be simpler, unless Mick or Tom need relieving up at Camp V, to hold Martin back at IV.

NICK: I think you will find that Martin is going very strongly at the moment. I mean—I'm not going very strongly but it's possible to argue the pros and cons of this. There's certainly arguments in both directions.

CHRIS: Roger, out to you. Hello, Camp V. Come in please.

MICK: Hello, Chris. I've been listening to all the argument. If you bring Don and Dougal up the hill who's going to take it between IV and V?

CHRIS: Between IV and V: Martin and Nick up to the col for the time being, you and Tom from the col, or rather from the bergschrund down to the col.

MICK: I can see absolutely no point in bringing Don and Dougal when they are in a really good position to carry from IV to V, when there is nobody else apart from Martin fit enough to carry through IV to V.

CHRIS: But the trouble is we do want to push out progress as quickly as possible, and I think their freshness will be of value in this direction. It is here that one has got to make a firm decision. Don and Dougal carrying heavy loads will move straight through to V and then you and Tom can do some carrying, which will give you a rest, back down to the col picking up loads there. Martin and Nick can do some carrying just to the shoulder which will also give them a rest.

MICK: The thing is, Chris, you don't realize what it is like up here. It's much easier to lead than to carry loads. I honestly think that I have been so long out of Base Camp that if I have to go back to carrying I'm going to have to go back to Base for a rest, and I think that Tom feels the same way.

CHRIS: O.K. That's entirely your decision if you want to do that.

MICK: Chris, you are taking it completely the wrong way, you are taking it as though I'm being awkward; we are not, it is much easier to lead and I think we can push forward as quickly as Don or Dougal, but to go back on the carrying from IV to V when we've been out of Base Camp for twenty-five days would be too much. It's very, very difficult to carry and I don't think that we are fit enough to do that carrying day after day. I think it will be much more sensible for Don and Dougal who've just had a rest to do the carry from IV to V for two or three days to just stock up the equipment here.

CHRIS: Except I think we are in a very strong position now for a summit push. It is not as though Tom and you are being pulled back; what I want to avoid at this stage is moving people more than it is absolutely necessary. Now once Don and Dougal are up at Camp V it means that you have just got half a carry to do, in other words, down to the end of the snowfield and back again. I realize that this is quite hard but provided the Rock Band goes fairly easily I think this is something that we'll be able to do fairly quickly. If the Rock Band proves a siege there is no shadow of doubt in my mind that most probably you and Tom, Nick and Martin are going to have to be pulled back for a rest and the thing's going to be very much slower.

NICK: Chris, this is Nick at Camp IV—can I butt in please?

CHRIS: Yes, sure, shoot.

NICK: Chris, I don't think you can possibly realize how fast equipment is building up at Camp IV here. Two of us carrying together could barely support Tom and Mick when they were working together, let alone four people up above us. We've hardly taken any pegs up—it's as much as we can do to take up the rope and food that they need in a day.

CHRIS: But remember though once we've got the upward-downward carrier although we're still only getting two loads per day through, it will be a great deal easier for all four of you and you will be able to take up heavier individual loads.

NICK: Yes, but what you're forgetting, Chris, is those two up to the shoulder from here, and from the shoulder to the new Camp V, are very nearly as much as a normal load carry is, anyway, and you're still expecting two people to support four people living above them plus the lead pair which is all we ever succeeded in doing before.

CHRIS: You're four people, though, four people in front, two ration packs per day plus a small quantity of fuel. This isn't that much.

NICK: Yes, but there's all the other odd bits and pieces which all add up like film, pegs, rope, the camp kit for Camp VI, oxygen which you need for the final push. You get through oxygen very quickly once you start using it.

CHRIS: I appreciate that but, in fact, pushing Don and Dougal straight through or holding them back is not going to make very much difference. If we don't start this broken carry it simply means we shatter everyone, including Don and Dougal. I think we've got to a stage at the moment where we need to make fairly quick progress out in front. This might or might not be possible. Now, if it isn't possible, in other words if the technical difficulty is so great, I think we're going to have to think again and perhaps pull people back for a rest before we all go back, but in the meantime, I think to push them up fast and keep them going out in front gives us probably the best chance of success. I realize that all four of you up there at IV and V have done a hell of a lot and are bloody tired and you know I can fully appreciate your point, but I think that to move Don and Dougal through fairly quickly, try to get some progress with fresh people out in front, provided you can just keep the trickle of supplies going, should help. I hope I'll be up in another couple of days' time. Ian's set out today so these are two more reinforcements.

NICK: Well, the point is, Chris, we're not tired. There's just . . . there is just too much job here, at least we're not tired all the time, there's too much job in carrying loads up to the summit pair, up to the in front pair.

CHRIS: Well, on this I'd be glad to compromise and say if Don and Dougal do one carry up to V to shift some stuff up and we will see how you get on tomorrow as well and then from there we can come to our decision.

NICK: O.K. We agree to that.

CHRIS: Hello, Dougal. Did you hear that?

DOUGAL: Yes, sounds O.K. Don wants to say something.

I should have ended there. In retrospect, I realize I made a mistake in agreeing to change my original plan when Dougal suggested that Don and he should move straight through to Camp V without spending a day carrying loads up to V. I was in complete sympathy with Don and Dougal's sense of urgency, and being down at Base Camp, and not having made the punishing carry from IV to V myself, I could not fully appreciate just how hard it was.

There was a great deal of truth in Nick's appreciation of the situation, for they could barely cope with the day-to-day supplying of Camp V, let alone ferrying up the dozen or so oxygen bottles that at this stage it seemed we should need, in addition to the gear for Camps VI and VII. This, however, could as easily have been done by Nick and Martin from Camp IV, working up to the Col, and Mick Burke and Tom Frost working down, leaving the rested and thrustful Don and Dougal to push out in front—it all came down to a question of morale and endurance. In this respect I believe I made the right decision.

Anyway, I seemed to have won a measure of agreement from the team and, by agreeing to the compromise solution that Don and Dougal should complete one carry before moving up to V, had returned in principle to what I originally directed. And then Don dropped his bombshell:

DON: I thoroughly agree with everything you said. Dougal and I left that place Camp V a week ago. Camp V isn't even consolidated and the progress of all towards Camp VI is so poor that it's had me and Dougal depressed all the way up the mountain. I don't know what Mick thinks he's playing at but Camp V is short and we want to get the route pushed out and unless they get their finger out, push it out and establish VI or at least find a site, they should make way for somebody else to try. He's had a week and progress seems very poor.

CHRIS: But, Don—here you must be fair and, in fact, except for today they've been running out the full five hundred feet of rope each day. They've certainly been doing their best. I can appreciate their feelings. We do need to build up a bit out in front and we'll see what happens tomorrow. I definitely don't want you to do more than one carry from IV to V. I think this one day of carrying will be well worth while and then, come what may, the day after that one carry you and Dougal should move up to V.

DON: All right, we're agreeable to that. We establish the camp and fix the rope. The plan for splitting the carry should have been put into operation about five days ago. They were told about that but they still persisted in exhausting themselves and therefore they came back half-way today on the full carry; it was just too much.

NICK: Look, how on earth do you think that with four people we could have split the carry and carried on pushing the route ahead?

CHRIS: Stop, all of you. Cut it out. Let's not have an argument here. Everyone's trying their bloody guts out to do this climb, and I think we can sort this out without any of this kind of argument. So we'll go firm on this. Don and Dougal move up to Camp IV tomorrow, the day after that they do a carry up to V, the day after that they actually move into V. I think it would probably be better if Martin and Nick for the time being stayed at IV. The moment we've got four people in at V we can split the carry which is going to mean that people will be left exhausted, but for heaven's sake let's not have a kind of a bloody great argy-bargy argument. We've managed to be a happy expedition up to now—let's keep it that way. Over and out.

We then got down to the practicalities of agreeing to the flow of supplies from camp to camp. Mick and Tom wanted some more porridge and coffee sent up to Camp V. We agreed that Nick and Martin should make yet another carry to Camp V. Kelvin Kent was at Camp II with two Franco-Swiss visitors who had wandered into our camp two days before. Since they were climbers he had promptly recruited them for the lower carries on the mountain and was on his way up to Camp III. Our local porters had now taken over the carry from Camp I to II completely, and Kelvin was even thinking of using them all the way up to III.

Once we went off the air, each group scattered in the camps on the mountain, plunged into discussion over my decision. Mick Burke and Tom Frost understandably were the most outraged. They had made excellent progress on difficult ground in the last three days and this seemed to have been completely ignored. Tom, in his diary, recorded that evening:

> On the 9.0 p.m. call Chris outlined the plan of attack; Don and Dougal now at Camp III would be pushed up the mountain right to the front.

240

Being fresh they could push the route the fastest and move on the summit bid. From my view O.K. for a long shot, quick success (only it won't work), but the biggest problem is morale. It will shatter the hopes of the carriers who had hoped for their fair turn out in front; particularly Nick and Martin presently trying to cope with the physically devastating carry from IV to V who will be passed up with little hope for more than a supporting role.

For the first time for me politics and personality problems rear their ugly heads and it ceases to be an idyllic, but becomes a normal expedition. As in life these schemers will drink from their own cup of wrath— time will tell.

Mick responds to challenges and so after the insults hurled by Whillans and the apparent plan to de-phase all climbers but he and Dougal, we resolved to fix the next day the entire eight hundred feet of rope that we had, just to show them the progress we could make.

Nick and Martin, the ones who had been passed over, were less outraged, since they realized just how tired they now were. Nick had protested on straight tactical grounds that he believed we should build up Camp V before trying to move on to VI.

The next morning Mick and Tom set out early, but it took them fully four hours to reach the top of the fixed ropes, on the edge of the couloir leading up the side of the Flat Iron. Mick swung into the centre of the couloir, using tension from the rope, and gazed up the steep gully. The walls on either side were steep and compact; and the ice in the bed of the couloir ran out into overhanging rock at its head. There was no route there, but across to the right on the flanks of the Flat Iron the rock seemed more broken and was seamed with ice-gummed cracks and snow-piled ledges.

Mick chose this line and edged his way across the gully and then over steep, snow-covered ice slopes to the foot of the Flat Iron, where he managed to find a belay and bring Tom Frost up. Tom followed slowly, laden down by the weight of five hundred feet of rope and a quantity of spare rock-pitons. From their stance at the foot of the Flat Iron it all looked steeper and more difficult than it had from the other side of the gully; the rock reared above them, vertical and overhanging. Mick took the lead again and teetered across the steep ice into a groove that seemed to lead towards the top. Slowly the rope ran out through Tom's hands, as Mick edged his way from hold to hold, clearing ice as he went. He did not dare use too many pitons for protection because of the problem of rope drag. His arms were beginning to tire, calf muscles to ache. He could hardly control the judder of his heels for they were constantly tensed across the groove in a series of wide bridging moves.

He had run out nearly two hundred feet of rope when he reached the final wall which barred his way to the crest of the Flat Iron. The rope behind him was dragging badly and each inch upwards seemed a battle against it. The rock now arched up into the vertical, there were no footholds and an icy armour encased every crack. He draped a sling over a rock flake and tentatively stepped into it, swung across out of the groove and onto another line of holds—rocky encrustations sticking out of the ice. As he delicately balanced from one to the next, his ankles were trembling like those of a jitterbug, threatening to dislodge him from his holds. His arms barely had the strength left to make those last final pulls towards his haven, a small ledge on the crest of the ridge. When he reached it, Mick had run out two hundred feet of rope and had undoubtedly climbed the most exacting stretch of rock that we encountered on the South Face of Annapurna. Driving himself to the limit, he had also made more impressive progress on difficult ground than anyone had during the entire expedition. In doing so he made our eventual success possible.

He pulled up the rope between him and Tom anchored it to a couple of pitons. While Tom followed up on jumars, Mick started to work his way up towards the crest of the Flat Iron ridge. He ran out of rope when still a hundred feet or so below it, wondered whether to continue climbing solo just to see the other side of the ridge, but prudence prevailed and he returned to find Tom just emerging onto the ledge immediately above the steep side of the Flat Iron.

They had had a magnificent day's climbing, fixing all their eight hundred feet of rope in position, but in doing so they had exhausted themselves. That night on their return to Camp V they told me over the radio that they would have to come down for a rest the next day. Mick had now been twenty-eight days on the Face; Tom a few days less. They were certainly due for a rest. On a cynical level, one could argue that Don Whillans's needling on the wireless, however unfair it might have been, had been effective, for Tom and Mick had done in one day what they would probably have taken at least two to complete if the row had never taken place.

It was fairly obvious that once they had completed their spell out in front, with the best will in the world, they would not have been able to stay on in a ferrying role. I asked them if they could do just one more carry, dropping down to the dump and ferrying back a couple of loads before their descent, but they told me they were too tired. Mick had severe pains in his chest and Tom felt near the end of his tether.

This left Don, Dougal, Martin, Nick and Mike Thompson at Camp IV. The same day (15th) that Mick and Tom had made their big push on the Rock Band, Don and Dougal had made a carry right through to Camp V, carrying heavy loads, while Martin, understandably tired from his two successive carries to Camp V, only went as far as the col. Nick Estcourt, who was not going as strongly as Martin, spent the day resting at IV. The most serious blow, however, was Mike Thompson's retreat. That morning he set out to reach the col with Martin, but on the first fixed rope felt a trickle of blood running down his leg; he was feeling weak and tired anyway, but this was the last straw—an appalling cluster of piles had burst. He felt he had no choice but to return to Base for a rest.

In some ways it looked as if Nick Estcourt's diagnosis of the situation could have been right—on the other hand, I still felt that in the very limited time we now had available we had to ensure fast progress out in front and that Don and Dougal were the only pair that could ensure this. The 15th was a busy day. I also started back up the mountain. The pain in my chest had settled into a dull but bearable ache. I felt tired and lackadaisical, yet seemed to be moving quite strongly. I had decided to

243

reach Camp II in a single push, and on my way up met the others as they came down. First there was Mick Burke who looked desperately tired and haggard.

'Don't think we came down out of spite,' he told me. 'We're exhausted—we couldn't possibly have gone on any longer.'

Tom was a long way behind him, and I had been at Camp II for an hour or so when he arrived.

'I hope you'll allow me to say this as an outsider. I think you've destroyed the spirit of the expedition by pushing Don and Dougal in front out of turn; it was a real stab in the back for Nick and Martin.'

'Look, Tom, I can appreciate how you feel, but there does come a time when you've got to choose expedience rather than fair turns for all, if you're going to climb a big mountain like this one. Martin and Nick have done a terrific job, but I think they've burnt themselves out in doing it. We must have some real poke out in front, and I just don't think they've got it any longer. They've already given too much, while Don and Dougal are well rested.'

'I'm not so sure,' he replied. 'Even on a level of expedience, I think you've destroyed their morale to such a degree that you might not get much more carrying out of them anyway. It's no good having a pair going strongly out in front if there's no one to support them.'

'You could be right, but I'm convinced that unless we get things moving fast in a final push for the summit, we could grind to a halt. I'm sure Nick and Martin will keep going as best they can—after all, this is what teamwork is all about, isn't it?'

'But *is* this teamwork? Up to now we've kept roughly in turn, though Don and Dougal have done less carrying than anyone else and have definitely nursed themselves for the summit. I'd rather risk failure and yet have everyone feeling that they had had a fair share of the leading which, after all, is the real reason why we have all come together on this climb.'

'I'm sorry, Tom, I just can't agree with that. I don't think you'll ever get complete fairness in any function of life. Look at Hillary and Tensing on Everest—they were nursed by John Hunt for their summit

Dougal Haston on fixed rope going up from camp 5 to 6 to take over the lead.

bid, and I think we must do the same if we're to be successful. I stand by my decision. I think it's the only thing we can do if we want to pull the climb off.'

We carried on for a long time, going over the same old arguments—I think of all members of the team, I respected Tom's selflessness and judgement the most. I was desperately disturbed by how upset he had been by my decision. I think both of us wanted to avoid an acrimonious argument.

That night at Base Camp, Tom wrote in his diary:

> *Chris and I have the appointed discussion regarding his decision to push Don and Dougal out in front of Nick and Martin. He was unaware of their disappointment in this. Although we were of opposing views on the subject for once I felt a good spirit present and I think we ended closer friends than before.*

That evening the radio call was short and to the point. The following morning Don, Dougal and Martin were going to move up to Camp V, while Ian and Dave would join Nick at Camp IV. Kelvin and I planned to move up to Camp III. In this way I hoped to plug the gap left by Mick Burke, Mike Thompson and Tom Frost, but I couldn't help wondering just how long Martin and Nick would be able to keep going.

CHAPTER 15

Attrition
(16–20 May)

On 16 May Martin, Dougal and Don moved up to Camp V; Ian and Dave Lambert to Camp IV; Kelvin and myself to Camp III. I was hopeful that this might be for the final push, but it all depended on the weather, and that afternoon, after three perfect days, the old pattern of afternoon snow recurred. At this stage we did not know how far we were to be extended, but in the next fortnight every member of the team was going to drive himself to his own personal limit and beyond.

In Chapter 17, Dougal Haston describes his personal experience over this period; in the next two I shall describe mine. I never got out to the front, yet, simply in a support role, drove myself harder than I have ever before done in the mountains. My own story could be duplicated by that of Martin, Nick or Ian. Dougal's and my stories cross on several occasions in the final days of the expedition when we met at camps, and yet we saw the same situation from different points of view, often interpreting the same events in different ways. I have therefore allowed our two accounts to complement each other.

That morning I set out from Camp II with Kelvin and the two Franco-Swiss climbers who had called in at Base Camp three days before. They had a tale of woe. Jean-Louis Pallarton came from Geneva and Jean-Marie Hagenmuler from Strasbourg; they had travelled out to Nepal overland, using public transport—a mixture of trains and buses—hoping to make a serious reconnaissance and perhaps an unofficial attempt on Machapuchare. They seemed blissfully unaware of all the hazards of high-altitude climbing. Anyway, they had been thwarted through the theft of all their gear on the train from Delhi.

'We were travelling for two days and nights,' Jean-Louis told me; 'we couldn't keep awake all the time, and as soon as we both dropped off to sleep some of the passengers stole everything we had.'

They had managed to buy some boots and light sleeping-bags in Katmandu and had decided to trek to the foot of Machapuchare. When they arrived at our Base Camp Kelvin promptly recruited them, kitted them out with borrowed gear and marched them onto the mountain. He hoped to use them for the carry to Camp III, and they were coming with us that morning. They both had severe headaches and were feeling very sorry for themselves as they plodded up the long gully leading to the camp. They had only managed about twenty pounds each, but Kancha, who was due for a rest at Base Camp, made up for this by carrying a double load of sixty pounds.

When we reached Camp III we met the four other Sherpas who had just got back from their carry up to Camp IV. Although they were very impressed by it, saying that it was the most difficult ground they had ever been on, they were now so used to monkeying up the fixed ropes that they were able to get up to the camp and back in under three hours.

I was hoping to persuade Ang Pema and Pemba Tharkay, the two most experienced of the Sherpas, to move up to Camp IV and undertake the arduous carry up to V. This stretch was technically very much more difficult than the one to Camp IV, but once they had mastered the necessary jumar techniques I hoped they would be able to cope with it. They undoubtedly had greater endurance than we had and could probably have kept open this exacting carry, enabling us to ferry the necessary oxygen and tent kits up to Camp V.

Kelvin put this to them when we arrived at the camp, but did not get a favourable response. Pemba and Ang Pema felt that they needed a rest. They had been carrying loads up to Camp IV for over a week.

'After we've had a rest at Base Camp we might go up to Camp IV,' Pemba, the main spokesman, said. They had already done a great deal more for us on difficult ground than Sherpas had ever done in the past, so we had no choice but to agree. Even so, they agreed to drop back to Camp II that afternoon and then do one double-load carry up to III next morning before going back for their rest. This meant we should have enough food and paraffin at Camp III to last for the next ten days, enabling us to concentrate on the upper part of the mountain.

After Pemba and Ang Pema had left, Nima, rather diffidently, approached Kelvin and said, 'Sahib, Mingma and I have been talking things over and we realize how much you need to carry stores above Camp IV. We are prepared to have a go.'

But we couldn't accept their generous offer: having lost Pemba and Ang Pema we needed Nima and Mingma down at III to ferry gear up to Camp IV. The three-cornered discussion with Pemba and Ang Pema through Kelvin, acting as interpreter, had taken over an hour, and while we were talking our two Franco-Swiss Sherpas staggered into camp and collapsed exhausted into one of the Whillans Boxes. This was their only carry up to Camp III, and it was all we could do to persuade them to stagger back down to Camp II that night. They would have liked to spend the night where they were.

I had hoped to get up to Camp IV the following day, but the weather seemed to have set in, and the stormclouds gusted in before we had reached the foot of the fixed ropes. The two Sherpas were out in front and complained that their jumars were slipping on the iced ropes. I was glad of the excuse to retreat, for I was going very badly, finding upward progress almost as exhausting as I had two weeks before when I had retreated to Base Camp.

This was Kelvin's first visit to Camp III and he had been struck down by the familiar Camp III headache, spending the day in his sleeping-bag. On the evening radio call, John Edwards and the television team at Base sang to Don at Camp V a special rendering of 'Happy Birthday': it was Don's thirty-seventh birthday that day—to be celebrated with lambs'-tongue stew and Christmas pudding in the cold comfort of the Whillans Box.

But the following morning was fine and we set out once again for Camp IV. Kelvin had recovered from his headache and was able to come with us—the highest he had ever been and the first time that he had ever used jumar clamps or crampons. He could not have had a worse tutor: I tend to be impatient and failed to check details which to me were commonplace. As a result I did not notice that Kelvin's crampons were about three sizes too big for his boots and needed adjustment. We waded through deep, fresh snow to the foot of the fixed ropes and muttering to Kelvin a few words about clipping his two jumars onto the fixed rope and pulling up on each alternately, I started up, hoping to film him as he came towards me. I stopped at the first snow anchor and waited for Kelvin. He came up slowly, was obviously having trouble with his crampons, both of which were falling off his boots—and then one of them came right off; he dived for it, but missed it, and it went cartwheeling down the slope, to be fielded by Mingma. Kelvin was now near helpless, enmeshed in a cocoon of rope, his two jumars jammed together. I shouted down instructions, which I suspect were of little value, but eventually he managed to untangle himself and somehow slid back down the rope. I'm afraid I hadn't taught him how to abseil (the method used for descending a rope). As he reached the end of the fixed rope he reached for a rucksack that Mingma had left on a ledge and dislodged it, tried to grab it, but missed; it slid beyond his reach and went bouncing down the steep snow slope and over the edge of an ice cliff some hundreds of feet below. I knew that my sleeping-bag was in one of the Sherpas' rucksacks, and thought this was it. I called Kelvin just about every name I could think of and ordered him to go back to Camp III to get his own bloody bag and bring it up to me. It was typical of Kelvin's loyalty and patience that he did so without a complaint, racing back down and then plodding slowly up again. By the time he got back I had discovered that the fallen sack did not hold my sleeping-bag but was merely full of food and carried Kelvin's own anorak.

Rather chastened, particularly as Kelvin's mishap was largely my fault through my failure to check his crampons and teach him a little more about basic mountaineering, I apologized.

Getting up to Camp IV on this and subsequent carries was a real achievement on Kelvin's part, for he had never been climbing before and the route up to IV was both difficult and spectacular. It brought out the fact, however, that once one has fixed ropes in position, completely inexperienced climbers can quickly learn how to negotiate them. On the other hand, should anything go wrong they would not have the experience to cope with an emergency.

We found Ian Clough and Dave Lambert at Camp IV. Nick Estcourt had now moved up to Camp V, bringing the strength there up to four, and that day Ian had made a carry to the dump at the end of the ridge, while Dougal and Nick had come down from Camp V to pick up some more gear, leaving Don and Martin to sort out Camp V.

At this stage I intended to stay at Camp IV ferrying up to Camp V until Don and Dougal were established at VI; I then intended to move up to Camp V myself. But that evening we were forced to alter our plans yet again. Martin had made a carry to the site of Camp VI, the day before, with Don and Dougal. Up to this point he had been going as strongly as anyone on the expedition, but the six trips to Camp V from IV now took their toll. On the way up the fixed ropes on the Rock Band his feet had become numb with cold and he only managed to bring them back to life on his return to the tent by immersing them in warm water. That day he had rested, but in the evening he felt no better and was beginning to suffer from blood-poisoning. His hands, burnt by the sun and lacerated by snow and rock whilst he had been out in front on the Ice Ridge, had never really recovered. He was now in such a badly run-down state that it was as if his entire bodily functions were going to pieces. He warned us over the radio that he thought he might have to go down for a rest the next day and the following morning he confirmed it.

This meant we were extended to the limit once again. Don and Dougal were planning to move up to Camp VI that day, which would leave Nick on his own at Camp V with the difficult job of supplying them. Obviously either Ian or myself would have to go up to Camp V to reinforce him, though this would leave only two at Camp IV for the exhausting carry to the foot of the Rock Band. I immediately decided to move up to Camp V myself. Ian did not demur, though in a letter to Nikki he wrote:

> *Yesterday Chris went up to V. He was very, very slow; I was going far better than him and he should have put me through if he was thinking of the team success. Dave did the carry to the end of the ice ridge with three oxygen cylinders, a good effort, thirty-three pounds. I did the same, held up by Chris and his personal gear all the way, and then continued from the end of the ice ridge with a five-hundred-foot rope as well as the oxygen cylinders—over fifty pounds—up the main snowfield as far as the foot of the ice wall where I had to leave it because of lack of time. If I hadn't been held up by Chris all the way I could have got the fifty-pound load right up to V. Oh well, the rope was pretty vital so Chris had to suffer for his slowness and took the rope up with his own personal gear.*

At the time I had no idea how strongly Ian felt, though I should probably have been a little more sensitive and have guessed. I don't think I believe in premonition, but throughout the climb Ian seemed different to the person I had climbed with on the Central Pillar of Freney and the North Wall of the Eiger. He never seemed happy or at ease. The solitary trip across India escorting our gear had undoubtedly taken a great deal out of him physically, and perhaps mentally as well. I think it was probably too heavy a strain for anyone on the expedition to have borne by himself, and that I should have sent out a pair. On the other hand, we had needed every available person during the early stages of the climb.

I think he also found it particularly difficult to accommodate himself to my own style of leadership. Nick Estcourt put it to me one evening after our return from the mountain, saying, 'The trouble is, Chris, you tend to think things out aloud. That's why you often appear to change your mind and seem overimpulsive. I think all of us—anyway, Don, Martin, Mike Thompson and myself—knew this about you and took it into account.'

This observation is probably true, but I suspect Ian found this trait of mine more difficult to come to terms with, particularly in his own state of uncertainty. Inevitably, this eroded our relationship on the mountain. He tended to distrust my judgement, and, because of his seeming lack of confidence, I had preferred to push through past him to Camp V. My own motive in wanting to get up to Camp V probably had a touch of the prima donna in it, in wanting to be nearer the front, but my prime reason was to be in a position to have contact with what was going on and therefore have some measure of control over a changing situation. That day I was undoubtedly going slower than Ian, finding it exhausting work swinging along the flanks of the Ice Ridge and then up the long slopes of the snowfield leading to the foot of the ice cliff.

Ian and I occasionally caught up with each other at anchor points and rested at the site of the dump, where he picked up the extra rope, but each of us was marooned on his own self-centred island, unable to understand the motives of the other. Ian resented the fact that I was moving on up to Camp V carrying only my personal gear; I could not understand why he insisted on taking such a huge load up from the dump—true, we needed as much as possible up at V, but equally we could not afford to have anyone burning himself out. We ended up by sharing the extra load, for I had to carry the five hundred feet of rope up through the ice cliff, dangling on the steep rope and then up the last few hundred feet to the lip of the bergschrund.

I was surprised to find Dougal as well as Nick there—he should have been at Camp V with Don.

'What's happened to you?' I asked.

'Dropped my bloody rucksack. It had everything in it, sleeping-bag, spare clothes, duvet, the lot.'

It never occurred to me, and I don't think it occurred to Nick, that one of us should take Dougal's place—it certainly never occurred to Dougal. He was going so much more strongly than either of us, and had such a single-minded drive to reach the top of Annapurna.

Dougal had left Don ensconced in solitary state at Camp VI and had returned to Camp V hoping to replace his lost gear. That night we agreed that Dougal should take my sleeping-bag and Nick's down jacket back up the mountain with him, while we should have replacement gear sent up to us from Camp IV, who in turn would have theirs replaced by a sleeping-bag and down jacket from Camp III.

After eating a stew prepared by Nick, I retired to the other tent, a RAFMA, leaving Dougal wearing all our spare down clothing in the Whillans Box with Nick. That night it was bitterly cold in a sleeping-bag; it must have been very much colder for Dougal. Perhaps partly because of this, but largely through his own personal drive to get back to the front to make up for any time wasted by his loss, Dougal was away from Camp V by seven o'clock in the morning, leaving the box vacant for me to move in.

Nick was very tired from his carry to the site of Camp VI the previous day and warned me that it was even more tiring than the pull up to Camp V. He therefore was going to go back down to the dump to pick up a load, while I was to carry some rope and a radio up to Don and Dougal. Dougal had taken with him a little food, but had wanted to travel light to enable him to get up quickly and put in a day's work, pushing out the route above Camp VI.

Nick and I sat in the box, brewing hot drinks and delaying the moment of departure to the last possible minute. Getting ready was made still more difficult through the fact that the tents were in perpetual shade, shielded from the sun by the huge cave of snow thrust over the top of the gendarme. From time to time a small powder snow avalanche would flow over it, like a dainty lace curtain between ourselves and one of the most magnificent mountain views I have ever seen.

Hiunchuli was little more than a wedge of ice far below us, and even the rounded summit of Modi Peak, with its fluted walls of ice, seemed on the same level as ourselves. We could look across the curtain wall of the Basin into a giant amphitheatre formed by the north-west slopes of Modi Peak. At dawn, heavily shaded in contrast to the brilliant high-lighting of the retaining walls, it resembled the segment of an extinct volcano, while at dusk, with the sun dropping away to the west, the amphitheatre was lit a brilliant gold, and the retaining walls in their turn were in deep shadow—it then resembled a giant stage, suitable setting for a Greek tragedy.

But I found it difficult to appreciate the magnificent setting any longer—I had been on the Face too long, was surfeited by over-exposure to the same mountain scenery and, above all, was too tired and cold to do much more than keep going, day after day after day. I moved out onto the edge of the bergschrund into the glare of the sun, which gave so little real warmth yet dazzled the eyes and burnt the skin. Even so, it was warmer and more cheering than the chill gloom of the camp-site. Crampons on, harness fitted round my thighs and I was ready for the long slog up to Camp VI.

It was a strange feeling being on my own—stimulating, yet frightening. The thread of rope I was following was my only reminder that there were other people on this huge face, or for that matter in the vast bowl of the Sanctuary. On this first carry there was the stimulus of the unknown, for the rope, like the thread in the caves of the Minotaur, wove its way across icefields, round rock spurs and up gullies. I could rarely see more than fifty feet in front of me at any one time.

It was impossible to build up any kind of rhythm, the soothing balm of all high-altitude climbing, for one moment the rope was stretching away up a vertical groove and the next it was snaking round a corner, or even dropping down into a minor gully. The horizontal sections were even more exhausting than those going straight up, for on these I had to swing across hand over hand, feeling, at this altitude, like a senile Tarzan trying to make a hopeless comeback onto the big scene.

I was moving desperately slowly—every now and then I'd glance up at the next feature, a corner in the rock, the top of a groove, the crest of a spur. It might be fifty feet away, and that fifty feet would take over an hour to cover. I climbed the initial icefield, then up the first rock groove, across the next icefield, up another groove—and so it went on. I was now below the final headwall of the Flat Iron. Nick had warned me of this stretch, telling me that Mick and Tom had left the rope dangling free of the rock for fully two hundred feet. It was as he said. With this length of rope hanging free, I had to haul in about twenty feet before I had pulled out all the stretch. Glancing up I could see it rubbing over countless sharp rock edges; a stone whined down from somewhere high on the Band. What if it hit the rope, or if one had already hit it, fatally weakening it? I could only find out by trusting my weight to it and if it did break, then I should die. I thrust out of my mind a vivid picture of my body hurtling down the rocks trailed by a useless rope, my jumars peeling from it; and then the rocks tearing at me, red blood and brains, falling spinning, down and down the endless snow slopes—red bloody horror—get a grip of yourself; drive the thought out of your mind. Concentrate on the next few feet; push one jumar up, straighten out on your leg; push the other one up. This is the occupational therapy of the mountaineer; you can't afford to let your imagination wander.

And then on this long, devastating jumar pitch, sheer exhaustion drove out fear. I tried to pick my way up a line that would minimize any swing across sharp flakes and also one that would at least allow me to touch the rock with my feet, to keep balance and make the exhausting task a little easier. I was nearly there; only fifty feet to go to the top. I was beginning to congratulate myself that it wasn't as bad as I had feared, but the rope dropped now over a jutting roof overhang, pulling me away from the security of the rock. I was spinning helpless, the rope at a slight angle from the vertical which somehow made it even more awkward. It took me over an hour to climb that last fifty feet; an hour of lung-bursting, demoralizing effort, where progress was measured in inches and heart-tearing pants for breath. At last I pulled myself over the top and collapsed onto a small ledge. The angle now eased off into a long snow ridge, dotted in its lower part with boulders, leading up to the top of the Flat Iron, where I could just see the blue cover of a RAFMA tent.

It was about four hundred feet of comparatively easy going above me, but I did not think I had the strength left to get there. I shouted up at the tent, the small blue blob in an expanse of cruel white snow slope and upthrust brown of the Rock Band, but there was no response. I had hoped that I might persuade one of them to come down and pick up my load, but I had no choice. Somehow I had to get there.

I started plodding up the snow, pulling on the fixed rope. Each step required a separate effort of will. Time seemed to have clicked into slow-motion—a special slow-motion hell, all of my own. I reached the last boulder, still about two hundred feet below and a full four-hundred-foot rope length away from the tent. I shouted again and again up at it, but it remained silent and still, like a little blue eye, watching my struggles. I decided I could not go any farther, took the rope and radio out of my rucksack and tied them to the piton. I was about to start down when my conscience began prodding. Don and Dougal had neither rope nor radio. Unless I could tell them that I had left the rope just below they might waste tomorrow waiting for it to arrive. Anyway, it was essential they got a radio as soon as possible.

And so I untied the radio and dropped it into my sack—it only weighed six pounds, but with each step I took it seemed to become a greater dead-weight, hauling me back. It was a strange feeling, for I did not feel short of breath—I simply seemed to have no strength, or even the will to make my muscles function. I took a step, rested one minute, two, three, and then forced myself to take another step. The rope described a long arc off to one side, which meant that if I had slipped I should have swung across the Face. The snow was unpleasantly soft, and though I had some help from the relics of Dougal's footsteps, I had to punch out each hold.

I was going too slowly—it was already half-past five in the afternoon and I hadn't even reached the camp. I resolved to take five steps at a time before resting. One, two, three, keep going you bastard, four, and I stopped for a rest. Next time I only managed three. But I was now just below the tent. The fixed rope, anchored to a piton hammered in above and behind it, ran over the tent. Its bouncing on the roof, caused by my own convulsive heaves, brought Dougal out.

'You're nearly there, Chris,' he called out, and his words of encouragement gave me the strength to take those last exhausting steps.

As I pulled over the edge of the tiny platform they had carved in the snow at the very crest of the Flat Iron, Dougal thrust out a mug of hot orange drink. The warmth of their welcome and thoughtfulness in preparing a drink made all the effort seem worth while. I know this sounds clichéd, but it was true. At this stage I knew I was not going well enough to go out in front and that my performance was not nearly as good as that of Don or Dougal, but the fact that I could still be in a position to give them real support meant a great deal to me.

We sat and talked for a few minutes. They warned me that they had very little food—just the odd scrappets that Dougal had taken up that morning. I told them that Nick would probably do the carry next day and started back down.

It was now nearly seven o'clock; I was in a limbo of thin cloud, where snow merged into cloud and rock looked like ghostly islands or the walls of a huge, demon fortress. But there was no wind and it hadn't started to snow, and so I decided on the way down to try to improve the route, breaking up the long jumar pitch into several separate pitches, following an easier line. I became enthralled in the work, untying knots, working out how much slack I should allow for each rope length. Only the gathering dark reminded me of how late it was getting.

Nick was getting worried back at Camp V. It was pitch dark and half-past eight when I finally swung down the last fixed rope into the camp. The box suddenly seemed very homely. Nick had already made a stew and lit the gas stove we were now using as an alternative to paraffin, and I was able to wriggle into my sleeping-bag and listen to the somnolent purr.

That night, in spite of our fatigue, we were full of optimism, talked of making the second summit bid together—a Bowdon team (we both live in this suburb of Manchester) for the top. We touched on the crisis caused by Don and Dougal moving through to the front over Martin and himself.

Nick was very positive that neither he nor Martin had felt resentment in the way that Tom and Mick obviously had.

'Both Martin and I were more worried by the practical logistic problem,' he said, 'of how on earth you were going to ferry enough oxygen and gear up to Camp V. We felt it would have been better to have used Don and Dougal's freshness to get two or three carries up to here so that we could have been fully stocked for the push to the summit. As it is, we've barely got any oxygen up here and not much in the way of food.'

Nick might have been right. We only had three bottles of oxygen and one set at Camp V, another three bottles dumped by Ian at the foot of the ice cliff. The carry to VI from V, however, was obviously going to be even tougher than the one from IV to V. At the moment Don and Dougal had the bare essentials for Camp VI, practically no food and only five hundred feet of rope. That day it had been all I could do to carry about thirty-five pounds to a point three hundred feet below VI. We were undoubtedly extended to the very limit, but time was also running out. It was now 20 May and the monsoon could not be far off. I felt that it was essential that we should somehow maintain our momentum towards the summit.

Camp VI, at 24,000 feet, could only be about a thousand feet below the top of the Rock Band—and once we had reached its top we knew that the going to the summit would be comparatively straightforward. But if that last stretch of the Rock Band should prove even more difficult than the lower stretch which Mick Burke had led, we should be in real trouble. That day Don and Dougal had managed to get round into the foot of a gully leading up towards the top; the lower part looked straightforward, but they could not see all the way to the top. The one encouraging factor was that they seemed able to climb on this difficult ground without oxygen.

That night we agreed that Nick should do a carry up to VI the next day, while I went down to the dump to pick up a load. I dropped off to sleep quickly, too tired to worry. We seemed so close to success, and yet so very far from it.

The Rock Band was climbed and success was within reach, but the weather broke, making movement up or down the mountain very difficult. Mick Burke is ferrying a load up the Face in support of Whillans and Haston out in front.

'll never make it to Camp VI,' said Nick. 'I feel dead rough.'

We were lying in the chill, green gloom of the Whillans Box—it reminded me of a nightmare deep freeze, with its heavy encrustation of ice on the roof and down the green walls. Both of us were feeling lethargic, putting off the unpleasant moment of decision when we should set out for another day's grinding repetitive work.

'I feel pretty shattered myself,' I admitted. 'I'm not sure I could even get down to the dump.'

'I certainly don't fancy it,' said Nick. 'One thing we could do is for you to sort out the site here, dig out the gear and the RAFMA tent for Camp VII, while I just go down and pick up the oxygen bottles below the ice cliff.'

'O.K. Let's do that.'

And we relaxed back into our sleeping-bags, comforted by the thought that we had awarded ourselves an easy day. It was ten in the morning before we next emerged from the Whillans Box. The familiar cloud sea had already engulfed the bottom of the Sanctuary and was fast rising up the Ice Ridge and lapping round the foot of the snow slope leading up to our camp. Nick, spurred by the threat of changing weather, set off down the fixed ropes, while I pottered round the campsite, finding even the simple job of digging out the spare RAFMA tent and sorting out our clutter of supplies extraordinarily difficult. But after an hour I had finished and was able to burrow back into the Whillans Box, feeling a sense of security in its dark gloom. By this time the cloud had crept in over the bergschrund and it had begun to snow. Spindrift avalanches were pouring over the top of the lip of the snow cornice protecting the box, in a continuous hissing torrent. I zipped up the door of the box and retired to my sleeping-bag, but Nick was still struggling to get back up to the bergschrund. The snow poured round him, over him, penetrating every chink in his clothing, filling his mouth and nostrils with its fine, ice-cold powder. His jumar clamps were almost useless, icing up on the rope so that they would no longer hold his weight. It was only three hundred feet of easy going back up to the bergschrund, but it took him over three hours of terrifying struggle to fight his way back.

That night on the wireless we heard the good news that Don and Dougal had managed to climb four hundred feet up the gully, but they were now completely out of food and urgently needed rope and the camp kit for Camp VII, which they hoped to establish at the top of the Rock Band. Nick and I hoped to carry up the necessary gear the next morning.

We also heard tantalizing news from the other side of the mountain. The Army expedition had had its share of tribulations, with one member of the team evacuated by helicopter after he had contracted pneumonia, another injured in an avalanche and a complete camp swept away. But they had kept up their assault, and on the previous day (20 May) Henry Day, the climbing leader, and Gerry Owens had reached the top of Annapurna using oxygen. We were happy for their sakes, but could not help feeling all the more impatient to get there ourselves.

We only had one oxygen set at Camp V, but I decided we should use this the next day, taking turns with it, in an effort to reduce the strain of the journey. The following morning we loaded up our sacks with food, the tent, a ciné-camera for the summit push and five hundred feet of rope. We agreed that Nick should have first go with the oxygen set. The bottle weighed eleven pounds and the regulator which controlled the flow of oxygen another two. This meant that a load was going to be about thirteen pounds heavier, so that if one was carrying a rope and some food, it would weigh fifty pounds altogether. In return for this increase of weight, one had the benefit of a flow of oxygen which one could control to one, two, three, four or five litres per minute. I was the only person on the expedition who had used oxygen on a mountain before, during the ascent of Annapurna II, and as a result of this I was convinced that the extra weight was amply compensated by the benefit conferred by the oxygen. Nick was less convinced. The rubber mask, clamped hard over his face, gave him a claustrophobic feeling, and it was even difficult at times to believe that any oxygen was flowing at all.

Nick set out first, pulling out of the bergschrund and up the fixed rope alongside the rocks of the first icefield. He was moving very slowly, but I was even slower. Head slumped; one step after another. It was a discouraging thought that there were fifteen hundred feet of fixed rope to negotiate up to Camp VI. And then I noticed that Nick had stopped; he was slumped on the rope. As I reached him he gasped, 'It's no good, Chris, I've had it. I'll have to go down.'

'Can't you increase the flow of oxygen?'

'I've already put it to full blast, but it doesn't seem to have any effect. I just don't seem to have any strength left.'

'Why don't you go back and rest up for the day in the box? You might feel better tomorrow.'

'It's no good, you just don't recover up here. I'm bloody sorry but I'll have to go down.'

I knew he was right. Nick had driven himself as hard as anyone on the expedition. He and Martin had somehow kept open the carry from Camp IV to V, but in doing so he had now burnt himself out.

We swopped around the load. I took the oxygen set and some food, but then had to make up my mind whether to take the rope or the tent. Since Don and Dougal had still not reached the top of the Rock Band, and I did not know how hard it was going to be, I chose the rope. There were eight hundred litres of oxygen in the cylinder—at a flow rate of three litres per minute this would give me just over four hours of climbing—not enough to get me to Camp VI, for it had taken me six hours the previous day, though I hoped that the oxygen might speed me up a little.

As Nick slid, disconsolate, back down towards the camp, I carried on up the fixed ropes. It was a never-ending treadmill, barely relieved by the grandeur of the situation. But the oxygen did help: I found I could keep going, admittedly very slowly, without taking rests. When I reached the final steep pull to the top of the Flat Iron I set the regulator valve at five litres per minute and almost felt a surge of power as I pulled up the fixed rope, taking only half an hour to reach the top, as opposed to two on the previous day.

By the time I had reached the crest of the Flat Iron the steady hiss of strength-giving oxygen had almost vanished, the pressure-gauge registered zero, and I was carrying eleven pounds weight of useless metal on my back.

Each cylinder cost fifty pounds, but without a qualm I pulled it out of the sack and hurled it down the mountain.

My load was eleven pounds lighter but I immediately noticed the lack of oxygen; once again my progress stalled into a crawl with rests at almost every step. It took me a further two hours to climb up to the tent.

Don and Dougal were already back from a day in the gully. They had reached the top of the Rock Band.

'Have you got the tent?' Dougal asked me.

But I had to admit that I had left it behind in preference for the rope. That day they had run out all their rope, reaching a point about two hundred feet short of the top. They had then climbed solo to the crest of the ridge.

'It got us out on top of the Mini Rock Band,' Dougal told me. This was a small cliff just above the main Rock Band. 'It looks quite easy to the summit; can't be more than fifteen hundred feet.'

I promised to bring up the tent the following day.

'I could move up myself and help you establish Camp VII,' I suggested.

'In that case, why not move up with us and come to the top?' Dougal said.

I was tremendously moved by his suggestion. I had always felt that, as leader, I should concentrate on pushing another pair to the summit, but had hoped that I should be in a position to do the carry to the top camp. Dougal's invitation was significant of the very close feeling of accord that we all had in those last days on the Face. At the start of the expedition, Don and I had not got on well, partly the result of our very different personalities, partly through the stresses of organizing the expedition, and yet during the climb I think we had come to have the same respect and liking for each other that we had had on other climbs in the past.

Without thinking I agreed. Ian was due to reach Camp V that evening to help with the difficult ferry to Camp VI. This would leave Dave Lambert on his own at Camp IV, but Mick Burke and Tom Frost were now on their way back up the mountain and were due to reach IV two days later on the 23rd. We had just enough food at Camp V for the next few days, and now that we were in sight of the summit, we could afford to make an all-out push.

I was thinking of this on the way back down to Camp V, hoping to find Ian ensconced in the box, gas stove purring under a panful of melting snow, but as I swung down into the bergschrund I saw that the place was still and silent.

It had been a beautiful day on the upper part of the mountain, but the cloud tide had rolled in early, filling the Basin up to the top of the Ice Ridge. That morning Dave Lambert and Ian had set out for Camp V, but it had started to snow almost immediately; jumars had iced up, fingers and toes had frozen, and they had been forced back to their box. At the same time, Kelvin and Kancha had forced their way up to Camp IV from III. The easy stretch up to the foot of the fixed ropes was getting increasingly difficult in face of the daily build-up of powder snow. Kancha had been suffering from toothache and seemed more worried by the steepness of the route up to the crest of the ridge than the other Sherpas. On the way up he fell on the difficult stretch between the top of the arête and the crest of the ridge proper, where an awkward traverse led across to a chimney of flaky ice. He dropped down onto the fixed rope and panicked. It was all Kelvin could do to talk him up and help him to the box at Camp IV, where they gave him oxygen to give him strength for the return journey; even our Sherpas seemed to be running out of power.

And so that night I had Camp V to myself. It was a grim and depressing spot to be alone. I cooked myself a stew from our fast vanishing stock of food, drugged myself heavily with sleeping-tablets and dropped into a fitful sleep. I woke early and started cooking, then waited for the sun at least to strike the top of the bergschrund before dragging myself out of the box to pack my load. I had to take up my own personal gear, the ciné-camera, the tent and a stock of food. By the time I had added the oxygen cylinder it must have weighed over sixty pounds—it certainly felt as if it did.

I got half-way up the first little icefield just above the bergschrund and realized that I could never carry this all the way up to Camp VI. Somehow I had to reduce the weight. I slid back down the ropes and tried to cut down on gear, but what on earth could I cut out? My own personal stuff—yes; I threw out spare gloves and socks, even my diary—but what else? The ciné-camera? It weighed about seven pounds, but the T.V. team were depending on the summit shots. I threw it out all the same, then realized I couldn't possibly go to the summit myself at that kind of sacrifice. The sack was still too heavy—there seemed no choice but to dump all my own personal gear and probably my chances of going to the summit, certainly all chances of being on the first ascent. I felt so helpless I sat down and cried. Then, ashamed at my weakness, I shouted at the walls around me, 'Get a grip of yourself, you bloody idiot!'

I reduced the load to the tent, ciné-camera and a bagful of food, about thirty pounds in all, or forty-three with the oxygen cylinder, and set out once again. By the time I was half-way up the fixed ropes I cursed myself for not taking my sleeping-bag, a mere four pounds extra; after all, that was all I needed since I was wearing every bit of clothing I had, it was so cold.

In a way, I think my instinct had stopped me, for I was not fit enough to go to the summit with Don and Dougal; I should only have held them up. In addition there was barely enough food for the three of us. That day it was all I could do to reach Camp VI. They had spent the day in the tent resting, since there was nothing they could do until I brought up the lightweight RAFMA tent for the top camp. I dumped it and returned to Camp V, praying all the way down that Ian would have made it, dreading spending another night by myself. As I came down over the bergschrund I saw tracks leading up through the deep snow from below, sure sign that Ian had reached Camp V. Immediately I felt better and shouted, 'Am I glad to see you!'

Typically, Ian had struggled up through deep snow, carrying a huge load—oxygen masks and, luxury of luxuries, a packet of Readi-Brek and a bottle of instant coffee on top of his personal gear. He had started out at 9.30 that morning and had only reached the bergschrund a few minutes before me, at about 4.30. Dave had tried to carry a load of oxygen cylinders all the way up to Camp V, but had been going so slowly that it was obvious to Ian he was not going to make it. Even so, Dave told him, 'I know I'll never get back tonight, but if you really need these cylinders I'll bivouac.' Ian dissuaded him and Dave left them at the dump at the top of the ridge.

I have not often mentioned Dave in this account. He never went out in front, was slow to acclimatize and found the carry up to the dump at the end of the Ice Ridge his limit, yet he spent more days carrying loads than any other person on the expedition. This is a grim, monotonous task, with no glamour in it and one that tends to gain very little recognition; and yet without his steady, willing effort, particularly towards the end of the expedition when everyone was getting badly run down, we should have been even more severely extended.

Once in the box with a brew in my hand I quickly recovered my resilience and began to plan the summit assault over the next few days. It now seemed that nothing could stop us; we had fixed ropes in place almost all the way to the top of the Mini Rock Band, and the front pair were confident that the way to the summit was straightforward. Tom Frost and Mick Burke had now reached Camp IV, and Mike Thompson, with the Sherpas Mingma and Pemba Tharkay, were at Camp III. Martin Boysen had set out but felt so shattered on the way up to III that he had to return. Although we were still badly extended on the mountain we had somehow managed to stock each camp and they were all fully occupied. On many expeditions, by the time the summit push takes place there are a couple of people in the top camp and practically no one else above Base Camp. This had been the case on Nuptse, which I had climbed in 1961.

That night I wrote out my orders, planning to give them on the radio the next morning.

> *Don and Dougal will move up to VII today (24th) and hope to reach the summit tomorrow, returning to Camp VI and getting farther down still if possible. They will then move straight down to Base Camp leaving all radios, etc., in situ. Don and Dougal will leave Camp VII stocked with foam mattresses, stove and cooking-pot.*
>
> *Ian and I will move up to Camp VI today, VII tomorrow, and hope to hit the summit on the 26th. Mick Burke: We shall stock VI with foams and cooking-pot; there is a primus for you here at V, but you will have to bring up foams.*
>
> *Mick and Tom will move up to V today, VI tomorrow, VII on the 26th and should reach the top on the 27th. They should bring down with them the Camp VII radio and pick up anything they can on the way down.*
>
> *Mike at III and Martin [I did not realize at this stage that he had been forced to retreat]: I should like the two of you to move up to Camp IV and stay there as an advanced reserve in the event of an emergency.*

It all sounded very neat and simple, but the next morning it was gusting hard and the sky was laced with high cloud, sure sign of bad weather. I wondered about going up to Camp VI, since if Don and Dougal failed to make VII it would have been embarrassing, but on the radio Don, who told me afterwards he also had reservations, said they had decided to try to establish VII, and so Ian and I began to get ready.

I was feeling weak and tired from my three carries up to Camp VI. In addition I had an attack of diarrhoea. The higher one gets on a mountain the more unpleasant become the problems of relieving oneself. I had had to get up twice during the night. Dragging oneself out of the warmth of one's sleeping-bag and going out into a night temperature of around -20F is a grim experience. If we wanted to urinate during the night we just pulled up a corner of the entrance or even used an empty tin. One had to be careful to remember which side of the tent one had used as an outdoor lavatory when one collected snow for melting.

That morning I had to drop my trousers three times during the slow and painful process of packing. Crampon straps were frozen like wire hawsers and even our harnesses were encrusted in ice. Both Ian and I were going to use oxygen for the move up to Camp VI, but would then have to go without. This did seem feasible, since the gully leading up to the top of the Rock Band sounded straightforward compared to the stretch below the Flat Iron.

I set out first and Ian immediately behind me, but after going a few yards he returned to take off his oxygen set. He felt enclosed and claustrophobic wearing it and preferred to do without, carrying, of course, a lighter sack as a result. The weather broke by the time we reached the first rocks; the wind hammered at our clothes, drove ice particles into our faces and great clouds of spindrift across the Rock Band. The mask of the oxygen set was now quite useful, protecting my face from the blast.

Half-way up I had an irrepressible urge to relieve myself—I was in the middle of a gully swept by powder snow avalanches. This was both a tricky and an exceedingly unpleasant operation. I was dangling on the fixed rope and somehow I had to remove my harness, tie a makeshift one to my chest and bare my backside to the icy blast. And at that point a powder snow avalanche came pouring down, filling my trousers, infiltrating up my back.

I ran out of oxygen at the top of the difficult jumar pitch and struggled up the last few hundred feet, hammered by winds that were driving across the Face with a terrifying force. I arrived about half an hour before Ian, who was going a good deal slower than myself, largely, I suspect, because he was not using oxygen. When he did arrive he was almost an exposure case, shivering uncontrollably and with numb hands. About five minutes after he arrived I heard a shout from above— Don and Dougal had been forced back. Their clothes were encased in ice, and Don was sporting a magnificent pair of drooping moustaches formed of pure ice.

And so there were now four of us in a two-man tent. It was too late for anyone to go down, and anyway Tom and Mick were already ensconced in the solitary Whillans Box at Camp V. The four of us had to stick it out at Camp VI for the night. I have had more than a hundred bivouacs in the mountains, but that night was the most uncomfortable of all. Ian was the worst off and uncomplainingly spent the night huddled into a corner.

Next morning the weather was even worse. There seemed no choice but for Ian and myself to drop back down to Camp IV, since V was now occupied, and then try to keep Don and Dougal supplied with food till we got a break in the weather. As the two of them were undoubtedly much fitter than Ian or myself there was never any question as to who should stay out in front.

It snowed non-stop for the next two days. The following morning (26th) Ian, Dave, who was waiting for us at Camp IV, and myself fought our way up to the dump at the end of the Ice Ridge with a load of food, which Tom and Mick Burke came down from Camp V to collect. The next day they were going to carry some of it up to Don and Dougal, who had now run out completely.

The mountain below Camp IV was completely cut off. The easier-angled sections, which had no fixed ropes, were impassable because of the build-up of snow. We spent 27 May in a state of deep gloom—we were so near to success, but the monsoon seemed to have arrived. I was determined to sit out until we did have a break, but we only had a week's food at the most on the mountain.

After a nightmare night, with Whillans, Haston, Bonington and Clough squeezed into a two-man tent at Camp VI (24,000 feet), Clough tries to thaw out frozen hands frostbitten when putting on crampons.

Don and Dougal had told us that they were going to try to establish Camp VII that morning and then return to VI, but it seemed unlikely that they would have got that far. When I opened up the radio at five o'clock, Dougal came on the air.

'Hello, Dougal, this is Chris at Camp IV. Did you manage to get out today?'

'Aye, we've just climbed Annapurna.'

CHAPTER 17

The Final Push

[17—27 May]

Dougal Haston

In this chapter Dougal Haston describes his own experience from 17-27 May, when Don and he reached the top of the South Face.

I come back to the subjective above the col, doing what I'd been doing so often in the last few weeks. Moving slowly. Knee-deep snow to be broken, a strange effort to lift one leg and place it in front of the other. It seemed so stupid. After all I'd been making the same motions for most of my life. I often wondered if my willpower was going to be strong enough. I'd spent many years training it to work in climbing situations. Yet trailbreaking at altitude is one of the hardest things to put up with. There's Don behind, but he can't help me. This kind of thing you have to go alone. Slowly as I look around, the doubt clears. The mind is a shattering brilliant firework display of incredible impressions battling with unforgettable memories. I'm not on a bed looking at a kaleidoscope of psychedelic colours and verging on the borders of insanity. I'm at 23,000 feet and sane, I hope—though many would question this. I've been asked so many times why I climb but in the ultimate analysis I often wonder if I know myself. Is this pleasure?

I am now at Camp V—lung-heaving tiredness—standing in a

crevasse with spindrift pouring over me. There are three of us now. I lie making tea with Don and Martin inside the RAFMA tent, putting off the decision to go outside and erect a box. One thing seems good, the weather is still fine. This is one of the few days when there hasn't been a storm in the afternoon. The dying sun hangs fire over the Fang and out to the left we are beginning to level off high up on Machapuchare. It takes time to erect the box. When one isn't under the pressure of actual climbing lethargy soon sets in. But Don and I have clocked many hours in boxes to date and reckon them the most comfortable rest-houses on the mountain. We do it and crawl in. The rest is routine. Morning has to be awaited. Martin has a lonely night in the RAFMA.

The morning comes and it is not so fine. I ponder the day's pro-gramme over breakfast tea. The aim is an establishment of Camp VI. This means fairly heavy packs. Tent, stoves and camp-kits. Mick had been fairly vague about the possibilities of a good site. The Flat Iron had been his high point but he had been unable to reach the point where it rejoined the main cliff. From a distance it had looked like a possible, indeed the only, camp-site. The amount of work they had done on the Rock Band was impressive, I thought, as I pushed my jumars ever upwards. But oh, the traverses! Upward jumaring is at least rhythmic, but going sideways is a constant strain on the arms and legs and at least one-third of this sec-tion between V and projected VI was on traverses. Then suddenly I was at the end of the lifelines and also the good weather. Mick and Tom's high point was a rock about a hundred feet below the crest of the Flat Iron and about four hundred from the proposed camp-site. The cloud was swirling around bringing intermittent gusts of snowflakes. We three stood talking on the belay. Martin's feet had already gone numb. He was thinking of turning round and going back as I set off for the top of the Flat Iron. It was a long and tortuous pitch done in one run-out on one of our big ropes. Firstly knee-deep mushy snow, then hard ice to exit, with one mis-erable knifeblade for protection. The one thing to remember not to do on the Annapurna South Face is fall off. Then the big disappointment. What had looked like a platform was a knife-edge ridge. So narrow that I broke through and nearly fell over the other side as I pulled up the last few feet.

However, it looked as if we might manage something with a lot of work. Don started to come up the fixed line. Curiosity got the better of me and I ran out the rest of the rope on a self-belay to see what was round the corner. The rope ran out so I tied all my aid slings and runners together. It was just enough to see into a big gully. It looked good. There was certainly a way ahead for a few hundred feet. Don arrived and we went back to normal roped climbing. Yes, it was a good continuation line. I could see upwards for about five hundred feet, then it swung to the right. This was the important news. It made the fact that we didn't have a camp-site fall into the back of our minds. It had been a long day. We turned round in the gathering snowflakes leaving our loads at the crest of the Flat Iron and down the ropeway to Camp V.

Nick was there with Martin and we all sat in happy squalor in the box and ate the evening meal. But outside, the elements were anything but happy. The roof of the box began to sag as the spindrift built up. Soon it had drifted half-way up the entrance. In choosing our site we had had the option of placing the box right under the lip of the bergschrund—which was the most sheltered, but this lip had looked as if it might drop off and there would have been no survival for anyone sleeping underneath—or placing it just outside where we were in the path of spindrift slides coming from the icefield above. We had opted for the latter and were now suffering the effects of our fear. Nick tried to make a break for his own tent which was only six feet away—he just got outside when we heard an agonized choke—'Christ, I'm suffocating.' Quick as a flash Don shouted, 'Get your head back in here, quick!' and an agonized distorted face appeared back in the tent. All was well. Nick had been having trouble with his breathing anyway and in gasping he had caught a lungful of spindrift. Finally everyone was in their sleeping-bags. No sooner done than Don and I had to get out and put our feet against the roof of the box and started a series of exhausting heaves to clear the snow from the roof. After our long day this was the finishing trick and we collapsed into comatose sleep.

Meanwhile next door the drama was not over. Around five in the morning I heard Martin and Nick get up and thought, They are keen: if they make breakfast then we can shoot up and establish Camp VI in good time. Then a brew came through our blocked-up door and I peered out to see two shaken faces and a scene of devastation. They had decided to sleep with their heads to the door because of the avalanches. Some time during the night the pressure of snow had collapsed the back of the tent, smashing the rear frame and ridge pole. If they hadn't turned round? Nick was particularly shaken up and could hardly stop talking. Two suffocation experiences within a night at 23,000 feet. Trying things on one's will? There was no question of going upwards. The debris had to be straightened out. The box was almost completely covered. All the supplies were buried. It took a supreme effort to dig out the entrenching-tool and start the excavation. But Nick and Martin still had to have a tent. The lightweight RAFMA for Camp VII was down at the col, so Nick and I went down to collect this plus food while the other two moved the box and made a platform for the tent. The weather was still wild and windy but despite the setbacks I felt in a strange happiness state coming back up the ropes. I was moving fast and having no breathing troubles. Acclimatization was obviously working. I suddenly had time to think about life again. Often at high altitudes one's mind is working so hard that one cannot appreciate the surroundings fully. It all came rushing back. The things I wanted most. Big mountains, savage surroundings, difficult climbing, with body and mind completely in tune with the situation. I popped into the bergschrund in such a state to find a cheerful enough Don but an unhappy Martin. He was feeling really low. To add to his tiredness from heavy load-carrying he had developed an infection from the open cuts on his hands. I felt that when he made this decision it would be the last time we would see him high on the mountain. I think Martin knew it as well but it's the kind of thing one leaves unspoken. Each to his own problems, hopes and despairs. One less load in the morning and one more problem in establishing Camp VI. The tent and box were much better sited under the lip of the schrund so we slept a better sleep that night.

Even so, in the morning we still had to dig out the ropes and gas cylinders again. Enough said about the fixed ropes between V and VI.

The clouds and snow set in around twelve. Don and I were bewildered and lost at Nick and Tom's old high point. He thought the situation bad enough to warrant digging-in as soon as possible. The light was such that you couldn't recognize a flattish spot until you were standing on it. He traversed to the ridge and started to dig. I prussicked up to get the tent from the top of the Flat Iron. Out of interest I started to clear a small platform. There didn't seem to be too much ice. Out of the storm a cry from below: 'It's no bloody use here, I've struck hard ice.' I told him that I thought we could get something in my position and he started up towards me. Slowly a platform materialized. Nick gave a shout from below and said he was leaving his load a few hundred feet beneath us and couldn't go on any farther. I went down a few rope lengths to pick up my rucksack, which I'd left at the point where Don had been digging. On the way up I stopped to pick up Nick's load. Took off my rucksack—a careless movement and that was the last I ever saw it. It contained all my personal gear and food for Camp VI.

For a few minutes I knew total despair. I was going well—the summit seemed possible. Now it looked as if I would have to go right down to get reserve gear. Then the mental clouds cleared and I began to rationalize. Perhaps if I went back to V I could borrow two duvets, then bivouac in them until a sleeping-bag could be sent. I could also talk the situation over with Chris. Don just looked at me: he probably knew how I was feeling. He just suggested that I should bivouac with his duvet and keep the stove going all night. This was fine—maybe for one night but it would also have weakened me and we also didn't have a radio to communicate my plight to the others and Nick had disappeared before it happened, so I just said, 'See you in the morning,' and turned round. The descent took only twenty minutes as I was so enraged with myself. I caught Nick up on the last rappel. He swung into Camp V expecting to find Chris and Ian but there was only silence and the swish of spindrift. More despair, we had no food. I—no equipment. Don was doing his foodless sentry duty above. It was late. It looked as if Chris and Ian had been unable to make it because of the storm. At least we had a radio. Perhaps we could get a little enlightenment. Even in this field we were having no luck. Atmospherics were terrible—I could barely make myself understood. After about five tries Kelvin at Camp III realized I needed a sleeping-bag. Selflessly he said he would send his up the mountain to Camp IV and someone else could take one up the mountain in the morning. It seemed a reasonable solution, but one that still left me at Camp V for a day. What about Don above? Then radio communications became slightly clearer. Chris and Ian had set out. Ian had dumped his too heavy load and set off downwards. Chris was still on his way. I got out and peered over the edge. There in falling light was Chris coming up the last rope. A good sight for my mind. He had a load of ropes. Scavenging the last of the existing Camp V food, we talked. It all seemed to fall into place. I was willing to set off in the morning to try and reach Don and push onwards. Chris offered me his sleeping-bag and we established by radio that someone would bring one up to Camp V to replace his. It all seemed so simple. Why had I ever had any problems? It was teamwork working to reach the ultimate object. Sleep wasn't so good that night. I slept in the rolled-up, frozen interior tent of a Whillans Box with all the spare down I could muster. Cold but bearable, and always the thought that I could go on instead of having to go down, defeated by a careless, silly move. Nick and I talked for a little. He reckoned he would have to have another rest day. Here was someone struggling hard with problems of altitude. I wondered how long it would be before the obvious tiredness would turn into complete exhaustion.

Morning again, and I set off to reach VI in a happy state of mind. At 11 a.m. I could see Don from the old Burke and Frost high point. It took me two more hours to reach him. The snow was in an atrocious state. Jumars couldn't help. If one leant back for a rest it incurred a great swing on the rope. The snow was deep, wet and sliding all the time from the ice beneath. One was so frustrated as to be reduced to cursing the surroundings. A futile gesture. I could talk to Don and he knew that I had some food and was willing me to get up quickly. Yet my slowness was as quick as one could move. I got there feeling a boredom that I'd seldom felt before. We talked and ate some porridge. That had been the only spare food at Camp V. Don had had a pensive night on cigars and snow-water. I was weary. Two rope lengths in the couloir was the total progress. Don reached the high point but still couldn't see round the elusive corner. Back to bed seemed to be the order of the day. That's where we went. Around 5.30 we felt the tugging of the fixed rope that went over the roof of the tent. Chris was on his way up but in a pretty tired state. He had had to dump his load of rope three hundred feet down and only our radioless state kept him coming up to VI. It was good to be in radio contact again, I had really felt the lack of one when my rucksack had dropped. At first it had been a chore to use them and the jargon of Roger, Over, etcetera, had seemed artificial, but sitting in the specific loneliness of Camp VI it was a good feeling to communicate with others.

A word about Camp VI. The platform was not quite wide enough and the outside of the tent hung over the edge. That meant that we had to sleep crossways. The front door gave out onto the veranda, which was about three feet wide. On all three sides there were impressive drops. That night the wind started to blow seriously. Down below we had been protected from the full blast by the Annapurna-Fang ridge but now we were above that level, conditions began to get slightly rough. It would come in sharp gusts. During the lulls you would doze off thinking that it had at last stopped. At the crucial nod the whole tent would billow and shake, I often wondered what kept it on the ledge. There were only two tent-pegs and a fixed rope which ran over the roof. The only other thing that kept it down was the build-up of spindrift on the back wall plus our body weight. At one time it got so violent that Don said, 'We'd better sleep with our boots on in case we have to get out of here fast.' This we did, and from that night onwards we always slept in a bebooted state.

Sleep that night consisted of a series of interrupted dozes and a stormy morning was conducive to staying in bed. However, we were so eager to see what lay round the corner in the gully that we decided to go out anyway. There was nothing much to keep us in the tent. Food level was porridge, mint cake and assorted synthetic drinks. Comfort level was a frozen sleeping-bag and a rime-filled tent. I dropped down for the rope that Chris had left while Don jumared up to the high point. As I reached him an hour later the surroundings were becoming impressive. The wind was blowing and though it hadn't yet started snowing, last night's fresh stuff was being blown hundreds of feet upwards. Every so often a patch of blue sky would appear, but it was quickly wiped out of vision by a grainy stinging white cloud. As I moved into the lead it started to snow again. The whole gully then began to move. It started with little avalanches coming down the centre. These were O.K. as I could climb out on the side. The snow started to get heavy as I reached a stance and I had just planted a piton when everything started to go. Powder snow avalanches were rushing over me and as I stuck my head up to breathe, the spindrift would whip into my mouth and nose. I just hung there waiting for a lull but none came so I fastened off the rope and slid down to find a similarly ice-encrusted Don. We didn't think the storm would last all day so decided to go back to the tent and see if it would clear a little. The snow was now coming down the gully like a raging highland torrent. It was a sobering thought. If it got very narrow then there could be no progress after a snowfall. At this time there was a snowfall every day. So we sat rather thoughtful in the tent pondering the problem. Slowly the day brightened and even the wind decided to give up for a bit. Early afternoon saw us back at the high point. There was still the odd small avalanche coming down but after the morning's effort we hardly noticed them. It was the same old style of climbing, a kind of swimming and sprawling motion in the loose snow. Don had had the brilliant idea of using an entrenching-tool in conjunction with the ice-axe. I now felt like a member of the Pioneer Corps doing a heavy penance as I lurched and slithered upwards. Trail-breaking in that type of snow demands a special state of mind. You must shut off completely and only think of the next few feet. It is better to keep up a continuous rhythm, no matter how slow, than to stop and take frequent rests. After a rest it is that much harder to start again. Slowly and methodically I rounded the corner and there was the continuation. After about two hundred feet of ascending traverse the gully narrowed to a chimney which didn't look as if it held anything to stop us. That afternoon we reached the start of the chimney.

Back at the tent it was a lonely night. No one had made it up from below. We were down to a few handfuls of porridge but feeling happy at the day's work and the knowledge that the route continued at least a little farther. Radio time produced the day's news. The weather had been really atrocious below and no one had managed to get anywhere. Various parties had set out but all had been beaten back. There seemed to be a lot of surprise when I said we had made a lot of progress. Considering the conditions I think we were slightly surprised as well. That night wasn't too much different from the previous. Sudden violent gusts of wind seemed to like wandering around our tent. But like most mountain hazards the mind eventually begins to accept them as a normal part of the environment and after that happens the particular danger never quite seems so bad again. The most troublesome thing about the nights was the sleeping position. Being forced to sleep crossways I could never quite get my legs straight and Don was curled up in a cocoon in the corner. But night passed as it has done for many years. By this time we were getting really wound up and I had the stove going at the freezing hour of five. This could be a crucial day. Would the gully lead us out onto easy ground or were there some hidden major difficulties?

Going round the traverse into the gully was like entering a special kind of refrigerated hell. Don had never felt it so cold in the Himalayas and I had never experienced anything like it in the hardest Alpine winters. The weather still wasn't good and the wind was still whipping clouds of spindrift around. But at least the avalanches had stopped. On the way up to the high point we were stopping every few minutes with frozen hands and feet. The cramped hand position needed for moving jumars is not conducive to good blood circulation. I eventually reached the high point and waited for quite a time before Don came up. 'I had to take me boots off to warm me feet.' Enough said. I started off on the chimney. At this time we were badly short of rope and ironmongery. I had about three hundred feet of rope, four pegs and about six karabiners. The climbing was difficult; downward-sloping slabby rock covered with loose snow. Every strenuous move brought me gasping to a halt. One runner for a hundred and fifty feet. Then it eased to a steep snow gully and I swam my way to the end of the rope. The way ahead

View across the Annapurna range looking east from the top of the Rock Band at a height about 25,000 feet. A spur of the Face is on the left, with Fluted Peak in the centre foreground. Along the main spine of the Annapurna Range from left to right are Gangapurna, Annapurna II and in the far right background Annapurna II (climbed by the author in 1960).

was blocked by a chockstone, but there still looked to be some distance to go before the gully ended. Don lung-heaved his way up. What to do? By this time we had been together so long, that we hardly needed to speak about obvious decisions. We were both desperately eager to see how the gully ended. The whole way to the summit depended on this. So we just untied our belays and carried on climbing. This is where mutual confidence in ability shows. I was leading but Don was only about ten feet behind. One bad move and I would have taken us both to oblivion. Round a small rock rib up the gully a little farther—a difficult chockstone with slabby snowy holds. Spindrift and cloud whipping around. Cold hands and tired lungs. More straight snow gully. Out. We couldn't believe it. It was the best moment of the climb so far.

There we were sitting on an easy snowfield obviously well above the Rock Band and between glimpses of cloud we could see the east summit of Annapurna. The main summit was hidden but we knew from careful binocular study that there wasn't anything outrageously difficult on the final section. If Camp VII could be set up in the vicinity of the top of the gully then we could make a reasonable try for the summit. Happily we turned and started to climb down as the usual afternoon storm came in. We didn't want the snow to fill in our steps so moved as quickly as possible. Light-headed elation soon gave way to grim concentration. Going back round the chockstone was breath-holding work. Soloing down steep mixed ground at 25,000 feet isn't the best way to enjoy a climbing holiday. But we reached the tent again so why should I complain too much?

Soon after we were back in the sleeping-bags, Chris arrived with more worrying news. We had lost the services of yet another high-altitude climber. Even oxygen had not been able to get Nick up to Camp VI again and he set off for the lower camps completely exhausted leaving Chris to make a lonely journey to VI. He had brought us enough gear to fix-rope to the top of the gully but there was no tent for the projected Camp VII or any food. Sprawled dejectedly in the stormy sunset we talked it over. Chris said that he would make yet another carry on the morrow to try and get us the tent and some food. It was the only way that a summit bid seemed possible at that time. I didn't think that such an effort should be made merely for Don's and my sake, so suggested that Chris join us in the summit bid by bringing his personal gear at the same time as the other things. His answer was an obvious yes and as he set off down the ropes the dejection began to fade away again. The odds were high against but everyone remaining was still giving everything they had. Teamwork was working at a maximum. Now there was nothing to do but wait for the Camp VII tent. We had enough rope to finish off the gully but it did not seem worth making two journeys so we decided to take a rest the next day and wait for Chris to come up with the necessary gear.

There isn't really such a thing as a rest day at 24,000 feet. The morning saw the usual rime-filled tent and frozen sleeping-bag. I tried to spin out making the porridge. We had been left a bar of chocolate and some nuts. These were added to the mixture to try and make something tasty. To our jaded palates it almost assumed the proportions of a treat. The sun didn't come around to Camp VI until around 9.0 a.m. A vague warmth began to creep into the tent but with it came the melting rime. Soon the inside was dripping. But we didn't really care too much. Talk was at a minimum as we had already discussed most of our hopes and plans. We knew that the morrow would be an important day. As the sun grew hotter and the inside started to dry our eyelids began to close. I lay in a half-sleep state feeling incredibly relaxed in the warmth. It must have been some kind of reaction from the long, cold, tense, cramped nights. Those few hours in the sun were more pleasant than all the nights I had previously spent at this spot. The afternoon clouds soon rolled up but we continued to lie and doze. There was nothing else to do except wait for the tug of Chris coming up the fixed rope. Late in the afternoon he fixed the last tired jumar stroke over the edge. Tiredness was all over his face. We had our tent and some food but he had been unable to carry his personal gear as well. A bitter disappointment for him. But Ian Clough was due to come up to V that day so they could at least make the second summit bid. A weary farewell left us to a change in menu—a mixed grill, with some nuts and chocolate left for the next day. Given good weather the summit seemed a possible two days away. Even the lack of stars in the sky couldn't curb our happiness at the chance to launch out fully again. Sleep was good.

I was once again up at five making the reviving drinks. Throats were raw from gasping in the thin cold air. During the night my whole mouth would dry up and I had to suck on a precious fruit-gum to get the saliva working again. Consequently we had to get the first drink down before we could begin to think of talking other than in monosyllabic grunts. This particular morning there was nothing much to discuss. It was the day for establishing Camp VII. Once again it was cold with snapping spindrift-laden wind. The sun was two hours away from the gully when we started the upward jumar. I had thought previous mornings cold but this was the one that was way out ahead. Every few minutes saw us stopping to warm one extremity or another. For the first time my nose began to freeze and even with my face covered with a duvet hood plus balaclava I still had to stop and bury it in my gloved hands in order to regain some vestige of warmth. Don had his boots off and on but was still suffering. It took a long time to reach the end of our fixed ropes. By this time the weather had closed in completely. My immediate prospect was a three hundred foot run-out to the top of the gully. At first thought this didn't seem too bad as we had soloed it two days previously. But things were slightly different on this day. I had only gone fifty feet when I could barely see any more. Goggles were ripped off in a rage but then I found my eyelids freezing solid. I tried to clean my goggles and put them on again but they were totally useless by this time. There was no way of cleaning my eyelids. Dachstein mitts were completely covered in snow and to take them off would have meant instant frostbite. Powder avalanches were sloughing down the gully and the swirling wind was blasting spindrift both up and from the sides. It was a nightmare climbing situation—yet the strange thing about it was that I never contemplated turning back. There was only one thought and that was to reach the end of the gully and pitch the tent for Camp VII. I had never thought I could get into as testing a situation as doing a hundred-and-fifty-foot run-out on hard ice in a storm on the Eiger with only an ice-peg and no axe or hammer but this seemed even more harrowing. It was twice as long and difficulties very similar. My eyes were so glued up and painful that I couldn't think of looking for a place to put a runner-peg. There was no contact with Don. The wind had drowned out shouted sounds after five feet. I fumbled onwards and only once did a brief thought break the terrible concentration. A flash of the possibilities of a fall. This was quickly cut dead. One doesn't even contemplate going for six hundred feet.

After I don't know how long the end was in sight. Ten feet to go when the rope went tight. I just had to ram in my axe and tie off the end as I was sure Don would interpret the pull as a signal to come up and I didn't want him to start jumaring with my body as anchor. I just sat there numb and empty as I felt the movement begin on the rope. It was a total dream state and it could have been minutes or hours before Don arrived. It was in fact a long time. His appearance on the stance broke the dream state, face completely crusted with ice. Even then we didn't say anything about retreat. I fixed a peg, tied off the rope then we both turned and began to move upwards looking for a flattish spot to dig out for the tent. Don took over and we front-pointed into the clouds. Soon we reached some rocks and this was where Don had reckoned to place the camp. He started digging but each time the snow was taken off the surface, the entrenching-tool struck hard ice. Nothing doing there so he wandered upwards but the slope still continued steeply.

As I stood waiting I suddenly realized that the whole of the outside of my left hand had gone numb. I quickly stuck it under my armpit. Slowly it dawned on us that things were serious. Retreat and defeat were right there with us. Still our minds would hardly let the thoughts begin to flow. We were so keyed up for the upward push. Down we had to go. Even that was a struggle. Our tracks were completely wiped out and in the whiteout and wild storm it was hard to know which way to turn to rereach the top of the gully. As we stumbled in the estimated direction there was an amazing ten-second break in the clouds and there it was about three hundred feet beneath us. Once there we still didn't want to give in and I tried to beat out a platform where the gully led out onto the icefield. Still no go. Every stroke met hard ice. Then it was suddenly inevitable and Don turned round, climbed down to the top of the fixed rope and started to abseil. Every foot we descended life seemed to get easier. Even though the storm was still at full blast it seemed relatively sheltered in the gully compared with the holocaust on the upper plateau. Retrospective analysis is interesting. We had been bewildered, lost, weary but still capable of making rational decisions.

Back at VI we found Chris and Ian. Shelter had been reached but the thought of four in the tent was something else again. Everyone was totally covered in ice. The spindrift had infiltrated the rucksacks and sleeping bags were frozen and ready to become sodden. Somehow we packed in out of the storm. Ian was bent double in the far corner. Don and Chris facing each other with legs bent and intertwined. I was in an icy pool at the door. This meant I had to do most of the chores but it was a relief to be occupied because sleeping was going to be difficult. Once I had to stagger out and clear the snow from the back of the tent. One good thing was that four bodies at least gave the tent extra ballast and there seemed little likelihood of it blowing away on this night. Discussion and tea-making was the solution to the night. It had been a defeat but already we were contemplating bouncing back for more. Chris and Ian reckoned they weren't going well enough to try for the summit. Their decision was to drop right down to Camp IV, leave us with the food they had brought up and then leave Mick and Tom who were already at V to support us while they in turn supported them. Don and I were to sit out the bad weather and then have another try at establishing VII.

The morning light flashed on our rime-coated bodies dozing in strange contorted positions. Chris and Ian eventually extricated themselves and left us alone once again with the wind and the swirling snow. There was no improvement in the weather. Sleep was about the only urge left in our bodies but the tent had to be cleared if we were going to do any surviving at all. Hours later we had all the surplus snow thrown out and the rime scraped from the bags. Our underclothes were still dry and with the stove burning constantly we fell into deep stupors. Thus passed the day. From the radio it turned out that nearly all activity had stopped on the mountain. There had been heavy snowfalls at all the camps. It looked like being a sit-out period. Most of the other really bad weather had passed reasonably quickly but this spell looked as if it had set in for a few days. Conversation came in spasms. Slight depression was beginning to set in again. If the snow got too heavy on the lower level there would be no carries. No carries meant no food and even at our present low consumption level we only had enough for two more days at the very most. When we did move it looked as if we would have to try and establish Camp VII then come down again for supplies before we could actually occupy it. The summit was once again beginning to fade into the vague future. We were alone with our sombre thoughts and the wind. Without the extra weight, being blown away again became a distinct possibility. The usual night passed. There was a gap where the entrance zip didn't quite close and each gust or jet of spindrift would seek out any exposed part of flesh. I slept with everything on, even overboots, and had the sleeping-bag tied right up with only a small breathing space. During the night the moisture from breathing would freeze round this hole and moustache and beard hairs would stick to it.

The new day was no better than the old. We passed it in the usual way. The only good news was that Mick and Tom had gone down to the dump at the end of the Ice Ridge to meet Chris, Ian and Dave Lambert, who had brought up loads of food and would try to make a carry the next day to alleviate our food situation. After the radio call I looked out. There wasn't so much wind activity. Some stars were actually visible and the Fang came into sight for the first time in three days. At least it looked as if we could try to establish the camp on the morrow. We were off by seven. Don left a few minutes before me as I was trying to organize the movie camera. It seemed like a good idea to take some film of the gully and also the establishment of VII so I stuck one cartridge in the camera and a spare in my pocket. The weather was by no means perfect. Spindrift and cloud were still making their presence felt. But compared to the other days in the gully it seemed relatively mild. Eleven o'clock saw us once again on the plateau. An exciting moment. In the clear spells we could see the summit of Annapurna at close quarters for the first time. I picked up the RAFMA and we had a short discussion. Don said, 'I think we should press on and find a campsite as close to the final wall as possible.' I was in complete agreement but we were both obviously thinking of greater things.

Here's the way it looked. There was an icefield leading up to a sharp snow ridge which in turn led to a mixed face of around eight hundred feet. At the top of this face? Annapurna. Once again we just turned to movement without any more discussion. It didn't need telepathy to communicate our thoughts. The summit was a real possibility. The big question was the weather. There was no way we wanted to get into a situation similar to our previous attempt. True, we could probably erect the tent on the ridge but it would be a bivouac without food, stoves or sleeping-bags. Certainly survival would have been O.K. but the weakening factor would have been enormous. Don led, I carried the tent and rope. Front-pointing up the ice slope the ridge was there. I just set the tent down on a platform and on we went. Time was pressing and there seemed no point in taking belays. Each moved upwards in his own special world. The climbing on the face was reasonably difficult. Little steep ice pitches combined with scattered rock moves. The mind was still working well. I got out the camera and shot off the first cartridge. Through the lens it looked sensational. A lone figure carving his way upwards towards the twin summit ridge cliffs, occasionally being blotted out by clouds of spindrift. I kept having trouble with my right crampon. It came off three times on the summit wall. But I was thinking clearly and stopped each time in contorted positions and fixed the straps. Due to this Don was about a hundred feet ahead.

The wonderful thing was that there was no breathing trouble. I had imagined great lung-gasping effort at 26,000 feet but I was moving with no more difficulty than I'd experienced four thousand feet lower down. Likewise Don was having no such problems. He picked a beautiful line through towards the summit ridge. Then he disappeared over the edge and I was alone for a brief spell. The final fifty feet needed care. Big flat

Whillans on the summit of Annapurna, which he and Haston reached at 2.0 p.m., on 27th May 1970.

unsolid snowy rocks which had to be scraped clean. Over the ridge and suddenly it was calm. There was no wind on the north side. Long, relatively flat spaces led down into the cloud. Don was already fixing a rappel peg. We didn't speak. There was no elation. The mind was still too wound up to allow such feelings to enter. Besides the supreme concentration was needed to get down. The real problem was the actual summit. We were on a ridge. The snow peak to the left looked highest so Don plodded up the thirty feet or so to its top while I filmed the historic moment. Vague traces of what must have been army footprints showed beneath the snow. I, in turn, stood on the peak. The view was disappointing. Only the east summit was clear. I had looked forward to seeing Dhaulagiri on one side and right down to Base on the other but there was only a vast sea of grey cloud about a thousand feet beneath us. The greatest moment of both our climbing careers and there was only a kind of numbness. But we knew the elation would come when we unwound. Meanwhile there was still the face to climb down. Fortunately I had carried up a hundred and fifty feet of rope in my pack so the hardest section could be bypassed by abseiling. That was our summit monument. A fixed rope. It seemed appropriate as it was the last of fifteen thousand feet of such.

The down climb took all the concentration we had. Twice again my crampon came off. Once on the summit wall and once on the icefield leading down to the top of the gully. Going down the fixed ropes the tensions started to wear away. It was turning into a good late afternoon. Everything seemed beautiful. Inside and out. I got back to Camp VI to find Don just about to tune in on the radio. He handed it to me muttering, 'You've made all the bloody communications till now, so you may as well make this one!' A serious-sounding Chris came on, 'Chris calling Camp VI. Did you manage to get out today?' I answered, 'Aye, we've just climbed Annapurna.' Atmospherics were so bad that he asked me to repeat. I was just about to do so when bedlam broke loose on the set. Base Camp had been listening in and it had come across loud and clear. Then Chris got the message and all the other camps and you could almost feel the relief and happiness vibrating along the sound waves.

Don Whillans (above) and Dougal Haston (next page) photographed here on their way down. Both climbers stayed at Camp VI for nine consecutive nights, with very little food and battered by storms before they succeeded in fighting their way to the top.

CHAPTER 18

Tragedy

[27–30 May]

It should have been over. But then, after all the excited talk over the radio between Dougal and the other stations on the mountain, Mick Burke came up with: 'Is it all right if Tom and I move up to VI tomorrow for our summit bid?'

We had always worked on the assumption that as many people as possible should go to the summit. It seemed only fair, for this is the natural, personal climax to an expedition for the individual. Mick and Tom had already done so much to help Don and Dougal reach the top.

Without thinking I agreed, but that night, once the euphoria had worn off, I began to worry. We had made it, but only just. The weather was appalling and progress upwards from the lower camps impossible. If Tom and Mick had an accident there was nothing we could do about it. Ian, Dave and I had barely managed to fight our way to the top of the Ice Ridge the previous day. I very much doubt if we could have got any farther.

I didn't sleep that night: the joy of success was gone in the worry of what I should do about Tom and Mick. If I stopped them going on, they would undoubtedly have a deep feeling of betrayal and grievance that could erode some of the very real unity the entire team felt—on the other hand, I was responsible not just for their lives but for those of others who might have to attempt a rescue if anything went wrong. By dawn I had resolved to pull them back.

On the morning radio call, Camp V was late in coming onto the air, and I had already told Dougal to strip Camp VI before coming down. But then Tom came on the radio.

'Look, Chris, you're planning to spend three days stripping the mountain. Couldn't we go up today to VI, and have the chance of going for the top tomorrow? We won't be slowing your evacuation of the mountain at all.'

He sounded so very reasonable, and what he said was true. I had a high regard for Tom's judgement and therefore relented.

'O.K., Tom, you can go up to VI today, but can I have your promise to come back down the day after tomorrow whether or not you have made a summit bid?'

'That sounds fair, we agree to that, Chris.'

'Roger. But remember you will be on your own. There is nothing we can do to help you if you get into trouble. Is that understood?'

'We understand that. Don't worry, we shall take very good care of ourselves.'

I decided that Ian, Dave and I should pull back down to Camp III, since we had almost run out of food at Camp IV. The way down was frightening. The ropes were all covered in a thick mantle of snow that had to be laboriously cleared, foot by foot, as we went down. At the bottom of the fixed rope the snow was thigh-deep and it was all we could do to wade downwards—upward progress was completely impossible. It was snowing hard; a heavy moist snow that surely must be the monsoon. There was a feeling of indefinable menace in the air. It was as if the whole mountain was ready to reject us, as if we were tiny foreign bodies or parasites clinging to a huge, living organism, whose automatic defensive mechanism had at last come to life.

Mike Thompson was waiting for us at Camp III, his box as always immaculately tidy, a real haven of order and comfort—not to remain so for long, I'm afraid, once I had moved in with him.

Don and Dougal, on their way down, reached us at about mid-day. We were very British, tremendously excited and pleased to see them, yet a little stilted and formal in offering our congratulations. Don mirrored my own feeling about the state of the mountain.

'You want to get everyone off the mountain as quickly as possible,' he said. 'It's falling apart. The whole place feels hostile somehow.'

I agreed with him; bitterly regretted letting Mick and Tom go for the summit. The strange thing was that the lower one got down the mountain, the more dangerous it felt, probably because of the greater precipitation of snow and higher temperatures. Don and Dougal floundered on down to be met by the T.V. team at the edge of the glacier, while Mike, Dave, Ian and I took up our vigil, waiting for Tom and Mick to make their attempt and come back down.

That evening they missed the five o'clock radio call—they still hadn't reached Camp VI. Tom described their passage in his diary:

> The weather was worse than the previous day with snow, wind, cloud and huge avalanches pouring down the Face and gullies. Mick was so slow that I finally passed him about three-quarters way up. The tent at VI was invisible until close up because of the huge mass of snow covering it. Mick flaked out crosswise in the back and I began cooking our dinner on the Bleuet gas cartridge stove. In spite of the high standard of the cuisine, Mick ate very little (one cup of soup) and I suspect he might not be up to tomorrow's ascent.
>
> But our big moment was at hand and I planned for an early pre-dawn start. By 10.0 p.m. I completed the cooking detail and stretched out diagonally, barely warm enough with everything on in my Erve bag.
>
> I woke up for the second time at 1.0 a.m. on 29 May and with excitement in my heart began preparing to leave. By 4.0 a.m. it was complete. I had made a cup of porridge with some honey we had specially brought up, for Mick and myself, heated up a tin of herring fillets in savoury sauce and boiled hot water for our bottles to drink during the day.

I put on my clean socks, inner and outer boots (laced loosely), wet suit, rubber overboots and proofed nylon outers. I also put on my crampons while still inside the tent. Worse than anything else I am afraid of frostbitten toes, having had numb feet many times already. The weather is bitterly cold with a high wind. Also I wore long johns, down pants, wool trousers and wind pants. On the top it was underwear, three sweaters, down jacket and windproof parka. On my hands silk gloves and Dachstein mitts.

Mick was moving slow in the sleeping-bag and admitted there was little chance of his making the summit. Here is a graphic example of the blessings that come from the obedience to the Word of Wisdom. A smoker for fifteen years, Mick Burke was failing with the altitude while I, not naturally strong at altitude, was still pulling at 24,000 feet. [One must remember that Don Whillans, who had smoked for at least twenty years and drunk an average of three pints a night, was going even more strongly than Tom.]

I borrow Mick's ice-axe head fixture for mounting my camera on the summit for solo photographs, shake hands and push out into the crisp, cold air; it is beautiful and clear with a partial moon. I notice for the first time that at this height the stars near the horizon are equally bright as those above.

Tom, totally involved in his purpose of reaching the summit and confident in his own judgement, was in a state of mental tranquillity, but back at Camp III I was tortured with worry. I slept very little that night, wondering whether Tom and Mick would be all right. I had never worried like this before on the expedition, mainly, I suspect, because until Don and Dougal actually reached the summit, this aim completely blocked out the possible consequences of an accident. In addition, I was spared worry during the summit bid because I knew nothing about it until they got down. I was used to taking risks myself, less accustomed to taking the responsibility for those of others.

At the seven o'clock call I immediately tried to get into contact with Camp VI but got no reply, went on to talk to Kelvin at Base and then, as a last chance, called VI before closing down—and back came the reply.

'Hello, Chris, this is Mick. I've only just got back. I set out last night but my feet froze up on me, so I decided no mountain was worth my toes.'

'Hard luck, Mick, but have you got Tom with you?'

'No. I think he's going for the summit on his own.'

My momentary relief was washed away. Tom going alone for the summit sounded even worse.

'In that case, let's have radio calls on the hour till he gets back. How are you feeling, Mick?'

'Shattered, but I'll be all right when I've had a bit of a rest.'

And then the long wait started. Eight o'clock: we opened up the set, but there was no reply; Mick had dropped off to sleep. Nine o'clock: he came on the air: 'no sign of Tom.' Ten o'clock: 'no sign of Tom.' And so it went on. I don't think I have ever felt so helpless, been so agonizingly worried.

But Tom, striving for the summit on his own, knew nothing of our worry. He wrote in his diary:

After hefting my Kelti pack frame containing sleeping-bag for emergency, water-bottle, camera and odds and ends, I attach jumars to the fixed rope above our tent and begin the traverse into the gully, reach it and begin the thousand-foot fixed-rope ascent. Shortly, a tremendous wind begins blowing down the steep snow gully I am ascending, creating its own blizzard of windblown snow. My toes are numb and for the first time my fingers are desperately cold. Don and Dougal said they needed two pairs of Dachstein mitts up here and I found they were right.

At 8.0 a.m. I reached the top of the gully and stepped out onto the summit snowfield at about 25,000 feet. It was disappointing to see the long distance to the summit, the high wind here and above blowing snow wildly, the bitter cold, the knee-deep snow and the penetrating tiredness which I now felt as a result of my four-hour climb.

After a couple of hours of indecision, some eating of wheat-germ and drinking from my now cold water bottle; feeble attempts at warming fingers and toes, half-hearted, frightened efforts at photographing the now puny peaks piercing the cloud layer, I realized the jig was up; that I could not reach the summit and survive. The only alternative was to turn back.

Was it the Lord's will that I reach the top? Unthinkable! I have prayed sincerely and repeatedly that the Lord's will and not mine should be done. 'Behold this is my will; ask and ye shall receive; but men do not always do my will.' I was determined for once to do his will and as an additional testimony to me, as I spent my nearly three hours on the summit snowfield, the wind gradually increased in ferocity and the cold continued to pierce my body. I spent the best part of an hour lost in a dream world, collecting beautiful rock specimens for my Love's and my own world-wide collection. A last look round through the blowing snow, and I began my descent.

At the twelve o'clock call Mick Burke gave me the good news that Tom was back. There was an overwhelming feeling of relief—all we had to do now was evacuate the mountain. They were going to try to get down as far as possible that day but it seemed unlikely that they would get farther than IV. I was anxious to get back to Base to catch up with the various administrative problems associated with our success and projected departure. I now felt free to descend and therefore, leaving Dave, Ian and Mike to wait for Tom and Mick, I set off for the last time down the long snow gully below Camp III. At its foot I found the debris of a monster ice avalanche that had swept away the tracks of Don and Dougal over an area of about three hundred yards. The mountain seemed to be falling apart.

Back at Base there was little feeling of uninhibited celebration, rather one of tiredness and relief that it was all over. It was good to take off crampons for the last time, relax into the comfort of a warm sleeping-bag in the communal base tent, but somehow I did not feel at ease.

In the morning I started writing the account of our success, to be radioed back to our committee of management. From time to time I went out and looked up at the Face through the binoculars. Tom and Mick should be down at Camp III by this time; the others would be at the foot of the long gully.

I remember Martin saying, 'Relax, Chris, it's all over. Nothing can happen now.'

'I don't think I'll be really happy till everyone is down.'

I very much doubt if this was premonition, for I have always been nervous on any descent after a hard climb, never relaxing until I get down to ground level.

I had returned to my typewriter when I heard someone rush up to the tent calling, 'Chris, Chris!' and the rest was incomprehensible. I ran out and found Mike sitting on the grass, head between knees, sucking in the air in great, hacking gasps. He looked up, face contorted with shock, grief and exhaustion.

'It's Ian. He's dead; killed in an ice avalanche below Camp II.'

Everyone had run out of their tents on hearing Mike's arrival; they just stood numbed in shocked, unbelieving silence for about five minutes as Mike gasped out his story; Mike is one of the most emotionally restrained and balanced people that I know, but that morning he was crying. I held him, my arm round his shoulder, barely restrained my own tears as I tried to find out exactly what had happened.

Mike, Ian and Dave Lambert had decided not to wait for Mick Burke and Tom, but set out from Camp III early that morning, hauling down as much gear as they could manage. We had arranged for the Sherpas at Camp I to come up to the now cleared site of Camp II to meet them.

Mike and Ian reached the site of Camp II at around 9.30, and since the Sherpas had not yet come up they decided to press on down. Ian suggested that they stop for a rest and something to eat, but Mike was impatient to get off the mountain and pointed out that they would be down at Camp I in half an hour if they pushed on quickly.

And so they carried on down the side of the glacier, into a narrow corridor between some small ice towers and then out onto the start of the ramp which led across the ice cliffs. This was the spot that we had always realized was dangerous, but the most obvious threat had been removed earlier on in the expedition when the Sword of Damocles had fallen. There was still an element of risk, for there were some ice towers farther up the glacier, but their threat was not so obvious and it seemed unlikely that these would collapse in the space of the few seconds it took to cross the danger zone. Even so, we all tended to hurry across this section of the glacier.

Ian was in front and Mike immediately behind. Dave Lambert was about five minutes behind them. They had just come out of the narrow, enclosed corridor that led down to the ramp and they could see the five Sherpas, who were coming up to meet them, resting on a small mound just short of the sérac wall.

There was practically no warning, just a thunderous roar and the impression of a huge, dark mass filling the sky above. Mike ducked back into the side of the ice wall where a small trough was formed. He thought that Ian, slightly farther out than he, had tried to run away from the avalanche, down the slope. But Ian hadn't a hope and was engulfed in the fall.

'It went completely dark,' Mike told me later. 'I thought I'd had it; just lay there and swore at the top of my voice. It seemed such a stupid way to die.'

The fall seemed to last for several minutes, though it was probably considerably less. Mike was buried in small ice blocks but had been protected by the wall at his side from the torrent of huge blocks that had come pouring directly over him.

When the cloud of ice particles had settled and the last grating rumble had died away into the silence of the glacier, the survivors picked themselves out of the debris. The Sherpas had had to run for their lives, but fortunately had been sufficiently far from the base of the cliff to get out of the direct line of fall. Even so, Mingma had been hit by an ice block, though he was not injured.

They then started to search for Ian and found him near the foot of the avalanche debris, his body protruding from it. Death must have been instantaneous. The accident had occurred at 10.0 a.m. and Mike had run straight down to warn us, leaving Dave and the Sherpas with the body. They had a walkie-talkie set with them and he had told Dave to open up on the hour.

Back at Base Camp it was now just after mid-day and I opened the set. Dave came on the air and told me that they had managed to get Ian's body clear of the ice.

I immediately decided that we should carry him back to Base Camp and bury him there. The Rognon was somehow too bleak a place, and I felt that we should try to have some kind of ceremony as a tribute to so close a friend of us all. At this stage we were all numbed by the very unexpectedness, the enormity of the accident. In a strange way it would have been easier to come to terms with during the actual course of the ascent, but now, the whole climb seemed to have been over, success achieved, the risk passed. And then this.

I couldn't help having a feeling of guilt, that if I'd brought everyone off the mountain the accident might never have happened. I could dismiss this on logical grounds for the sérac could have collapsed at any point of time during the expedition and presented the type of risk that climbers face as a matter of course in the Alps. If it had fallen one minute earlier, Ian would be alive now; but equally, if it had collapsed two minutes later, Mike and all five Sherpas could also have been engulfed. It was a risk that we all knew and had accepted—you must accept this type of risk if you go climbing on any Himalayan peak—but the knowledge of this did not make the tragedy, when it occurred, any easier to understand or accept.

But the risks were not over. Mick and Tom were still on the mountain, probably somewhere below Camp III, we still had to carry Ian's body back across the lower glacier below the Rognon, another place that was fraught with peril. I could not bring myself to just sit and wait for the rest of my expedition to get back to Base Camp and therefore, taking Nick Estcourt with me, set out to meet the carrying party, and to find Mick Burke and Tom Frost.

I met them just starting across the glacier. It was terribly difficult to believe that the inanimate bundle tied in a tarpaulin, strapped to a ladder, had only an hour or so before been an active, living person. Pasang Kami had taken charge and was directing the Sherpas and Gurkha porters with a cool competence, as they manoeuvred the makeshift stretcher through the chaotic icefall. One could not help being aware of the ice cliffs frowning above. At this stage Mick Burke and Dave Lambert arrived down, but Tom Frost was still on his way. They had left Rob, one of our London Sherpas, to wait for him, but I felt I had to go back up the Rognon to assure myself that he was all right. I plodded up through the mist, my mind a mixture of grief and shock; still no sign of Tom; could something else have happened? I was nearly at Camp I and heard a rattle of stones below; they had nearly passed me in the cloud. I set off back to Base Camp with them; at least we had now got everyone else off the mountain.

That night everyone was subdued and silent, buried in their own thoughts and reaction to the tragedy. Next morning, the 30th, our porters were due to arrive from Pokhara to carry out all our gear. We buried Ian about a hundred feet above Base Camp, at the foot of the slab of rock where he had spent so much time teaching the T.V. team and our Sherpas and cookboys how to jumar and abseil. I said a few words of tribute; Tom said a prayer and we filled in the grave. It was a very short, simple ceremony and yet it had a beauty and dignity, enhanced by the depth of feeling of all who were present.

The Sherpas placed a wooden cross at the head of the grave and decked it with wreaths made from alpine flowers collected by the porters. The tents had been pulled down, the porters were waiting with their loads and all that was left of two months' occupation, with all its struggle, drama and laughter, were a few piles of empty tins and the lone grave of a close friend.

We turned our backs on the South Face of Annapurna and set foot, for the first time in nearly ten weeks, on the glacier below Base Camp. When we had walked up it everything had been hidden by a mantle of snow, but now that the bare bones of rubble were exposed, a dusty path worn through it, it reminded me of a vast junkyard. And then we reached the other side of the glacier, dropped down into the shallow valley at the side of the lateral moraine through lush meadows sprinkled with an ever widening variety of flowers. I don't think any of us felt regret at leaving Annapurna as we turned down into the gaping jaws of the Modi Khola gorge. We had been there too long and had given too much, and yet we had known some of the most exciting climbing of our lives, had reached a level of unity and selflessness that had made success possible. As we walked down the Modi Khola we felt a mixture of grief at the death of a friend and an extraordinary elation, not solely from our success, but also because we had managed to become such a close-knit team.

I can't attempt to evaluate the worth of our ascent balanced against its cost in terms of the loss of a man's life, of the time devoted to it or the money spent on it. Climbing, and the risks involved, are part of my life and, I think, of those of most of the team—it was certainly a very large part of Ian's life. It is difficult to justify the risks once one is married with a family, and I think most of us have stopped trying. We love climbing, have let a large part of our lives be dominated by this passion, and this eventually led us to Annapurna.

Maurice Herzog, in his story of the first ascent of Annapurna, finishes up his book with the words: 'There are other Annapurnas in the lives of men.' This is still true today, both in the realm of mountaineering and in one's own progress through life. Our ascent of Annapurna was a breakthrough into a new dimension of Himalayan climbing on the great walls of the highest mountains in the world—this represents the start of an era, not the end. Climbers will turn to other great faces, will perhaps try to reduce the size of the party, escape from the heavy siege tactics that we were forced to employ and make lightweight assaults against these huge mountain problems.

And then, on a personal level, each one of us who helped to climb the South Face will find new challenges. For Don and Dougal it is the South Face of Everest; for Tom Frost, it is living within the moral code of his Mormon faith; for Mick Burke, perhaps carving out a career in films; for myself—I know not, at the moment, but I know my life will be a constant search for Annapurnas and, having found one, I shall feel forced to seek the next.

APPENDIX A
Diary and Statistics
NICK ESTCOURT

Expedition Diary

23 January 1970	Gear leaves by s.s. *State of Kerala* for Bombay
27 February	Whillans and Lambert fly to Bombay, and find that *State of Kerala* has been delayed
17 March	Main party flies out from England
22 March	Main party leaves Pokhara
28 March	Main party reaches Machapuchare Base Camp
2 April	Camp I (16,000 ft) occupied by Bonington and Burke
6 April	Camp II (17,500 ft) occupied by Haston and Whillans
7 April	Haston and Whillans reach site of Camp III (20,100 ft)
13 April	Camp III occupied by Bonington and Frost
23 April	Camp IV (21,300 ft) occupied by Boysen and Estcourt
3 May	Haston and Bonington reach end of Ice Ridge (21,500 ft)
7 May	Haston and Whillans reach foot of Rock Band
9 May	Camp V (22,750 ft) occupied by Frost and Burke
14 May	Frost and Burke reach Flat Iron
19 May	Camp VI (24,000 ft) occupied by Whillans
22 May	Haston and Whillans reach top of Rock Band
27 May	HASTON AND WHILLANS REACH SUMMIT (26,545 ft)
29 May	Frost and Burke attempt to reach summit
30 May	Clough killed by ice avalanche below Camp II
4 June	Expedition back in Pokhara
11 June	Expedition back in London

A Few Statistics

Table I shows a breakdown of the performances of the members of the expedition. At first glance one might get the impression that Chris Bonington spent the whole expedition rushing from one camp to the next, Kelvin Kent organizing Base Camp, Mike Thompson resting at Camp III, Don Whillans and Dougal Haston climbing the mountain and a stolid Dave Lambert humping loads. In fact the figures for days resting above Base Camp are unfairly swollen for those people who were on the mountain during the last two weeks or so of the expedition, as during this period the weather was bad and movement often very difficult. Dougal, for instance, had only taken two rest days on the mountain before this period, and anyway it is debatable whether rest days at Camp VI count as rest days.

	Bonington	Boysen	Burke	Clough	Estcourt	Frost	Haston	Kent	Lambert	Thompson	Whillans
Total days at or above Base	63	63	63	53	62	63	63	53	63	53	63
Total days at Base	12	16	14	10	13	8	10	28	8	12	10
Total days resting above Base	5	5	7	5	6	7	5	1	12	16	8
Days in lead	13	5	8	4	5	10	22	—	—	—	19
Days moving camp	24	15	18	17	16	16	16	7	13	13	19
Days carrying loads	9	22	16	15	22	21	10	17	29	12	7
Total days at or above 20,000 ft	31	25	27	27	29	32	33	6	20	21	32
Total non-rest days at or above 20,000 ft	26	20	22	22	23	27	29	5	11	8	25
Longest continuous period at or above 20,000 ft	13	16	19	15	20	19	15	6	18	14	15
Total days at or above Camp IV	16	15	18	18	21	18	21	—	12	3	19

	Bonington	Boysen	Burke	Clough	Estcourt	Frost	Haston	Kent	Lambert	Thompson	Whillans
Total non-rest days at or above Camp IV	14	13	15	15	17	15	18	—	6	2	15
Longest period at or above Camp IV	10	11	12	12	17	12	14	—	12	3	14
Total days at or above Camp V	6	3	11	2	5	11	14	—	—	—	14
Total non-rest days at or above Camp V	5	2	9	2	5	9	11	—	—	—	10
Longest period at or about Camp V	6	3	6	2	5	6	12	—	—	—	12

Table I

Don, Dougal and Ian Clough are notable in that they tended to take very few rest days on the mountain: they stayed above Base for comparatively short periods and did their resting at Base. Mick Burke on the other hand, after his early illness, spent the longest single period above Base (twenty-nine days); no one else spent more than three weeks. I spent the longest continuous period high on the mountain. Another fact that emerges is that, until the final push, Don had spent nearly the *least* time above Camp III, and yet was going strongest on the final day when most other people were burnt out. Perhaps this shows that deterioration of the body due to altitude sets in only just slower than acclimatization, and in fact Don, the wily old mountaineer, had timed things just right.

The figures for load-carrying are not really a true guide to how much each individual did, as some of the carries were very much harder than others. Those to Camps III, V and VI, for instance, were long and hard, whilst those to II and IV were comparatively short, though even the carry to Camp IV involved a lot of steep jumaring. Taking this into account, Mick, Tom, Martin and I did the most load-carrying. One other surprising fact was the number of days spent moving camp—most people spent over a quarter of the expedition doing this. It is very diffi-cult to get the right balance between going low for resting and wasting more days and energy moving back up again, and taking more rest days on the mountain.

Camp	Weight carried there*	Man-nights spent there	Man-days to force route from previous camp
III	3,160 lb.	183	6
IV	2,220 lb.	89	15
V	800 lb.	32	24
VI	225 lb.	22	8

* Exclusive of personal equipment.

Table 2 gives a little basic information on how much the various camps were used and how much equipment reached them. Unfortunately it was not possible to get the weights that reached the lower camps, nor was it possible to break the weights down accurately into food, rope, oxygen and so forth. The weight of food that reached Camps III to VI respectively was around 1,600 lb., 700 lb., 200 lb., and 60 lb. 240 lb. of oxygen reached Camp IV and 60 lb. reached Camp V. From this it can be seen that roughly half the weight that reached Camp III was food, the proportion getting lower as one goes higher. Thus a saving in the weight of the food ration of, say, 25% would have reduced the weight needed to reach Camp III by 12%, but that to reach Camp V by only 6%. From this it could be argued that if one is to have a different ration for eating very high on the mountain, then, contrary to what might be imagined, it can be heavier than the normal ration. The only significant way to reduce weight very high on the mountain is by careful choice of equipment and economizing on such items as fixed rope, pegs, etcetera, which is probably unacceptable for other reasons.

To summarize, there are two ways in which our logistic problems could probably have been eased:

(a) use of a lighter dried food based ration above base camp and below, say, Camp V.

(b) use of one of the more modern, very lightweight, artificial-fibre ropes for fixed rope above, say, Camp V.

Note on Survey

During the first few days at Machapuchare Base Camp I carried out a very limited survey of the Face and its surroundings. A baseline of 500 feet was established on the moraine near point 13,070 (General Survey of India, 1963). The heights of the summit of Annapurna and some points on the Face above the baseline were fixed by theodolite, and the actual heights were obtained assuming a height of 26,545 feet for Annapurna and working backwards. The theodolite used was a Kern, very generously lent to us by the Royal Geographical Society. It was both light and easy to use. The heights obtained for various features on the Face were:

Small Peak above Camp III	20,250 (±50) feet
Top of Ice Ridge	21,650 (±50) feet
Bottom of Rock Band	22,750 (±50) feet
Top of Rock Band	24,750 (±50) feet

From this approximate heights of the camps were:

Base Camp	14,000 feet
I	16,000 feet
II	17,500 feet
III	20,100 feet
IV	21,300 feet
V	22,750 feet
VI	24,000 feet

All these heights were checked using an altimeter.

The average angle of the Face from Camp III to the top of the Rock Band was 55°; this compares with the Brenva face of Mont Blanc (44°) and the Walker Spur (61°).

The Team

ORGANIZATION IN ENGLAND

Patrons

Lord Tangley of Blackheath, K.B.E.

Lord Hunt of Llanvair Waterdine, C.B.E., D.S.O.

Sir Charles Evans, M.A., F.R.C.S.

Committee of management

Sir Douglas Busk, K.C.M.G.	Chairman
Lt.-Col. C. G. Wylie	
P. Pirie Gordon	Williams & Glyn's Bank, Ltd
T. S. Blakeney	Secretary, Mount Everest Foundation

Agent

George Greenfield	John Farquharson, Ltd

Secretarial

Mrs Joan Clare	Office secretary
Mrs Sylvia Davies	Postcard secretary

ON THE MOUNTAIN

Climbers

Chris Bonington	35	Leader, and organizing co-ordinator in Britain
Don Whillans	37	Deputy Leader, and designer of specialist equipment
Ian Clough	30	Assistant equipment organizer
Martin Boysen	27	
Mick Burke	28	In charge of filming
Nick Estcourt	26	

Tom Frost   33

Dougal Haston   27

Dave Lambert   30   Doctor

Mike Thompson   32   Food organizer

Kelvin Kent   30   Base Camp manager and communications officer

High-altitude porters

Pasang Kami (Sirdar)   31

Pemba Tharkay   29

Ang Pema   35   High-altitude Sherpas recruited through

Mingma Tsering   37   the Himalayan Society, who carried loads

Nima Tsering   20   up to Camp IV

Kancha   27

Auxiliaries

Alan Hankinson   44   T.V. team, but ferried loads as high as Camp III

Frank Jackson   'London Sherpas', who carried to

Robin Terrey   Camp III (once to Camp IV)

Jean-Louis Palarton (Swiss)

Jean-Marie Hagenmuler (French)   One carry to Camp III

2 V.S.O. men (English)

1 Peace Corps man (American)   One carry to Camp I

1 climber (Japanese)

Radio Operator and foreman of local porters

Signalman Gambahadur Pun   Gurkha signals—att. from Brigade of Gurkhas

Local Porters

Birkahadur Pun

Bombahadur Pun

Hiralal Kharkay   Retained from approach march and used

Jitbahadur Lama   for carries on lower portion of the face and

Manbahadur Ghale   to collect fresh rations from Ghandrung

Tirkhamuni Pun

BASE CAMP STAFF

T.V. team

John Edwards	34	Thames—reporter/director
Jonathan Lane	33	I.T.N.—cameraman
John Soldini	46	I.T.N.—sound recordist

Nepalese liaison officer

K. B. Rana

T.V. Sherpa

Nima Norbu

Kitchen staff

Ex-L/Cpl. Tukte — Cook—recently made redundant from 6th Gurkha Rifles

Nima Noru
Sonam Tensing } Cookboys
Phur Gyalgen

Auxiliaries

Miss Cynthia Gilbey } Came with London Sherpas, and
Mrs Barbara Jackson } helped with typing and mending

8 Mailrunners — Recruited in Katmandu and the Tibetan refugee camp, Pokhara

BETWEEN BASE CAMP AND POKHARA

Ex-Lt. (Q.G.O.) Khagbir Pun — Former R.S.M., Gurkha Signals; Chief Naik

Ex-Sgt. Cheesbahadur Gurung — In charge of local purchase arrangements and Ghandrung porters. (House used by mailrunners)

AT POKHARA

Lt. (Q.G.O.) Bishnuparsad Thapa — Gurkha Signals—att. from Brigade of Gurkhas. I/c communications, mail systems and local purchase requests for both A.S.F. and A.M.A. expeditions

Ex-Cpl. Surjabahadur Gurung Radio operator and local assistant

AT KATMANDU

Miss Elizabeth Hawley Main office agency, Reuter outlet and
i/c mail/film/requests
Miss Jennifer Yoder   Finance liaison and cash withdrawals

APPENDIX B

Equipment

Chris Bonington

Our equipment consisted of a combination of well-tried conventional gear and some specially designed items; most of the latter proved satifactory, but I should strongly recommend any other expedition organizer to ensure that he has plenty of time once he starts trying to design new items of equipment. Inevitably there are considerable delays while improving prototypes, and it is all too easy to slip over packing deadlines while trying to get an item of clothing or tentage just right. We secured all foreign items through Pindisports who saved us a great deal of time and money in handling all the paperwork involved in importing equipment.

In discussing the equipment we used I have listed the various items under general headings and have included a list of the gear we took, in the hope that it might be useful to other expeditions.

Personal Gear

I have included below a complete list of gear issued to individual members. In almost every instance we issued the same gear to the Sherpas as we did to ourselves: this is undoubtedly the best policy since they are very quick to notice any discrepancies, and an expedition can start on a bad footing if they feel they have been inadequately equipped.

To them it is not just a matter of having sufficient gear to carry out their job, it is also a question of status and hard cash, since they regard the sale of their gear at the end of the expedition as one of their perks.

(a) *Headwear*

ITEM	MANUFACTURER	COMMENTS
1 bonnet	Functional Clothing	Proofed nylon outer, Borg fur inner
1 balaclava		Wool
1 face-mask		Similar to balaclava with holes cut for eyes and mouth, providing greater protection to face
1 crash-hat	(At climbers' discretion)	Joe Brown, Romer and A.G.V. used. Joe Brown helmets issued to Sherpas

(b) *Body Covering*

ITEM	MANUFACTURER	COMMENTS
1 outer parka	Functional Clothing	4-oz. Dunloprufe nylon with open-cell foam liner
1 pair overbreeches	"	4-oz. Dunloprufe with zip-up leg to allow putting on over crampons
1 anorak	R. L. Harrison, Ltd	Ventile
1 overtrousers	"	Ventile
1 Borg fur jacket	Functional Clothing	Four pockets— artificial fur on side next to skin

1 Borg fur breeches	"	
3 sweaters	St Michael	Lightweight to medium
1 set long underwear	Damart (British)	
1 set long underwear	Rhovyl (American)	
1 pair breeches	H. Pickles & Sons, Ltd	Ski-trouser material
1 sheepskin jacket	Morlands	For Base Camp wear

(c) *Down Gear*

1 double down jacket	Hutchinson Mountain Eqpt	Two jackets fitting over each other: the inner to be used as a climbing jacket, the outer as an addition in extreme cold or at night
1 pair down breeches	"	With zip-down side to allow putting on over boots and crampons
1 pair down boots	"	For use in sleeping-bag
1 Sleeping-bag	Erve Expedition	Super lightweight at 4½ lb., yet very warm

(d) *Foot Covering*

1 pair double boots	Galibier-Hivernale	2 prs inners, leather outer
1 pair closed-cell	Singleton & Green	foam overboots Knee height—same material as wet suits

315

1 pair proofed nylon overboots	Karrimor	Worn over closed-cell foam boots, zip-up back
1 pair vapour-barrier boots	Mishawaka Rubber Co.	
1 pair basketball boots	Dunlop	
1 pair camp boots	Morlands	
3 pairs stockings	Nanga Parbat	Nylon wool mixture
1 pair Borg fur socks	Functional Clothing	For use inside tent and sleeping-bag

(e) *Hand Covering*

2 pairs Dachstein mits	Dachstein	Shrunk wool
2 pairs overmits	Functional Clothing	Proofed nylon with Velcro grips on palms
1 pair overmits	"	Proofed nylon with Borg fur liner
2 pairs mittens	Millarmit	String construction
2 pairs silk gloves		

(f) *Eye Protection*

1 pair ski-goggles	Carrera	Choice of two tinted eye-pieces
2 pairs	sunglasses	British American Optical Co., Ltd

(g) *Personal Climbing Gear*

1 ice-axe	Stubai for Sherpas and spare; personal choice for climbers	
1 ice-hammer	Whillans Whammer [issued to climbers]	An all-purpose modern tool combining a descendeur,

		ice-pick and ham-merhead
2 pairs ascendeurs	Jumar for climbers Clogger for Sherpas Prussikers for all	See Notes below
1 head-lamp	Achil Wonder	
1 pair crampons	Chouinard for climbers	12-pt rigid construc-tion, fully adjustable
	Salewa for Sherpas and spare	12-pt partly adjustable
1 rucksack	Karrimor, designed by Whillans	See Notes
1 sit harness	Troll, designed by Whillans	Nylon tape with adjustable waistband
1 chest harness	Troll	Nylon tape

Notes

I included a wide choice of gear to enable individual members to make up their own permutations. In addition, individuals brought items of their own equipment. Tom Frost, for instance, was entirely kitted with gear to his own specification. The fact that no one suffered from frost-bite or severe exposure is indicative that the system worked.

(a) *Headgear:* All the varieties were used by different members at dif-ferent times. Crash-hats were worn on the Rock Band and wherever there seemed to be risk of stonefall. The Sherpas always used theirs on the run from Camp I to II, where there was some stonefall from the ridge. It is essential that crash-hats are a sufficiently loose fit to go over a balaclava or bonnet.

(b) *Body covering:* The requirement is that the *outer layer* should be light and completely windproof. For high-altitude work it is not essen-tial that it should be waterproof, but it needs to be water-resistant, since an absorbent material collects powder snow which can melt and then form into ice. The functional jacket and breeches designed and manufactured specially for the expedition were completely waterproof with a novel construction, having a thin layer of open-cell foam in the sleeves between 4-oz. proofed-nylon walls and a detachable foam liner of one, two or three thicknesses in the body, giving up to seven layers of air, once again within the double skin of the jacket, through which air was allowed to flow. This insulation meant that there was no precipitation of ice from condensation on the inside of the jacket. Water vapour must have been trapped inside the jacket, but this did not make the inner clothing damp and ensured great warmth. The waterproof nature of the cloth also ensured that the material never froze up or became over-stiff: the hood of the jacket fitted over a crash-hat and had a Wolverine trim. the jacket zipped all the way down the front and had four pockets closed by Velcro. We also used Ventile anoraks which were completely windproof and, of course, 'breathed', though they did tend to freeze up in bad weather, becoming stiff to handle.

As for the *inner layer*, everyone used different combinations, but most of us wore a suit of long underwear next to the skin, with a light wool sweater and the Borg fur jacket on our top half, and the Borg breeches on our lower half. On a sunny, windless day, even up to about 22,000 feet, this was sufficient without any windproofs, but on the upper part of the mountain, when the weather turned, we wore our down gear as well as windproofs.

(c) *Down Gear:* The Hutchinson down jackets were so successful that we found we needed only the single jacket either for climbing in or for wearing inside the sleeping-bag at night. They had the advantage of being quite close-fitting and did not make one feel like the Michelin tyre man. The breeches were worn inside the sleeping-bag and while climbing on the upper slopes of the mountain. The Erve Expedition sleeping-bag was an outstanding success, being both light and extremely warm; it is constructed on a double-layer principle, though it is a single bag.

• • •

(d) *Footwear:* The Galibier-Hivernale boots proved both warm and suitable for high-standard climbing. On the upper part of the mountain Neoprene overboots, covered in turn by proofed nylon overboots, gave the necessary insulation to save feet from frostbite even in extreme cold. The leather outer boot froze at nights, but the design of the Galibier boots makes it possible to slip them on in a frozen state. They thawed out quickly once on, since the overboots gave them good protection from external moisture and the leather never became saturated. We also used rubber vapour-barrier boots, manufactured in the United States for winter hunting. These have the advantage that they never freeze up and are very light. They are not a climbing boot, however, and even with crampons strapped to them are insufficiently rigid for high-standard climbing. They are fine for the traditional Himalayan snow plod, but unsuitable for serious face routes.

(e) *Hand Covering:* Dachstein mits proved the ideal covering, being robust and warm, though on the upper parts of the mountain Don Whillans and Dougal Haston found they needed two pairs. We also found that they tended to wear through, largely as a result of friction while abseiling. We could therefore have done with an allowance of at least four pairs each of outer Dachstein mits and two pairs of the lighter inner glove.

(f) *Eye Protection:* Ski-goggles, manufactured by Carreras, which covered the upper part of the face, proved ideal in bad weather conditions. It is essential to ensure that the eyepiece is sufficiently well tinted to give protection from the excess of ultraviolet rays at altitude. In still weather the specially fitted sunglasses, manufactured by the British American Optical Company, proved adequate. They had blinkers at the side to stop strong rays of light getting in. If glasses are worn it pays to leave a piece of safety string round them to save them if they are knocked off your ears.

Martin Boysen and Mick Burke, who wear glasses normally, had pairs of optically corrected dark glasses of a revolutionary design. These spectacles automatically adjusted to ambient light, absorbing ultraviolet rays. They darken and clear as light conditions change, transmitting the same amount of light at any given time (between two fixed limits). They were totally successful; both climbers were enthusiastic about their performance.

(g) *Personal Climbing Gear*

Ice-axes: everyone used his own. Ian Clough had a prototype of the new MacInnes/Peck all metal ice-axe which was nicely balanced with a well-angled pick. The pick, however, was too thin and tended to stick in the ice. The Chouinard axe brought by Tom Frost had a curved adze and a better head than any of the other axes brought out by expedition members. No axe broke on the expedition, though several were dropped.

Peg hammers: although everyone was issued with a Whillans Whammer, climbers tended to use their own. The Chouinard ice-hammer was particularly effective, its curved pick biting into the ice and acting as an effective hold when front-pointing on crampons.

Ascendeurs: Jumars were undoubtedly the favourite, for the handle gives a much better grip than that provided on the Clogger. Both Jumars and Cloggers start slipping on iced ropes; this is where the Hiebelers come into their own, for their construction ensures they will not slip. The Hiebeler, however, is not nearly as easy to use as the other two types on dry rope. On easy-angled slopes a single Jumar was used, attached to the sit harness by a tape sling. On steeper slopes two were used, one attached to the sit harness and the other, by a longer sling, to one foot.

Head-lamps: the Achil Wonder has the advantage that it can be used as a hand torch as well as a head lamp. There is little requirement for torches on a Himalayan climb since one rarely practises Alpine-style starts. A hand-torch is easier to manipulate round the tent than a head-torch. We used standard Ever Ready batteries and these proved entirely adequate in spite of very cold conditions.

Crampons: the Chouinard crampons were ideal for high-standard ice climbing and had the great advantage that they could be closely fitted to boots, but they tended to ball up badly—this could probably be counteracted by using a plastic sheet wrapped underneath them as recommended by Pemberthy. Salewa and Grivel crampons were also used by members and these were not as prone to balling up as the Chouinard crampons, but the points became a good deal more blunt.

Rucksacks: Don Whillans designed a frame rucksack that had excellent capacity, but unfortunately it did not hang well on the body and as a result tended to increase fatigue while carrying it. Karrimor have now rectified the design faults on the Annapurna rucksack.

Harnesses: the sit harness designed by Don Whillans was an outstanding success, for it enabled one to rest back in the seat whilst jumaring up snow slopes. It was less comfortable on vertical stretches but these were in the minority. It was not designed to act as a leader's harness and a Troll chest harness was provided for this purpose.

Communal Climbing Equipment

ITEM	DESCRIPTION	SIZE	QUANTITY
Rope	Viking Kernmantel	9 mm. in 500-ft reels	18,000 ft
	"	11 mm. in 150-ft lengths	9,000 ft
Cord	Nylon	5 mm.	3,000 ft
Bootlace	Nylon		2,000 ft
Tape	Tigers Web (stiff)	1 in.	500 ft
	"	½ in.	500 ft
	Spanset (soft tubular)	1 in.	1,000 ft
	"	½ in.	2,000 ft
Snow-anchors	Dexion strips	3 ft	20

	Alloy stakes	Between 2 ft and 3 ft	50
	Clog dead men		40
	Clog dead boys		40
Ice-pitons	Cassin channel		50
	Salewa screw	12 in.	60
		8 in.	40
	Salewa spiral pitons	21 cm.	20
Rock-pitons	Clog assorted—chrome molybdenum (?)		200
Bolt kits	American rawl stud bolts for hard rock	1 ½ x ¼ in.	4
	'Star Dryvin' for soft rock	2 x ⅜ in.	
	Drills—2 flute	¼, ⅜ in.	
	Hangers—leeper		
Karabiners	Bonnaiti alloy, non-screw gate		200
	screw gate		200
Winch, capstan	M.S. Gibbs, Ltd, hand-operated by winding in two different gears		1
Winch, lever	Tiofor, Ltd		2
Sledge for winch	Turner Bros. Asbestos		1
Hauling-sacks	Millet		6
Hauling-sacks	Karrimor		6
Sectionized ladders	Clifford L. Brown, wooden	5-ft sections	4
Flares	Dyak emergency,		1 set

	firing from pocket	
	clipholder	
Snow-saws	Norwegian (Pindisports)	4
Snow-shovels	Pindisports	6
Entrenching-	Ex-W.D.	6
tools		

Notes

Rope: We used the 9-mm. rope both as climbing rope and as fixed rope; the leader ran it out from the five-hundred-foot reel, pulling it all in at the end of each pitch and securing it. The second man then jumared up. As a result, we did not use the 11-mm. climbing ropes at all. There are terylene ropes on the market which are slightly heavier but with less stretch than nylon; these would probably have been more suitable as fixed ropes, but would have been less safe as climbing ropes.

As a guide to others in estimating the quantity of fixed rope to take, we had fixed rope in position to give a vertical height gain of 7,500 feet, yet used approximately 17,000 feet of rope.

Tape: We used huge quantities of tape for everything from tie-offs on pitons to belts for trousers. The tubular soft variety is more adaptable, being easier to knot. Great care is required to check all tape knots for they tend to become undone very easily.

Snow anchors: The 'dead men' were an outstanding success and undoubtedly gave by far the most reliable and least bulky or heavy snow anchor we were able to use on the expedition. We did not use many 'dead boys', since we preferred to go for the larger surface area of the dead man for fixed-rope anchors. The Dexion strips were effective but very heavy. In most instances dead men are preferable to any type of conventional stake, though there are some places, such as traverses, where stakes might be preferable.

• • •

Ice-pitons: All three types of ice-piton were used extensively. The Cassin Channel can double up as a rock-peg, while the long 12-in. Salewa, once in, gives a real feeling of security. The Salewa spiral piton, copied from a Russian model, goes in easily as it can be pounded home, and is easy to extract since it has a form of thread and can be screwed out.

Rock pegs: We took a complete assortment of Clog pegs and found the King pins particularly useful. We had very few over at the end of the expedition. We did not use any expansion bolts and therefore were unable to try them out. However, I used these bolts on the Eiger Direct in 1966 and found them very effective. They are obtained in the United States and work on a split-pin principle.

Pulleys: The capstan winch was mounted on an alloy frame and worked excellently. However, the 9-mm. nylon rope we used for hauling had too much stretch, and on the one occasion that we tried to winch gear up the long gully below Camp III there was so much stretch in the rope and drag through the snow that the entire process was much too slow. If we had used a non-stretch rope or wire cable it would have been more effective. Don Whillans designed a sledge made of fibreglass to use for this type of hauling, but it weighed sixty pounds and seemed too heavy. As a result this was not taken beyond Pokhara.

The other winches were not used. The hauling-sacks were not really suitable for dragging through snow, but were extensively used as rucksacks.

Snow-clearing tools: We had both a folding shovel and a small solid one, both purchased at Pindisports. The former was insufficiently robust and in choosing a shovel we found that it was essential to have one that was well made. Don Whillans discovered the value of the ex-W.D. entrenching-tool as an alternative to an ice-axe in very soft snow, using one in conjunction with his Whammer all the way to the top of Annapurna. The snow-saws are undoubtedly effective for cutting out blocks in very hard snow, but we did not use them during the course of the expedition.

Tentage

ITEM	MANUFACTURER	DESCRIPTION	QUANTITY
Whillans Box	Karrimor	2-man	6
Standard RAFMA tent	Pneumatic Tent Co., Ltd	2-man cotton tent	4
Lightweight RAFMA tent	"	2-man, in ripstop nylon	1
Annapurna tent	Brigham	2-man, in ripstop nylon	2
Igloo tent	Pneumatic Tent Co., Ltd.	4-man	1
Everest Meade tent	Edgingtons	2-man	4
Frame tent	Marechal Commodore	Base tents	3
Coated nylon tarps.	Carrington & Dewhurst		3
Plastic tarps.	British Visqueen, Ltd	24 x 24 ft.; 15 x 15 ft.; 10 x 10 ft.	3
Closed-cell foam pads	Karrimat	To fit all tents and boxes	
Open-cell foam mattresses	Spatzmolla	For use at Base Camp	18
Hand brushes		For sweeping out tents	10
Camp tables			4
Camp stools			20

Notes

We based our mountain tentage on a combination of Standard RAFMA tents and Whillans Boxes, while at Base Camp we used Marechal Commodore frame tents: two were specially modified and the third was standard. We had a variety of other tents which were used on the lower part of the mountain and at Base Camp.

Whillans Box: This was first developed by Don Whillans on the South Patagonia Survey Expedition, when he found that conventional tents would not stand up to the wind. He prefabricated a small, box-like hut made from timber and heavy tarpaulin; he later designed a more sophisticated model with a framework of Dexion for his Gaurishankar expedition. It was also used on the Fortress, in South Patagonia, by Ian Clough in 1967, but the model used on Annapurna was the most successful yet; in fact, without the box our problems would have been considerably greater, since conventional tents tended to collapse under the weight of powder snow building up on the steep face. The present model was manufactured by Karrimor.

The advantage of the box was that it had a rigid frame and could be slotted into a ledge cut into a steep snow-slope. Powder snow then built up around it and this made it more, rather than less, secure.

The box was 6 ft 6 in. long, 4 ft wide and 4 ft high, with a tubular aluminium alloy frame and socket joints at the corners. The long side was divided in the middle to give sections of 3 ft 3 in. The covering was a single piece that dropped over the top of the box and was laced up underneath until the covering round the box was fully tensioned. The roof was made from 7-oz. proofed nylon, the walls from 5-oz. cotton terylene and the floor from 7-oz. proofed nylon. There was one zip doorway, with Ririe nylon zips, taking up the entire front of the box, and a sleeve entrance, which was rarely used, at the back. There were two small ventilators.

Nylon webbing tensioning straps going diagonally from corner to corner across the two long sides and the roof gave added rigidity to the frame and prevented the canvas flapping or sagging unduly. There was also an inner tent of 2-oz. nylon which hung from the frame. This was not always used, since members of the expedition found the frame useful for hanging their gear, and the boxes seemed sufficiently warm without the inner. Even with the inner there was still a fair amount of condensation on the roof at night. A very useful side-product of the box was the fact that snow in the roof melted during the day to give a supply of water.

On steep ground, or wherever accommodation was exposed to spindrift build-up, the box was superior to conventional tents. It could support a considerable weight of snow on its roof and never showed any signs of failure during the course of the expedition. Its weight was 30 lb. greater than that of a mountain tent, but this was amply compensated for by the feeling of security one had while sleeping in a box. Its weight could probably be reduced still further, though care would have to be taken to ensure that it remained sufficiently robust.

RAFMA tent: This is a single-skin tent in cotton weighing approximately 18 lb., though the lightweight RAFMA in ripstop nylon only weighed 10 lb. The simplicity of design and lack of numerous guyropes makes this tent ideal for high-altitude use. It was used for Camp VI, and the lightweight RAFMA was taken up to the possible site of Camp VII. The hooped shape of the tent gives it plenty of room inside and three can sleep in it if necessary. The nylon zip entrance proved reliable and easier to use than the traditional sleeve entrance.

Annapurna tent: This tent is a double-skin ridge tent and light for its size—13 ½ lb. We used it at Base Camp and Camp I. While ideal for roughweather camping below the snow-line, the number of guylines it requires make it less suitable as a high-altitude tent.

P.T.C. igloo tent: This is a four-man tent, shaped rather like a beehive and depending on inflated tubes instead of conventional poles for its support. Because of the extremes of temperature and rarity of the atmosphere experienced at altitude, it is not really suited to the Himalayas. We used it at Camp I (16,000 ft), but the Sherpas, ever zealous, overinflated it in the evening when it was cold, and in the morning when the sun came up it exploded with a spectacular bang. The inner tube was irreparably damaged; however, we made a makeshift frame and the tent was used throughout the expedition.

Marechal Commodore tent: This is a conventional frame cottage tent seen in its thousands in camping-sites round Europe. It was ideal for Base Camp living, enabling climbers to relax from their efforts in the front line. Two of the tents were specially modified with extra guylines, but even the standard tent stood up to the test very well.

Tarpaulins: These proved invaluable, not only for covering supplies but also as shelters. The heavy-duty plastic tarpaulins with reinforced eyes were particularly useful in this respect and formed the walls and roof of a commodious kitchen at Base Camp. Small tarpaulins were also used on the mountain as high as Camp III for covering supplies dumped outside the tents, making unnecessary the tiring chore of digging out fresh snow each morning.

Floor insulation: On the mountain we used closed-cell foam Karrimats designed to cover the entire surface area of the tent or box. They are 3/8 in. thick, do not absorb moisture and were extremely effective, acting as insulation from the cold of the snow yet also giving a firm floor. They were superior in this respect to the open-cell foam mattresses, which are softer and more comfortable but absorb moisture and inevitably become waterlogged from melted condensation. We used the Spatzmolla foam mattresses at Base Camp and on the approach march to provide a little extra luxury.

Hand brushes: A small item but extremely useful for clearing snow both from the tent and clothing. We packed one in each tent kit.

Cooking

ITEM	MANUFACTURER	DESCRIPTION	QUANTITY
Paraffin stoves	Primus	1-pint	6
"	"	2-pint	7
Double burners	"		2
Spares	"		6
Solid fuel	Meta Fuel		50

	and Profol		boxes
Containers		½-gallon	4
		1 gallon	5
		4½-gallon	13
"Funnels"			10
Cartridge gas stoves			3
Gas cartridges			36
Pressure-cookers	Prestige	Large	2
		Small	3
Knife, fork and spoon sets			18
Melamine mugs	Melaware	1 pint	18
Melamine plates/bowls	"		40
Washing-up bowls			6
Can-openers			5
Water-containers		5-gallon	2
Pan-scourers	Plastic		24
Toilet paper			50 boxes
Water-bottles	Plastic	1-pint	20
Midget tin-openers			100
Penknives	Swiss Cutlery, Ltd		18
Sets of billies		2 nesting billies with lids— 8-pint	3
		4-pint	7
Large detichies or pans	Purchased locally		20
Large kettle			1
Butcher's knives	Swiss Cutlery, Ltd		1 set

Notes

We had originally intended to use paraffin stoves for all cooking on the mountain. The stoves themselves, which were fitted with special silent

329

burners, functioned well, but we had a great deal of trouble with faulty paraffin. As a result we decided to use the butane cartridge gas stoves for the top two camps. We had been led to believe that these would not function well in extreme cold. However, we found their performance entirely satisfactory, even when the cartridges were still very cold and had been taken from the supply dump outside the tent. Gas is undoubtedly much easier to use than paraffin, avoiding all the troublesome business of preheating the element and the inevitable blockages occurring from impurities in the fuel. The quality of the locally purchased paraffin was so poor that the gas stoves seemed to give off as much heat.

From our experience I should recommend the use of paraffin on the lower camps and gas for the top camps. If gas were used throughout the mountain I suspect one would find one used too much, and there could be a risk of running out. One would also have to take it out from home. Paraffin has the great advantage that it is readily available in most regions of the world.

At Base Camp, wood was used for almost all the cooking. Large cooking pots were bought locally for use at Base Camp and on the lower part of the mountain, while nests of canteens were used in the upper camps, with a capacity of around four pints.

We made up tent kits which stayed with their respective tents wherever they went. These consisted of a cooking-stove, nest of canteens, solid fuel, funnel, tent brush and spare parts for the stove. Paraffin was carried in plastic containers of between one and five gallons, purchased in Nepal. We found that it would pay to take at least two cutlery sets, plates and mugs for each member of the expedition, so high is the wastage.

Pressure cookers were used by the Sherpas on the mountain to enable them to cook rice and fresh meat stews. The rations Mike Thompson had devised made it unnecessary for the climbers to use them.

We used both Meta fuel and Profol for preheating the Primus stoves. Meta was infinitely superior, lighting more easily and being virtually fumeless.

Heating and Lighting

ITEM	MANUFACTURER	QUANTITY
Paraffin pressure lamp	Willis & Bates	2
Spare glasses and mantles		
Bleuet gas cartridge lamps		3
Torch-batteries	Ever Ready	100
Spare bulbs		50

Navigational

Altimeters	(Borrowed from the R.G.S.)	2
Wrist-watches	Omega Seamaster	11
Fieldglasses	Zeiss 6x	1
Monocular	Zeiss 8x	1
Theodolite	(Borrowed from the R.G.S.)	1
Tripod	"	1

Hygiene

Soap	Fairy	20 bars
Soap powder		12 packets
Glacier cream	Savory & Moore	120 tubes
Lip-salve		50 tubes
Washing-up liquid		10 bars
Toilet soap		36 bars

Stationery

Packs of cards	2
Airmail envelopes	50
Airmail paper pads	5
Ballpoints	20
Pencils	20
Portable typewriter	1
Erasers	2
Typing-paper	1 ream

Stapler		1
Staples		1 box
Brochures		100
Clothing labels (each)		50
Magic markers		20
Expedition stamp		1
Paper-clips		1 box
Stencils		1 set
Paint		1 tin
Stencil brushes		2
Carbon paper		1 packet

Miscellaneous

Padlocks		100
Kitbags		100
Boot polish		120 cans
Cigarettes	Wills & Gauloises	14,000
Lighters	Ronson	18
Gas cylinders	Ronson	36
Spring scale		1
(weighs up to 100 lb.)		
Poly bags (assorted)	British Visqueen	1,000
Flag		1
Identification tags		250

Notes

Lighters: These were gas lighters and were more than luxuries, since it is very much easier to light Primus stoves with a lighter than with matches. They proved very reliable.

Poly bags: You can't have too many of these. In size they ranged from 6 ft x 2 ft down to 6 in. x 2 in.

• • •

Repair Kits

ITEM	MANUFACTURER	QUANTITY
Housewives		18
Boot repair kit with assorted adhesives		1
Tent repair outfits		
—small		10
—large		1
Baling-wire		500 ft
Baling-machine		1
Rivets		200
Riveting kits		2
Nails (assorted)		5 lb.
Screws—wood		2 lb.
Tool-kit		1
Adhesive tape (various widths)	'Lasso'	60 rolls

For Porters

Cheap goggles		300 pairs
Gym-shoes		300 pairs
Walking-boots	Hawkins Astronaut	20 pairs
Anoraks		20
Trousers		20 pairs
Gloves		40 pairs
Socks		40 pairs
Sweaters		20

Notes

If one is likely to go above the snow-line to reach Base Camp, gym-shoes and goggles are essential for all porters. It also pays to take a stock of old clothes and sleeping-bags for cookboys, mailrunners and any locally recruited porters. Another useful item would be plain plastic sheets of 6 ft x 6 ft to give to each porter for protection from rain.

APPENDIX C

Oxygen

CHRIS BONINGTON

Although Annapurna had been climbed in 1950 on the first ascent from the north without the use of oxygen, it had seemed possible that oxygen might be necessary to contend with technically difficult climbing at a height of over 23,000 feet. The French had used it on their ascent of Jannu in 1962 and had found it essential. I had used oxygen on the first ascent of Annapurna II in 1960: this had been based on the type of set used for the Kangchenjunga expedition of 1955, and was extremely effective, but the set was both bulky and heavy. The French company l'Appareil Médical de Précision had since developed another set which was both simpler and more compact, as well as being lighter. This set had been used extensively by Himalayan expeditions in the preceding years, including the American Everest expedition. I therefore chose this set, getting all the equipment from l'Appareil Médical de Précision; even though there were indications that the British mask used on Kangchenjunga and the American mask used on Everest were superior in design, I preferred to keep things as simple as possible, eliminating any risk of parts failing to marry up. The French equipment consisted of:

an aluminium alloy bottle weighing 11 lb. full and containing 800 litres of oxygen;

a robust and compact regulator valve screwing into the bottle with various settings-closed, ½-litre per minute, 1, 2, 3, 4 and 5 litres per minute;

a rubber mask attached to the head by webbing straps, with a bladder hanging beneath it.

We ordered 40 bottles, 6 regulators, 6 masks and 4 medical sets. Chesterfield Tube Co., Ltd then very kindly loaned us a further supply of cylinders as a reserve.

Oxygen Plan

One of the problems associated with using oxygen on a mountain is the weight of bottles one must take up to the upper camps, doubling the total weight that must be carried, thus protracting the siege or requiring more people to carry loads. It is also very expensive. The oxygen listed above cost £2,500—with the cost of porterage it comes to considerably more.

I hoped to reduce the number of bottles required by limiting their use to the lead climbers, leaving the load-carriers on the fixed ropes to struggle up without. I planned to start using it at 22,500 feet, at the foot of the Rock Band. Even so, it was difficult to say how many bottles would be required, since this would depend entirely on the length of time we took to climb the Rock Band—something that it was impossible to predict. In the event, we found that the lead climbers could manage without the help of oxygen, while I very much doubt if I could have managed the four trips I made between Camps V and VI without its help. Since I was the only person besides Dougal Haston to make more than two complete trips, this is not entirely a fair test, since others, going stronger than I, might have managed without oxygen. The only time I was with another person on this carry was on 24 May with Ian Clough. He made the trip without oxygen, whilst I used it. A few days before he had been going more strongly than myself between Camps IV and V, yet on the carry up to VI using oxygen I reached the camp about half an hour in front of him.

I have little doubt that oxygen materially helped performance. Our problem was in carrying it to the place where it was needed, we were so extended on the carry between Camps IV and V.

We carried 24 bottles up to Camp I, of which 17 reached Camp III, 12 Camp IV, 6 Camp V, and none Camp VI. I used three bottles on three successive carries up to Camp VI and these were the only bottles used on the entire expedition to aid movement.

Oxygen, however, was frequently used for medicinal purposes at Camps III, IV and V, when climbers became unduly fatigued. It seemed to have a beneficial effect.

• • •

Performance

On the three occasions that I used the set I found its extra weight was amply compensated for by the help I had from it. There were times when I thought the flow was being interrupted; this could have been psychological, though the French mask has a reputation for icing up. The mask was also uncomfortable to wear, biting into the bridge of the nose. The British mask I used on Annapurna II was certainly more comfortable and easier to use.

Recommendations

In the light of our experience on the South Face, I should not recommend anyone to encumber himself with oxygen equipment for use while climbing or ferrying on mountains of up to 26,500 feet; but it is as well to have some oxygen in reserve for medical purposes or for a last-ditch effort similar to my own ferrying on the South Face of Annapurna. For this type of operation it is advisable to have an oxygen set and at least one bottle at each camp, with half a dozen held as spares on the mountain itself.

APPENDIX D

Food

MIKE THOMPSON

Both the rations chosen for the expedition and the basic philosophy that underlay their selection were fairly revolutionary, and were related to the principles of composition, packaging and dietetic theory of previous Himalayan expeditions only insofar as they rejected them. As it turned out, the low altitude ration was an unqualified success but the high altitude one was less successful. The special strategy and techniques required in climbing Himalayan faces create a pattern of residence, work and movement very different from that of the traditional Himalayan expedition. For example, most members spent at least four weeks above 20,000 feet, and—since the Sherpas were unable, because of the technical difficulty, to carry above Camp IV—were engaged day after day in monotonous and strenuous load-carrying on the fixed ropes. Under these conditions the traditional fare of dehydrated meat bars and reconstituted mashed-potato would have led to a complete collapse of morale, and the mountain might well have remained unclimbed. It was only the thought of the Crunchie bar you were going to consume at the top of the next fixed rope, and of the elaborate five-course meal that you would prepare when you returned to the tent, that kept you going.

Food was the consuming passion and obsession of the expedition, and if the members were not actually engaged in eating it or getting rid of it, from one end or the other, they would be talking of it or dreaming of it. Hour after hour was passed in ecstatically recalling past meals and in planning and contemplating those that lay in the future. At Base Camp recipes and tips were continually being swapped as if it were some remote branch of the Women's Institute, and passionate arguments would rage over the relative merits of the chips in 'trannies' and 'chippers' along the length and breadth of the British Isles. With glazed eyes and drooling lips one would recall the trannie at Beattock Summit where 'steak pie and two veg' announced over the loudspeaker meant 'steak pie, chips and mash'; another would invoke an 'egg in a dry cake' in Dot's Cafe in Craven Street, Hull; and a third the 'sausage toad and double bubble, bread pudding and custard' of the Double L in the Liverpool Road, Islington. Even sleep did not bring release, and the night air would often be rent by Mick Burke's anguished cries for the meat and potato pies of his native Wigan. Burke was perhaps the most deeply affected of us all, and at times it seemed that, like one of the Knights of the Round Table, his whole life was a ceaseless quest not for the Holy Grail but for the Perfect Chip. A soul in torment, it seemed that he would only find peace (and the Perfect Chip) on that far-off day when he finally pulled his clapped-out artic of life into the lorry-park of the Great Trannie in the Sky.

Planning

A newsletter setting out the basic food philosophy and the general form of the rations was sent to each member of the expedition. There were to be three types of ration:

> High Altitude: for use by Europeans and Sherpas above Base Camp;
>
> Low Altitude (European): for use by the European members on the approach march, at Base Camp and on the return march;
>
> Low Altitude (Sherpa): for use by the Sherpa members on the approach march, at Base Camp and on the return march.

As it turned out the Low Altitude (Sherpa) rations were abandoned, and the Low Altitude (European) rations made sufficiently flexible so that, by varying the local purchase supplement, they were suitable for both Sherpas and Europeans.

The policy was that on the approach march, in Base Camp, and on the return march, the food should be as 'normal' as possible, and that it should be plentiful, appetizing and varied. Luxury items such as tinned fruit, smoked oysters, sauerkraut and pickled onions would be included in these rations, and separate luxury boxes would not be taken. The only supplementary boxes would be those containing alcohol. These Low Altitude rations were to be supplemented by a flexible amount of local purchase of potatoes, onions, eggs, dal, rice and flour.

The High Altitude rations were to be broken down into two-man-day packs and, within the limits of a fairly generous four pounds per man-day allowance, were to be appetizing, tempting and easily cooked.

The calorific content was considered to be of secondary importance and priority was given to including items that were likely to get eaten. Thus tinned fruit, tinned new potatoes and cream were included, and meat bars and most dehydrated food excluded.

Attached to the newsletter was a list of all the foodstuffs that could possibly feature in the rations. This list ran to over 200 items, and was compiled by spending a morning in a large supermarket with a notebook and pencil. Alongside this list were three columns headed LIKE O.K. and HATE, and members were requested to place ticks in the appropriate columns and to add to the list any items to which they were partial and which had been omitted. There were surprisingly few 'hated' items, and it was possible to omit these from the rations entirely. Most members were almost omnivorous and very catholic in their tastes, though Estcourt not only objected to peanut butter but, because of its 'nauseous' smell, objected to anyone else's consuming it in his presence.

Using this list as a basis, the detailed composition of the various ration packs was worked out. Both the Low and High Altitude rations were made up from five different menus. A further category, Kitchen rations, was added. These consisted of items useful for stocking the Base Camp kitchen, such as baking-powder, yeast, mixed herbs, garlic powder, chilli sauce, etc. Also, since wholesalers supply goods in grosses or dozens, there were a lot of 'overs' once the packs had been made up and all these surplus items were consigned to the Kitchen rations. (They were all eaten.)

LOW ALTITUDE RATION PACKS—MENU "A"

1 x 8 oz. tin	Ovaltine
1 x 14 ½ oz. tin	Condensed milk
5 x 7 oz. tins	J. West kipper fillets
1 x 2 lb. tin	Marmalade
1 x 1 ¼ tin	Whole tomatoes
1 x 2 ½ lb. tin	Fruit salad
1 x 16 oz.	Austrian smoked cheese
1 x 10 oz. jar	Keddie mango chutney

10 x 2 oz. bars	Milk chocolate
20 x 2 oz. pkts	Nuts and raisins
10 pkts	Assorted Spangles
1 doublet	Toilet roll
4 boxes	Safety matches
1 x 8 oz. pkt	Salt
1 x 8 oz. pkt (72)	Teabags, Brooke Bond
1 x 2 oz. tin	Instant coffee
3 x 1 lb. pkts	Cube sugar
2 x 7 oz. tin	Marvel milk
2 x 1 lb. pkt	Porridge
1 x 1 lb. bag	Soft brown sugar
1 x 1 lb. tin	Butter
4 x 1 lb. tins	Stewed steak
1 x 1 lb. tin	Baked beans
2 x 6 oz. tins	Cream
1 x 11 oz. jar	Branston pickle

LOW ALTITUDE RATION PACKS—MENU "B"

1 x 14 oz. tin	Condensed milk
3 x 1 lb. tins	Heinz baked beans and sausages
1 x 2 lb. tin	Strawberry jam
3 x 5 oz. tins	Tomato paste
3 x 1 ½ oz. pkts	Parmesan cheese, grated
3 x 1 lb. pkts	Spaghetti 'II'
1 x 2 ½ lb. tin	Pears
4 x 4 oz. tins	Pâté Plumrose
1 X 11 oz.jar	Tomato chutney
10 bars	Mars bars
20 x 2 oz. pkts	Peanuts
10 rolls	Polo mints
2 x 20 oz. tins	Mornflake oats
1 doublet	Toilet roll

4 boxes	Safety matches
1 x 8 oz. pkt	Salt
1 x 8 oz. pkt (72)	Teabags, Brooke Bond
1 X 2 oz. tin	Instant coffee
3 x 1 lb. pkts	Cube sugar
2 x 7 oz. tins	Marvel milk
1 x 1 lb. pkt	Soft brown sugar
1 x 1 lb. tin	Butter
4 x 1 lb. tins	Minced beef with onions
2 x 6 oz. tins	Cream

LOW ALTITUDE RATION PACKS—MENU "C"

1 x 14 oz. tin	Condensed milk
5 x 7 oz. tins	Tuna fish
1 x 2 lb. tin	Apricot jam
8 x 8 oz. tins	Fray Bentos steak and kidney pudding
3 x 3 oz. pkts	Surprise peas and carrots
1 x l6 oz.	Austrian smoked cheese
1 x 14 oz. tin	Herring in tomato sauce
3 x 5 ¼ sachets	Olives de Nice
1 x 16 oz. tin	Potato salad
1 x 20 oz. bottle	Pickled onions
5 x 3 ¾ oz. packs	Kit Kat chocolate
10 x 4 oz. pkts	Mixed nuts
10 pkts	Assorted Spangles
1 doublet	Toilet roll
4 boxes	Matches
1 x 8 oz. pkt	Salt
1 x 8 oz. pkt (72)	Teabags, Brooke Bond
1 x 2 oz. tin	Instant coffee
3 x 1 lb. pkts	Cube sugar
1 x 7 oz. tin	Marvel milk
2 x 16 oz. pkts	Porridge

1 x 1 lb. bag	Soft brown sugar
1 x 1 lb. tin	Butter
1 x ¼'s lb. tins	Sardines in tomato

LOW ALTITUDE RATION PACKS—MENU "D"

1 x 14 oz. tin	Condensed milk
3 x 16 oz. tins	Ravioli
1 x 2 lb. tin	Raspberry jam
2 x 16 oz. tins	Frankfurters
2 x 16 oz. tins	Ham
1 x 2 ½ lb. tin	Sauerkraut
3 x 3 oz. pkts	Surprise beans
1 x 6 ½ oz. jar	French mustard
1 X 10 oz. jar	Hot pickle
5 x 8 oz. pkts	Xmas pudding
10 bars	Crunchie chocolate
20 x 2 oz. pkts	Nuts and raisin
10 pkts	Polo mints
1 doublet	Toilet roll
4 boxes	Safety matches
1 x 8 oz. pkt	Salt
1 x 8 oz. box (72)	Teabags, Brooke Bond
1 x 2 oz. tin	Instant coffee
3 x 1 lb. bags	Cube sugar
2 x 7 oz. tin	Marvel Milk
2 x 16 oz. pkts	Porridge
1 x 1 lb. bag	Soft brown sugar
1 x 1 lb. tin	Butter
1 x 11 oz. jar	Piccalilli
2 x 6 oz. tins	Cream

LOW ALTITUDE RATION PACKS—MENU "E"

1 x 14 oz. tin	Condensed milk
5 x 8 oz. tins	Red salmon

1 x 2 lb. tin	Gooseberry jam
2 x 3 lb. 10 oz. tins	Chicken (whole)
3 x 3 oz. pkts	Surprise peas
1 x 1 ¼ lb. tin	Tomatoes
1 x 11 ½ oz. tin	Mexicorn 'Green Giant'
1 x 14 oz. tin	Mushrooms
1 x 4 oz. tin	Brisling
1 x 2 oz. tin	Anchovies
1 x 3 ½ oz. tin	Smoked oysters
1 x 5 oz. tin	Shrimps
1 x 16 oz. tin	Potato salad
10 x 2 oz. bars	Plain chocolate
20 x 2 oz. pkts	Nuts and raisins
10 pkts	Assorted Spangles
1 doublet	Toilet roll
4 boxes	Safety matches
1 x 8 oz. pkt	Salt
1 x 8 oz. pkt (72)	Teabags, Brooke Bond
1 x 2 oz. tin	Instant coffee
3 x 1 lb. pkts	Cube sugar
2 X 7 oz. tins	Marvel milk
2 x 16 oz. pkts	Porridge
1 x 16 oz. pkt	Soft brown sugar
1 x 16 oz. tin	Butter

HIGH ALTITUDE RATION PACKS—MENU "A"

1 small drum	Salt
1	Candle
4 double cubes	Instant tea with milk (Tisa)
2 double cubes	Instant tea with lemon (Tisa)
2 double cubes	Instant Cola drink
2 double cubes	Instant grapefruit drink
2 double cubes	Instant lemon drink
2 double cubes	Instant orange drink

50 sachets (approx.)	Kuwait Airlines sugar
1 x 7 oz. tin	J. West kipper fillets
1 x 8 oz. pkt	Pumpernickel
2 bars	Mars bars
2 x 2 oz. pkts	Peanuts
1 sachet	Maggi onion soup
2 x 7 oz. tins	Chicken supreme
1 x 11 ½ oz. tin	Mexican 'Green Giant'
1 x 3 ½ oz. pkt	Swiss cheese spread (3 assorted)
2 x 1 oz. Pkt	Jam
1 x 8 oz. tin	Fruit salad
½ box	Paper tissues
1 box	Safety matches
1 x 8 oz. bar	Rum fudge
1 x 6 oz. bar	Kendal mint cake

HIGH ALTITUDE RATION PACKS—MENU "B"

1 small drum	Salt
1	Candle
4 double cubes	Instant tea with milk (Tisa)
2 double cubes	Instant tea with lemon (Tisa)
2 double cubes	Instant Cola drink
2 double cubes	Instant grapefruit drink
2 double cubes	Instant lemon drink
2 double cubes	Instant orange drink
50 sachets (approx.)	Kuwait Airlines sugar
1 x 8 oz. tin	Heinz West End grill
1 x 8 oz. pkt	Pumpernickel
2 x 2 oz. bars	Hazelnut chocolate
4 x I oz. pkts	Cashew nuts
1 sachet	Maggi chicken noodle soup powder

1 x 8 oz. tin	Plumrose frankfurters
1 x 8 oz. tin	Libby Spanish rice
2 x 1 oz. pots	Jams
1 x 3 ½ oz. pkt	Swiss cheese spread (3 assorted)
1 x 8 oz. pkt	Xmas pudding
½ box	Paper tissues
1 box	Safety matches
1 x 8 oz. bar	Rum fudge
1 x 6 oz. bar	Kendal mint cake
1 x 4 oz. tin	Cream

HIGH ALTITUDE RATION PACKS—MENU "C"

1 small drum	Salt
1	Candle
4 double cubes	Instant tea with milk (Tisa)
2 double cubes	Instant tea with lemon (Tisa)
2 double cubes	Instant Cola drink
2 double cubes	Instant grapefruit drink
2 double cubes	Instant lemon drink
2 double cubes	Instant orange drink
50 sachets (approx.)	Kuwait Airlines sugar
1 x 8 oz. tin	Red salmon
1 x 8 oz. pkt	Pumpernickel
2 x 2 oz. bars	Fruit and nut chocolate
2 x 2 oz. pkts	Mixed nuts
1 x 8 oz. pkt	Roast beef and gravy, 'Tyne'
2 x 1 oz. pots	Jams
1 x 3 ½ oz. pkt	Swiss cheese spread (3 assorted)
1 x 8 oz. tin	Pears, Smedley
½ box	Paper tissue
1 box	Safety Matches
1 x 8 oz. bar	Rum fudge

1 x 6 oz. bar	Kendal mint cake
1 sachet	Oxtail soup
1 x 10 oz. tin	New potatoes
1 x 8 oz. tin	Baked beans
1 x 4 oz. tin	Cream

HIGH ALTITUDE RATION PACKS—MENU "D"

1 small drum	Salt
1	Candle
4 double cubes	Instant tea with milk (Tisa)
2 double cubes	Instant tea with lemon (Tisa)
2 double cubes	Instant Cola drink
2 double cubes	Instant grapefruit drink
2 double cubes	Instant lemon drink
2 double cubes	Instant orange drink
50 sachets (approx.)	Kuwait airlines sugar
1 x 8 oz. tin	Heinz beans and frankfurters
1 x 8 oz. pkts	Pumpernickel
2 x 2 oz. bars	Cadbury's whole nut chocolate
2 x 2 oz. pkts	Nuts and raisins
1 x 10 oz. tin	Dana pork in juice
1 x 11 ½ oz. tin	Mexicorn 'Green Giant'
1 x 3 ½ oz. pkt	Swiss cheese spread (3 assorted)
2 x 1 oz. pots	Jams
⅓ box	Paper tissues
1 box	Safety matches
1 x 8 oz. bar	Rum fudge
1 x 6 oz. bar	Kendal mint cake
1 sachet	Mushroom soup
1 x 10 oz. tin	New potatoes

• • •

HIGH ALTITUDE RATION PACKS—MENU "E"

1 small drum	Salt
1	Candle
4 double cubes	Instant tea with milk (Tisa)
2 double cubes	Instant tea with lemon (Tisa)
2 double cubes	Instant Cola drink
2 double cubes	Instant grapefruit drink
2 double cubes	Instant lemon drink
2 double cubes	Instant orange drink
50 sachets (approx.)	Kuwait Airlines sugar
1 x 7 oz. tin	J. West herring fillets
3 x 3 oz. pkts	Service ration biscuits
2 x 2 oz. bars	Toblerone chocolate
2 tubes	Rowntree's fruit gums
1 x 12 oz. tin	Lamb's tongue
1 x 7 oz. tin	Sanfayna salad
1 x 3 ½ oz. pkts	Swiss cheese spread (3 assorted)
2 x 1 oz. pots	Jam
1 x 8 oz. pkts	Xmas Pudding
⅓ box	Paper tissues
1 box	Safety matches
⅓ box	Paper tissues
1 box	Safety matches
1 x 8 oz. bar	Rum fudge
1 x 6 oz. bar	Kendal mint cake
1 satchet	Chicken soup
1 x 4 oz. tin	Cream

Estimating Quantities

The original estimate was for rations for 20 men (11 climbers, 6 Sherpas, 1 liaison officer, 1 cook, 1 spare) for 73 days (20 March to 1

June) giving a total of 1,460 man-days. The need for a safety margin plus the suspicion that there might be more than 20 people to feed led to an increase in the estimate by almost half, to around the final total of 2,200 man-days. These rations filled 122 tea-chests and weighed a total of 10,803 lb. gross. This gives a gross weight of roughly 5 lb. per man-day, though the net weight of edible material is probably around 3 ½ lb. per man-day.

To this must be added vast quantities of locally purchased rations: mainly rice, potatoes and flour, but also eggs, dal, onions and fresh meat (2 buffaloes, half a dozen goats and innumerable chickens). The buffaloes were slaughtered in the spectacular Gurkha style by having their heads lopped with one blow of the kukri, and the joints carried by porters up the last few miles to Base Camp. Fresh buffalo meat reached Camp III (20,100 feet) and ready-cooked chickens were a rare delicacy at Camps I and II. The goats and chickens made it live all the way to Base Camp, which at times looked more like a high-altitude experimental farm than the nerve centre of an expedition. One cockerel survived as an alarm clock until the very last day at Base Camp. Taking into account the local purchase, there was probably about 6 lb. per man-day gross, or 4 ½ lb. per man-day net.

In determining the balance between Low Altitude and High Altitude rations, the proportions were heavily biased in favour of the High Altitude, since these could easily be used at low altitude but not vice versa. Even the generous 70% increase over the original estimate was scarcely sufficient. The bias in favour of High Altitude rations was fully justified, and there were still enough of these at the high camps to last a further 10 days on the day we withdrew from the Face. The Low Altitude rations had however more or less run out several days before this, and for the last few days at Base Camp and on the return march we subsisted entirely on local purchase supplemented by what little we could scrounge from the Japanese ladies' expedition.

The number of persons living at Base Camp far exceeded the original estimate of 19. In addition to the 11 climbers, 6 Sherpas, 1 cook and 1 liaison officer, there were 4 television teams, 1 T.V. Sherpa, 3 cook-boys,

2 or 3 mailrunners, 1 radio operator, 2 London Sherpas, 3 camp-followers, the odd visitor and an average of 8 porters, all of whom had to be fed from Tukte's kitchen. The porters, cook-boys and mailrunners subsisted mainly on local purchase, but nevertheless drew upon the Low Altitude rations for chocolate, nuts, raisins, tea, milk, sugar and tinned meat, and so the total number of mouths fed came to roughly 43—more than double the original estimate.

Our experience shows that it is impossible to estimate with any degree of accuracy the quantity of food one will require, and it seems advisable to allow a large safety margin and to devise flexible Low Altitude rations that can easily be 'stretched' by increasing the local purchase. It is absolutely vital that the proportions should be strongly biased in favour of the High Altitude rations since, whatever happens, one must not run out of food on the face itself. To run out of food at Base Camp is inconvenient but not disastrous—at a pinch one can live on rice and water.

Cost

The pre-expedition publicity laid great emphasis on the luxurious nature of the rations we were taking, and there was much talk of smoked oysters, pâté de foie gras, and herrings in white wine. Dave Pearce summed it all up in *Mountain* when he said that 'the High Altitude menus would do justice to the catering of most bachelor, flat-dwelling climbers at home, let alone whilst camping'. The rations certainly were varied, but it is doubtful whether 'luxury' also implies 'expense'. One obvious economy is that all the food was eaten—there was no waste.

It is difficult to obtain an accurate estimate of the real cost of the food since much of it was given to us free of charge: all the sugar was donated by Tate & Lyle, and Fine Fare gave us something like £250's worth of groceries, which included the excellent instant porridge breakfast cereal, packet soups and tinned cream. Everything else was bought through Andrew Lusk & Co., who also carried out the highly specialized packing so vital to the intricate logistics of the Face. The total cost of the food (including packing but excluding the whisky), had we had to pay for it all, would have been around £2,000, which means that the cost per man-day was just under £1—not a very high price to pay for 'luxury'.

Suggested Modifications

The Low Altitude rations were virtually perfect. There was only one unsatisfactory item—the Smedley's ravioli, which formed the basis of the breakfast in Menu D and seemed to be completely tasteless. Heinz ravioli has some taste and would be an acceptable substitute, but better still would be tinned sausages, and best of all Morning Glory tinned hamburgers. There were perhaps too many nuts and raisins, and it would be a good idea to reduce these a little and increase the chocolate and sweets accordingly.

Tukte Sherpa, the cook, built a magnificent kitchen by stretching some large polythene tarpaulins over several conveniently arranged boulders. A range of cooking-fires ran along one side and the gaps between the boulders were filled with shelves made from tea-chests and empty oxygen boxes, and stocked with the kitchen rations. From this kitchen there issued an almost continuous stream of excellent meals— breakfast, morning coffee, lunch, afternoon tea, dinner and, finally, a bedtime brew. So efficient was this catering that a pint mug of tea always reached climbers returning from the Face even before the television camera did. Perhaps the most delightful meals of all were the al fresco lunches, normally taken lying stretched out on Spatzmollas in the blazing sun. On one occasion this meal featured some seven different kinds of sea-food: brislings, anchovies, smoked oysters, prawns, salmon, tuna fish and herrings in white sauce, not to mention the potato salad, olives, Piccalilli, mango chutney, pickled onions, chappattis and Austrian smoked cheese.

The Low Altitude rations were designed to give main meals of curry and rice (based on the stewed steak), spaghetti and meat sauce (based on the minced beef and onions), steak and kidney pudding and potatoes,

cold meats and potatoes (based on the ham, frankfurters and sauerkraut) and chicken casserole (based on the tinned chicken, sweet corn,
tomatoes and mushrooms). However, thanks to the built-in flexibility
of the rations, and to Tukte's virtuosity, the range of dishes was enormously extended and included chicken and ham fried rice, beef stew
with dumplings, salmon fishcakes, delicious fish curries, roast chicken,
liver and onions, trifle and cream, and even fresh bread and doughnuts.
Base Camp, with its green grass and gurgling streams, its superb food
and casual efficiency, was a wonderful convalescent home for exhausted
climbers returning from the Face. For the T.V. team, who were there all
the time, it must have approached heaven on earth. It is probably safe
to say that in Base Camp we lived better than any previous Himalayan
expedition. Our closest rival might be the 1922 Everest expedition,
which took crates of Champagne and chickens in aspic.

The High Altitude rations, due to the rigours of the Face and the
effects of altitude, were subjected to a much tougher testing than the food
at Base Camp, and a number of defects became apparent on the mountain
despite the unanimous approval they had received in Snowdonia. These
were defects in detailed composition rather than basic conception, and the
High Altitude rations were certainly ideal in principle.

The most important modification suggested by our experience is the
need for a separate lightweight Assault ration for use above a certain
point on the Face. The exact location of this point will probably vary from
one mountain to another; for us it clearly lay between Camps IV and V. It
was here that the carrying became really difficult, Sherpas could not be
used, and the feasible payload became critically small. Also, at Camp V
and above appetites declined rather, and we found that it was possible to
continue making the route, and to climb the mountain, on a very small
intake of food. Burke and Frost lived largely on scraps at Camp V, and
Whillan and Haston had only Readi-Brek, sweetened with Kendal Mint
Cake and washed down with hot water, for the three days leading up to
and including their successful summit bid. Above this critical point the
climber is living on his reserves and has only a limited period of time in
hand before exhaustion sets in and he must return to Base Camp.

Suitable Assault rations would be simplified and lightened versions of the two-man-day High Altitude packs, and could weigh as little as 4 ½ to 5 lb. gross. These would enormously reduce the supply problem high on the mountain, yet would be ample to support life and morale over the limited period for which it is possible to operate at these altitudes.

Below this critical point fairly substantial and varied rations are essential. Between Base Camp and Camp V is where the real work of the expedition is done. The fixed rope on this section of the route is like the M.I. Every day vast quantities of food, tents, rope, paraffin, pitons and whisky must be lifted from camp to camp to allow the two tiny dots at the top of the pyramid to continue making the route. Climbers and Sherpas spend anything up to three or four weeks at a stretch on this section, every day making a carry to the next camp. This carry, though always strenuous, often takes a surprisingly short time—four hours on average for the round trip, and occasionally as little as two and a half. The rest of the twenty-four hours is passed in chatting, reading, brewing, eating and sleeping; and boredom, not altitude, is the real enemy. It was here that the High Altitude rations received their severe testing, which revealed the defect that had remained hidden at sea-level.

From the literature of Himalayan mountaineering one gains the impression that climbers suffer from altitude sickness continually, heroically forcing themselves to swallow a few tiny morsels only to vomit them up minutes later. The pages of *The Untrodden Peak*, the account of the successful ascent of Kangchenjunga, are awash with regurgitated meals and indeed, only one meal is described as successfully completing its journey through the digestive tract. Likewise one reads of gorges rising at the sight of fat, porridge, meat, stodge, indeed all the goodies that make life at sea level so delightful. Apparently one goes off everything except sugar and hot liquids, and all one can face is a little hot soup and the odd square inch of Kendal Mint Cake. What is more, on the rare occasions when one fancies something to eat the effort of raising oneself onto one's elbow becomes so herculean that one immediately falls back exhausted and the meal goes uncooked and uneaten.

All this is complete nonsense. Admittedly, altitude sickness puts you off your food and off your work. No mountain could be climbed by people suffering continually from altitude sickness. It is an unpleasant condition that we all experienced for a number of days, after which we were acclimatized and able to do our work. Once acclimatized we ate huge meals and maintained our morale by contemplating those that lay ahead.

Although always ravenous we were far from omnivorous, and many items (especially sugar) became unattractive. The instant tea-with-milk cubes unfortunately underwent some chemical change during their journey across India, becoming almost undrinkable, and this left just the instant fruit drinks which, though pleasant now and then, soon began to pall when they were the only available brew. Kippers were too much first thing in the morning, though they went down a treat later in the day. Pumpernickel was a complete failure—its taste seemed revoltingly strong at altitude and this meant that the cheese spread and pots of jam also went uneaten as there was nothing to put them on. The high-fat-content 'Army' biscuits were much better, especially when crushed and fried up with salmon or tuna fish to make a kind of fish cake. There was far too much sugar and too much fudge and mint cake. The Kendal Mint Cake really came into its own at very high altitude, when it was greatly appreciated, but the rum fudge—at sea level the most delicious any of us had ever tasted—became quite sickly and unattractive.

Some items became more popular as new ways of cooking them were devised. At first the Christmas pudding did not get eaten, except by Tom Frost who regularly ate two at a sitting, but Christmas Pudding Boysen—thinly sliced, fried, drenched in whisky and served *en flambante* with cream—was universally appreciated (except by Frost, who disapproved on religious grounds and, anyway, was quite content to chew his way through any pudding even if it was frozen into a solid brick). Christmas Pudding Bonington—a thin gruel made by stewing the pudding with melted snow, sugar and whisky—was really only appreciated by its inventor, who nevertheless forced it upon anyone unfortunate enough to share his tent.

The whole lambs' tongues were a disastrous last-minute substitute for roast pork and stuffing, which could not be obtained in time. They were the most intractable items on the mountain and we soon learnt to avoid like the plague the 'E' packs which contained them. The result was that 'E' packs were passed on and on from camp to camp whilst the more appetizing packs got eaten. At Camps IV and V there was almost nothing to eat except whole lambs' tongues, which we tried cold, boiled, fried, stewed and devilled—all equally revolting. Finally, when it was almost too late, the master chef Boysen produced the first palatable dish by dicing the tongues, frying them with pounded chillis (stolen from the Sherpas' goodie-bags) and frying for an hour or two until really crisp. The recipe, a small bag of chillis and a few more 'E' packs were carried the next day to Camp V, where Burke and Frost, subsisting on an unvarying diet of soggy stewed tongues, were near breaking-point.

Far from being too exhausted even to light the Primus, we found that the cooking of long and elaborate meals was the main cultural activity of high-altitude life. At Camp IV the person whose day off it was would busy himself with ambitious puddings such as whisky trifle, made from high fat biscuits soaked in whisky, tinned fruit salad, jelly and cream, prepared during the morning and placed outside the Whillans Box to set. There was also a rather nasty rum-fudge-and-cashew-nut-ice-cream.

Many of the defects in the High Altitude rations were overcome by sending up specially prepared goodie-bags from Base Camp, containing such things as instant porridge, Nescafé, condensed milk, Oxo cubes, olives and steak-and-kidney puddings. These made an enormous difference and enabled us to prepare some memorable meals. For example, dinner at Camp III on 7 May consisted of seven courses spread over five hours, the menu reading:

Olives and smoked Austrian cheese
Tukte's bread (baked at Base Camp) and pâté de foie gras
Thick onion soup and croutons (made from Tukte's bread fried in
fat from Dana pork)
Fried pork, fried new potatoes and Surprise peas

Fruit salad and cream
Christmas pudding Boysen flambé
Coffee with whisky and cream

Probably the most appreciated items were 'kiddy foods' like baked beans, Readi-Brek, condensed milk, chocolate, Surprise peas, packet soups and tinned fruit, and large trannie-type noshes such as steak-and-kidney pudding, new potatoes and peas, fried corned beef and potatoes, salmon and biscuit fishcakes, frankfurters, ham and pickles.

The presence of unattractive items in the rations at high altitude is exceptionally irritating and demoralizing and tends to ruin one's appreciation of the attractive items. It is, of course, impossible to devise rations which will please everyone all the time—it is easier to change the composition of the team to suit the rations than vice versa—but, even so, there was a vague consensus on what was wrong with the rations and how they should be modified. Since food was the main topic of conversation, it was not too difficult, over the weeks, to work out the desirable modifications and to devise the ideal High Altitude rations.

Ideal High Altitude Rations

Items common to all packs

> Readi-Brek *or* Muesli
> Condensed milk (8-oz. tin)
> Sugar (8 oz. approx.)
> Salt
> Nescafé (sachets)
> Teabags
> Instant fruit-drink cubes
> Oxo cubes
> Ovaltine
> Horlicks
> 2 packets soup

Sweets (boiled, toffees, mints) ⎫
Nuts   ⎬ about 1 lb. total
Chocolate   ⎪
Mint cake (6 oz.)   ⎭

Tube margarine (Blueband—spreads straight from the
    crevasse)

Tinned fruit: mandarins, fruit salad, blackeurrants, pears,
    raspberries, strawberries

Dried apple flakes

Tinned cream

Candle

Matches (Bryant & May)

Tissues

MENU A   Steak and kidney pudding (16 oz.)
Packet Surprise peas
3 oz. smoked cheese
Fruit cake (12-oz. tin)

MENU B   Roast beef and gravy (Tynebrand, 8-oz. tin)
New potatoes (Smedleys, 10-oz. tin)
Baked beans (8-oz. tin)
Salmon (8-oz. tin)
Ryvita (6-oz. tin)

MENU C   Roast pork with stuffing (Tynebrand, 8-oz. tin)
Mashed potato (powder)
Baked beans (8-oz. tin)
Christmas pudding (8-oz. packet)

MENU D   Frankfurters (12-oz. tin)
Sanfayna salad (7-oz. tin cucumber, green and red peppers
    in brine)
New potatoes (10-oz. tin)

High-fat biscuits (6 oz.)
Tuna fish (8-oz. tin)

MENU E   Chicken breasts in jelly (Maid Marian, 8 oz.)
Surprise peas
Mashed potato (powder)
Pâté (Plumrose, 4-oz. tin)
Ryvita (6-oz. tin)

MENU F   Corned beef (12-oz. tin)
Surprise peas
Mashed potato (powder)
Ryvita (6-oz. tin)
Salmon (8-oz. tin)

NOTE: Make up packs to desired weight with odd goodies such as small tins of pâté, crabmeat, prawns, and a few jellies.

Suggested Assault Rations
Items common to both packs

Salt
Condensed milk
Sugar
Coffee
Teabags
Fruit cubes
Oxo cubes
Ovaltine
2 packets soup
Chocolate
Mint cake
Spangles

Small tin fruit
Candle
Matches (Bryant & May)
Tissues (1/3-box)

MENU A   Readi-Brek
Steak and kidney pudding (16 oz.)
Surprise peas

MENU B   Muesli
Corned beef (12 oz.)
Tin beans (8 oz.)

NOTE: A more lightweight expedition, hoping to pare down weight, would be recommended to investigate the possibility of substituting dried foods for some or all of the tinned foods listed in the proposed High Altitude menus.—C.B.

APPENDIX E

Communications

KELVIN KENT

Radio

Negotiations started in August 1969. Chris Bonington had left the running of this side of things entirely to me, but had indicated that walkie-talkie communications between Base Camp and the upper camps were vital, whilst some form of rear-link radio to civilization would be desirable if we could get it. This latter facility was equally applicable to the joint British-Nepalese Army expedition on the north side of the mountain, who also planned to use the British Gurkha pension paying-post ground for their Pokhara base, and for obvious reasons I undertook their requirements in my overall plan for rearward communications. It was for this reason also that I requested an officer from the Gurkha Signal Regiment (Lt. Bishnuparsad Thapa) to run the Pokhara end of the link, which was common to both expeditions.

The next stage was to select suitable radio sets capable of performing well over the distances and at the same time light, manpackable, simple and robust. For the walkie-talkies I obtained specifications from several Japanese firms, and Chris approached British firms. After examining the factors concerned we jointly agreed that the Pye Bantam set was the most suitable. We were proved correct because they gave us no trouble at all, and the special Mallory Cells provided ample power to last each set for about two weeks of use without a battery change, even at the higher altitudes.

The rear-link radios had to be h/f sets capable of voice/cw and able to utilize a sky-wave and surface-wave mode of operation. I chose Racal Squadcal sets and asked for four with necessary ancillaries and antenna equipment. Here again our choice could not have been better.

Next to arrange was the actual plan of operation, Government clearances and schedules. I acted on behalf of the Army expedition in this respect and submitted the appropriate application to the Ministry of Foreign Affairs in February. This showed sets at both our own and the Army Base Camp, one at Pokhara and the fourth one at Katmandu. We showed this last set as being located at the Royal Nepal Army headquarters so that it could provide a link for them direct to the two Nepalese officers on the Army expedition and also to enable the Nepalese authorities to monitor the whole net should they require to do this.

The day before I left for Pokhara to see off the main party, the clearances came through and I was both relieved and pleased. We knew that it was not normal for the Nepal Government to grant the use of h/f sets in Nepal to expeditions, and were most grateful for their approval. This had now become even more important to us for several reasons.

First, our main team now included a television team whose success depended largely on the speed with which they could get their film back to England. Communications could thus quicken the administration and control of mailrunners as well as providing cablegram information on quality reports, etcetera, within hours of arrival in Nepal. And vice versa.

Secondly, the possibility existed that the two teams climbing Annapurna could meet at the top or even traverse down the other side. Communication between the two regarding progress was therefore advantageous.

Thirdly, the Army team were trying to arrange air supply drops and needed radio for this purpose.

Finally, information, progress reports and requests for casualty evacuation for both expeditions could be sent quickly and efficiently, avoiding much loss of time.

A few technical details are given below:

	WALKIE TALKIES	H/F SETS
Type	Pye Bantam HP1	Racal Squadcal TRA 906 (SSB)
Number	6	4
Weight	4 ½ lb.	18 lb.
Power Source	Mallory ZM 9 batteries, output 0-1 watt	14 x U2 batteries or 3 x 6 volt dry cells (all Ever Ready). Output PEP and CW 5 watts with 550 MA at 18 volts on speech, input
Frequency	84 MHz	11 crystallized channels (out of 20) between 2 and 7 MHz. Actual frequencies used were 4-135 and 5-235 MHz
Antenna	Telescopic Whip	Dipole cut length wire antenna supported by 2 Army 27-ft telescopic masts loaned by the British Gurkha L. of C.H.Q. in Dharan

Schedules   0700 and 1700 hrs   0900 and 1600 hrs (later
             (or later as required)   changed to 0800 and 1500)

In addition to the radios listed above, Phillips kindly provided an excellent All World Receiver which gave good reception at Base Camp for general listening and was especially useful in picking up the special All India Radio weather forecasts which had been arranged previously for both expeditions on Annapurna I.

Mail Systems

Apart from ordinary private mail the system had to cater for television film and sound dispatches, reports to the Nepalese Government, the Mount Everest Foundation, the Chairman of our Committee and George Greenfield, as well as the passage and replenishment of hard cash rupees and small local-purchase items. We decided on six mailrunners: four for the television team and two for us. This accurately reflected the relative use we made of them, although all six were used on a mutual basis for general mail.

The route up to Base Camp from Pohkara had taken the main party seven days. The mailrunners, fully laden with sleeping-bag, food and dispatches, were expected to do it in two and a half to three days. The journey down was slightly quicker.

Most of the mail and other items leaving Base Camp were for onward dispatch to Katmandu, although some private Sherpa mail was re-routed to the Army expedition (using their mailrunners) and other instructions were specifically for Lt Bishnuparsad or Khagbir at Pokhara.

The onward despatch to Katmandu was by Royal Nepal Airlines Corporation DC3s as air documents. Lt Bishnuparsad controlled this part of the system on behalf of both expeditions and also met the incoming aircraft. All bags were marked for Miss Elizabeth Hawley of Tiger Tops, Katmandu. When mail arrived at Katmandu the airline staff would telephone Miss Hawley and she would collect the bags, open them and sort out the mail for onward posting through the Nepalese postal system, as well as that for local delivery and action in Katmandu. It was in this way that requests for cash, stamps and other things could be met.

Miss Hawley's postal address in Katmandu was also used as the expedition postal address for us and the Army. Consequently bags going out from Katmandu to Pokhara (possibly containing telegrams or Army signals for both expeditions) were met at Pokhara by Bishnu and opened, and if necessary texts of important messages were transmitted direct to one or both Base Camps.

Throughout the expedition our six mailrunners covered a total distance of 3,500 miles; the quickest run was done by one 'Tibetan Joe', who covered the sixty-odd miles from Base Camp to Pokhara in exactly twenty-six hours.

Conclusions

Radio communications rearwards to the mounting base or Katmandu played a not insignificant part in the success of this large expedition. The time saved in requesting certain important items such as high-grade paraffin and fresh rations was a distinct advantage, as was the reassurance that a request for help, in emergencies, could reach Pokhara or Katmandu in a matter of hours. In addition, the administration of Base Camp and general organization during and at the end of the expedition was made more efficient and easier. To the T.V. team these communications were vital, and both types of set used were ideal for the purpose. Indeed, with this type of expedition, where the supply-line up the mountain is extended to such an extent that it takes five days for a piece of equipment to reach Camp V from Base, VHF communications are essential. Without them, implementation of the logistic plan, medical advice from the doctor and overall control of the progress and climbers by the leader would be virtually impossible.

The mailrunners were excellent and the system functioned smoothly. To the best of my knowledge, nothing was lost between Base Camp and Katmandu.

The physical communications within Nepal are very much better now than a few years ago, and the combination of Royal Nepal Airlines and present road systems virtually allows an expedition to drive in direct to Pokhara or Katmandu. A new road is about to be opened linking Katmandu with Pokhara itself, and the local airline operates at least two daily flights between these valleys. Even the Sherpas are able to fly home, to the Hillary strip at Lukla just south of Namche Bazar.

A further expedition of this type could save time and money by driving out in two or three large vehicles. Main expedition equipment would have to be sealed and bonded up to the Nepalese border. At least one member should be Nepali-speaking—ideally the Transport-Base Camp manager—and either he or someone else who understands Nepal should arrive in Katmandu at least three weeks before the main party if subsequent delays are to be avoided.

In the not too distant future it should be possible for expeditions to think in terms of air supply dropping at or near Base Camp. At least 50% of the normal equipment could be dropped in this way, and fresh rations could also be brought in. This would save the cost of many porters, reduce administration and probably work out cheaper overall. But the element of risk with weather conditions and inaccurate drops should also be borne in mind, as should the understandable difficulty in obtaining clearances for authorized sorties near the northern border.

APPENDIX F
Photographic
MICK BURKE AND CHRIS BONINGTON

Ciné Photography

Mick Burke

Perhaps the most important aspect of the filming on the South Face of Annapurna was that for the first time people back in Britain were able to follow a Himalayan expedition whilst it was actually in progress. It was shown at least once a week on *News at Ten*. Viewers were able to see interviews by John Edwards of Thames Television with the climbers and hear the climbers' opinions of their progress on the mountain. This was backed up by film actually shot on the Face. Generally we were able to show film one week after it had been shot: the summit shots were shown five days after the summit had been reached. The problems which we overcame in filming were only challenged in difficulty by the climb itself.

We first contacted Don Horobin of I.T.N. in October 1969, to find out if I.T.N. were interested in taking part in what at that time must have seemed a terrific gamble against all odds. Throughout, Don Horobin had the utmost confidence in us, and he eventually persuaded Thames Television to come in and take over part of the cost. At that time we were of course far from certain of our success on the mountain, let alone of our ability to get interesting footage or even get the film back to London before the news became stale. To assist us and in fact take the brunt of the logistic work from us we had John Edwards; Alan Hankinson, in charge of I.T.N.'s interest and general factotum; Jon Lane, I.T.N.'s cameraman; and John Soldini, an I.T.N. sound recordist. I was to be in charge of the film on the mountain, though all members of the expedition shot some footage at different times.

We had decided to use Ektachrome EF 7242 stock for a number of reasons. It was the stock which the I.T.N. labs were used to; it could be pushed to 1000 ASA quite successfully; and we could also get it at short order from Rochester in the fifty-foot magazines for the Autoloads.

We had in total seven cameras. For the interviews we used an Auricon CineVoice with a perfectone 12-volt conversion. It was generally either mounted on an Arriflex 16-mm. tripod or used with an I.T.N. shoulderbrace. For more flexibility we then had two Beaulieu R16s, one for Jon in and around Base Camp and the other for myself in static situations on the mountain. My Beaulieu went as high as Camp IV (23,000 feet), but wasn't too successful. With it I had a Dixons lightweight tripod. We were later to have a third Beaulieu sent out to us. For stand-by we had a Bell & Howell 70DR, and on the mountain we used mainly the Bell & Howell Autoloads, two 603s and a 603T.

The CineVoice had an Agénieux 12-120 zoom lens, which was later damaged in an avalanche and replaced by the lenses from the Bell & Howell 70DR. For that we had 10-mm., 1-inch and 2-inch lenses. The Beaulieus had the same lens arrangement. The Bell & Howell Autoloads had 10-mm. lenses, and the twin turret one also a 2-inch lens. We also had a 400-mm. lens with tele-converters for the Beaulieu, but this seemed to have been damaged in transit and we were never able to get it to focus on infinity, so it was replaced by a Russian 1,000-mm. mirror lens supplied by Technical & Optical Equipment, Ltd. However, this arrived just before we left and we were not able to use it to best advantage. All lenses had C mounts and were interchangeable.

The CineVoice used the sound-on-film system. The Beaulieus were used in conjunction with either a Nagra 3 or a Bell & Howell Filmosound cassette recorder; both worked superbly. We also used a Philips EL3302 cassette recorder for conversations on the mountain, and this too worked very well (especially playing back prerecorded Beatle tapes).

Harrison's provided front filters, which protected the lenses not only from scratches but also from both dust and snow. Our anoraks had pockets made of an antistatic material. Whilst on the mountain the Autoloads were used with Harrison front filters and Wratten gelatine back filters. These were placed in the recess behind the lens. Jon Lane and I both used Gossen Lunasix exposure meters. The only trouble we had was when I had the U.V. filter crack because of cold. For the Beaulieus and the CineVoice we had nickel cadmium 12-volt batteries. Because of the altitude at Base Camp we did not take a generator, but left a charger for the batteries in Pokhara. As they were used, the batteries would be sent back with a runner and charged there.

John Edwards and Alan Hankinson left first to build up our line of communications between Pokhara and London. The film and reports would come to Pokhara by runner. In theory, from our high point on the mountain, we could get our film back to I.T.N. House in six days: one day on the Face, to Base Camp; three days from Base to Pokhara by mailrunner; one day into Katmandu and on to New Delhi by air; and one day from New Delhi to London. In actual fact our fastest time was four days from the Face to London.

Our first problems came on the march in to Base Camp, when the power lead on my Beaulieu came loose, and that was that for the duration. Just after we reached Base Camp the second Beaulieu went for a burton—this time it was the socket for the sync. generator which came loose. From then on this one was usable only as a silent camera. It was followed a few days later by the CineVoice, which had a mechanical seizure, and now we were without a sound camera.

John Soldini very pessimistically stripped the CineVoice down. The shutter had to be taken out and then replaced; the difficulty came in replacing it in the correct position. Jon ran test rolls. Normally, with the aid of the radio, we would have had results back from London in six days, but unfortunately just around that time the radio was out of action—it had been struck by lightning. This meant it would be at least twelve days before we got results back from London: a disturbing time. All Jon could do was to carry on using the CineVoice and just hope that everything was working.

A few days later, more trouble. The television crew were filming by the side of the glacier when a small avalanche caught them; the camera was swept away and the zoom lens damaged. Eventually the reports on the shutter came back—everything was O.K.—but now of course we had to sit and wait for another report to see if the CineVoice had suffered any undetected damage in the avalanche.

On the mountain the light was fantastic. I had never been in such bright conditions—even in South America we didn't have as much light as this. With the sun and the great expanse of snow we were getting constant exposure readings of f22 with the Harrison 85N6 filter, and the 10-mm. lenses had a smallest stop of f16. Luckily I happened to have some Wratton filters left over in my bag from Switzerland, and it was possible to cut out the gelatine and fit it into the recess behind the lens. Using a Harrison 85N6 screwed onto the front of the lens and a Wratton ND3 behind the lens we were back in business again.

On the mountain the Autoliads worked well. We had had slight alterations made in London: slightly larger lugs had been fitted on the hinged back, enabling the back to be opened with gloves on, and we had also had the backs padded with foam to save the operator's face from frostburn.

Because of the steepness of the Face we handheld the cameras on most occasions. Higher up the mountain we had a problem holding the cameras steady, due to our irregular breathing which was caused by the lack of oxygen.

When the new Beaulieu came up the mountain, it wasn't kept warm enough and the motor froze. It never really recovered. If I kept it inside my duvet coat, and that inside my sleeping-bag, all night, the next day it would run a hundred-foot spool before refreezing. The speed control of the Autoloads occasionally slipped, and this led to a couple of 'slow motion' rolls of film. On odd occasions a lens would get snow on it and not be noticed, if snow had got into the pocket which the camera was in. I had my anorak made with the pockets big enough to carry an Autoload in: it was less tiring than carrying it round the neck.

In all we shot around 65,000 feet of film and recorded nearly forty hours of tape. The finished product will be an hour-long documentary for Thames Television. As we have already shown over an hour of film on *News at Ten*, the filming will eventually have had about two hours of coverage, probably a record for an undertaking of this type.

• • •

Still Photography
Chris Bonington

Each member of the expedition owned a camera, and there was sufficient film for everyone to shoot as many rolls as he wanted. In this way
the keen photographers were able to get a very full coverage, while the
not so keen shot very little. In terms of sheer quantity of pictures taken
I headed the list, with 89 rolls of colour and 33 of black and white; at the
bottom was Martin Boysen, who took one roll of film which, sadly, he
had loaded incorrectly so that it came out blank. In terms of quality,
Tom Frost undoubtedly earned the accolade: his results were consis-
tently good and some of his pictures rank amongst the best mountain
colour pictures I have ever seen.

Equipment: Of the eleven climbers in the team, nine used Pentax SV
cameras, generously donated by Rank Photographic; of these, five had
35-mm. lenses fitted as standard. Ian Clough used a 28-mm. wide-angle
lens and an 85-mm. lens with two bodies, one for black and white and
the other for colour. This made an excellent combination. Tom Frost
used his own battered but well-tried Leica IIIg with 35-mm., 50-mm.
and 90-mm. lenses. I used 2 Nikon bodies, with 24-mm. and 35-mm.
perspective-control lenses, a 55-mm. Macro lens, and 105-mm., 200-
mm. and 500-mm. reflex lenses at Base Camp and on the lower slopes.
I also had a Leica Mk 2 with 21-mm., 35-mm. and 90-mm. lenses which
I favoured on the upper part of the mountain for colour because of its
ruggedness and lack of bulk, in conjunction with a Rollei 35 for black
and white. The Rollei 35 has a fixed 40-mm. lens, and the great advantage that it is smaller than most ½-frame cameras.

All the cameras functioned well, and although only the Nikons were
winterized, there was no trouble from freezing up. Ultraviolet filters were
fitted at all times. Tom Frost used one with a slightly green cast, which
gave his pictures a rather special atmospheric quality. We all had trouble
at times, especially in bad weather when snow got onto the lens, with
moisture getting in between the filter and the lens, causing condensation.

Film: The expedition used 350 rolls of Kodachrome II, 20 of High Speed Ektachrome, 100 of Plus-X and 20 of Tri-x. Since all but Ian Clough and myself were limited to one camera, almost everyone used the Kodachrome II. In the bright light available at altitude this proved amply fast enough, and gave transparencies of excellent brilliance and definition. We have since had many of these made into quarter-plate black and white negatives with excellent results—so good that in future I should be tempted to shoot only in colour. Each member of the team was also issued with a special clamp to fit on the head of an ice axe with a ball-and-socket attachment for the camera, which made a very useful and compact monopod.

Exposure: Several members did not bother to use an exposure-meter; two had Westons and two Lunarsixes. We all had exposure problems. Tom Frost was an underexposure man, very often using direct reflected-light readings, giving exposures of around 1/250 at f11 and f16 in full sunlight. This turned out to be on the high side. I erred on the other side, using incident-light readings and giving an average of 1/250 at f8. Above 20,000 feet a mean exposure rating would appear to be around 1/250 at f11 for good, strong results retaining some texture in the snow. At this speed figures would become dark, and for close-ups it pays to open up a stop, or even more. Using an incident-light meter, which is probably the most accurate way of assessing exposure above the snow-line, it pays to close down one stop on the given reading. As a general rule, if you are going to err, it is much better to do so on the side of underexposure, which at least ensures you get striking pictures. Even half a stop overexposure gives very wishy-washy results. Wherever possible it certainly pays to bracket exposures.

Sending film back: This is always a problem on an expedition, especially when it comes to ensuring that a record is kept of who took what and returning originals to each individual photographer. As film was shot on the mountain, the photographer marked each cassette with his name and numbered it, keeping a record of the number. The film was sent back down the mountain, packed into linen bags addressed to the expedition secretary and sent back to England with the T.V. film consignments. The expedition secretary had the film processed, and stamped every single cardboard mount of the transparencies with the name of the photographer and the number of the film—each black and white negative strip was similarly marked and a complete record was maintained on file. This ensured that transparencies could eventually be returned to the photographer after they had been sent around to magazines, book publishers and so on.

Conclusions: We managed to get a very full photographic coverage up to the first half of the Rock Band, but practically nothing above. Part of the problem was that neither Don Whillans nor Dougal Haston was particularly photographically minded, and therefore they did not take any pictures once the going became really rough. Even the devotees such as Ian Clough, Tom Frost and myself, all of whom reached Camp VI, were so cold and exhausted that we never took a photograph of the Camp site, even though it was the most spectacular of the lot—each one of us thought, Oh, well, one of the others is sure to take it. It was fortunate that Tom Frost did take a series of magnificent pictures from his solitary high point at 25,000 feet. The trouble was, though, that he had no one with him to act as foreground and therefore got no pictures of the gully leading up to the summit ridge.

For summit coverage we had to rely on a clip of film taken from that shot by the Autoload. For any future expedition it is essential to ram home to members the importance of everyone taking photographs— even if they are not very good they might fill an irreplaceable gap. To make it easier, it is more important to have simple, compact, easy to handle cameras, rather than bulkier, sophisticated ones. Once a camera is put away in a rucksack to be out of the way, it is most unlikely that it will come out again, and certainly not in time to record any dramatic incident. From this point of view, cameras like the Rollei 35 have many advantages, for they can be slipped into a pocket, always ready to hand,

and don't get in the way. If the climber wants a more sophisticated camera with interchangeable lenses, the Pentax SV is robust, very compact for a single-lens reflex camera, and is set at a reasonable price.

APPENDIX G

Medical

DAVE LAMBERT

This medical appendix is principally intended for those with the problem of organizing an expedition. Our team was big enough to have its own doctor, and much of the equipment and many of the drugs which we took would be too specialized for those without this advantage. Such expeditions would be well advised to find a non-travelling medical adviser with some experience in the field, but further sources of information will be found in the references at the end.

The essence of good organization is anticipation. All the medical problems likely to arise must be thought through and prepared for. It is no use having the right drug at Base Camp when it is needed by a climber at 25,000 feet, or inoculating that climber against polio and having no method of getting him down the mountain when his feet are frozen. The mortality rate amongst Europeans climbing in the Himalayas is said to be about 6%. Although there will always be natural hazards such as avalanches and ice-falls, the figure seems unacceptably high, and could probably be reduced by more careful preparation.

Preliminaries

As the team came from a wide area, there was no full medical examination of the members, it being assumed that men with their reputations could have nothing basically wrong. In fact, we might have been saved a lot of trouble: particularly in the case of those suffering from piles, had they been picked out beforehand and encouraged to get treatment. A questionnaire was sent out asking about respiratory, intestinal, skin and other common complaints and for any medical history. Any special drugs needed were then added to the list.

A circular advised people about minor ailments. Respiratory troubles are exacerbated at altitude, so smokers are advised to stop and those with green or yellow sputum should have a course of antibiotics. Abnormalities of sinuses and nasal passages are corrected, ear infections settled and wax syringed out. A visit to the dentist will save amateur attempts at extraction in the field. Also, small pockets of air in tooth fillings expand due to low pressure at altitude and can cause severe toothache, so doubtful fillings are best replaced. Piles should be treated by injection or surgery. Appendicectomy is done routinely on members of expeditions to the Antarctic, and although climbing expeditions are for a shorter period of time there is a good case for members having it done; appendicitis is a pretty lethal disease where surgery is not available. Attention should be paid to skin conditions, such as sweat rashes which may develop during the march in, as climbers will not be washing and changing at higher camps and skin lesions become worse. Feet tend to sweat in the warm lower valleys and previously tough skin becomes softened and athlete's foot becomes worse. Toenails should be kept short; spares of medical accessories such as spectacles should be taken.

All members of the team had a blood sample taken which was grouped and cross-matched against others with the same group. It happened to work out that if anyone had needed blood after an accident there would always have been at least two climbers who could have donated it.

Vaccination

The legal vaccination requirements for an area such as Nepal are small, but the range of diseases one may contact is fairly large. Reasonable advice would seem to be to obtain vaccination against as many diseases as is conveniently possible in the time available. International certificates are needed for cholera and smallpox but not yellow fever (unless one is travelling via an affected area, such as Africa). Such certificates are issued by the Local Health Authorities (L.H.A.). Vaccination may be carried out by general practitioners or by the L.H.A., which can be contacted through the Town Hall. Doctors' evening surgeries are usually more convenient than the 9 a.m. to 5 p.m. clinics of the L.H.A., but doctors will need to get supplies of vaccine specially, and are also entitled to charge a fee. Those who were vaccinated as children probably had the triple vaccine against diphtheria, whooping cough and tetanus; they may also have had polio cover, and for this and tetanus they should have a booster. Smallpox may have been done, but the international certificate is only valid for three years and this will have to be repeated.

Yellow fever: This was the fever with jaundice which killed so many workers when the Panama Canal was being built. An international certificate is not needed for the Himalayas but is needed for South America. Such a certificate is valid for ten years. Vaccination is carried out only in special L.H.A. centres and is usually done first on a vaccination programme.

Smallpox: A certificate is needed and is valid for three years. The inoculation needs to be checked for a satisfactory response at about seven days.

Cholera: This was the lethal disease in Japanese prisoner-of-war camps during the Second World War, and is characterized by a profuse watery diarrhoea. A certificate is needed for the Middle and Far East including Nepal, but is only valid for six months. Two injections are needed.

Diphtheria: The disease is practically never encountered in this country now, but is still common elsewhere. Potentially a killer, it starts as a severe sore throat. Children after about 1940 received the vaccine, but it should be given to anyone who missed out. A test known as the Schick Test may have to be done beforehand.

Tetanus: This is lockjaw, which may go on to inability to breathe and asphyxiation. It is acquired through dirty, particularly soil-contaminated wounds, and is common abroad. The vaccine is now commonly given to anyone attending hospital with a cut, but three injections are needed for the full course and a booster is advisable after five years.

Tuberculosis: This is widespread in the less developed areas of the world, and is most likely to be picked up from the coughing porter or by drinking local milk. The vaccine, B.C.G., is given in the forces and some schools, and does not need repeating. Immunity is tested first by the Mantoux Test, and this is examined after three days.

Poliomyelitis: Adequate protection against this ailment is essential for anyone travelling in less developed areas, as it is common and we do not have a naturally developed resistance to it, unlike the indigenous inhabitants. It is caused by a virus transmitted by water and food. The Sabin vaccine given on sugar lumps is usually used now, and a full count is three doses, though as with all these agents a partial course is better than none. A booster is advisable before a trip such as this for those who have had the course.

Diarrhoea and dysentery: Everyone knows about the danger of these when travelling abroad, and that they are picked up from local food and water. T.A.B. gives protection against the more serious of the causative organisms. Two injections are preferred. This is the one which upsets some people. Protection lasts for a year only.

Typhus: A fever transmitted by lice which may subsequently go on to pneumonia. It became endemic in the trenches during the First World War and a lot of people died. It has not been so serious since the advent of antibiotics. The vaccine has to be obtained from the few L.H.A. centres which keep supplies. Two shots are needed and immunity lasts six months.

Jaundice: Gamma Globulin, an extract of human blood, confers some protection against infective hepatitis, or jaundice. Only recently universally available, it needs to be given within a month before departure.

Immunization programme: The above list is a rather terrifying one, and is a reflection of how well we have done in the Western world to eradicate such killers from our society. It is worth the trouble involved to obtain immunity from them. There are two programmes listed below; one covering all the above possibilities, and the other a crash course for those with limited time. They will both need to be modified according to what the individual has already had.

FULL PROGRAMME

WEEK	VACCINE
1	Yellow fever, Mantoux Test, Schick Test
2	Read test results; smallpox
3	Check smallpox
4	Poliomyelitis, diphtheria, tetanus, typhus
5	T.A.B., cholera
6	B.C.G.: leave a clear 10 days afterwards
7	
8	Second injections of polio, diphtheria, tetanus, typhus
9	Second injections of T.A.B., cholera

NOTE: A third dose of polio may be given a month later, and Gamma globulin just before departure.

SHORT COURSE

Taken from 'Protection and Prevention, Immunization Products and

Procedures' (Wellcome Services). This does not include tuberculosis and diphtheria.

DAY	VACCINE
1	Yellow fever, cholera, polio
5	Smallpox, T.A.B., tetanus
11	Cholera (second), typhus
13	Read smallpox results
28	Second dose of T.A.B., tetanus, polio
35	Second dose of typhus

NOTE: The courses of poliomyelitis and tetanus should be completed later.

Hygiene

Hygiene is an unattractive word; maybe because it conjures up memories of having to scrub knees and fingernails as a child. Yet it merely means ways of avoiding disease, and is as much a matter of common sense as vaccination.

Water near any inhabited area should be considered as infected, even the fresh-looking streams of Nepal. It is probably safer to boil it, but we used Halazone tablets in our water-bottles. These release chlorine, which is effective against bacteria, viruses, and the amoeba, a common contaminant, which causes a form of dysentery that can be very difficult to treat. Filtering the water through Millbank bags was not found to be necessary. Water obtained by melting snow is not always sterile, as it can be fouled by wind-blown frozen faeces, and in higher camps care must be taken to get snow for water well away from the latrine area.

Food may also carry infection, usually because it has been handled by people with unclean hands. Most of our food we took with us from England, but we relied on the locals for rice, potatoes, meat and eggs. As these are all cooked before being eaten, this was satisfactory. Food which is not cooked, such as fruit, must be cleaned and preferably peeled before being eaten, and it is probably better to avoid such produce as milk and butter, which may come from animals infected by tuberculosis.

Latrine arrangements are important. Bushes serve their purpose during the march in, but slit trenches, well away from the water supply, must be dug at more permanent camps. This requires a definite effort higher up the mountain, and collapsible shovels have to be carried up. Disinfectant should also be taken for the latrines, at least at Base Camp.

We were not much troubled by insects, which was fortunate as they are important vectors of disease. A recent campaign by the World Health Organization has practically eradicated from Nepal the mosquito and the malaria which it carried. We started by taking anti-malarial tablets, then decided that they were unnecessary. Lice and fleas can be picked up by sleeping in villages, and we carried D.D.T. powder, but were not in fact troubled. Leeches can be troublesome, particularly after the monsoon has started; they drop off if a lighted cigarette, salt or alcohol is applied.

Local Population

Treatment of the local population did not constitute much of a problem to our expedition as the march in was short and only the first part through an inhabited area. About forty attended those clinics held in villages. Treatment was necessarily superficial, as it was not possible to investigate or follow up cases and we could not carry enough drugs to be a travelling dispensary.

Wounds were cleaned and dressed; patients with an infection were given an injection of Triplopen, a long-acting penicillin. Those with worms or who were anaemic were given a dose of Alcopar and a few iron tablets. Many were suffering from a chronic conjunctivitis, as their houses have no chimneys to let out the smoke from their fires, and Otrivine-Antistin eye-drops were used. We had dental equipment and a few extractions were performed under local anaesthesia, but no demands were made of the obstetric forceps. Above the snow-line, many porters complained of cough, and codeine phosphate acted as both a cough suppressant and an analgesic. The majority who attended had to be given some form of placebo, and panadol or aspirin were found best for this purpose.

Rescue

Rescue from the South Face of Annapurna above Camp III would have been very difficult indeed. Above this point the route traversed a very steep face, below the crest of a ridge, and it would have been virtually impossible to retreat this way with a climber unable to help himself. A stretcher would have had to be lowered down one of the dangerous couloirs of the Face. At Camp III was a medical pack, together with splints, oxygen, and a canvas stretcher lined by a sleeping-bag which unzipped 180°, allowing easy access to a patient. At Base Camp we were equipped to give general anaesthesia and carry out emergency surgery.

All camps were connected by portable radio, on which calls were made twice a day and more often during assaults, and this meant that all members of the party could soon be notified in the event of an accident. There were also connections from Base Camp to Pokhara and so to Katmandu, and the means of rescue from Base by helicopter were assessed before the team left Katmandu. In the event we did not need such help, but the Army team did get helicopter rescue for one of their members who developed pneumonia.

Medical Problems of High Altitudes

The lack of oxygen causes altitude sickness and pulmonary oedema, depression, insomnia, loss of appetite and weight loss leading to the general picture of high-altitude deterioration. The cold may cause frostbite or exposure, and climbers become dehydrated from lack of water. The liability to snowblindness, respiratory and intestinal complaints completes the picture.

Acclimatization

It is necessary to have a simple understanding of the mechanics of breathing. At rest the lungs are like a couple of partially inflated balloons containing about two and a half litres (that is, five pints) of gas, which is trying to reach a state of equilibrium with the oxygen and carbon dioxide carried by the blood flowing through the lungs. A normal breath is only half a litre, so the lungs are not emptied and then filled with fresh air. Breathing more frequently and more deeply means more fresh air and a higher percentage of oxygen in the lung air. This breathing also blows off more carbon dioxide, which is useful in exercise as more is being produced, but if the shortage of oxygen is due to altitude there is a loss of carbon dioxide. In the blood this gas forms carbonic acid and its loss leaves an alkaline state. Maintenance of the correct pH—a measure of acidity—is essential to life, so the body corrects this state of affairs by excreting alkalis in the urine, a process taking two or three days. This is the first stage in the process of acclimatization and merely means adapting to breathing more deeply in rarefied air. In spite of this the oxygen concentration in lung air starts dropping below normal from 10,000 feet upward, and the blood which is normally 100% saturated with oxygen becomes less and less so. Acclimatization means becoming used to this, and the process is not understood. Normal people are exhausted when the saturation drops to 65% and unconscious at 55%, but climbers have been found to have 65% at rest and 45% during hard exercise when acclimatized to 19,000 feet. One way in which the body adapts to this is to increase the number of red cells, as these carry the oxygen. There is a 50% rise and this takes some seven weeks.

Acclimatization has its limitations. There is a mine at 19,000 feet in the Andes, but the miners walk up daily from 17,500 feet rather than live in the village there. In 1961 a scientific team spent six months at 19,000 feet and was less fit than newly arrived men at the end of this time. On these grounds it is felt that 18,000 feet is probably the upper limit for permanent acclimatization, and lower for a number of people. Above this, general condition declines, a process known as high-altitude deterioration, which is more severe the higher one goes.

From these facts, and from practical experience, a few guide lines for acclimatization can be worked out. Individuals vary enormously, but, roughly, those who are younger and fitter and have been to altitude previously are likely to acclimatize better. Ascent from about 10,000 feet onwards is best taken gradually. At each height it takes two days to make the basic adjustment, and a rise of another 3-4,000 feet will require a further period of adjustment. Above 18,000 feet this adaptation still occurs, but there is an underlying slow process of deterioration and above 24,000 feet this is so rapid that one hardly has time to benefit from acclimatization, so that the time spent above this height is probably best kept to a minimum. Climbers developing altitude sickness should descend, and the farther down they go the quicker they will recover. From this point of view, Base Camp is best below 18,000 feet, but this is often dictated by the mountain. One of our climbers who was unwell at 23,000 feet felt better on coming down to 20,000, but after three days' rest was insufficiently recovered and had to descend to Base at 14,000, where he soon became fit again. On the other hand, many expeditions have had Base Camps at about 20,000 feet. How quickly a climber can re-ascend after a rest at Base depends on how well acclimatized to the higher altitude he was previously. We had planned for re-ascent from Base Camp V (14,000-23,000 feet) in five days, but this was hardly ever achieved, though how far this was due to logistic considerations it is difficult to say.

Full acclimatization to a particular height takes some seven weeks. In part this is due to the increase of the red cells in the blood, but there are little understood factors such as the control of breathing and the adjustment of the body cells to the low saturation of oxygen in the blood. There are no rules and each individual must find out what is best for himself.

• • •

Mountain Sickness

When the unacclimatized person ascends to altitude he develops a splitting headache, can't sleep, loses his appetite and feels sick, is tired and weak, and may behave strangely. Though basically this is due to lack of oxygen, the changes occurring in the body are not yet fully elucidated and are the subject of much research and controversy at the moment.

Singh considers that the body tends to retain fluid. This could cause swelling of the brain and hence headache, and could lead to that dreaded disease of altitude, acute pulmonary oedema. In the latter condition, water suddenly accumulates in the lungs, giving intense breathlessness and perhaps resulting in the 'drowning' of the sufferer. Singh found that in over 400 cases of mountain sickness in unacclimatized soldiers transported quickly to over 12,000 feet, considerable improvement resulted from administering frusemide, better known by its trade name Lasix. This is a diuretic, a drug which makes the kidneys excrete a large volume of water.

No one would disagree with this treatment in the case of acute pulmonary oedema, and results in fit young soldiers with mountain sickness sound very good. However, climbers have the additional complication of a tendency to dehydration, which throws a doubt on this whole concept of altitude sickness. Our limited experience was that frusemide proved very unpopular. By enhancing dehydration it made sufferers worse and they all had to descend as is conventional.

At the moment therefore, careful acclimatization and descent when ill remains the answer to this problem.

High-Altitude Deterioration

It seems hardly surprising that men living in tents in the snow and working hard every day should begin to feel run down after a while, but it has been found that this happens at altitude even when conditions are made as near normal as possible, and this is ascribed to the lack of oxygen. The symptoms are like those of a gradual return of a low-grade mountain sickness. The climber is tired and apathetic, goes off his food, loses weight, and cannot sleep. He recovers only by descending again.

The condition may be delayed if not avoided by careful attention to the basic necessities of life, as was pointed out by Pugh in 1954.

Climbers become dehydrated. The air is dry and breathing is rapid and heavy so that a lot of fluid evaporates this way. Also it is often hot on the snow, so sweating can be profuse. Pugh said that the 1953 Everest climbers should drink seven pints daily, and this was satisfactory. As snow has to be melted to get water, which is a tedious business, it takes a determined effort to achieve this intake. Snow melted if left on top of our Whillans Boxes during the day, and this proved a great asset. Any similar arrangement is to be recommended. As a screw-top plastic urine bottle is in any case very useful on a stormy night in a tent, it is worth having a calibrated one and recording urine output. An output of two or three pints a day indicates a satisfactory intake of water.

Salt deficiency is also probably common, but its effects are masked by lack of water. A simple test of the urine will reveal it, and the reagents are worth having at one of the higher camps.

Fanlus Test: Take ten drops of urine and one drop of 20% potassium chromate, and add 2.9% silver nitrate drop by drop. At least three drops should be needed before the colour turns brown, otherwise salt deficiency is indicated. This assumes a normal urinary volume. Salt tablets taken routinely naturally increase thirst and are therefore not popular. Anyone who gets cramps should take them but a deficiency may initially just show itself as malaise.

The problem of food has been discussed in Appendix D. Everyone loses weight, but this is minimized if an adequate intake of calories can be maintained. Problems of transport, loss of appetite caused by altitude and dehydration, and the sheer lack of energy to struggle with the Primus all mitigate against this. Taking a vitamin tablet has become a traditional daily ceremony, although it is doubtful if anyone can become vitamin deficient during the period of a climbing expedition.

Altitude causes insomnia, particularly in the unacclimatized. At high camps, Everest climbers have used a slow flow of oxygen whilst sleeping and this has had good results. Keeping warm is very important, and our team had closed-cell foam mattresses under their sleeping-bags. Most of us took sleeping-pills and found the choice of a medium- or a short-acting barbiturate very satisfactory.

Frostbite

When fingers and toes become very cold the small arteries supplying them go into spasm, further reducing blood supply and allowing tissue cells to become frozen. The cells are recoverable at first, but eventually die, making gangrene inevitable. This is exacerbated at altitude because of the lack of oxygen in the blood, and also by its increased viscosity due to the increase in red-blood cells, dehydration, and changes in the plasma volume associated with acclimatization.

Prevention: The injured climber is particularly liable to frostbite as he cannot move to keep his circulation going, and care must be taken to keep him warm.

Gloves with waterproof over-mitts are standard, and we used a balaclava which covered nose, cheeks and ears, as these parts are also liable to frostbite. The problem of boots is still not fully solved. Leather boots with inners and over-boots do become wet through and liable to freeze eventually, and we found vapour-barrier boots (like glorified wellingtons, with rubber inners) were quite popular, though sweat accumulated in them and socks became soaked. Recently socks electrically heated by battery have become available and are an interesting possibility.

First aid: A great difficulty is that there is no clear-cut sign heralding the onset of frostbite. All snow and ice climbers are used to cold and numb feet, yet after numbness there will be no further sign, so this should be taken as the danger symptom. The best treatment is the application of warmth and the only convenient source on a climb is likely to be another part of the body. Hands are easily put under one's own armpits, but when to decide to take off crampons and boots to put the feet under one's colleagues' armpits must depend on circumstances. The old treatment of massaging and beating frozen extremities definitely damages frozen cells and must be avoided.

There is argument about the benefit of vasodilator drugs at this stage. Experimental studies have not shown them to be any use, but many people have experienced a subjective sensation of warmth after taking a dose. We used Ronicol, taken when the feet felt very cold. This is not as powerful as some of the other drugs which dilate blood vessels, but nor does it have the same danger of side-effects. Alcohol also has some dilating effect on vessels. It must be remembered that such drugs cause more blood to circulate through the skin and cool the body, which may be a disadvantage.

Treatment: Initial treatment is by rewarming in a water-bath at a temperature which can just be borne by the elbow without discomfort. It takes at least twenty minutes, and the water should be kept hot. Do not warm a limb directly over a flame. The treated part becomes painful, swollen and discoloured, and if the feet are affected the victim will not be able to walk. He should therefore get himself out of any dangerous situation whilst his feet are still frozen and numb.

The patient should be kept warm so that he has a good skin circulation. At higher camps he should be given oxygen, as the lack of oxygen aggravates the condition. The part is kept warm and clean without pressure on it, and an antibiotic is given, as the risk of infection is high. If a doctor is present, the possibilities of intravenous low-molecular dextran, anticoagulation, and a lumbar sympathetic block should be borne in mind.

• • •

Snow-blindness

Snow-blindness is a severe conjunctivitis caused by ultraviolet light. The eyelids feel gritty, then painful, and it becomes impossible to open the eyes against the light, hence the 'blindness'.

The treatment is avoidance of light, hydrocortisone and antibiotic drops to diminish the inflammation, and 1% amethocaine drops for pain.

Amethocaine is an anaesthetic, and our climbers carried it to enable them to open their eyes if they became snow-blind in a dangerous situation. It was accepted that this would allow the conjunctivitis to become worse, and that there is a slight risk of bleeding into the eye. Also, when anaesthetized, the eyes need protection against dust and the casual brush of the hand.

Other Complaints

Respiratory: Infection of the respiratory tract is particularly liable to occur in high mountains, and the results can be serious. Heavy breathing in the dry air at altitude causes sore throats, and throat lozenges are very useful. We used Merocets, which are sweet and tasty. Bronchitis and pneumonia cause impairment of the ability to oxygenate the blood, with resulting shortness of breath, which can be very severe and lead to death. It is difficult to distinguish such an infection from acute pulmonary oedema. Our climbers carried both tetracycline and Lasix to be used in such an emergency, but it is even more important to have oxygen available. The necessity for oxygen cannot be too strongly emphasized, as it can be lifesaving in this condition. We had oxygen and masks at all our camps, though fortunately no emergency occurred.

Two of our team developed a sharp pain in the chest, worse on deep breathing and coughing, which is known as a pleuritic pain. There were no signs of an underlying pneumonia and both men recovered in two or three days. Although this may have been muscle strain, a more interesting possibility is that small adhesions between the lung and the chest wall were torn by the excessive respiratory effort.

Haemorrhoids: More commonly known as piles. These gave us a lot of trouble. As well as causing irritation and soreness, they are prone to two painful complications. Bleeding just under the skin near the anus gives a peri-anal haematoma, and the term 'prolapsed piles' is used when they descend below the anus, become swollen, and will not return. They are treated by rest and ointment, and usually incapacitate the climber for a while. No less than four of our team of eleven Europeans, and one Sherpa, developed these complications, although they were not severe sufferers beforehand. This emphasizes the need to obtain treatment before the expedition starts.

Thrombosis: As has been explained, the increase in red cells and the changes in the volume of the other component of the blood, the plasma, result in an increased viscosity, and the blood flows more sluggishly. It is therefore more liable to clot in the arteries and veins, and this is known as thrombosis. Cerebral, pulmonary and deep leg-vein thrombosis have all been recorded in climbers.

Drugs and Equipment
The expedition was greatly helped by the generous donation of drugs and equipment from the firms listed at the end of this Appendix, and we owe them a special debt of gratitude.

Packing: Packs have to fulfil widely differing criteria for transportation by ship and porter, storage in the snow and easy accessibility. It is probably best to have them specially made, but we solved the problem in a satisfactory way.

Drugs were taken out of their bottles and repacked in two sizes of plastic containers, which were then carefully labelled. The main containers were Benesto boxes supplied by W.C.B., each of which carried about 30 lb., so that two made a rather heavy porter load. (Porters carry about 50 lb., to which they add their own personal possessions and food.) Most of these boxes we used for storage, but two were specially subdivided for readily accessible medical supplies. One of these was fitted with plastic luncheon boxes, each containing drugs for a particular system; the other was used for dressings. For transportation by ship, these boxes would have to be repacked in crates. They were not wholly waterproof but would stand exposure to snow for a period of time. Aluminium boxes would probably have been better.

Individual Packs: Each mountaineer was given a small First-Aid pack. This was made up into a plastic box and weighed only 4 oz. It contained the following drugs (plus instructions on their use): codeine phosphate tablets for headache, cough and diarrhoea; Ronicol tablets for cold feet and frostbite; Fortral tablets for severe pain and Fortral injection with a syringe for use in the event of an accident; amethocaine eyedrops for snowblindness; and sleeping-tablets, which in our case were Tuinal, lasting about eight hours, and Seconal, lasting four hours. For a respiratory emergency, Lasix and tetracycline tablets were included as explained in an earlier section.

Camp Packs: It was found convenient for each camp to have a small stock of commonly used drugs, from which individuals could replenish their supplies. They included vitamins, iron, salt, sleeping-tablets, analgesics, Ronicol, throat lozenges and dressings.

A special mountain-rescue pack was made up for Camp III, for use in the event of an accident. This included a selection of drugs for doctor's use, dressings, slings and splints. We used inflatable plastic splints for convenience; the trouble with these is that they are liable to occlude the skin circulation of blood, which is especially dangerous to climbers because of the risk of frostbite. Equipment for maintenance of the respiratory system was included, and this consisted of an oropharyngeal airway, endotracheal tube with laryngoscope, foot suction-pump and manual inflating bellows, together with oxygen and the necessary connections for the endotracheal tube or a mask. An additional refinement was a hot-water bottle.

Recommended Drugs

Quantities are those recommended for an expedition of the same size with the same number of porters and local inhabitants to treat.

	DRUG	QUANTITY
Respiratory	Merocets	1,000 lozenges
	Faringets	1,000 lozenges
	Otrivine nasal spray	12
	Soframycin nebulizer	4
	Triominic	100 tablets
	Rhinamid drops	2 bottles
Gastrointestinal	Nulacin	30 tubes
	Aludrox	400 tablets
	Senokot	500 tablets
	Anusol ointment and applicator	20
	Scheriproct ointment	20
	Scheriproct suppositories	100
	Pro-banthine	200 tablets
	Kaolin powder	500 grammes
Cardiovascular	Ronicol	1,000 tablets
	Ronicol timespan	500 tablets
	Priscol	200 tablets
	Heparin 25,000 units/ml.	10 vials
	Protamine sulphate	5 ampoules
	Digoxin	20 ampoules
	Digoxin	200 tablets

	Hydrocortisone	50 vials
	Lasix	50 ampoules
	Lasix	500 tablets
	Aminophylline	5 ampoules
	Adrenaline	5 ampoules
	Pronestyl	50 tablets
Eyes and ears	Otrivine-antistin eyedrops	10 vials
	Hydrocortisone/chloramphenicol eyedrops	10 vials
	Novocain eyedrops	10 vials
	Amethocaine eyedrops	50 minims
	Chloramphenicol eye ointment	5 tubes
	Xerumex eardrops	1 bottle
	Corlan	200 lozenges
	Glycerine and borax	100 ml.
Skin	Betnovate	40 tubes
	Betnovate N	5 tubes
	Tinaderm	10 tubes
	Mycota powder	10 tins
	Uvistat	50 tubes
Antibiotics	Chloramphenicol	200 tablets
	Tetralysal	1,000 tablets
	Penbritin	500 tablets
	Septrin	100 tablets
	Triplopen	500 vials
	Nystatin	100 tablets
	Tridia	200 sachets
	Lomotil *and* neomycin	100 packs
	Orastrep	500 tablets
	Emetine hydrochloride	50 ampoules
	Emetine-bismuth iodide	200 tablets
	Furamide	500 tablets
Parasites	Alcopar	200 sachets

	Nivaquine	100 tablets
Dietary	Multivite	1,000 tablets
	Ferrous gluconate	1,000 tablets
	Sodium chloride, lime flavoured	1,000 tablets
Analgesics	Cyclimorph	20 ampoules
	Fortral	20 ampoules
	Fortral	200 tablets
	Codeine phosphate	2,000 tablets
	Aspirin	1,000 tablets
	Panadol	2,000 tablets
	Lingraine	50 lozenges
Sedatives	Largactil	50 tablets
	Valium	100 tablets
	Tuinal	1,000 tablets
	Seconal	1,000 tablets
	Phenobarbitone inj.	10 ampoules
Anaesthetics	Lignocaine 2% with adrenaline	200 dental cartridges
	Xylocaine 2%	100 ml.
	Xylocaine 4% topical	50 ml.
	Atropine	5 ampoules
	Tubocurarine	25 ampoules
	Neostigmine	2 ampoules
	Scoline	10 ampoules
	Epontol	5 vials
	Brietal	5 vials
	Fluothane	250 ml.
Intravenous agents	Normal saline	10 pint bags
	5% dextrose	10 pint bags
	Plasma	2 bottles
	Lomodex	10 bottles
General	Water-sterilizing tablets	50 tubes
	Zinc oxide	

Oil of cloves	
Avomine	100 tablets
Dexamethasone inj.	10 ampoules
Ergometrine inj.	5 ampoules
Dexadrine	500 tablets
Sterile water	300 ml.
Hibitane 20%	1,500 ml.
Mercurochrome	500 ml.
Polybactrin spray	2 tins

Recommended Equipment

Dressings
- Elastoplast
- Sterile-sofratulle
- Bandages
- Melolin
- Crepe bandages
- Gauze
- Cotton wool

Surgical
- Small general surgical set
- Hudson brace and burrs
- Obstetric forceps
- Towels
- Steridrape
- Nail-brushes
- Gloves
- Masks
- Swabs
- Packs
- Needles
- Sutures, etc.

} ready sterilized

Dental equipment

    Syringe

    Probes

    Forceps, etc.

Anaesthetic

    Oxford miniature vapourizer

    Heidbrink valve

    Flow meter

    Suction-pump

    Inflating bellows

    Plastic laryngoscope

    Connections

    Endotracheal tubes

    Rubens valve

    Oropharyngeal airways

    Anaesthetic masks

General

    Thermometer

    Inflatable splints

    Stethoscope

    Thomas splint

    Sphygmomanometer

    Skin traction set

    Intravenous giving sets

    Plaster of Paris

    Blood-donor Packs

    Cellophane bags for dispensing

    Syringes

    Nasogastric tube

    Needles

    Urethral catheter

• • •

References

O. G. Edholm and A. L. Bacharach (eds.), *Exploration Medicine* (John Wright, 1965)

L. G. C. E. Pugh, 'Animals in High Altitudes', *Handbook of Physiology: Adaptation to Environment* (American Physiological Society)

M. P. Ward, 'High Altitude Deterioration' (*Proc. Roy. Soc.*, B-143, 40) (1954)

L. G. C. E. Pugh, 'Himalayan Rations with Special Reference to the 1953 Expedition to Mount Everest' (*Proc. Nutr. Soc.*, 13, 60) (1954)

B. Bhattacharya, *Mountain Sickness* (John Wright, 1964)

Singh *et al.*, 'Acute Mountain Sickness', *New Eng. J. Med.*, 280: 175–184 (1969)

James Wilkerson, *Medicine for Mountaineering* (Veil-Ballou, Washington, D.C.)

Acknowledgements

We would particularly like to thank the following for their generosity in supplying the expedition:

Mr McGuckin, Mawson & Proctor Pharmaceuticals, Newcastle

B.D.H. Pharmaceuticals, Ltd

Boots Pure Drug Co., Ltd

Beecham Group, Ltd

Ciba Laboratories, Ltd

Charles Thackary, Ltd, surgical instrument supplier

Dales Pharmaceuticals, Ltd

Dista Products, Ltd

Ethicon, Ltd

Eli Lilly & Co., Ltd

Fisons Pharmaceuticals, Ltd

Glaxo Laboratories, Ltd

Johnson & Johnson, Ltd

Longworth Scientific Instruments Co., Ltd

May & Baker, Ltd

Minnesota Mining & Manufacturing Co., Ltd
Merrel National, Ltd
Parke, Davis & Co.
Smith & Nephew, Ltd
W.C.B. Containers, Ltd

APPENDIX H
The People of Nepal
KELVIN KENT

These notes are compiled to enable the reader to get some idea of the Nepalese people themselves, in whose rugged yet beautiful country we lived for nearly three months as a team, though some of us had been there longer, in the planning stages and on previous visits.

The views expressed are intended not necessarily as an authoritative guide but mainly as impressions and opinions of the day-to-day aspects of life in Nepal, as conveyed to us by the Gurkhas, local hillmen and town dwellers of the places with which we came into contact. Without a little knowledge of their philosophy of life and some of the local customs it is difficult to understand the mentality and outlook of these basically happy, cheerful people, who can endure so much for so little with patience, dignity and sufferance.

Philosophy

The Nepalese people believe in fate, destiny, 'writing on the wall' and reincarnation. If one had to put on paper what religion they are, the nearest would be Hindu, although farther up in the hills Buddhism is common, and this has intermingled with Hindu rites and ceremonies and the general way of life.

In addition many of the older tribes in Nepal still possess their own customs, which have traces of a pre-Hindu culture. Hence the fact that Brahmins are not required on some occasions by some *jhats* (clans) to perform ceremonies.

Hinduism itself is more of a civilization than a religion. It *is* the way of life, and it is also the spiritual culture of the whole Indian subcontinent. It is tolerant of other beliefs and is by no means fixed or immovable in its own.

One of the governing rules is that of *Samsara*, or the belief that all living things have a succession of lives. This chain of births is governed by the law or principle known as *Kharma*, or action. In other words, the result of virtuous deeds in this life is to be reborn in a higher plane or state, while the result of bad deeds is to be reborn in some lower unpleasant plane, which could be that of an insect or animal or just lower in the caste strata.

Everything they do is tied up with Kharma, because their present position is a direct result of the good or bad deeds of their forefathers. Thus a low-caste individual is resigned to his position, but by striving hard for his Kharma may accept this life as a sacrifice or transient phase in the cycle of rebirth towards a higher plane. Most Hindus (and Buddhists) strive to escape from this wheel of life and death by clocking up as many points as possible for their Kharma and eventually extinguishing the flame of life in the way that the cessation of fanning a fire can result in its dying out. To the Buddhists this is *Nirvana*, or 'bliss unspeakable'. The Hindu may strive to achieve this, as in the case of holy men (sadhus, gurus, purohits, and bhagats) and practitioners of yoga, but for the normal hillman, who for practical reasons cannot devote his life and time to more pious beliefs of self-denial, it is merely something that he is conscious of, and accordingly he tries to behave in such a way as to go forwards rather than backwards in the cycle of existence.

To a certain extent, the higher-caste Brahmins (top caste, 'priests') and Chhetris (traditional warrior caste) have power to control the destinies of the other lower-caste people and are therefore feared and often hated because of their exploitation of this belief.

An unfulfilled Kharma would bind a person still more closely to the wheel of rebirth or Samsara. A fulfilled Kharma at least ensures that the person is reborn a Hindu and perhaps in a sphere more close to that of realization and eventual Nirvana.

Interpreted into everyday life, the Nepali accepts the situation as it is and not necessarily as what it ought to be, what it might have been or what he would like it to be. He is resigned to disaster, failure and loss and accepts it with a type of *c'est-la-vie* complacency. The state in which he finds himself is his problem and no one else's. It is his own personal state and *Dharma* (religion,) and an inevitable consequence of previous acts or retribution. This is *his* Kharma. Therefore it is assumed that he has lived before and will live again to try and achieve the mystical final liberation from material things. This is basic and fundamental to the way in which he conducts his life.

Caste

The system is Hindu, and was probably originally introduced by the Aryan high-caste population who sought refuge in Nepal at the time of the Moslem invasions of India or even before. It divides the society into certain grades or strata:

CASTE	CHARACTERISTICS	NOTES
Brahmin	Pure-bred Indian blood	Wear the *janai* or sacred thread.
Kshatriya	Originally the Indian (Rajput) Warrior Cast	Do not eat meat or eggs
Vaishya	Common man or merchants. Normal	The Gurungs and Magars of the West Nepal area are in this

Hillmen farmers   group, although it is thought
they may really be between it
and Kshatriya

Sudra   Menial caste—artisans

The clan name of Nepalis (Gurkhas) is not a caste. It merely indicates to which *jhat* the individual belongs. Our own organizers, porters and helpers consisted of:

Head Naik	Khagbir Pun (sub-jhat)	Magars		3rd Group
Radio Operator	Gambahadur Pun (sub-jhat)	Magars		3rd Group
Pokhara Base Officer	Bishnuparsad Thapa (sub-jhat)			
Chief Naik under Khagbir	Cheesbahadur Gurung	Gurung		3rd Group
Local HA	3 Puns (sub-jhat)	Magar		3rd Group
Porters	1 Karke (sub-jhat)	Chhetri	High Caste	2nd Group
	1 Ghale (sub-jhat)	Gurung		3rd Group
	1 Lama	Tamang		3rd Group
Other Porters	Gurungs	Gurungs		3rd Group
	Damais / Kamis	(Menial Caste)		4th Group
	Puns	Magars		3rd Group
	Chhetris / Brahmins (2)	(High Caste)		1st and 2nd Group

NOTE: Magars are usually found to the west of the Kali Ghandaki river; Gurungs to the east.

• • •

What is eaten, not eaten and worn is purely relative to caste position. It becomes a question of being 'clean' or 'unclean', and every other festival, daily act and action is connected with this caste position. However, the fact that Brahmins and Kamis carried identical loads alongside each other on the approach march adequately shows that both *jhats* have to work to earn a living. Later, when a high-caste Chhetri lived and worked closely with the other lower-caste Base Camp local porters, he mixed in well and accepted the situation by adapting to it. He ate most things in the end.

History

In the mid eighteenth century a prince of Gorkha—a small hill town midway between Katmandu and Pokhara—raised an Army consisting of Indian-blood Rajputs from that area (Chhetris) and local hillmen of the Gurung and Magar tribes and moved eastwards to besiege Katmandu. After many struggles with the Newar inhabitants and rulers the conquest was complete by 1768. The Prince's name was Prithwi Narayan Shah, and his army became known as the Gorkhas.

Later-generation rulers expanded and consolidated this success, until the whole of Nepal was subjected and the Gorkha (or Gurkha) kingdom extended from Sikkim in the east to the borders of Kashmir in the west. They then went south to the plains of India, but came up against the East India Company and its British troops. An armistice was declared after heavy fighting in 1815, which resulted in the Nepalese borders being redesignated and the Nepalese units being raised to serve the British Crown. A treaty of everlasting friendship was signed (in 1816) and from that point onwards the Nepalese soldiers (Gurkhas) became part of the British Army, to which, to this day, they still come to enlist.

Later, the Eastern tribes (Rail and Limbus) were also recruited, and, together with some lesser-known but other martial tribes, also became known under the general title of *Gurkha*; the language of the Gurkhas became adopted as the national language of Nepal. In 1846 Jangbahadur came to power after what has been recorded in history as the Kot massacre. He was a likely contender for Prime Minister and caught between intrigues of the King, Queen and other nobles and ministers. A fantastic scene resulted, in which sixty-five nobles and ministers with hundreds of other top officials were massacred. Jangbahadur and his own private armies emerged almost unscathed, and the Queen made him Prime Minister. The next day he was appointed Commander-in-Chief by the King. A little later, after further assassination attempts, the King and Queen departed to Benares, leaving an heir as Regent. Before going they gave Jangbahadur supreme authority over all departments, civil and military. This put him in a position whereby he was even able to overrule the King and Queen themselves.

Jangbahadur married his daughters to the King's sons. He visited England, went himself with 12,000 Gurkhas to assist in the Mutiny (1857), and later became absolute in power. He was knighted by Queen Victoria and added the title of Maharaja to his name. He then decided on male agnate as a means of succession. This included a system of hereditary Prime Ministers; thus was established the Rana regime which was to completely dominate all positions of influence in Nepal.

After support to and from the British Crown in both world wars, the local people became displeased, and certain factions grew both from within and from outside. The country itself was virtually closed to the outside world. In November 1950 the King sought refuge in the Indian Embassy, and left for India. An insurrection was launched by the Congress Party (Nepalese), supported by India. Negotiations began, and in early 1951 a democratic form of government was established by proclamation. It kept the existing Rana, Sir Mohan Chamsher, as Prime Minister, but in November 1951 a revision replaced this last Rana Prime Minister with Mr M. P. Koirala of the Congress Party.

In 1955 the old King was succeeded by his son, the present King Mahendra, who shortly afterwards formed a Government under a new Prime Minister. But it remained unstable, and the King took over himself in 1957 in a period of direct rule until the first elections ever held in Nepal took place in 1959. A new Prime Minister was selected by the King, and the Constitution was formally inaugurated in June that year. At the end of 1959, after a period of near chaotic rule, the King dissolved Parliament and suspended the Constitution. He assumed direct rule through a Council of Ministers. He decided that a Western type of Government was unsuitable, and introduced the ancient and proved Indian system of democracy based on village *Panchayats*, or councils. The country was reorganized into zones (14) and districts (75) with village panchayats as necessary in all districts. *Rashtriya*, or National Panchayat, meetings are held quite frequently in Katmandu and are presided over by the King.

Food

The main foods are:

Rice (*dhan*)	Lower terraced slopes
Maize or corn on the cob (*makai*)	Middle region
Wheat (*gahan*)	Middle region
Barley (*jau*)	Middle region
Millet (*kodo*)	For beer or *raksi*
Potatoes (*aln*)	Farther up (about 8,000 ft)
Bananas (*kera*)	Each house up to about 7,000 feet has a small plantation
Oranges (*suntala*)	Plentiful in season in the Pokhara valley area

MEATS	RESTRICTIONS ON EATING ACCORDING TO CASTE			
	Magar	*Gurung*	*Ghale*	*Pun*
Goat (*kasi*)	YES	YES	NO	YES
Chicken (*kukara*)	YES	YES	NO	YES
Buffalo (*rango*)	NO	YES	YES	YES
Pig (*sungur*)	YES	NO	NO	NO
Long-tailed sheep (ram) (*dumba*)	YES	YES	YES	YES

The Sherpas

The name *Sherpa* means 'people from the East'. They have more ties
with Tibet than other eastern tribes, and their true home now is the Sola
Khumbu area, on the upper reaches of the Dudh Kosi river in north-
eastern Nepal, where altitudes range between 10,000 and 13,000 feet.
The main trading centre is Namchhe Bazar. The tribe is very small,
numbering only about 3,000 in Sola Khumbu, but due to their trading
ability and reputation as high-altitude load-carriers they have earned a
lot of money and are probably better off than most people in Nepal.
(This is also the result of various aid programmes, such as Sir Edmund
Hillary's.) Many of them have moved to Darjeeling, over the Indian
border to the east, and a lot more are now earning money through
tourism and trekking organizations in Katmandu.

Sherpas are a hundred per cent Buddhist, with 'Red Hat' sect Lamas.
All of ours, including Tukte, were from Sola Khumbu.

Property and Villages

Nowadays the Land Reform (*Bumi sudar*) officials control the amount
of land that any one family can possess. The average homestead usually
consists of two or three terraced fields, with a grazing area on the *lekh*
farther up. It is a self-contained unit with a few farm animals and its
own crops. But sugar, salt, spices and other material things have to be
bought and the small profit made from a little crop-selling or animal
barter is just enough to pay for this. Some men work on other people's
land for their keep, and may get a percentage of the yield themselves.

Each village will have a *panchayat* (literally 'council of five', but in
practice seven, eight or more men), and the head man on the panchayat
called the *Pradhan Panch*. The panchayat is recognized as an official
Government body and is elected. In addition the old hereditary system
mukya, or village headmen, is still found and they can be a powerful
force in more remote areas. This system, however, is dying out.

• • •

Rest-places

En route to Base Camp several conveniently sited resting-places were seen as a welcome sight to a party rounding a corner after a sweaty struggle uphill.

The rest-places are either stone benches or platforms, usually constructed, under a peepul tree (a large Indian fig-tree of the banyan family, which is regarded as sacred) for the purposes of resting weary travellers and their loads. These rest-places, called *chautaros*, are normally constructed at strategic places up a long hill, and offer shade as well. They may be constructed by a whole village for everyone's benefit, or by a single family to commemorate a relative. Sometimes a long flat stone bench with seats on both sides is made for the same purposes. It may have prayers inscribed on some of the upright stones, and is Buddhist in origin (a *mane*) but often now built in a simplified form by a family or group of people for the benefit of others (and their own Kharma). Rest-houses for travellers are also found: these are known as *dharamsalas* and are merely simple stone and wood buildings for the shelter of animals and travellers. *Dharma* means religion and hence *dharamsala* means a charitable institution, a rest-house built with the aim of religion in mind. (The town of Dharamsala in north-western India, also known as Bakloh and for a time the headquarters of the Dalai Lama and Tibetan refugees, was no doubt built up on the same principle.)

Music

It would be optimistic to expect to hear selections of *sitar* serenades in Nepal. Instead music normally consists of flutes and huge metal horn-type instruments played by the low-caste Damais, although most boys learn to play the flute and *madal*—a double-ended drum, with one end slightly smaller than the other. Both ends are covered in skin held tight by leather thongs; the smaller produces a slightly higher note. The rhythms can vary, but one of the most popular is the quick, pulsating beat of the *juwari nautch* (dance). Some *gits* (songs) are national, but many are peculiar to specific *jhats*, such as Gurung, Magar and Chhetri gits and nautches. Young men called *marunis* impersonate girls in the dancing; the man who takes the real male part is known as the *phursunge*.

Names

Sometimes parents who have lost children in infancy consider that some sort of evil eye or controlled fate is the cause. To protect a new-born child they may associate the child with a lower menial caste by feeding it unclean food or giving it a metal or leather belt to wear (produced by low-caste artisans). They then call the child by one of the menial-caste clan names such as Sarki (leather-worker) or Kami (metal-worker). Our Sirdar, Pasang Kami, was in this category even though he is a Sherpa. At home, children are called according to their title of seniority—i.e., Jetho (oldest son), Sainli (third daughter), etcetera. The Brahmin will however give a formal name, usually associated with religion, astrology, war or the manly virtues. *Bahadur* (brave) is almost an honorific, and follows most names, e.g., *Gambahadur*. However, this is dying out now and most children have more Indian-sounding names.

Death and Burial

All ceremonies cost a lot of money, but the death ceremony can be crippling financially, especially to the sons of a family when their father dies. The formal ceremony need not be carried out immediately and often the sons must save up for years or sell their own possessions to see it through. It must be done.

Apart from the purely religious side, which is expensive, the Gurungs in the west also perform the elaborate *argan* ceremony, which involves buying animals for sacrifice and throwing a huge party worthy of the father. It is very much a 'keeping up with the Joneses' thing, but tradition forces observance of it even when the sons cannot afford it. It can involve the spending of a life's savings or selling of much valuable property.

Holi

Among the many festivals in Nepal we encountered one called Holi. This is a two-day holiday in the month of Phagan (February—March) in honour of Krishna. It is often accompanied by the throwing of red powder after four days. It is a very joyous affair, and the powder (nowadays different psychedelic colours) is thrown and rubbed into anyone passing a village where festivities are in progress. The main party were caught as they left Pokhara on the approach march, and few of them escaped the uninhibited joy of the occasion.

Conclusions

These few words are but a glimpse into the hazy world of oriental enigmas. Many will already understand it more clearly than it is expressed here, but those of us who came to know the people during the expedition will doubtless retain the memories of a warm association with the friendly, hospitable and generous people of Nepal. Several of them became very much part of the expedition, and their contribution was invaluable.

APPENDIX I

Acknowlegements of Assistance in Launching this Expedition

KELVIN KENT

In addition to those mentioned in the text of the book we wish to give our special thanks to the following, who gave us exceptional assistance in various ways.

Individuals

In Nepal

Mr. G. B. Rajbhandari, Minister for Foreign Affairs

Mr. G. P. Burathoki, Minister for Defence

Mr. B. P. Remal, Chief of Protocol

Mr. N. P. Raj Bahandari, Under Secretary for Home Affairs

Mr. S. B. Shah ⎫
Mr. G. B. Shah ⎭ of the department in charge of mountaineering

Mr. Parajuli of the Himalayan Society

Mr. Tokbahadur Lama of the Himalayan Society

Mr. T. J. O'Brien, M.C., British Ambassador in Katmandu with all his staff

Brigadier A. B. Taggart, M.C., Commanding British Gurkha line of communications

Lt.-Col. A. M. Longlands, M.B.E., O/C British Gurkha Recruiting Centre, Paklihawa

Lt.-Col. A. C. Dexter, Commanding Officer, 17 Gurkha Signal Regt.

The Manager, Nepal Bank, Katmandu

In India

We should especially like to express our gratitude to the following for their help in locating Nikki Clough, who was leading an expedition in Kashmir, after the tragic death of her husband:

405

Mr. H. C. Sarin, Chairman of the Indian Mountaineering Federation and Secretary for Defence

Mr. J. A. G. Boon of the British High Commission, New Delhi

In Britain

Major-General H. A. Lascelles, C.B., C.B.E., D.S.O., Director-General of the Winston Churchill Memorial Trust

Major-General A. G. Patterson, C.B., D.S.O., O.B.E., M.C., Director of Army Training

Major-General M. Forrester, C.B., C.B.E., D.S.O., M.C., Chairman, Army Mountaineering Association

Mr. R. D. Lavers of the South-East Asia Department of the Foreign and Commonwealth Office

Mr. H. M. Evans, Editor, *Sunday Times*

Mr. D. Nicholas, Deputy Editor, Independent Television News

Mr. D. Horrabin, Assistant Editor, Independent Television News

Mr. J. Issacs, Controller of Features Programmes, Thames Television

Mr. A. Bridge, Advisor on oxygen equipment

Mr. J. G. Simpson ⎫
Mr. C. D. Brown   ⎬ Williams & Glyn's Bank Ltd.
Miss Esther Roland ⎭

Organisations which gave cash grants

The Winston Churchill Memorial Trust

Whitehall Securities

Organisations and Firms

Abridge Overalls Ltd.	Manufacturers of Borg Fur Suits
Air India	Flight of entire team
Anglo Overseas Transport Co.	Agents handling shipping
L'Appareil Médical de Précision	Oxygen equipment
Ashton Bros. & Co. Ltd.	Ventile cloth
Bahco Condrup Ltd.	Primus stoves
Belwoven Labels	Pictorial clothing labels

Borg Fabrics Ltd.	Suppliers of Borg cloth
F. Ellis Brigham	Tentage
British American Optical Co. Ltd.	Dark glasses
British Fish Canners (Fraserburgh) Ltd.	Tinned fish
British Melamine Tableware Co. Ltd.	Bowls and mugs
British Oxygen	Filling oxygen cylinders
British Ropes Ltd.	Nylon rope
British Visqueen Ltd.	Plastic bags, sacks and tarpaulins
Clifford L. Brown	Sectionized ladders
The Joe Brown Shop	Helmets
B. C. Buhariwala & Sons	Agents in India
James Carr & Sons Ltd.	Nylon tape
Carrington & Dewhurst Industrials Ltd.	Tarpaulins and cotton terylene for Whillans Boxes
Chesterfield Tube Co. Ltd.	Oxygen cylinders
Chouinard	Crampons
Clan Tent Co. Ltd.	Casualty bag
David Clark Co. Inc.	Rhovyl underwear
Clogwyn Climbing Gear	Pitons, Dead Men, etc.
Crosse & Blackwell Ltd.	Tinned fish
Damart	Thermal underwear
John Dewar & Sons Ltd.	Whisky
D. E. Dewhurst	Storage and road transport in Britain
F. Diak & Son	Flares
Dodwell & Co. Ltd.	Agents for Erve bags
Dunlop Ltd.	Material for outer garments and basket-ball boots
Ets Roger Egger	Erve sleeping bags
Ever Ready (G.B.) Ltd.	Batteries
Fine Fare Ltd.	Wide variety of provisions

Functional Clothing Ltd.	Design and supply of special clothing
Gauloises	Cigarettes
M. S. Gibb Ltd.	Windlass winch
R. L. Harrison & Co. Ltd.	Making up Ventile suits
John Harvey	Whisky
G. T. Hawkins Ltd.	Boots
Herring Industry Board	Tinned fish
Karrimor Weathertite Ltd.	Whillans Boxes, rucksacks, overboots, Karrimats
Kodak Ltd.	Film
Robert Lawrie Ltd.	Agents for 'Jumar'
Lloyds Machinery Packing Co. Ltd.	Packing for air freight
Lockwood & Brown	Nanga Parbat socks
Andrew Lusk & Co. Ltd.	Food packers
Macarthy's Ltd.	'Savory & Moore' glacier cream and lip salve
Mallory Batteries Ltd.	Wireless batteries
Marks & Spencer Ltd.	Sweaters and underwear
Marshall & Co. (Aberdeen) Ltd.	Tinned fish
Walter Marti	Manufacturer of Jumars
Millar Gloves Ltd.	Millarmitts
Sacs Millet S.A.	Hauling bags
Mishawaka Rubber Co. Inc.	Vapour-barrier boots
Morlands	Sheepskin coats and boots
Mountain Equipment Ltd.	Down gear and light tents
Omega Watch Co. (England) Ltd.	Wristwatches
Philips Electrical Ltd.	Tape recorder, radio, electric shavers and transcriber
H. Pickles & Sons Ltd.	Breeches
Pindisports Ltd.	Sole retail supplier
Pneumatic Tent Co. Ltd.	Tentage and camping gear
Richard Pontvert S.A.	H.A. Boots

The Prestige Group Ltd.	Pressure cookers and knives
Price's Patent Candles Co. Ltd.	Candles
Pye Telecommunications Ltd.	'Bantam' walkie-talkie radios
Racal-BCC Ltd.	H.F. Radios
Rank Audio Visual Ltd.	Pentax and Nikon cameras
Red Rose Products Ltd.	Kite and bags
Riri	Nylon zips
Ronson Products Ltd.	Lighters
Shelley Press Ltd.	Printing
Shirley Institute	Consultation and advice on material
Smith & Nephew	Lasso Proof adhesive tape
Spanset Ltd.	Nylon tape
Stewart & Son of Dundee Ltd.	Whisky
P. & C. Suswin Ltd.	Manufacturers of outer clothes
Swiss Cutlery (London) Ltd.	Knives
Tate & Lyle Ltd.	Sugar
Third Eye Tours & Travel (P) Ltd.	Travel agents in Katmandu
Troll Products Climbing Equipment	Harnesses
Turner Bros. Asbestos Co. Ltd.	Fibreglass domes and sledge
Willis & Bates Ltd.	Pressure lanterns
W. D. & H. O. Wills	Cigarettes

GLOSSARY

Abseil Method of descending by sliding down the rope (in our case always on the fixed rope, using a karabiner brake attached to the sit harness to create friction and slow down the rate of descent).

Acclimatization The process of becoming accustomed to climbing at altitude where the air is thin.

Anchor The point where fixed ropes are anchored, on rock by a piton hammered into a crack, on ice by an ice-screw, on snow by a dead man or snow-stake. Anchor-points are close together on traverses—where possible, every ten feet or so—and even on straight-up sections are placed every sixty feet or so to avoid too much rope stretch.

Arête A ridge—used specifically in this book for a narrow, very sharp ridge.

Belay The safeguard of all climbers in a party who are not actually moving. On the South Face, with the extensive use of fixed rope, the only time a belay was used was when the climber going out in front to make the route for the first time was belayed by his second man. This entails the second man's attaching himself to the mountain by one of the methods mentioned under **Anchor**, and then paying the rope out either around his waist or over his shoulder, so that he can hold the leader if he happens to fall. The leader can also protect himself by **Running Belays**.

Bergschrund The last big crevasse beneath a rock face or steep slope at the head of a glacier or ice-slope.

Bridging A method of climbing chimneys and corners by using opposing pressure of arms and feet against the two sides. This can also be used on an open face by using the same technique on holds.

Bulge A rounded overhang.

Chimney A fissure in a rock or ice wall which will admit the body.

Col A pass or, as in the case of the Col on the Ice Ridge, a major dip in a ridge with access on at least one side.

Cornice An overhanging lip of snow.

Couloir A gully.

Crampons Forged strips of steel fitted with spikes which are strapped to the soles of climbing-boots for climbing ice or snow. All the crampons we used had twelve points, with the front pair sticking forwards.

Crevasse A split in the surface of the glacier caused by a change in the angle of the slope underneath that of its course.

Dead man A snow anchor shaped rather like the blade of a shovel, with a spliced wire running through two holes in it. The dead man is pushed or hammered into the snow and the wire pulls it deeper into it, so that the harder you pull the more secure it becomes.

Exposure The feeling of a long drop below the climber's feet; also the effects of being exposed to severe weather and exhaustion in the mountains, which can lead to rapid collapse, particularly at altitude.

Fixed rope This is the method used on long climbs to enable climbers in a party to ferry equipment up a mountain, passing up and down over a period of time. The rope is attached by different kinds of anchor and remains *in situ* for the entire course of the climb.

Glacier A river of ice.

Harness A nylon webbing harness used to sit back in whilst jumaring up fixed ropes, and also as a waist or chest attachment for the climbing-rope.

Ice-piton A piton specially designed for use in hard snow or ice. This is hammered into the ice.

Ice-screw This is a piton equipped with some kind of screw formation so that it can be screwed into the ice and easily removed for unscrewing. This gives the most secure ice anchor.

Jumar A device for climbing fixed ropes. It works on a ratchet principle, sliding up the rope but gripping it under tension. We also used Cloggers and Hiebelers for climbing the fixed ropes; these are described in Appendix B.

Karabiner A metal snap-link, in our case made from alloy, which used to clip the rope into pitons or anchors and for carrying pitons and other gear. Karabiners, linked together, can also be used as a brake whilst abseiling.

Layback A method of climbing cracks and flakes by gripping the edge with the hands, leaning back and placing the feet against the rock and pressing onto it.

Leader The climber going out in front with the rope.

Monsoon An annual front of warm, wet winds which hits Nepal around the end of May, making climbing extremely dangerous if not impossible. The climbing season is limited by the thawing of winter snows at one end and the arrival of the monsoon at the other. There is also a climbing season after the monsoon in September and before the arrival of the winter snows around November.

Objective dangers Dangers over which the climber has no control, such as stonefall, ice avalanches and crevasses.

Overhang Rock or ice beyond the perpendicular.

Pitch Section of climbing between two stances or belay points. These might be of any length, depending on the length of the climbing-rope. Since we usually climbed on the 500-foot-reels of the fixed rope, pitches were often as long as 200 feet.

Piton A piece of metal designed to be hammered into a crack in a rock face to serve as a belay, anchor-point for fixed rope or running belay.

Protection The quantity and quality of running belays used to make a pitch safe to lead.

Ridge The line on which two sides or faces of a mountain meet.

Rognon An island of rock or solid ground in the middle of a glacier.

Running belay This (also known simply as a runner) is an intermediate belay point where the rope runs through a karabiner attached to the anchor-point so that a fall by one of the climbers—usually the leader— is reduced. In other words, if the leading man is fifty feet above his second he would fall a hundred feet if there were no runners in position, but if he has a running belay six feet below him, although he is still fifty feet above his second, he will fall only twelve feet before the rope is brought tight.

Sérac A wall or tower of ice in an icefall or glacier.

Slab A stretch of rock inclined at roughly between 30° and 70° to the vertical.

Sling A short length of nylon tape or rope tied into a loop and carried over the shoulder or round the neck for use on running belays, belays or anchor-points for fixed rope. It can also be used to carry karabiners and pitons.

Snowfield An expanse of snow, sometimes set at quite a steep angle.

Soloing Climbing without the security of a rope.

Stance The place where the climber makes his belay, ideally somewhere where it is possible to stand or sit comfortably.

Step-cutting Cutting steps in snow or ice with an ice-axe.

Tension traverse Leaning out on the rope to allow the climber to edge his way across a holdless section.

White-out A condition when either driving snow or cloud on a snow face makes it impossible to distinguish between solid features and cloud.

Index

Abominable Snowmen, 63, 71–75
acclimatization, 9, 15, 92–93, 115,
    122, 134, 180, 194, 379–81
Alaska, 3, 6, 25
Alpine Club, 31
Alps, climbing in, 4
altitude sickness, 91, 99–100, 103, 138
Ang Nyima, 22
Ang Pema, 16, 54
    Base, 91, 207
    I to II, 192–93
    II to III, 113, 116, 134
    III to IV, 202
    IV to V, 248–49
    background, 55
    eye infection, 207
    role in expedition, 55–56
Ang Temba, 55
Annapurna, South Face
    ascent. See approach march; summit
        from Base Camp, 87
    campsites. See Base Camp; camp
        siting strategy; Temporary
        Base Camp; specific Camps
    description and views on, 6–7, 69,
        70, 81–82, 88
    expedition team. See team aspects
    first sight, 78
    preparations, 30–49
    reconnaissance, 23, 46, 70–71
    selection, 18–29
    strategy for ascent. See strategy;
        team aspects
    televised account of expedition.
        See photography; television
        team
Annapurna Glacier, 63, 81–82, 92, 196

routes across, 89–91, 93, 97–99
    'Sword of Damocles,' 103, 116,
    147, 176, 299
    view from Camp I, 96–97
Annapurna I, 18, 52
    1950 French expedition, 18, 20–21
    1969 German expedition, 22–23, 75
    1970 Army expedition, 262
    description, 21
Annapurna II, 6, 22, 59, 122, 263, 282
Annapurna III, 21, 22, 52, 83–84, 122
Annapurna IV, 22, 122
Annapurna South. See Modi Peak
Annapurna South Glacier, 222
Apollo XIII moonshot, 177
approach march, 50–69, 58
    Temporary Base to Base, 112
    Base to I, 91–97
    I to II, 100–104
    II to III, 110–11, 118–27, 149–50
    III to IV, 127–33, 143–47
    IV to V, 147, 150–51, 165–75
    V to VII attempt, 263–89
    Ice Ridge, first attempt, 118–22,
        125–26, 137, 144, 152–61, 156
    Ice Ridge, second attempt,
        166–87, 179
    statistics, 306–10
    summit, 289, 289–90
    summit ascent, 247–60, 272, 273–92
    summit ascent support, 261–72
Ardgour, Great Gully, 12
Argentière, North Face, 5
Army Mountaineering Association
    (A.M.A.), 34–35, 47, 50, 51, 95
assistance, acknowledgements of,
    405–9

avalanches
    between II and III, 147
    at V, 197, 229, 262
    death of Ian Clough, 299–300
    at Fang, 127, 129
    on Ice Ridge, 169
    threat, 6–7, 69, 77, 82, 87, 89,
        110, 114, 127–31, 142, 149

Baltoro, Paigu Peak, 19
Base Camp, 52, 86
    on ascent, 83, 84–88, 103
    daily routine, 56, 139–40, 145
    description, 57, 84
    reconnaissance for, 71
    return of Clough's body to, 300–302
    South Face from, 87
    supplies to, 113, 140
    team returns to, 136–51, 162–64,
        180, 243, 298, 300–302
    view from Camp I, 96
Bhutan, 19
Bishnuparsad Thapa, Lt., 40, 48, 131
Blakeney, Tom, 31
Blue Nile expedition (1968), 2
Bonington, Chris, 16
    Temporary Base, 108–12
    Base, 298–99
    I, 91–97, 99–100, 203
    II, 100–101, 103–4, 116–17, 146,
        147, 149
    III, 122–26, 127, 160, 161, 189,
        247, 294, 296
    III to IV, 128–33, 194–96
    IV, 152, 160, 164, 165–87
    IV to V, 191, 252
    V, 253–55, 261–63, 265–66, 278
    V to VI, 247–60, 265–67, 269,
        279, 284
    VI, 283, 286–87
    across Glacier, 89–91
    administrative duties, 81, 133, 146
    Annapurna II 1960 expedition, 6,
        22, 59
    background, 1, 28
    on the challenge of climbing, 26–28
    decision not to try for summit, 267
    on the feel of the expedition, 145–46
    gear list and statistics, 313–33
    health problems, 104–5, 203, 207,
        243
    on Ian Clough's death, 303
    Ice Ridge, first attempt, 118–26,
        161
    Ice Ridge, second attempt,
        166–87, 179
    impressions of South Face, 7, 38,
        69, 78, 81–82, 87
    on leadership, 28–29, 30, 126
    lecture activities, 31, 33
    preparations, 30–46, 66. See also
        approach march
    returns to Base Camp, 136–51,
        196, 203, 207
    strategy development. See strategy
Bonington, Wendy, 2, 124
Boysen, Martin, 16, 46–47, 224
    I, 103–4
    II, 111, 113, 116, 268
    III, 134, 135, 138
    III to IV, 194
    IV, 146–47, 150–51, 160, 191,
        203, 209, 228, 231, 232
    V, 204–5, 213, 225, 247, 251, 274,
        275–76
    VI, 251
    across Ice Ridge, 152–61, 156,
        166, 167
    background and style, 3–4
    at the Col, 113
    conception of expedition, 3
    health problems, 115, 251, 276
    preparations, 54
    on South Face, 7
Breitenbach, John, 55
Broad Peak, 25
Brown, Joe, 69
Buhariwala, Freddie, 38
Bühl, Hermann, 25
Burke, Mick, 16, 46–47, 78, 190, 211,
    260
    Temporary Base, 81, 84

Base to I, 91, 92, 93
I, 95–97, 99–100, 103, 134
II, 150, 244, 299
III to IV, 161, 171–72, 191, 199, 268
IV to V, 198, 202, 203–4, 243
V, 198, 204, 204–5, 207, 225–29,
    232, 270, 287
VI, 295–97
across Glacier, 89–91
background, 9–10
bid for the summit, 293–98
on death of Ian Clough, 299–300
diary entry, 228–29
Flat Iron, 241–42
health problems, 99, 103, 115,
    134, 146, 171–72
on Ice Cliff, 189
request for lead, 180
Rock Band, 207, 214–29, 219
Busk, Sir Douglas, 31, 66

Camp I, 83, 94, 95, 309
    as advanced base, 203
    on ascent, 91–97, 99–100, 145, 176
    view from, 96–97
Camp II, 102, 114
    avalanches, 142
    establishment, 83, 101–4
    statistics, 309
    as supply base, 146–47
    team movements through, 109, 113,
        116, 122–23, 138, 142, 147, 150
Camp III, 111, 114
    establishment, 83, 111
    as resting base, 171, 189
    statistics, 309
    team movements through, 115,
        125–27, 131, 135, 138, 142,
        145, 147, 150, 160
Camp IV, 83, 309
    on Ice Ridge first attempt, 132,
        145, 146, 150, 156, 160, 164
    on Ice Ridge second attempt,
        167–75, 168, 184
    preparation for the summit, 243,
        251

shunts to Camp V, 200–202, 209,
    212–13, 234–35, 243, 252–53,
    270
camp siting strategy, 83, 101,
    309–10
Camp V, 208
    establishment, 83
    movement of team through, 189,
        191, 197, 224–29, 243, 253–55,
        261–63, 273–76
    statistics, 309
    transfer to new site, 200–203
Camp VI
    establishment, 83, 191, 228, 229
    movement of team through, 251,
        258–59, 267, 270, 278–80,
        283–88, 295–97
    statistics, 309
Camp VII attempts, 212, 261, 262,
    265, 276, 285–89
caste system, 396–98
Chacaraju, 119
Cheesbahardur, 56, 112
Cheney, Mike, 41, 45
Chicheter, Sir Francis, 30
Chogolisa, 25
Chomro, 64, 106
Chondracot, 60
Cho Oyu, 18
Chorley, Roger, 6
Chouinard, Yvon, 215
Chusan, 34
clothes and footwear, 96
    boots, 159, 319
    Dachstein Mitts, 110, 285, 297, 319
    eye protection, 319–20
    for final summit attempt, 296
    list and statistics, 314–16, 317–19
    of porters, 76, 77, 107, 133
Clough, Ian
    Temporary Base, 106–8
    Base Camp, 180, 210
    I, 134, 232
    II, 142, 147, 149, 299
    II to III, 138, 142, 147, 161, 199
    III, 160, 196, 294

III to IV, 202
IV, 160, 164, 209, 247, 251
V, 207
VI, 269, 270, 271, 286–87
across Ice Ridge, 169–75, 177–78
background and style, 9, 12, 31,
    252–53
burial ceremony, 302
death, 299–302
health problems, 115, 210, 271
preparations, 32, 37, 47, 49, 66, 79
Clough, Nikki, 106, 210, 252
Col, The, 106–17, 230. *See also*
    Camp III
    first approach, 110–11
    second approach, 186
    supplies to, 116, 206
    communications
    mail systems, 63, 361–62
    radio, 39–40, 45, 65, 109, 112,
        199–202, 208–9, 233–40, 257,
        358–61, 362
Coolie Lama, 41, 106, 112
Cordillera Blanca, 14
Cox, David, 6, 7, 21

Davies, Dennis, 22
'dead man,' 97, 99, 120, 125, 131,
    132, 158–59, 186
Dhaulagiri, 20
Dienburger, 25
Dix, Paul, 25
Downes, Bob, 100
drinking water, 96, 102
Droites, North Face, 5
drugs, 99–100, 105, 386–91
Drus, South-West Pillar, 10

Edwards, John, 16, 16, 43, 133,
    141–42, 163, 176–77, 203, 225
Eiger, North Wall, 5, 9, 31
Eiger, Second Icefield, 11, 215
Eiger, Third Icefield, 215, 222
Eiger Direct (1966 expedition), 4, 5,
    10
equipment, 25, 32–33. *See also*

clothes and footwear; photography
    crampons, 149, 159
    Customs and import permits, 37,
        39, 41–42, 43, 45, 79
    Dexion strip/stake, 121, 125
    entrenching-tool, 185, 276, 280
    ice-axe ice-hammer combination,
        215
    ice-pitons, 125, 154, 184, 185,
        216–17
    ice-screws, 132–33, 152, 154, 157
    inventory and statistics, 313–33,
        325–28
    jumar clamp, 120, 130, 155, 166,
        190, 193, 242
    karabiner, 125, 184, 215
    ladders, 162
    preparation of, 32–33, 34
    radio, 39–40, 45, 65, 109, 112,
        199–202, 208–9, 233–40, 257,
        277–78, 358–61, 362
    RAFMA tent, 189, 205, 254, 257,
        274, 327
    rope shortages, 186, 198, 212,
        223, 264
    rope sling, 170
    shipping, 34–38, 49, 65, 66
    sit harness, 173
    tent inventory, 325–28
    theodolite, 82
    Whillans Whammer, 102, 198
    windlass winch, 161
Estcourt, Carolyn, 3
Estcourt, Nick, 16, 46–47, 224
    Base to I, 91, 92
    Base to III, 134, 135
    I, 95, 103–4
    II, 111
    III, 138
    III to IV, 194
    IV, 146–47, 150, 160, 191, 202,
        203, 209–10, 232, 243
    IV to V, 166, 168, 198, 204, 205, 263
    V, 228, 251, 254, 258–59, 261–63,
        275–76, 277
    across Ice Ridge, 155–61, 160, 166

background, 4, 82
chest pains, 210
at Col, 113, 116
conception of expedition, 3
diary and statistics, 305–13
near-suffocation from snowdrift,
275–76
preparations, 54
strategy development, 7, 81–82,
236–38
as surveyor, 82–83
use of oxygen, 263
Evans, Sir Charles, 22, 31, 82
expedition assistance, acknowledg-
ments, 405–9

Fang, 21, 52, 94, 127, 129, 279
financial aspects, 23, 30–32, 43, 60,
81, 405–9
Flat Iron, 214, 223, 227, 241–42, 256,
258, 264, 274, 277
Fluted Peak, 52, 87, 282
food. *See also* drinking water
Base, 55–57, 139
I, 95–96
II, 122–23
IV, 172, 178, 191
V, 204–5, 225, 230, 254, 266
VI, 279, 283–84, 295
from A.M.A., 95
on approach march, 60, 61, 77, 83
cooking gear inventory, 328–30
high-altitude rations, 122–23
of Nepalese, 59–60
organization, 32
of porters, 67
purchase of local, 40, 60, 63, 64–65
rations inventory and menu
plans, 336–58
France, 18, 20–21
Franco-Swiss climbers, 240, 248, 249
Frêney, Central Pillar (1961 expedi-
tion), 9, 11
Frost, Tom, 16, 46
Base, returns to, 136, 302
II, 113, 116–17, 147, 244

III, 119–26
III to IV, 130–33, 134–35, 161
IV, 268
V, 198, 202, 203–4, 224–29, 232,
270, 287
VI, 294, 295–96
background, 13–14
bid for the summit, 293–98
diary entries, 202, 221–22, 228,
229, 240–41, 246, 295–96,
297–98
fall into crevasse, 214–15
Flat Iron, 241–42
on Ice Cliff, 189
religious beliefs, 14, 123–24, 298
Rock Band, 207, 214–29
on strategy of front selection,
180–81
frostbite, 271, 383–84

Gambahadur Pun, 16, 40, 65, 203
Ganga Bahadur Pun, Corporal, 112
Gangapurna, 21, 22, 122, 173, 282
Gasherbrum III, 19
Gaurishankar (1964 expedition), 9,
11–12, 84
Germany, 22–23, 75
Ghandrung, 40–41, 56, 61, 62,
63–64, 79
Gilbey, Cynthia, 16
Glacier Dome, 21, 22, 23, 52, 87
Glen Coe, 9, 12–13
Gosainthan, 18–19, 20
Grandes Jorasses, 9, 88
Grant, Dick, 22
Greenfield, George, 13, 30–32
Greissl, Ludwig, 22–23, 81
Gurkhas, 39–40, 41, 112, 192
culture, 56, 397
pension paying-post, 48, 53
Gurung tribe, 56, 396

Haaser, Günther, 22
Hagemuler, Jean-Marie, 248
Hankinson, Alan, 16–17, 84, 103,
141, 203, 232

Harlin, John, 5
Harrison Rocks, Tunbridge Wells, 3
Haston, Dougal, 16, 46–47, 80, 292
  approach to Base Camp, 80, 81, 82
  Base Camp, 91, 150, 162–64, 203
  I, 99, 111
  II, 100–101, 103–4, 109–10
  III, 120, 125, 126, 127, 170, 295
  III to IV, 128, 130, 135, 138–39,
    142–43, 175
  IV, 143, 146–47, 151, 178, 243, 251
  V, 247, 253–54, 273, 275–78
  V to VI, 197–98, 199–201, 245,
    274–78
  VI, 258, 264, 270, 278–83,
    286–88, 290
  VII attempts, 284–89
  across Glacier, 89–91
  background, 4–5, 138
  the Col, 110–11, 121
  Ice Cliffs, 188–89, 197–98
  Ice Ridge, 144, 182–87
  loss of gear, 254–78, 277
  philosophy of climbing, 273
  on strategy of front selection,
    180, 181, 182
  at summit, 289–90
  summit ascent, 272, 273–92
Hauser, Günther, 23, 81
Hawkinson, Alan, 16
Hawley, Liz, 47
health aspects
  altitude sickness, 91, 99–100, 103,
    138
  altitude sickness pills, 99–100
  blood-poisoning, 104–5, 251
  chest pains, 203, 207, 210, 243
  diarrhoea, 176, 269
  dysentery, 176, 207
  effects of cold, 175, 185, 189, 269,
    284–85. See also frostbite
  exhaustion, 108, 170–71, 175,
    177, 195–96, 205, 213–14
  exposure, 109, 137, 270
  eye infection, 207
  influenza, 115, 138, 150, 189

  line of retreat, 26
  local population, 61–62, 377–78
  medications, 99–100, 105, 386–91
  paraffin fumes, 131, 138, 192, 229
  personal hygiene, 140–41
  piles, 115, 243
  pulmonary oedema, 99–100, 231
  recommended equipment, 391–92
  salt deficiency, 382
  sleeping-tablets, 168, 177, 266
  snow-blindness, 385
  supply organization and
    inventory, 371–92
  toothache, 266
  ulcerated tongue, 189, 191, 208
  vaccinations, 372–76
  vertigo, 131
Herbert, Wally, 30
Herzog, Maurice, 18, 20–21, 145,
  303
Hillary, Sir Edmund, 20, 115, 244
Himalayan Society, 41, 45
Himalayas, historical background of
  expeditions, 18–23
Hinko Cave, 52, 63, 67, 72, 106–7
Hispar Glacier, Ogre Peak, 19
Hiunchuli, 21, 51, 52, 255
Hunt, Lord John, 31, 244
Huntingdon, West Face, 25

Ice Cliffs, Annapurna South Face, 7,
  188–89, 194–98. See also Camp V
Ice Ridge, Annapurna South Face, 7,
  71, 98, 128
  elevation, 83
  first attempt, 118–22, 125–26,
    137, 144, 152–61, 156
  second attempt, 166–87, 179
Independent Television News
  (I.T.N.), 16, 48, 203, 364–66
India, 33, 34–35
International School of Modern
  Mountaineering, 5

Jackson, Frank, 16, 145, 176
Jannu, 26

Japan, 20, 22, 83–84
Jones, Chris, 25
jumars. *See* equipment, jumar clamp

Kancha, 16, 75, 81, 91, 248, 265–66
Kangchenjunga, 18, 22, 31, 82
Kantega, 14
Karakorum, 11, 19
Katmandu, 35–36, 37–45
Kent, Kelvin, 16
　　Temporary Base, 106–8, 112, 133,
　　　134
　　Base, 131, 137, 140, 203
　　I, 176
　　II, 240
　　III, 247, 249–50
　　IV, 250–51, 265
　　background, 15, 39
　　organization ability, 137, 140
　　preparations, 35, 39–46, 53, 65–66
　　role in the expedition, 81, 103
Khagbir Pun, Lt., 54, 79, 107
　　background, 41, 56
　　food purchase, 63
　　leadership ability, 50–51, 76, 79, 112
Khumjung, 115
Knox-Johnston, Robin, 30
K.2, 18

Lachenal, 21
Lambert, David, 16, 43, 107. *See also*
　　health aspects
　　II, 299
　　III, 232, 294
　　IV, 247, 251, 265
　　acclimatization problems, 134, 267
　　background, 14–15
　　healthcare to local population,
　　　61–62, 377–78
　　healthcare to porters, 76
　　healthcare to team, 91, 104–5,
　　　109, 207, 210
　　preparations, 35, 36
　　supply transport by, 191, 267–68
Lane, Jonathan, 16, 42, 142
Lhotse, 18

'London Sherpas,' 145, 162, 176,
　　191, 203, 207, 232, 302
Lumle, 58, 60

Machapuchare, 6, 21–22, 51, 52, 64,
　　65
　　Base Camp, 62, 63, 71, 76
　　Flats, 107
MacInnes, Hamish, 10
Magar tribe, 56, 396, 397
mail systems, 361–62, 363
Makalu, 18
Mallory, George Leigh, 26
Manaslu, 18
Masherbrum, 11, 15, 100
Matterhorn, 19
medications, 99, 105, 386–91
Mingma Tsering, 16, 113, 138, 142,
　　147, 203, 249, 268, 300
Mini Rock Band, 265, 268
Miristi Khola, 20
Modi Khola gorge, 21, 60, 62, 65, 68,
　　302–3
Modi Peak, 21, 51, 52, 85, 94, 255
monsoon season, 24, 223, 259, 271
Mountain Travel, 41
Mount Everest
　　1953 British expedition, 4, 15, 18, 20
　　1963 American expedition, 19
　　1960 Chinese expedition, debate, 19
　　1965 Indian expedition, 113
　　1969 Japanese expedition, 20, 116
　　accident at Khumbu Icefall, 116
　　Western Cwm, 103
　　West Ridge, 55
Mount Everest Foundation, 31–32
Mount McKinley, 14
Muktinath, 58

Naiks, 34, 41, 50, 51, 56, 112
Nally, Brian, 11
Namche Bazaar, 54
Nanga Parbat, 18, 20
Nautanwa, 40, 79
Nepal, 33, 59
　　access to climbers, 3, 5, 20, 22, 64

culture, 59–60, 61–62, 64, 79,
    394–98, 402–3
    education, 62, 115
    food, 400
    historical background, 44, 398–99
    names, 403
    property and villages, 401
    shipping equipment to, 34
    travel in, 58–59, 402
New Delhi, 47
Nima Tsering, 16, 113, 115, 138,
    141, 142, 149, 150, 203, 249
Nuptse, 6, 7, 8, 38, 268

Owens, Gary, 262
oxygen
    disadvantages, 26, 269
    effects of deprivation, 216,
        230–31, 378
    equipment used, 334
    loss of supplies in shipping, 66
    plan, 26, 181, 335
    recommendations, 336
    supply at Camp IV, 192
    supply at Camp V, 212, 252, 259,
        262–63, 267
    unaided climbing height, 8
    use of, 8, 181, 262–63

Pallarton, Jean-Louis, 248
Pasang Kami, 16, 54–55, 63, 78,
    108–9, 176, 207, 301
Patagonia, 80
    Cerro Torre, 5
    Fortress, 9
    Towers of Paine, 9, 11, 84
Patey, Tom, 12, 13
Pemba Tharkay, 16, 71, 75, 91, 116,
    134, 192–93, 202, 248–49, 268
photography. See also television
    team
    ciné, 225, 266–67, 364–67
    equipment and Customs, 39, 43
    need for a record, 182
    self-portraits on the summit, 296
    still, 368–71

Pirie-Gordon, Pat, 31
Pokhara, 35, 39–40, 41, 46–49, 84
porters, 51, 53, 65
    Temporary Base, 106–8, 111–12
    Base to I, 92, 95
    clothes and footwear, 76, 77, 107,
        133, 333
    daily life, 67
    Franco-Swiss visitors, 240, 248, 249
    'London Sherpas,' 145, 162, 176,
        191, 203, 207, 232
    personnel and statistics, 50, 311
    relationship with Sherpas, 116–17
    salary, 43, 60, 106, 112
    selection, 41, 56
preparation for expedition, 3–17,
    30–49
Pun sub-tribe, 56, 397

radio. See communications, radio
Rawlison, Anthony, 31
recreation, 60–61, 64, 75, 104, 141,
    162
religious aspects, 14, 56, 75, 123–24,
    298, 403–4
rescue management, 378
Ridlington, Peter, 131
Roberts, Dave, 25
Roberts, Lt.-Col. J.O.M. "Jimmy,"
    6–7, 21, 22, 41, 50, 55
Rock Band, 219–20, 260, 282. See
    also Camp VI; Flat Iron
    climb across, 198, 199–201,
        206–23, 264–65
    elevation, 26, 83
    strategy, 71
rock falls, 220–21
Roc Noir, 23, 52
Rognon, 76, 82, 91–93, 92, 95. See
    also Camp I
Ross, Paul, 10
Royal Geographical Society, 31

Sanctuary, The, 21, 22, 57, 63, 67,
    70–88
Seti Khola gorge, 51

Sherpas
  culture, 54, 56, 64, 75, 401
  relationship with, 116–17
Smith, Robin, 5
Sola Khumbu, 54, 56
Soldini, John, 16, 42–43
Sonam Tenzing, 16
South Col, 55
South Face. *See* Annapurna, South
  Face
South Ridge, Everest, 19
State of Kerala, 35, 47
strategy. *See also* team aspects
  across Ice Ridge, 169–70, 178
  ascent of the team, 115–16, 146,
    206, 212
  front members selection, 115,
    180–81, 235–38
  initial, 7, 8–9, 23, 71, 79–80
  line of retreat, 26
  size of party, 24–26
  summit approach, 191, 233–40,
    245–46, 259, 265
  supply lines, 26, 79
  timing, 24
summit, 289–90. *See also* Camp VII
  attempts
supplies. *See* clothes and footwear;
  drinking water; equipment; food
'Sword of Damocles,' 103, 116, 147,
  176, 299

Tangley, Lord, 31
Taylor, Tim, 40
team aspects
  leadership and discipline, 28–29, 107
  morale, 99, 241
  personnel and statistics, 310–13
  selection for expedition, 3–5, 8–17
  selection for summit ascent, 27,
    223–24, 235–40, 244–46, 265
  strategy of front selection, 115,
    180–81, 235–38
  tensions and grievances, 104,
    235–40
television team, 15, 47. *See also*

photography
  Base Camp, 140–41
  I, 203
  adaptations to Nepal, 67
  communication with Bonington,
    133
  filming sessions, 108, 142
  hardship of ciné-camera trans
    port, 266–67
  meeting Whillans and Haston on
    descent, 295
  personnel and statistics, 312
  radio contact with Pokhara, 112
Temporary Base Camp, 52, 73,
  111–12
  arrival, 78–79
  on ascent, 80–81, 83–84
  supply transport to, 76, 104, 106–8
Tensing, 20, 244
Tent Peak, 122
Terray, Robin "Rob the Gob," 16,
  144, 176, 302
Thames Television, 16
theodolite, 82–83
Thomo, 68, 106
Thompson, Mike, 16
Temporary Base, supply transport
  to, 107–8
  Base, 150, 299
  I, 134
  II, 138
  III, 142, 189, 196, 208, 268, 294–95
  III to IV, 194
  IV, 191, 208, 228, 231, 232, 243
  background and style, 14, 189
  health problems, 189, 191, 208,
    243
  Ice Cliff, 230
  organization of food, 32, 122–23
  oxygen deprivation, 230–31
  preparations, 35–36, 40, 46
  reconnaissance, 46, 62–63, 71, 72
'Tibetan Joe' mail carrier, 362
Tillman, Bill, 22
Tint Peak, 87
traverses, 274

"Terrible Traverse," 166, 167, 169, 170, 184, 230
"Traverse of the Devil," 160
Trivor, 11
Tukte, 16, 56, 57, 109, 137, 197

water. *See* drinking water
West Ridge, Everest, 19
Whillans, Don, 16, 291
 Temporary Base approach, 76, 77
 Base approach, 80, 81, 82
 Base, 91, 150, 162–64, 203
 I, 99
 II, 100–101, 103–4, 109, 111
 III, 119–26, 175–76, 295
 III to IV, 128, 130, 131, 134–35, 138–39
 IV, 146–47, 172, 243
 V, 247, 250, 251, 275–78
 V to VI, 197–98, 199–201
 VI, 264, 270, 278–84, 286–88, 290
 VII attempts, 284–86, 288–89
 on Abominable Snowmen, 63, 71–75
 background and style, 10–12, 15, 80, 138, 182
 birthday, 250
 the Col, 110–11, 121
 Glacier, 89–91
 health problems, 100, 131
 Ice Cliffs, 189, 198–98
 preparations, 32, 35, 36
 reconnaissance, 46, 62–63, 69, 70–72
 sit harness by, 173
 strategy development, 171–72, 181–82, 206, 239
 summit, 289, 289–90
 summit ascent, 272, 273–92
Whillans Box by. *See* Whillans Box
Whillans Whammer by, 102, 198
Whillans Box, 84–85, 99, 113, 121, 122, 147, 148, 156, 182, 192–93, 250, 326–27
wind
 adaptations, 84

on Ice Ridge, 167–68
near the summit, 297
V to VI, 270, 279, 287
Winston Churchill Trust fellowship, 32
Wylie, Lt.-Col. Charles, 15, 31

yeti. *See* Abominable Snowmen
Yeupaja, East Face, 25
Yosemite, 13

adrenaline classics ®

Other exciting titles from Adrenaline Classics ®

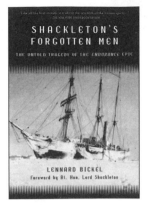

SHACKLETON'S FORGOTTEN MEN:
The Untold Tragedy of the Endurance Epic

By Lennard Bickel; foreword by Rt. Hon. Lord
Shackleton, K. C., P. C., O. D. E.

This thrilling account tells the tragic story of a supplementary expedition that Shackleton launched—
but did not lead—to lay support depots across the
Great Ross Ice Shelf in preparation for his own party.
$14.95 ($23 Canada), 256 pages

> "Like all the best stories, it is about the
> triumph of the human spirit."
> —*The New York Times*

EVEREST: Alone at the Summit

by Stephen Venables

When accomplished climber and writer Stephen
Venables and three companions set out to climb
Everest's fearsome Kangshung Face, the experts
predicted disaster. They were very nearly right.
$14.95 ($23 Canada); 288 pages

> "One of the most impressive climbs of the past
> three decades—my idea of true adventure."
> —Reinhold Messner

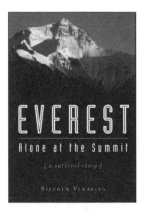

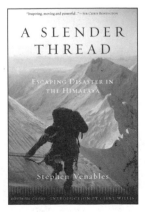

A SLENDER THREAD:
Escaping Disaster in the Himalayas

By Stephen Venables

A Slender Thread tells the gripping tale of the award-
winning author's against-all-odds survival after a
near-fatal plunge off one of the world's highest
mountains. This is not only a spellbinding account
of Venables' survival—but of his intense personal
struggle to understand the risks he takes for the sake
of his insatiable passion for climbing.
$14.95 ($23 Canada), 272 pages

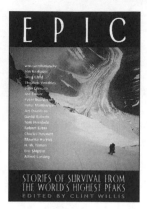

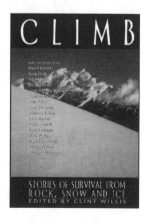

Exciting titles from Adrenaline Books

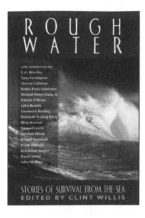

ROUGH WATER: Stories of Survival from the Sea

Edited by Clint Willis

A unique collection of 16 pieces of great writing about storms, shipwrecks and human resourcefulness. Includes work by Patrick O'Brian, John McPhee and Herman Wouk, as well as a Sebastian Junger story previously unpublished in book form.
$16.95 ($26 Canada), 368 pages

WILD: Stories of Survival from the World's Most Dangerous Places

Edited by Clint Willis

The wilderness—forest, desert, glacier, jungle—has inspired some of the past century's best writers, from Edward Abbey and Jack London to Norman Maclean and Barry Lopez. *Wild* contains 13 selections for people who love the wilderness and readers who love great writing.
$16.95 ($26 Canada), 336 pages

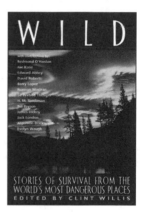

RESCUE: Stories of Survival from Land and Sea

Edited by Dorcas S. Miller; Series Editor, Clint Willis

Some of the world's best adventure writing tells stories of people in trouble and the people who come to their aid. *Rescue* gathers those stories from mountain ledges, sea-going vessels, desert wastes, ice flows and the real Wild West. It includes work by some of the world's best writers, from Antoine de St. Exupéry to Spike Walker and Pete Sinclair.
$16.95 ($26 Canada), 384 pages

adrenaline

Exciting titles from Adrenaline Books

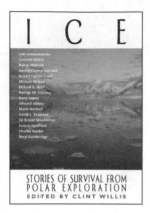

ICE: Stories of Survival from Polar Exploration

Edited by Clint Willis

The Arctic and Antarctica were the sites of many of the twentieth century's most gripping adventure stories. *Ice* features 15 of the best and most exciting accounts by the greatest explorers and observers of the polar regions—from Robert Scott, Ernest Shackleton and Richard E. Byrd to Barry Lopez, Nancy Mitford, and Beryl Bainbridge.
$16.95 ($26 Canada), 384 pages

STORM: Stories of Survival from Land and Sea

Edited by Clint Willis

Storm offers 18 gripping stories of people facing nature in all of its fury: blizzards, typhoons, windstorms, gales and hurricanes. These accounts come from all over the globe: from the South Pacific to Saskatchewan; from Everest's summit to Antarctica's wastes. Includes works by Sebastian Junger, Annie Proulx, Rick Bass, Barry Lopez, Richard E. Byrd, and Jack London.
$16.95 ($26.00 Canada) 384 pages

EXPLORE: Stories of Survival from Off the Map

Edited by Jennifer Schwamm Willis
Series Editor, Clint Willis

Adventurers endure storms, starvation, predators and disease for the thrill of discovery in 19 gripping stories. Selections from writers such as Edward Marriott, Tim Cahill, Andrea Barrett, Redmond O'Hanlon and Harold Brodkey bring readers to places where genuine discovery is still possible.
$16.95 ($26 Canada); 384 pages

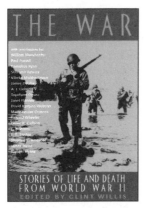